THE RISE AND FALL OF THE SOVIET NAVY IN THE BALTIC, 1921–1941

This book, based on extensive work in Russian archives, investigates how strategy, organizational rivalry and cultural factors came to shape naval developments in the Soviet Union, up to the invasion of 1941.

Focusing on the Baltic Fleet, the author shows how the perceived balance of power in northern Europe came to have a major influence on Soviet naval policy during the 1920s and 1930s. The operational environment of a narrow inland-sea like the Baltic would have required a joint approach to military planning, but the Soviet navy's weak position among the armed services made such an approach hard to attain. The Soviet regime also struggled against the cultural heritage of the tsarist navy and the book describes how this struggle was overcome. In a special Appendix dedicated to the purges of 1937–38, surviving party records from the Baltic Fleet intelligence section are used to illustrate the mechanisms of the Great Terror at a local level.

Gunnar Åselius PhD, Associate Professor, is a Historian at the Swedish National Defence College, Stockholm.

CASS SERIES: NAVAL POLICY AND HISTORY
Series Editor: Geoffrey Till
ISSN 1366–9478

This series consists primarily of original manuscripts by research scholars in the general area of naval policy and history, without national or chronological limitations. It will from time to time also include collections of important articles as well as reprints of classic works.

1. AUSTRO-HUNGARIAN NAVAL POLICY, 1904–1914
Milan N. Vego

2. FAR-FLUNG LINES
Studies in imperial defence in honour of Donald
Mackenzie Schurman
Edited by Keith Neilson and Greg Kennedy

3. MARITIME STRATEGY AND CONTINENTAL WARS
Rear Admiral Raja Menon

4. THE ROYAL NAVY AND GERMAN NAVAL
DISARMAMENT, 1942–1947
Chris Madsen

5. NAVAL STRATEGY AND OPERATIONS IN
NARROW SEAS
Milan N. Vego

6. THE PEN AND INK SAILOR
Charles Middleton
and the King's Navy, 1778–1813
John E. Talbott

7. THE ITALIAN NAVY AND FASCIST
EXPANSIONISM, 1935–1940
Robert Mallett

8. THE MERCHANT MARINE AND INTERNATIONAL AFFAIRS, 1850–1950
Edited by Greg Kennedy

9. NAVAL STRATEGY IN NORTHEAST ASIA
Geo-strategic goals, policies and prospects
Duk-Ki Kim

10. NAVAL POLICY AND STRATEGY IN THE MEDITERRANEAN SEA
Past, present and future
Edited by John B. Hattendorf

11. STALIN'S OCEAN-GOING FLEET
Soviet naval strategy and shipbuilding programmes, 1935–1953
Jürgen Rohwer and Mikhail S. Monakov

12. IMPERIAL DEFENCE, 1868–1887
Donald Mackenzie Schurman; edited by John Beeler

13. TECHNOLOGY AND NAVAL COMBAT IN THE TWENTIETH CENTURY AND BEYOND
Edited by Phillips Payson O'Brien

14. THE ROYAL NAVY AND NUCLEAR WEAPONS
Richard Moore

15. THE ROYAL NAVY AND THE CAPITAL SHIP IN THE INTERWAR PERIOD
An operational perspective
Joseph Moretz

16. CHINESE GRAND STRATEGY AND MARITIME POWER
Thomas M. Kane

17. BRITAIN'S ANTI-SUBMARINE CAPABILITY, 1919–1939
George Franklin

18. BRITAIN, FRANCE AND THE NAVAL ARMS TRADE IN THE BALTIC, 1919–1939
Grand strategy and failure
Donald Stoker

19. NAVAL MUTINIES OF THE TWENTIETH CENTURY
An international perspective
Edited by Christopher Bell and Bruce Elleman

20. THE ROAD TO ORAN
Anglo-French naval relations,
September 1939–July 1940
David Brown

21. THE SECRET WAR AGAINST SWEDEN
US and British submarine deception and
political control in the 1980s
Ola Tunander

22. ROYAL NAVY STRATEGY IN THE FAR EAST, 1919–1939
Planning for a war against Japan
Andrew Field

23. SEAPOWER
A guide for the twenty-first century
Geoffrey Till

24. BRITAIN'S ECONOMIC BLOCKADE OF
GERMANY, 1914–1919
Eric W. Osborne

25. A LIFE OF ADMIRAL OF THE FLEET ANDREW
CUNNINGHAM
A twentieth-century naval leader
Michael Simpson

26. NAVIES IN NORTHERN WATERS, 1721–2000
Edited by Rolf Hobson and Tom Kristiansen

27. GERMAN NAVAL STRATEGY, 1856–1888
Forerunners to tirpitz
David Olivier

28. BRITISH NAVAL STRATEGY EAST OF SUEZ, 1900–2000
Influences and actions
Edited by Greg Kennedy

29. THE RISE AND FALL OF THE SOVIET NAVY IN
THE BALTIC, 1921–1941
Gunnar Åselius

THE RISE AND FALL OF THE SOVIET NAVY IN THE BALTIC, 1921–1941

Gunnar Åselius

FRANK CASS
LONDON • NEW YORK

First published 2005
by Frank Cass, an imprint of Taylor & Francis
2 Park Square, Milton Park, Abingdon, Oxon OX14 4RN

Simultaneously published in the USA and Canada
by Routledge
270 Madison Ave, New York, NY 10016

Frank Cass is an imprint of the Taylor & Francis Group

Transferred to Digital Printing 2006

© 2005 Gunnar Åselius

Typeset in Times New Roman by
Newgen Imaging Systems (P) Ltd, Chennai, India

All rights reserved. No part of this book may be reprinted or reproduced or utilized in any form or by any electronic, mechanical, or other means, now known or hereafter invented, including photocopying and recording, or in any information storage or retrieval system, without permission in writing from the publishers.

The publisher makes no representation, express or implied, with regard to the accuracy of the information contained in this book and cannot accept any legal responsibility or liability for any errors or omissions that may be made.

British Library Cataloguing in Publication Data
A catalogue record for this book is available from the British Library

Library of Congress Cataloging in Publication Data
A catalog record for this book has been requested

ISBN10: 0–714–65540–6 (hbk)
ISBN10: 0–415–40777–X (pbk)

ISBN13: 978–0–714–65540–6 (hbk)
ISBN13: 978–0–415–40777–9 (pbk)

Printed and bound by CPI Antony Rowe, Eastbourne

CONTENTS

List of illustrations   ix
Series editor's preface   x
Acknowledgements   xii
List of abbreviations   xiii

PART I
Introduction   1

1 Preparing for war in the Baltic   3
2 Strategy   20
3 Organizational rivalry   29
4 Culture   41

PART II
The Old School, 1921–1928   55

5 'Mare Clausum' and the prospects of war   57
6 The meaning of 'small wars'   72
7 The navy of the military specialists   92

PART III
The Young School, 1929–1935   115

8 The era of collective security – and of coastal defense   117

9	Support for the Red Army	126
10	The navy of the red commanders	137

PART IV
The Soviet School, 1936–1941 — **155**

11	Toward the great oceanic navy	157
12	Ready for offensive operations?	175
13	The Navy of the Soviet admirals	198
14	The lessons of war and peace	221
	Appendix: the Great Terror in the Baltic Fleet	238

Bibliography	249
Index	262

ILLUSTRATIONS

Plates (between pages 114 and 115)

- I Sailors relaxing
- II 'The Sailor and his sailor-comrade'
- III Sailors eating soup
- IV Navy personnel listening to music
- V A soldier – orchestra
- VI Komsomol poster supporting the navy
- VII The anchor of a *Gangut*-class battleship
- VIII A seminar at the Naval War College
- IX Naval officers in the class room
- X A party representative addresses the crew of battleship *Marat*
- XI In the coal box
- XII Provisions deliveries
- XIII Engine personnel under instruction
- XIV 'Political Hour'
- XV Fresh recruits
- XVI 'Does our cook deserve a prize?'
- XVII 'The Battleship Marat Working School'

Maps

1	The Baltic region in the inter-war period	24
2	Theater of operations	81
3	Presumed enemy lines of advance, 1940	170
4	Baltic Fleet operations, 1939–1940	187
5	Presumptive Soviet counterstrikes, 1940	189
6	Naval operations in the Baltic, 1941	231

SERIES EDITOR'S PREFACE

One of the main issues for those interested in the former navy of the Soviet Union was whether it behaved just as any other Navy would have done in its particular circumstances, or whether it represented a novel and wholly unique maritime force with a distinct set of beliefs that set it apart from other navies. Protagonists in this debate would often assume, and sometimes state, that the model for the conventional, normal Navy was in fact Western [usually in fact an adulterated version of the American or British navies]. This could lead to the conclusion that the Soviet Navy was defective, or mistaken, when it departed from the norm – a navy run by land-lubbers and by a General Staff dominated by the Ground Forces. This argument could even be extended to the proposition that the Navy's 'weirdness' was emblematic, that it did not proceed from the need to defend the nation's maritime interests, that it was illegitimate, basically unnatural, offensive – a threat. According to this perspective the Americans, the British and most other West Europeans were entitled to large navies because of their many maritime interests and vulnerabilities. The economically autarchic and strategically self-contained Russians were not.

This constant debate over the past several hundred years provides the context for Gunnar Åselius' detailed study of the Soviet Navy during that key part in its development in the period between the two World Wars. The Soviet Navy's Baltic preoccupations at this time provide a case study, which admirably demonstrates that through depth comes breadth. He shows that in its response to circumstances, the Soviet Navy provides a unique means of exploring the origins of naval conduct. Geography, climate, the ambitions and preoccupations of Government, the political and social system, strategic culture, the technological and industrial state of the nation all had their part to play. They combined to produce a navy that was indeed distinctive at times, but which, more to the point, shifted in its orientation as the various sources of naval conduct themselves shifted. Broadly the pendulum swung from the 'traditional' [modified to suit Russian purposes] to the 'radical' and through the Great Patriotic War (and indeed the Cold War) back to the traditional. But for all that it always remained a navy with a difference.

And as to the central question of whether there was, and is, a central model of the Navy to which Russia conformed to varying degree, two competing tendencies can still be noted at the very end of the period. On the one hand, Admiral Isakov announces that '…we are no law-abiding dogmatists of the past, but the creators of a new way of life'; on the other, Admiral Belli reintroduces the study of Mahan and Colomb at the Naval Academy.

Gunnar Åselius has admirably situated this topic within the broader scholarly debate about the sources of, and influences on, military conduct and so provides us with a fascinating case study of a set of themes that are as broad as they are deep and that should fascinate anyone interested in the world's navies.

Geoffrey Till

ACKNOWLEDGEMENTS

I began working on this book in 1995. That it has taken so many years to complete is due to my work at the Swedish Defense College. Although the teaching of history to officers has delayed my writing considerably, it has also enriched it. My daily meetings with Swedish sailors, soldiers and airmen have helped me to understand better the inner life of military organizations, and the operational geography of the Baltic Sea. This in turn, has helped me to understand the Soviet Navy in the 1920s and 1930s.

My work has also profited from discussions with fellow historians at the Defense College through the years: Gunnar Artéus, Klaus-R. Böhme (now retired), Lars Ericson, Lennart Samuelson (now Stockholm School of Economics) and Kent Zetterberg. Professor Bo Huldt took the time to read the manuscript and contribute valuable criticism, as did Captain (N) Lars Wedin, head of the college's department of military history. I am also grateful to members of the 'Free Seminar' at the Department of History at Stockholm University, who took time to discuss some draft chapters in the fall of 2002.

My research in Russia (which took place during extended stays in 1995, 1997 and 2000) was considerably facilitated through the helpful staff of the Russian State Archives of the Navy (RGAVMF) in St Petersburg, and through assistance from Russian colleagues. I would like to mention Vladimir Baryshnikov and Pavel Petrov at the St Petersburg University and Alexey Komarov and Oleg Rzheshevsky at the Institute of Universal History at the Russian Academy of Sciences in Moscow. My fellow countrymen Magnus Haglund – former Swedish naval attaché in Moscow – and Gunnar Wärnberg – former liasion officer for the Swedish Police in St Petersburg – supplied me with books and photocopies from Russia. Alan Crozier reviewed the English text, and it has been copy-edited by Malcolm Ward. The maps have been drawn by Mark Evans.

My greatest thanks goes to my wife Ebba, who for many years listened to my complaints about not finding time to write. All the time, she assured me that I would eventually finish my book. She was right, so I dedicate it to her.

ABBREVIATIONS

ASW	Anti-submarine warfare
BOS	*Beregovoy Otryad Soprovozhdeniya* (Coastal Support Force)
BU	*Boevoy Ustav* (Naval Fighting Regulation)
Cheka	*Chrezvychaynaya Kommissiya* (Special Commission [for fighting counter-revolution and sabotage])
EU	European Union
FOA	Försvarets forskningsanstalt (Swedish Defense Research Establishment)
GDR	German Democratic Republic
GOR	*Glavny Oboronitelny Rayon* (Main Defense Area)
Gosplan	*Gosudarstvennoe Planovaya Komissiya* (State Planning Commission)
GPU	*Gosudarstvennoe Politicheskoe Upravlenie* (State Political Directorate)
GRU	*Glavnoe Razvedyvatelnoe Upravlenie* (Main Directorate for [military] Intelligence)
GUPP	*Glavnoe Upravlenie Politicheskoy Propagandy* (Main Directorate for Political Propaganda)
IUR	*Ikhursky Ukreplenny Rayon* (Ikhorsky Fortified Area)
KBF	*Krasnoznamenny Baltiysky Flot* (Red Bannered Baltic Fleet)
Komsomol	*Kommunistichesky Soyuz Molodezhi* (Communist Youth League)
LVO	*Leningradsky Voenny Okrug* (Leningrad Military District)
MSBM	*Morskikh Sil Balticheskogo Morya* (Naval Forces in the Baltic Sea)
MTB	Motor torpedo boat
NATO	North Atlantic Treaty Organization
NEP	New Economic Policy
NKID	*Narodny Kommissariat Innostranikh Del* (People's Commissariat for Foreign Affairs)
NKVD	*Narodny Kommissariat Vnutrennikh Del* (People's Commissariat for Internal Affairs)

ABBREVIATIONS

NMO	*Nastavlenie Morskikh Operatsii* (Instruction for Naval Operations)
OGPU	*Obyedinyonnoe Gosudarstvennoe Politicheskoe Upravlenie* (United State Political Administration)
OLS	*Otryad Legikh Sil* (Group of Light Forces)
OON	*Otryad Osobennogo Naznacheniya* (Special Mission Squadron)
OsoAviaKhim	*Obshchestvo Oborony, Aviatsii i Khimii* (Society for Defense, Aviation and Chemistry)
OVR	*Okhrana Vodnoga Rayona* (Aquatic Area Defense)
PU	*Politicheskoe Upravlenie* (Political Directorate)
PUR	*Politicheskoe Upravlenie RKKA* (Army Political Directorate)
RGAVMF	*Rossisky Gosudarstvenny Arkhiv Voenno-Morskogo Flota* (State Archives of the Navy)
RGVA	*Rossisky Gosudarstvenny Arkhiv Armii* (State Archive of the Army)
RKKA	*Raboche-Krestyanskaya Krasnaya Armiya* (Workers' and Peasants' Red Army)
RO KBF	*Razvedyvatelny otdel Krasnoznamennogo Baltiyskogo Flota* (Intelligence section Baltic Fleet)
RVS	*Revolutsionny Voenny Soviet* (Supreme Revolutionary-Military Council/Soviet)
RVSR	*Revolutsionny Voenny Soviet Respubliki* (Supreme Revolutionary-Military Council/Soviet of the Republic)
Shtab RKKF	*Shtab Raboche-krestyanskogo Krasnogo Flota* (Staff of the Workers' and Peasants' Red Navy, i.e. Naval Staff)
UMS	*Upravlenie Morskikh Sil* (Directorate for the Naval Forces)
UVMS	*Upravlenie Morskikh Sil RKKA* (Directorate for the Naval Forces of the Workers' and Peasants' Red Army)
UVMUZ	*Upravlenie Voenno-Morskimi Uchebnimi Zavedeniyami* (Directorate for Naval Educational Institutions)
VMF	*Voenno-Morsky Flot* (Navy)
VVS	*Voenno-Vozdushnye Sili* (Air Force)

Part I

INTRODUCTION

1

PREPARING FOR WAR IN THE BALTIC

About 22.00 hours on 21 June 1941, in his headquarters in Tallinn, the commander of the Soviet Baltic Fleet, Rear-Admiral Vladimir Tributs, received a long-expected telegram from the People's Commissariat for the Navy in Moscow. During the preceding weeks, tension had grown along the Soviet–German border with almost daily incursions by German ships and aircraft into Soviet territory. On the 19th, combat readiness had been raised to level 2, which meant readiness to go to sea within 4–6 hours. However, the forces along the frontiers were at the same time instructed to avoid countermeasures, which could provoke the Germans. Now, late in the evening on the 21st, Tributs was allowed to regroup his two battleships from Tallinn to the safer surroundings of Kronstadt, and to withdraw most of his remaining forces from Riga Bay to Tallinn. On the Latvian coast, only the cruiser *Maxim Gorky* and a squadron of destroyers were to remain.[1]

Shortly before midnight, Tributs was again contacted from Moscow, now by telephone. This time, the People's Commissar for the Navy, Admiral Nikolay Kuznetsov, personally gave the order to enter into full alert ('operational readiness level number 1'). The German invasion was to start in a few hours. Later, in his memoirs, Kuznetsov would complain about Tributs, who, on receiving this order, had asked if this meant the Baltic Fleet could now open fire against all intruders. However, when confirming that war could break out the next day, the People's Commissar still found it necessary to repeat the need for cautiousness. According to Kuznetsov, his conversation with Tributs ended at 23.35. The war diaries of the Naval Staff claim that the order to enter operational readiness level number 1 was issued two minutes later. Thus, the Baltic Fleet was the first branch of the Soviet armed forces to be alerted before Operation Barbarossa (the Nazi invasion of Russia). The People's Commissar's official order to increase operational readiness was issued at 23.50.[2]

Yet, with only a few hours' warning, the fleet was caught as unprepared by the German onslaught as the rest of Stalin's war machine.[3] After a disastrous campaign in 1941, the Baltic Fleet spent most of the remaining war behind mine-barriers outside Leningrad, supporting the besieged city with artillery fire, occasionally sending submarines into the Baltic and assisting in flank operations on the Leningrad and Karelian fronts, where sailors and naval infantry fought side by side with the Red Army. Only in the autumn of 1944, after the armistice with Finland, could the fleet escape from its imprisonment in the Gulf of Finland. During the following months, Soviet naval forces made a major contribution to the recapturing of Estonia and Latvia, supporting landing operations against Tallinn, Riga Bay and the Moonsund archipelago. However, in spite of their return to the Baltic, they failed to prevent the Germans from evacuating more than 2 million people out of the Kurland pocket during the last months of the war.[4]

Very little in the Baltic Theater turned out in the way the Soviets had expected. Notwithstanding the countless examples of individual bravery from officers and men, the World War II record of the Baltic Fleet was not entirely satisfactory. Over the years, there has been an intensive debate on whether things would have turned out differently had the Soviet government reacted earlier in the summer of 1941, issued the call for mobilization in time or even launched a preemptive strike against the Germans.[5] But most campaigns are won and lost before the fighting starts, and in June 1941 the Baltic Fleet had to make do with the equipment and training it had acquired during the preceding decades. If it is true that the Soviet naval forces failed in the Baltic during World War II, studying developments in a longer perspective seems more fruitful than scrutinizing decision making in the months immediately prior to the German attack. As David Glantz points out in his study of the ground campaign in 1941, 'the most serious Soviet failure was neither strategic surprise nor tactical surprise, but *institutional* surprise'.[6]

As pointed out by Jonathan Shimsoni, a true military entrepreneur is not only concerned with what the next war will be like, but also asks questions on how he can 'engineer' the next war away from that scenario, 'so as to maximize my relative advantages and bypass those of my competitors'.[7] What kind of war did the Soviet Navy men expect to fight in the Baltic before World War II? How did they prepare for it? These are the fundamental questions of the present study.

The investigation starts in 1921, when the Civil War was over and the sailors' revolt in Kronstadt had been crushed. For many years, the Bolshevik regime regarded its naval forces with the utmost suspicion. In the words of naval historian Donald Mitchell, this period represented the absolute 'nadir of Russian naval power'. J. N. Westwood characterizes the 1920s by labeling the chapter in his book on Russian and Soviet naval construction 'Picking up the pieces'. A British intelligence survey from the summer of 1921 describes the Baltic fleet as 'useless as a fighting unit, there are no officers, the old experienced soldiers have been sent away... and under the present conditions the reestablishment of the fleet is out of the question'.[8]

From this absolute low-point, we follow developments throughout the campaign of 1941, when the Baltic Fleet finally went to war against a Great-power enemy.

The end of the Cold War and the rewriting of history

There is already quite an extensive literature on the Soviet inter-war navy. Before the end of the Cold War, the most substantial work to appear in the West was Robert W. Herrick's *Soviet Naval Theory and Strategy* (1988), which analyzed

Soviet naval thinking up to the 1950s and used as sources contemporary Soviet naval literature, such as the maritime journal *Morskoy Sbornik*.[9]

Parallel to the Western literature there was a substantial Soviet historiography as well. The second volume of the official textbook on the history of naval warfare (1963) deserves mentioning, as do the above–cited memoirs by Admiral Kuznetsov (naval chief 1939–46, 1950–55). Another influential interpretation of the period was offered by Kuznetsov's successor, Admiral Sergey S. Gorshkov, in his writings on naval strategy during the 1970s.[10] Shortly after the appearance of Herrick's second book in 1988, the process of *Glasnost* in the Soviet Union and the opening of archives led to a flood of renewed research. Some of it was conducted by Russian scholars in commemoration of the 300th anniversary of the founding of the Russian Navy in 1696. Of special importance was a series of articles, mainly authored by Captain 1st rank Mikhail Monakov, which appeared in *Morskoy Sbornik* between 1990 and 1994. Monakov, who studied the discussions on doctrine and theory in the Soviet Navy between 1922 and 1939, was the first writer with a wide access to archival documents. Together with the German naval historian Jürgen Rohwer, Monakov in 2001 also published the volume *Stalin's Ocean-going Fleet*, which focuses on Soviet naval strategy and shipbuilding programs in the period 1935–53.[11]

Another officer of the Soviet Navy, Sergey Zonin, published a biography in 1991 on Admiral Lev Michailovich Galler, chief of staff in the Baltic Fleet 1921–27, fleet commander 1932–37 and chief of the naval staff in Moscow 1938–40. Zonin did not discuss Soviet naval policy in a wider context, and certain passages in his book give the impression of literary fiction. Nonetheless, his account is obviously based on archival documents and on interviews with Galler's contemporaries (even if the reader could wish for more detailed references to sources).[12]

Other important works to appear during the early 1990s were official histories of the Soviet Naval War College and of the Baltic Fleet during World War II, as well as V. I. Dotsenko's maritime biographic dictionary (*Morskoy biograficheskys slovar*).[13] The British historian J. N. Westwood treated the subject of ship construction during the period on the basis of primary sources, as did the Russian naval officer and ship constructor V. N. Burov.[14]

Among those who hurried to the newly opened archives in Russia from abroad were also Finnish historians, eager to study their own country's dramatic history in connection with Soviet naval strategy. Ohto Manninen wrote about Finland between Germany and Soviet Russia in 1939–41, and the Helsinki historian Jari Leskinen studied Finnish–Estonian military cooperation during the 1930s. In addition, the British historian Carl Van Dyke studied the Soviet–Finnish War of 1939–40 from a Soviet perspective, giving an overview of naval operations on the basis of a former classified Soviet study.[15] Later, the St Petersburg historian Pavel V. Petrov added further to the picture through his dissertation on the Baltic Fleet's operations during this war.[16]

Furthermore, in 1992 the Center of Military History of the Soviet General Staff published the first volume in a series entitled *Boevaya letopis voenno-morskogo flota* (The Combat Chronicle of the Navy). The volume in question deals with the period 1917–41 and had been compiled by N. Yu. Berezovsky, S. S. Berezhnoy and Z. V. Nikolayeva. Apart from battle accounts, *Boevaya leotopis* contains short notices on organizational changes, appointments, new regulations, maneuvers, naval visits and other important events in the life of the navy. The term chronicle in this case should not arouse associations to the well-known medieval literary genre of historical narrative. If *Boevaya letopis* is to be defined through medieval analogies at all, it bears more resemblance to the annalist history writing practiced in the monasteries. The short entries are organized in chronological order, and should be regarded as a kind of calendars or document summaries, complete with meticulous references to original documents in the archives of the Communist Party, various military agencies and government ministries.[17]

Finally, some volumes in the series of published documents on the history of the Great Patriotic War, which was initiated by the Center of Military History in the mid-1990s under the editorship of Alexander Zolotarev, contain material relevant to naval matters. Of special interest are volume 1 (2), treating the discussions of the naval high command in the autumn of 1940, and volume 10, containing the orders of the People's Commissariat for the Navy from 1941–45.[18]

In view of the vast amount of literature and document publications, the writing of yet another book on the inter-war Soviet Baltic Fleet may certainly call for some justification.

It could of course be argued that the geopolitical conditions in the Baltic region during the 1920s and 1930s in many ways appear similar to the situation at the beginning of the twenty-first century. The weakening of Russia after the Cold War, the reunification of Germany and the resurrection of independence in Estonia, Latvia and Lithuania have to some extent recreated the borders that existed in the region during the inter-war period. Although Russia today has a foothold in Kaliningrad (in former German East Prussia), it has again been deprived of most of its former coast along the Baltic, and sees its military power diminish. At the same time, its small neighboring states see this state of weakness as temporary and have tried to strengthen their ties to the West (Poland and the Baltic states joining the North Atlantic Treaty Organization [NATO] and Sweden and Finland the European Union [EU]).

Just as it did during the inter-war period, Russia during the 1990s regarded with some discomfort its neighbors' efforts at military integration with the West, fearing that NATO's extension westwards would mean isolation and eventually a threat to national security. In recent years, there has also been an intensive discussion on the navy's role in national defense–parallel to that of the 1920s and 1930s. Will a strategic deterrence force in the North Atlantic be enough in the future, or will ships that can 'show the flag' in foreign ports also be needed? If Russia is to remain a great power in the eyes of the world, must it reinforce its strategic submarine force with ships that can protect shipping and fishing interests at sea, and participate in international peacekeeping operations around the globe? Where could the means to create such forces be found?[19]

However, there are also important differences between the post-World War I era and the post-Cold War era. A more constructive international climate with less ideological and military confrontation, increased economic integration between states, a widened definition of national security, etc. are factors that make superficial comparisons between the two periods truly problematic. Furthermore, modern military technology has fundamentally changed the strategic conditions in the Baltic. Already during the latter half of the Cold War, the Baltic belonged to the rear areas in Soviet naval thinking, and the role of naval forces in controlling a confined water area like this is likely to become even less significant in the future.

The end of the Cold War is nonetheless a good reason for rewriting the history of the inter-war period. This is not only due to the increased access to archives, but also to the fact that much of the earlier literature on the subject is flawed, having been written in the shadow of the East–West confrontation. Western research was concerned with understanding Soviet naval developments during the 1970s and 1980s and tried to trace its origins back to the 1920s and 1930s. Soviet research aimed at pointing out proper historical lessons to justify present naval doctrine. For obvious reasons, the Baltic did not attract any special attention in any of this literature, as it was a rear area in Soviet Cold War strategy, a theater where crews were trained and new equipment was tested but mostly old or second-class ships were permanently stationed. From the 1960s onwards the Baltic Fleet's percentage of the total number of ships steadily decreased, while the main interest was focused on the Northern Fleet in Murmansk.[20]

However, during the inter-war period the Baltic's role was different. During the 1920s, the Baltic and Black Seas were the only theaters where the Soviets had any naval forces at all, and the Baltic was clearly where these forces were concentrated. In 1928, three out of three battleships, two out of four cruisers, 12 out of 17 destroyers and nine out of 14 submarines were stationed here.[21] During the 1930s, when new fleets were created in the Pacific and the Arctic and Soviet naval rearmament began, the Baltic remained a center of gravity. According to the naval construction program of 1936, the Pacific and Baltic Theaters were to get a third each of the planned tonnage. The only field in procurement planning in which the Pacific Fleet was given clear priority was the naval air arm. In 1941, at the time of the German attack, the Baltic Fleet still kept its leading position among the four Soviet fleets with two out of three battleships, two out of seven cruisers, 28 out of 54 destroyers, 71 out of 212 submarines and 656 out of 2,429 naval aircraft. About a third (311 million) of the 944 million rubles that Admiral Kuznetsov wanted for his budget this year were to be spent on the Baltic Fleet. The Pacific Fleet was 'only' to have some 230 millions.[22]

Thus, it is reasonable to assume that a reassessment of Soviet naval policy during the inter-war period from a Baltic perspective would yield new insights, especially in consideration of newly accessible documents. The pioneer user of this material, Mikhail Monakov, is indeed more appreciative of the Baltic's crucial importance during the period than were his Cold War predecessors. However, he studied naval policy of the era with the aim of discussing contemporary Russian naval policies. In spite of their great scientific value, his articles also belong in the context of the 1990s Russian defense debate.

Three levels of military doctrine

Apart from ambitions to increase our knowledge of military conditions in a particular part of the world in a particular historical period, I also want to increase our understanding of military thinking in general. What are the determining factors when military organizations formulate their doctrines? Here I see a second reason for writing this book.

A country's military doctrine is concerned with how its armed forces should be used to promote what national leaders identify as the country's security interests.[23] Ultimately, military power equals the capability to fight wars. Thus, a sound military doctrine should be based on a realistic estimate of what the next war will be like. Ideally, it should contain both an analysis of the international environment and possible threats to national security, a prescription of how these threats could be countered with military means and – at the lowest level – combat instructions to the country's military forces.

These three levels of military doctrine could also be labeled strategic, operational and tactical levels of doctrine. At the strategic level, general problems of national security are dealt with (What types of military threats face the nation? Who will the enemy be? How do we know that we have won the war?). The operational level regulates the organization and use of military forces (How should we compose our forces to attain our objectives? Where and when shall they be deployed?). The tactical level deals with the winning of battles (With what kind of weaponry should we equip our forces? How should we train them in order to be successful in combat?).[24]

In this book, I examine Soviet naval doctrine at all these levels. As will be explained below, some dramatic doctrinal changes occurred in the Soviet Navy between 1921 and 1941. Obviously, these changes could be explained in various ways, and I have the ambition to seek a different type of explanation at each level of doctrine: at the strategic level the balance of power, at the operational level organizational rivalry within the armed forces, and at the tactical level the role of cultural factors. The exact line between these different levels of doctrine is difficult to draw, and to some extent they overlap each other. Also, my investigation of the influence of cultural factors on Soviet naval tactics deals not so much with the evolution of tactical regulations – a subject that has already been treated extensively by others – but highlights such factors as training and morale, which are nonetheless important for the tactical performance of military forces.

It could well be argued that in treating a subject like this, an author should choose one of two paths. Either he should attempt a detailed reconstruction of the past and concentrate his energy on archival research. Or the author should devote his work to a discussion of the theoretical foundations of military doctrine and regard empirical data as merely instrumental, to be conveniently obtained from secondary literature. Traditionally, the difference between these two approaches corresponds to the disciplinary border between history and political science. For me as an historian, the choice would seem easy, especially since the existing literature has only to a limited extent made use of the archives that have become available in recent years. At the same time, however, it is impossible to reconstruct the past in a meaningful way without some preliminary assumptions and theoretical preconceptions. To do full justice to the complexities of historical reality, I have chosen to use rival theories, such as power realism, bureaucratic theory and cultural constructivism. My aim is not to compare their explanatory power, or to suggest that one perspective should be regarded as superior to the other. Rather, I find it hard to believe that we can satisfactorily understand either the inter-war Soviet Navy, or the foundations of military doctrine, without combining various perspectives and various types of sources.[25]

The development of naval doctrine during the inter-war period

It is often said that the inter-war period marked the transition from 'the age of the big guns' to 'the age of the aircraft carrier' in naval warfare. To illustrate the meaning of this, Wayne P. Hughes's 'cornerstones of naval tactics' could be cited:

- *Firepower*. On a tactical level, the goal of naval warfare is to deliver successful fire upon the enemy.
- *Scouting*. To deliver successful fire upon the enemy a capacity to detect and target him is required.
- *Command-and-control*. The transformation of firepower and scouting into successful fire upon the enemy requires an ability to direct your own forces effectively.
- *Attack first*. Naval victory is won through 'simultaneous force-on-force attrition'. Therefore, victory goes to the side which can attack effectively first.

What happened between the world wars was that superiority with regard to firepower could no longer compensate for inferior scouting and command-and-control functions. This in turn further accentuated the need to attack first. A symbolic confirmation of that development was the Battle of Midway in the Pacific in 1942 between Americans and Japanese. The Japanese were superior in firepower (four aircraft carriers with 277 aircraft against three American aircraft carriers with 233 aircraft). In a game of 'simultaneous force-on-force attrition', the Japanese should really have had the better odds, or at least managed to take most of the American force down with them. However, the Americans were superior in intelligence and staff work and managed to attack first. Consequently, the Japanese force was completely annihilated while the Americans, having failed to locate the fourth Japanese carrier in their first strike, lost only one of their own carriers. Since the end of World War II, the role of scouting and command-and-control functions in naval warfare has grown immensely. In the age of missiles and computers, a naval commander has to direct most of his time and assets to information-processing activities, while the importance of skilful maneuvering or accurate firing has decreased through precision-guided, long-range weapons. Today, the main reason for naval ships to operate in large formations is not to combine their firepower, but to combine their intelligence resources and their means of warning and protection against incoming missiles.[26]

At the beginning of the twentieth century, however, 'the age of the big guns' had just begun, and concentration of force – superiority in firepower – still seemed the key to tactical victory. The doctrines of the leading naval powers were strategically offensive, in line with the ideas of the American strategist Alfred T. Mahan (1840–1914). According to Mahan, throughout history command of the sea had laid the foundation of all great empires. In keeping with this thesis, it was argued that the primary task of any Great power navy should be to defeat the enemy in a decisive battle, or to paralyze him through an effective naval blockade. The principal tool to achieve this goal, it seemed, was the battleship, a huge weapon platform that could deliver as well as receive massive barrages of heavy shells. In the naval race between the Great powers, the number and caliber of guns were therefore believed to be crucial factors. Also, a 'Big Ship' navy could serve as an impressive and highly mobile instrument for diplomacy and colonial expansion.[27]

There were, however, also defensive notions of sea warfare at the time. Although American and British admirals saw the battle between heavy artillery ships as the apogee of naval conflict, admirals in other Great power navies thought differently. In France, for instance, naval thinking was for a long time dominated by the *Jeune École* (Young School), with Admiral Théophile Aube as its most prominent spokesman. France could not challenge the Royal Navy in battle, but according to Aube and his followers, a weak naval power could always fight a stronger enemy by raiding his shipping or coastal areas. Cruisers and torpedo boats would always be faster than heavy battleships, and those big, costly vessels always ran the risk of running aground in coastal waters or being sunk by comparatively cheap weapons, such as torpedoes and mines.[28]

On the other side of the English Channel, Julian Corbett (who taught history at the Royal Naval College in Greenwich from 1902) questioned that territorial control was at all possible to attain at sea. As long as an inferior power had a single ship left in operational condition, it could always dispute the stronger power's command of the sea. Instead, naval strategy must be directed at controlling the sea-lines of communication. This, Corbett believed, was certainly attainable, 'for in maritime warfare the lines of communication of either belligerent tend to run approximately parallel, if indeed they are not identical'. In contrast, on land the belligerents' lines of communication ran in opposite directions, joining only in the theater of operations. Therefore, to attack and threaten the enemy's supply lines in ground warfare always meant exposing one's own supply lines. At sea, however, the securing of one's own communications as a rule meant denying the enemy the use of his.[29]

Just like Carl von Clausewitz before him, Corbett argued that the defensive in fact represented a stronger form of warfare, as it had the potential for neutralizing an imbalance in strength. In naval warfare, this was especially true after the introduction of torpedoes and mines. Drawing inspiration from Clausewitz's distinction between limited and total wars as well as from his famous definition of war as a continuation of politics, Corbett also doubted that an encounter between two Great power battle fleets was likely to be decisive. Blockade warfare, in which the enemy was engaged at a distance, would be preferred instead, being less risky and with greater prospects of damaging the enemy's society as a whole. The main instrument of blockade warfare, however, would not be the battleship but the fast-going cruiser/surface raider. From Corbett's reading of Clausewitz also stemmed his refusal to see naval strategy in isolation from continental strategy. Apart from destroying the enemy's commerce, Corbett argued, one of the main advantages of controlling the sea was that it allowed for the safe and speedy deployment of armies. Here, in the projection of power ashore, he saw the principal role of the battle fleet: escorting troop transports, protecting amphibious landings or – as a 'fleet in being' – deterring the enemy from invading the homeland.[30]

To some extent, the experience of World War I proved Corbett right, although it was the submarine, not the surface raider, which came to revolutionize blockade warfare. Only one major engagement between battle fleets was fought during the conflict – the Battle of Jutland in 1916 between the British and the Germans – and it failed to produce a decisive outcome. Instead of fighting each other, navies made their main contribution during the war by fighting the supply lines of the enemy. During the inter-war period, Corbett's ideas were developed further by the British Admiral Herbert Richmond and the French Admiral Raoul Castex. German Rear-Admiral Wolfgang Wegener reasoned along similar lines when he criticized the battle-oriented German naval strategy during the war for having neglected the role of sea-lines of communications and the need for strategic bases.[31]

After World War I, the role of the battleship seemed uncertain, while the submarine and the aircraft carrier appeared as the future rulers of the oceans. The latter category of ship had been introduced during the final stage of the war, and in 1921 the US Army Air Force General William Mitchell made a spectacular demonstration of air power at sea against a captured German battleship (similar demonstrations were later repeated against other scrapped battleships). Furthermore, international treaties (Washington 1922, London 1930) for many years limited the number and size of battleships in the Great power navies. By the mid-1930s, however, when the obligations of the disarmament treaties had ceased and the naval arms race began with renewed speed, battleship construction was again prioritized. The defenders of battleships argued that anti-air artillery and sonar could protect them from dangers from the sky or from under the sea. Because of their superior size and firepower, battleships would also last longer in combat than any other type of warship. Only World War II effectively demonstrated that the battleship era was over.[32]

It was against this international backdrop that Soviet naval doctrine developed during the inter-war period. Indeed, parallel positions to those of Mahan, the *Jeune École* and Corbett could also be found in the Soviet debate.

The years before World War I had seen the predominance of Mahanian ideals in Russia. Although the country had no colonies overseas and most of its navy had been destroyed during the Russo-Japanese War, in 1912 the Duma approved a naval construction program which in 18 years would produce a navy of 24 battleships, 12 battle cruisers, 24 light cruisers, 108 destroyers and 36 big submarines.[33]

When the Bolsheviks came to power, they thus inherited the uncompleted remnants of an ocean-going fleet to be. Consequently, the early Soviet period (1920–28) was dominated by the Mahanian concepts of the Tsarist era, with dreams of a 'Big Ship' navy and command of the sea. Its opponents labeled this strand of thinking the 'Old School'. However, the severe losses of ships and competent people, the massive industrial devastation suffered during the period of war and internal turmoil (1914–21), as well as the reduction of Russia's coastline through the dissolution of the Tsarist Empire, made the idea of an ocean-going navy seem unrealistic. Although tradition continued to rule at the Naval War College in Leningrad, where most of the teachers had been educated in the tsarist navy, these ideals were gradually called into question. Open criticism of the 'Old School' began in 1927–28. By 1930, the struggle had been more or less won, when a new Naval Fighting Regulation (BU-30 = *Boevoy Ustav*) was issued.[34]

Now, the ideals of a light navy instead came to dominate – the 'Young School', not so different from its French predecessor *Jeune École*. The Young School completely redefined the notion of naval warfare, criticizing traditional Mahanian concepts of command of the sea and preaching the 'death of the battleship'. In future wars, it was argued, the airplane and the submarine would make sea control impossible. Consequently, the Soviet Navy should be designed for coastal defense, using submarines, torpedo ships, mines, coastal artillery and shore-based aircraft. Also, the importance of joint operations and unity of command was strongly emphasized. To some extent, the Young School could draw on Russia's own experience in World War I, when the Baltic Fleet had waged a successful defensive struggle against the Germans from the protection of minefields and coastal batteries in the Gulf of Finland.

However, the ideals of an oceanic navy suddenly returned with the gigantic naval rearmament program of June 1936, according to which a fleet of 1.36 million tons was to be created in ten years time. Over 53 percent of this enormous tonnage would consist of battleships, 24 units in all. At the same time, the Royal Navy counted 1.22 million tons, the US Navy 1.1 million tons and the Japanese Navy 0.8 million tons. Thus, the Soviet Union was to become one of the world's leading naval powers. This naval program was revised repeatedly in 1937–39, and in the final version the tonnage had grown to almost another million tons. Only in October 1940, when war with Germany appeared imminent, was the scheme canceled and production resources redirected to the construction of lighter vessels.[35]

New tactical regulations were also issued. In Soviet literature, the Naval Fighting Regulation of 1937 (BU-37) was generally described as a more mature version of the Naval Fighting Regulation of 1930 (BU-30), signifying a further elaboration of inter-service cooperation, specially designed task forces and of operations against enemy sea lanes of communications. BU-37 also emphasized the navy's role as an offensive weapon, stressing the importance of incessantly attacking the enemy. In June 1939, a special chapter was added to BU-37, dedicated to the problems of 'operations at sea.' The new operational guidelines were further developed in the temporary regulation for the conduct of naval operations (NMO-40 = *Nastavlenie Morskikh Operatsii* [Instruction for Naval Operations]), which was issued in the autumn of 1940.[36]

According to Robert W. Herrick, it is doubtful whether Stalin's naval policy really signified a turn toward genuine navalist thinking. Instead, what happened was that traditional Mahanian concepts of 'command of the sea' were fused with the operational principles of the Young School. Herrick labeled the new creed the 'Soviet School', and according to him, it came to dominate naval thinking in the Soviet Union throughout the Cold War.

The Soviet School maintained that the navy's task was still predominantly defensive, but that this did not exclude offensive operations in a local or regional context, in cooperation with the ground forces. Submarines and aircraft were the main weapon systems, but there was also need for major surface combatants to support them. Command of the sea according to Soviet School thinking did not imply command of the oceans, but control of a limited theater. The aim was not to achieve global domination, but domination over seas adjacent to the Soviet Union's own borders, in areas where the operations of Soviet ground forces could be actively supported. Thus, the Soviet School was more in tune with Corbett than with Mahan or, as Herrick argues, with the views of the French naval theorist Admiral Raoul Castex.[37]

In their recent study, Mikhail Monakov and Jürgen Rohwer come to a different conclusion. The decision in October 1940 merely signified a temporary halt in Stalin's grandiose scheme to challenge the maritime supremacy of the Western powers. After the war the gigantic construction program was again resumed. If there was a continuity between Stalin's and Brezhnev's navy, it was above all in the appreciation of an ocean-going fleet as a potent symbol of Great power status.[38]

Military doctrines

Thus, the evolution of naval doctrine during the twentieth century was characterized by a growing role for information-processing functions (scouting, command and control), while the relative weight of firepower gradually diminished. The ability to attack first appeared to be a greater advantage than superiority in weapon load or ship size. World War II formed a turning point in this development. However, during the period under study here, 1921–41, this outcome had not yet been decided. Whether the battleship, the airplane or the submarine was the main weapon system at sea was still open to debate.

In the same era, naval doctrine in the Soviet Union underwent dramatic change. The cult of big artillery ships (the Old School) was replaced by the concept of a light, coastal defense fleet, emphasizing the role of submarines, air power and joint operations (the Young School). In the final years of the period, big ships again became fashionable. According to some interpreters, what finally emerged was really an entirely new understanding of naval power (the Soviet School), adapted to Soviet needs, containing elements from both the previous strands of thinking. Others maintain that Stalin did desire an ocean-going fleet that could challenge Western global domination.

How then, should these developments best be explained?

A way of characterizing military doctrines is to see them as either offensive, defensive or deterrent. According to the definitions used by Barry R. Posen, an offensive doctrine aims at disarming an enemy and destroying his military forces. A defensive doctrine aims at denying the enemy the object he seeks, while a deterrent doctrine aims at punishing an aggressor – raising his costs for attacking – without regard for one's own losses. Classical examples of offensive ground warfare doctrines could be found among the European Great powers in 1914, in Nazi Germany as well as in modern Israel. A well-known example of an unsuccessful defensive doctrine is the French Maginot Line of the 1930s. Deterrent doctrines could be illustrated by the strategies of second-class nuclear powers like China and France, as well as by the territorial militia defense concept embraced by small, mountainous, non-aligned countries like Switzerland or Titoist Yugoslavia.[39]

One could argue that the Old School of the Soviet Navy was an offensive doctrine and the Young School was a defensive one. The Soviet School could either be seen as an offensive doctrine or as mixture between offense and defense. As we will see, however, such labels really contain gross simplifications. Seemingly, both the Old School and the Soviet School existed in offensive and defensive versions, while the Young School might very well be described as a deterrent doctrine. In reality, no military doctrine displays purely offensive or defensive elements. As Julian Corbett pointed out, every offensive requires a concentration of force at a decisive point, which implies assuming a defensive posture in other, less important directions. Similarly, the reason for assuming the defensive is to win time to prepare for a counterattack, once the enemy has exhausted himself. With regard to deterrent doctrines, they must contain both offensive and defensive elements.[40]

The structure of this book

What then, determines a country's choice of military doctrine, the choice between offense, defense and deterrence? The existing literature on the subject suggests at least three types of explanations: strategy (or balance of power), organizational rivalry and culture. The implications of these different perspectives will be explored in Chapters 2–4. Chapters 5–7 discusses the period of the Old School (1921–28), Chapters 8–10 the period of the Young School (1928–36) and Chapters 11–13 the period of the Soviet School (1936–40). In Chapters 5, 8 and 11 it is the strategic aspects of Soviet naval doctrine, which comes to the fore, while Chapters 6, 9 and 12 focus on the role of organizational rivalry and pertain to the influence of operational planning. Finally, Chapters 7, 10 and 13 discuss the role of national culture and identity, covering indirectly the tactical dimensions of naval doctrine by discussing such questions as training and morale. In sum, this book will tell the story of the rise and fall of the Soviet navy in the Baltic between the world wars from three different angles. In Chapter 14, we conclude by studying the 1941 naval campaign and how the Baltic Fleet developed after World War II. There is also an appendix, which examines how the Great Terror of 1937–38 affected the Baltic Fleet.

A note on archival records and the institutions that produced them

From the Russian State Archive of the Army (RGVA = *Rossisky Gosudarstvenny Arkhiv Armii*) in Moscow I have used material from the *fond* 33988, which contains documents from the RVS. The full name of this institution – *Revolutsionny Voenny Soviet* – is often translated into English as the 'Supreme Revolutionary-Military Council/Soviet of the Republic' (from 1923 'Supreme Revolutionary-Military Council/Soviet of the USSR'). Already in June 1918, the Bolsheviks had formed this decisional body, which, during the Civil War, replaced the Ministry (or People's Commissariat) for War and continued to serve as the supreme organ for supervision of the armed forces until 1934. Although a regular People's Military and Naval Commissariat was recreated in 1923, this ministry merely came to serve as an executive branch of the RVS. As a rule, the People's Commissar for War presided as chairman during RVS meetings. Other members were top military commanders and prominent party leaders. The RVS both formulated defense policy and collectively exercised the functions of a commander in chief.

An institution akin to the RVS was the Baltic Fleet Soviet, which played a similar role at the regional level. Such military soviets could be found in each of the armed services as well as in the various military districts, fronts, fleets, armies and air wings which made up the Soviet armed forces. As a rule, the Baltic Fleet Soviet consisted of the fleet commander, the commander of the fleet's political directorate and some figurehead of the Leningrad branch of the Communist Party.

Apart from the files of the RVA, Most of the archival records that I have used are to be found in the Russian State Archive of the Navy (RGAVMF = *Rossisky Gosudarstvenny Arkhiv Voenno-Morskogo Flota*) in Saint Petersburg. Some of them stem from the various state organs in Moscow, which – subordinated to the RVS – exercised central command of the Soviet naval forces. From 1920 to 1926, this function was chiefly upheld by the Staff of the Workers' and Peasants' Naval Forces (*Shtab Raboche-Krestiyanskogo Krasnogo Flota* = *Shtab RKKF*), which will be referred to in the text as the Naval Staff. Its archive can be found in *fond* r-1.

After 1926, when the navy was incorporated into the Workers' and Peasants' Red Army (*Raboche-Krestyanskaya Krasnaya Armiya* = RKKA) the functions of the abolished Naval Staff were divided between the Directorate of the Naval Forces of the Workers' and Peasants' Red Army (*Upravlenie Morskikh Sil RKKA*, or UVMS) in the People's Military and Naval Commissariat and the naval department of the RKKA General Staff. The records of these institutions are to be found in the *fonds* r-1483 and r-2041 respectively. Also originating from the same period are the documents in *fond* r-1543 used in this study, containing records of the voluntary Society for Defense, Aviation and Chemistry (*Obshchestvo Oborony, Aviatsii i Khimii* = OsoAviaKhim), which organized preparatory military training for navy recruits from 1929 onwards.

At the turn of 1937–38, the Naval Staff (*Glavny Shtab Voenno-Morskogo Flota* or *Glavny Shtab VMF*) and the People's Commissariat for the Navy (*Narodny Kommissariat VMF*) were recreated (VMF = *Voenno-Morsky Flot* [Navy]). The records of those agencies can be found in *fonds* r-1678 and r-1877 respectively. At the same time, an independent Political Directorate for the Navy was also established (*Politicheskoe Upravlenie* – or *PUR – VMF*), the records of which are preserved in *fond* r-1549.

To study events at the regional level, I have used the archives of the Baltic Fleet. For the sake of simplicity, I use the term Baltic Fleet to describe the Soviet naval forces in the Baltic Sea throughout the period, although they included air and coastal defense units as well, and from 1921 to 1935 bore the official name 'the Naval Forces in the Baltic Sea' (*Morskikh Sil Balticheskogo Morya* or MSBM). Some material from the pre-revolutionary period has been used (*fond* 479 – the files of the commander of the Baltic Fleet), but most documents stem from the fleet political directorate (*fond* r-34), the fleet staff (*fond* r-92), the intelligence section (*fond* r-1883) and the personnel section (*fond* r-2185).

Finally, I have also used the personal archive of a prominent Soviet naval theoretician of the period, Vladimir Belli, whose unpublished memoirs are preserved in *fond* r-2224.

Although some references are made in the text to Soviet naval literature and journals from the period, I have made no systematic study of this category of sources. Since it has already been thoroughly analyzed by other authors, there seems to be little to gain from such an undertaking. As has been indicated above, the main forum of Soviet naval debate was *Morskoy Sbornik*, a journal which has been published since 1848. It is one of the oldest naval journals in the world, surpassed only by the Royal Swedish Academy of Naval Sciences' *Tidskrift i Sjöväsendet*, which has appeared since 1836.

Notes

1 D. M. Vasiliev, 'Pervy boevoy pokhod Otryada legkikh sil', *Gangut*, vol. 9 (1995), pp. 50–1; N. G. Kuznetsov, *Nakanune* (Moscow: Voenizdat, 1966), p. 327.
2 Kuznetsov, *Nakanune*, p. 329; V. I. Dotsenko, *Flot–Voyna–Pobeda, 1941–1945* (St Petersburg: Sudostroenie, 1995), p. 64; A. I. Barsukov and V. A. Zolotarev (eds), *Russky arkhiv: Velikaya Otechestvennaya Voyna. Prikazy i direktivy narodnogo komissara VMF v gody Velikoy Otechestvennoy voyny*, vol. X (Moscow: Terra, 1996), p. 12.
3 Dotsenko, *Flot*, pp. 64–74.
4 Apart from Dotsenko, *Flot*, a recent Russian study is I. V. Kasatonov *et al.* (eds), *Krasnoznamenny baltisky flot v Velikoy Otechestvennoy Voyny sovetskogo naroda 1941–1945 gg.*, 5 vols (Moscow: Voenizdat, 1990–92); authoritative German studies are Jürg Meister, *Der Seekrieg in den osteuropepäischen Gewässern 1941–1945* (Munich: Lehmanns, 1958); Friedrich Ruge, *The Soviets as Naval Opponents, 1941–1945* (Annapolis, MD: US Naval Institute Press, 1979).
5 See Gerd R. Ueberschär and Lev A. Bezymensky (eds), *Der Deutsche Angriff auf die Sowjetunion 1941: Die Kontroverse um die Präventivskriegsthese* (Darmstadt: Primus Verlag, 1998).
6 David M. Glantz, *Barbarossa: Hitler's Invasion of Russia 1941* (Stroud: Tempus, 2001), pp. 31–2.
7 Jonathan Shimsoni, 'Technology, Military Advantage and World War I: A Case of Military Entrepreneurship', *International Security*, vol.15(3) (Winter 1990–91), p. 199.
8 Donald W. Mitchell, *A History of Russian and Soviet Sea Power* (London: André Deutsch, 1974), p. 355; J. N. Westwood, *Russian Naval Construction, 1905–1945* (London: Macmillan Press, 1993), chapter 5; Gunnar Åselius, '"The Unskilled Fencer": Swedish Assessments of the Soviet Navy, 1921–1928', *Militärhistorisk tidskrift*, vol. 11 (1991), pp. 161–2.
9 Robert W. Herrick, *Soviet Naval Theory and Strategy: Gorshkov's Inheritance* (Annapolis, MD: US Naval Institute Press, 1988); he had treated the subject 20 years earlier in *Soviet Naval Strategy: Fifty Years of Theory and Practice* (Annapolis, MD: US Naval Institute Press, 1968).
10 K. A. Stalbo (ed.), *Istoriya voenno-morskogo iskusstva: Sovetskoe voenno-morskoe iskusstvo v grazhdanskoy voyne i v period postroeniya sotsialisma v SSSR (1917–1941 gg.)*, vol. II (Moscow: Voenizdat, 1963); Kuznetsov, *Nakanune*; an uncensored appendix to Kuznetsov's memoirs appeared in 1995, *Krutye povoroty: Is zapisok admirala* (Moscow: Molodaya gvardiya, 1995); in 1969–70, Gorshkov published a series of articles in *Morskoy Sbornik*, some of which were translated into English and published in US Naval Institute's *Proceedings* 1974, later published in Herbert R. Preston (ed.), *Red Star Rising at Sea*, (Annapolis, MD: US Naval Institute Press, 1974); Gorshkov's interpretation of the inter-war period Soviet Navy in these articles can also be found in his famous book *Morskaya moshch gosudarstva* (Moscow: Voenizdat, 1976, 1979) – English translation *The Sea Power of the State* (Oxford: Pergamon Press, 1979).
11 Monakov's articles appeared in *Morskoy Sbornik* in a series of ten articles labeled 'Sudba doktrin i teory' (The fate of doctrines and theories). The publishers made a mistake with the numbering of the last two episodes in the series and the correct numbers appear in square brackets. Monakov's contributions to the series were: '1: "Kakoy RSFR nuzhen flot?" 1922 g.', vol. 143(11) (1990); '2: "Kakoy RSFR nuzhen flot?" 1923–1925 gg.', vol. 143(12) (1990); together with N. Yu. Berezovsky, '4: "Flot dolzhen byt aktivnym". 1925–1928 gg.', vol. 144(3) (1991); '5: K istorii voprosa o "maloy voyne". 1927–1928 gg.', vol. 144(4) (1991); '6: Tanki ili korabli? 1928–1930 gg.', vol. 145(3) (1992); '7: Razgrom staroy shkoli, 1930–1931 gg.', vol. 145(7) (1992), '8: K bolshomu morskomu i okeanskomu flotu (1936–1939 gg.)',

vol. 147(5) (1994); '8 [9]: flot dlya "maloy royny"', vol. 147(3) (1994); together with V. Gribovsky, '9[10]: Na poroge bolshoy voyny', vol. 147(12) (1994). The third article of the series was A. Yemelin's 'Voennaya reforma, 1924–1928 gg.', vol. 144(2) (1991). See also Jürgen Rowher and Mikhail Monakov, *Stalin's Ocean-going Fleet: Soviet Naval Strategy and Shipbuilding Programmes, 1935–1953* (London: Frank Cass, 2001).
12 S. A. Zonin, *Admiral L. M. Galler: Zhizn i flotovodcheskaya deyatelnost* (Moscow: Voenizdat, 1991).
13 V. N. Ponimarovsky *et al.* (eds), *Voenno-morskaya akademiya (kratkaya istoriya)* (Leningrad: [TsKF VMF], 1991); Kasatonov *et al.* (eds), *Krasnoznamenny baltisky flot*; V. D. Dotsenko, *Morskoy biograficheskty slovar* (St Petersburg: Logos, 1995).
14 Westwood, *Russian Naval Construction*; V. N. Burev, *Otetchestvennoe voennoe korablostroenie v tretiem stoletty svoey istorii* (St Petersburg: Sudostroenie, 1995).
15 Ohto Manninen, *Molotovin cocktail – Hitlerin sateenvarjo: Toisen mailmansodan historian uudelleenkirjoitusta* (Helsinki: Painatuskeskus, 1994); Jari Leskinen, *Vaiettu Suomen Silta: Suomen ja Viron salainen sotilaainen yhtestoiminta Neuvostoliiton varalta vuosina 1930–1939* (Helsinki: Suomen Historiallinen Seura, 1997); Carl Van Dyke, *The Soviet Invasion of Finland, 1939–40* (London: Frank Cass, 1997).
16 Pavel Vladimirovich Petrov, 'Krasnoznamenny baltisky flot v sovetsko-finlanskoy voyne 1939–1940 gg.', 'unpublished dissertation, St Petersburg State University, Department of Russian History, spring term 2000'.
17 N. Yu. Berezovsky, S. S. Berezhnoy and Z. V. Nikolayeva, *Boevaya letopis sovetskogo voenno-morskogo flota 1917–1941* (Moscow: Voenizdat, 1993).
18 A. I. Barsukov and V. A. Zolotarev (eds), vol. X; *Russky arkhiv: Velikaya Otechestvennaya Voyna, nakanune voyny: Materialy soveshchany vyshego rukovodyashchyego sostava VMF SSSR v kontse 1940 goda*, vol. I.2 (Moscow: Terra, 1997).
19 See the discussion on the Russian Navy of the 1990s in a report from the Swedish Defense Research Establishment – Försvarets forskningsanstalt, *Rysk militär förmåga i ett tioårsperspektiv* (FOA-R – 99-01151-170 – SE, May 1999), pp. 167–89.
20 John Skogan, 'The Evolution of the Four Soviet Fleets, 1968–1987', in John Skogan and Arne Brundtland (eds), *Soviet Sea Power in Northern Waters* (London: Macmillan, 1990); Göran Andolf and Bertil Johansson, 'The Baltic – a Sea of Peace? Swedish Views of Soviet Naval Policy in the Baltic', in Göran Rystad, Klaus R. Böhme and Wilhelm M. Carlgren (eds), *In Quest of Trade and Security: The Baltic in Power Politics, 1500–1990*, vol. II, *1890–1990* (Stockholm: Probus, 1995); Geoffrey Till, 'The Great Powers and the Baltic', in ibid.; Wilhelm Agrell, 'Strategisk förändring och svensk–sovjetiska konflikter i Östersjöområdet efter 1945', *Scandia*, vol. 51 (1985); Michael MccGwire, *Military Objectives in Soviet Foreign Policy* (Washington, DC: Brookings Institution, 1987), p. 137 n. 8; Bryan Ranft and Geoffrey Till, *The Sea in Soviet Strategy* (London: Macmillan, 1983).
21 Berezovsky *et al.*, *Boevaya letopis*, p. 562.
22 The strength of the Baltic Fleet in 1941 according to Dotsenko, *Flot*, p. 238, and Berezovsky *et al.*, *Boevaya letopis*, p. 675 – these figures include ships commissioned after 22 June; Kuznetsov's budget proposal, 28 December 1940, f. r-1678, o. 1, d. 162, list 955.
23 The definition is taken from Barry R. Posen, *Explaining Military Doctrine: France, Britain and Germany between the Wars* (Ithaca, NY: Cornell University Press, 1984), p. 13.
24 See Jack Snyder, *The Ideology of the Offensive: Military Decision Making and the Disasters of 1914* (Ithaca, NY: Cornell University Press, 1984), p. 27; Wilhelm Agrell, *Allianspolitik och atombomber: Kontinuitet och förändring i den svenska försvarsdoktrinen 1945–1982* (Lund: Liber, 1985), pp. 19–26; Anders Berge, *Sakkunskap och politisk rationalitet: Den svenska flottan och pansarfartygsfrågan 1918–1939* (Stockholm: Almquist and Wiksell International, 1987), pp. 13–15.

25 A similar approach was used many years ago by Graham T. Allison in his work *Essence of Decision: Explaining the Cuban Missile Crises* (New York: HarperCollins, 1971).
26 Wayne P. Hughes, *Fleet Tactics: Theory and Practice* (Annapolis, MD: US Naval Institute Press, 1986); idem, 'The Strategy–Tactics Relationship', in Colin S. Gray and Roger W. Barnett (eds), *Seapower and Strategy* (Annapolis, MD: US Naval Institute Press, 1989).
27 Mahan's central work is *The Influence of Seapower upon History, 1660–1793* (1890); a modern edition with selected texts is *Mahan on Naval Strategy*, John B. Hattendorf (ed.), (Annapolis, MD: US Naval Institute Press, 1991).
28 See Volkmar Bueb, *Die 'Junge Schule' der fransözösischen Marine: Strategie und Politik, 1875–1900* (Boppard am Rhein: Boldt, 1971).
29 Julian S. Corbett, *Some Principles of Maritime Strategy*, Eric J. Grove (ed.), (Annapolis, MD: US Naval Institute Press 1988 [1911]), p. 322.
30 Corbett, *Some Principles*; for a useful introduction, comparing Mahan and Corbett, see John Gooch, 'Maritime Command: Mahan and Corbett', in Colin S. Gray and Roger W. Barnett (eds), *Seapower and Strategy* (Annapolis, MD: US Naval Institute Press, 1989).
31 James Goldrick and John B. Hattendorf (eds), *Mahan Is Not Enough: The Proceedings of a Conference on the Works of Sir Julian Corbett and Admiral Sir Herbert Richmond* (Newport, RI: Naval War College Press, 1993); a selection of Castex's writings in English translation in Raoul Castex, *Strategic Theories*, Eugenia C. Kiesling (ed.), (Annapolis, MD: US Naval Institute Press, 1994); on Wegener see Carl-Axel Gemzell, *Conflict, Organization and Innovation: A Study of German Naval Strategic Planning, 1888–1940* (Lund: Scandinavian University Books, 1973), pp. 215–22, 266–71, 332–55.
32 Bernhard Ireland, *Jane's Battleships of the 20th Century* (London: HarperCollins, 1996).
33 Westwood, *Russian Naval Construction*, pp. 73–5; Mitchell, *A History of Russian and Soviet Sea Power*, p. 274.
34 Mitchell, *A History of Russian and Soviet Sea Power*, pp. 370–2; Jürgen Rohwer, 'Russian and Soviet Naval Strategy', in John Skogan and Arne Brundtland (eds), *Soviet Sea Power in Northern Waters*, pp. 6–7; Herrick, *Soviet Naval Strategy*, pp. 19–27; John Erickson, *The Soviet High Command: A Military-Political History, 1918–1941* (London: Macmillan, 1962), pp. 165, 353–5.
35 Monakov, 'Sudba doktrin i teory, 8', pp. 39–42; V. Yu. Gribovsky, 'Na puti k "bolshomu morskomu i okeanskomu flotu"', *Gangut*, no. 9 (1995), pp. 12–13; cf. Mitchell, *A History of Russian and Soviet Sea Power*, pp. 373–6; Rohwer, 'Russian and Soviet Naval Strategy', pp. 7–9; Herrick, *Soviet Naval Theory and Strategy*, pp. 28–46; Ranft and Till, *The Sea in Soviet Strategy*, p. 87; Erickson, *The Soviet High Command*, p. 475; the decree from 19 October 1940 on the revised naval plan has been published in English translation by E. Mawdsley, 'The Fate of Stalin's Naval Program', *Warship International*, vol. 27 (1990), pp. 402–4.
36 K. A. Stalbo (ed.), *Istoriya voenno-morskogo isskusstva*, pp. 148–151; V. I. Achkasov et al., *Boevoy put sovetskogo voenno-morskogo flota* (Moscow: Voenizdat, 1988), p. 140; Ponikarovsky et al. (eds), *Voenno-morskaya akademiya*, p. 86; Monakov and Gribovsky, 'Sudba doktrin i teory, 9 [10, see n. 11]', p. 31.
37 Herrick, *Soviet Naval Theory and Strategy*, pp. 59, 63–4 n. 53, 83, 86–140; some 20 years earlier, Herrick had seen things differently, cf. idem, *Soviet Naval Strategy*, pp. 41–6.
38 Rohwer and Monakov, *Stalin's Ocean-going Fleet*.
39 Posen, *The Sources of Military Doctrine*, pp. 14–15.
40 Corbett, *Some Principles*, pp. 310–11.

2

STRATEGY

Chapters 5, 7 and 11 address the strategic dimension of Soviet naval doctrine. A study along similar lines is Barry R. Posen's book on the developments of French, British and German military doctrines between the world wars. Posen investigates how such factors as the distribution of power in the international system, technological progress, geography or the organizational interests of the military shape the formulation of doctrine. As a key factor when a state decides what mission to give to its armed forces, Posen emphasizes the (perceived) balance of power in relation to possible adversaries. States with revisionist and expansionist foreign policy aims, like Nazi Germany, are likely to develop offensive military doctrines. States seeking to preserve the status quo in the international system – like France and Britain before World War II – tend to adopt defensive or deterrent doctrines. As a rule, a feeling of temporary superiority also seems to inspire an offensive doctrine.

Historically, countries that chose offensive doctrines have had in common their desire for a short war. For various reasons (diminishing resources in relation to adversaries in the case of Nazi Germany, domestic instability in the case of most European Great powers in 1914, a vulnerable geopolitical situation in the case of Israel) they were uncertain of their ability to sustain a protracted struggle. If they had to invest all their resources in a single battle, they at least wanted to decide when and where it was to be fought. Correspondingly, states perceiving themselves as comparatively weak tend to prefer defensive and deterrent doctrines. States needing to husband resources or to await the intervention of allies often adopt defensive doctrines. A state whose 'capabilities fall short of its aims or needs, may throw its "political" will into the balance', and resort to a deterrent doctrine.[1]

Factors such as technology and geography, although exerting important influence, are not in the same way independent factors, according to Posen. Rather, a state's need to enhance its security, its wish to improve the balance of power, tend to inspire the development of new military technology. Furthermore, technology can neither be offensive or defensive in itself. It can only be applied in offensive and defensive ways. In 1940, France and Britain possessed more modern tanks and aircraft than did the Germans, but they used them in a less effective way and consequently suffered defeat.

Of course, the influence of geography is less susceptible to engineering. Therefore, Posen chooses to integrate geography together with the balance of power as a systemic element into a state's security environment. However, he observes, various actors' appreciation of geography's role is often influenced by their perception of the geopolitical balance.[2] Also, one is tempted to add, geography's influence can in some ways be neutralized by technology (fortifications, improved communications, long-range weapons systems).

If we are to follow Posen, the preparations for war in the Baltic formed a rational response to a perceived threat. Soviet decision makers weighed external threats against technical possibilities and economic resources, and then elected the doctrine they found to be most effective. Of course, this does not mean that they were necessarily right. They may have ignored serious threats to national security, misinterpreted technological developments or been too slow in implementing their insights. Nonetheless, in Chapters 5, 8 and 11 we will regard the needs of national security as the main vehicle of Soviet naval doctrinal developments.

Soviet grand strategy

After their triumph in the Civil War, just like the Russian rulers before and after them, the Bolsheviks were confronted with their country's awkward maritime geography. Although Russia had the longest coastline in the world, its access to the high seas was limited and Russian ships could nowhere reach the oceans without passing through sounds and archipelagos controlled by other powers. Nor were the vast distances that separated the maritime theaters in the Baltic, the Black Sea, the Arctic and the Pacific easy to overcome.

The Pacific Theater was definitely out of reach from the maritime theaters in Europe. Although the sea lane along the Arctic coast could be used for redeployments from the Northern Theater, the distance to cover was gigantic and the aid of icebreakers would always be needed. Only in 1936 did the first voyage of Soviet warships through the Arctic Sea occur. It took the two destroyers *Voykov* and *Stalin* more than three months to cover the distance from Kronstadt to Vladivostok, needing continuous support from icebreakers, supply ships and reconnaissance aircraft. Moreover, parts of the crew did not travel aboard the ships but were sent by railroad through Siberia. Nonetheless, this passage was celebrated as an extraordinary achievement, with plenty of decorations bestowed upon the participants. Although the Communist Party in its congratulatory telegram assured the expedition that its 'victory in the Arctic' would be of great importance to the country's defense, it was hard to see how this long and cumbersome route could play a vital strategic role in the future.[3]

Thus, if naval operations were to be coordinated between different maritime theaters, that coordination had to be limited to European waters. In 1922, the peace treaty in Lausanne between the victors of World War I and Turkey reopened the Dardanelles to the traffic of naval ships, prohibited since the end of the Crimean War in 1856. The only remaining restriction was that no single ship entering the

Black Sea was to be larger than those already stationed in the area. When Mikhail Petrov argued for the role of Soviet naval forces in a debate with Mikhail Tukhachevsky in the RVS in May 1928, he made the existence of the Lausanne Treaty a special point. Now, the Soviet Union could start developing a global naval strategy, with the Baltic and Black Sea fleets cooperating as a joint force. Among Petrov's audience, however, there was little support for this optimistic view.[4]

Already in the following year, the practical problems of transferring forces between the two theaters were ostentatiously demonstrated. When Turkey decided to modernize the old battle cruiser *Yakuz Sultan Selim* (formerly the German *Goeben*), the Soviet government saw an excuse to redeploy one battleship and one cruiser—*Parizhkaya Kommuna* and *Profintern*—from the Baltic to the Black Sea. Although their journey did not meet with much diplomatic protest, it still took almost two months to complete. There were not many ports along the route where the Soviet ships were allowed to bunker, and the stormy Bay of Biscay put the crews to hard tests. Later, the voyage of the *Parizhkaya Kommuna* and the *Profintern*, just like that of the *Voykov* and the *Stalin* in the Arctic, was to be commemorated as one of the most remarkable feats of Soviet seamanship during the inter-war era. If the redeployment of ships between the Baltic and Black Sea seemed an extraordinary achievement in peacetime, it was unlikely to be easily repeated during times of war or crisis.[5]

During his appearance before the RVS in 1928, Petrov also mentioned the possibility of using Russia's inner waterways as routes for strategic redeployment. If a canal was dug between the Don and the Volga (this project was realized only in 1952), this link could be used to transfer light forces between the maritime theaters in the north and south. As late as December 1940, the People's Commissar for the Navy, Kuznetsov, would urge the political leadership to begin the works on the Volga–Don Canal. Kuznetsov was then prepared to budge from the required depth of 5 meters, as 3.65 meters would be enough to satisfy the navy's most urgent needs. An alternative solution would be to link the Baltic and the Black Sea through a canal between the rivers Dnepr and Dvina, but that stretch would run dangerously close to the western border and also be too shallow for the passage of destroyers.[6]

At least, the inner waterways were extended northwards in 1933 when the White Sea Canal ('the Stalin Canal') was completed and the Baltic Theater linked to the Northern Theater. However, because the White Sea Canal was shallow, narrow and blocked by ice for six months a year, communications remained problematic.[7] When the Soviets founded a naval flotilla in the north in 1932, the first units were transferred there from the Baltic Fleet. Two destroyers, two submarines and two patrol craft went up from Kronstadt to Murmansk, partly dismantled and towed by barges, needing more than three months to get there via the canal.[8] In the autumn of 1937, the submarine *Dekabrist* set a record in reaching Murmansk from Kronstadt in three weeks.[9] The poor navigability of the canal was further demonstrated during the war against Finland in 1939–40. As a result, in January 1940 the People's Commissariat for River Transports was ordered to prepare for complementary excavation works.[10]

Although there were many solemn declarations on the role of naval forces in protecting Soviet commerce and supporting the world revolutionary movement during the inter-war period,[11] there was thus no global Soviet naval strategy, nor any concrete plans for how fleets in different theaters were to support each other in the event of a general conflict.

The role of the Baltic

In reality, strategic focus came to be concentrated to the Baltic. The Northern Theater, although important, was too remote to become a decisive area of operations. In the Black Sea and Caspian Theaters, where the position of the imperialists was deemed insecure, the Soviets could easily gain local supremacy and then take a defensive posture. Although the threat of Japanese aggression in the Pacific seemed grave, Anglo-American influence for a long time acted as a deterring factor.[12]

What then, was the role of the Baltic? As the Swedish historian Alf W. Johansson has pointed out, the Baltic is at the same time a bay of the Atlantic and a secluded inland sea, and this fact is of fundamental importance when the region's geopolitical role is to be analyzed.[13] Traditionally, the dominating power in the Baltic has always argued that as an inland sea, this should be regarded a secluded 'mare clausum' to the navies of nonlittoral states. Erik of Pomerania, ruler of the three Scandinavian kingdoms, who introduced a Sound Toll in 1429 (which remained in force until 1857), first formulated this principle. In the seventeenth century, the 'mare clausum' idea was taken over by Sweden.[14]

In the late eighteenth century, when Russia had succeeded Sweden as the leading power in the region, the court in Saint Petersburg organized the states around the Baltic Sea into 'neutrality leagues' to prevent the incursion of foreign navies. By advocating the Baltic's status as confined inland water, this predominantly land-locked power saw a way to counter the threat of invasion. As we will see, the same historical pattern was discernible during the inter-war period, when Soviet Russia was challenged by some of the most powerful navies in the world and the exclusion of nonlittoral powers became a fundamental task for Soviet diplomats and naval strategists in the region. Later, during the Cold War, the Soviet Union would for similar reasons launch diplomatic campaigns to make the Baltic a 'Sea of Peace' or Scandinavia a 'nuclear-free zone.'[15]

Throughout history, however, the leading naval powers in northern Europe have just as stubbornly challenged the claims of the regional hegemonic powers in the Baltic, asserting their right of free access to the area and claiming this sea to be a 'mare liberum' and a continuation of the oceans. In 1658–60, Dutch navies prevented Swedish domination, and during the Napoleonic wars threatening Russian domination made the British intervene repeatedly (with Copenhagen as an unfortunate stop on the way – both in 1801 and 1807). A relatively late example of this behavior by Western sea powers was the Baltic tour of the US battleship *Iowa* in the autumn of 1985, intended to demonstrate the meaning of the Reagan administration's 'forward maritime strategy'.[16]

Map 1 The Baltic region in the inter-war period.

At least since the Napoleonic wars, when the imbalance between Russia and its northwestern neighbors became truly apparent, Western power projection in the region has been facilitated by the fact that the minor countries have supported the principle of the Baltic as a 'mare liberum,' welcoming the presence of nonlittoral fleets.[17]

Parallel to the wish to keep nonlittoral powers out of the Baltic, during the inter-war period the Soviets also wished to move their own frontiers in the region further west to protect the city of Leningrad. Apart from their ideological motives for defending the home of the Great October Revolution, they saw Leningrad as a major military industrial center – the capital of Russian ship construction and a vital supplier to the Red Army's mechanized forces. In July 1925, the People's Commissar for Defense, Mikhail Frunze, published a famous article in the commissariat's paper, *Krasnaya Zvesda*, entitled 'We need a powerful Baltic Fleet'. Although naval forces would always be of secondary importance to a land power like the Soviet Union, Frunze wrote, the country would always need a strong fleet in the Baltic to protect Leningrad and its factories.[18]

In 1925, before the five-year plans shifted Russia's economic geography eastwards, Leningrad housed 56 percent of the Soviet Union's rubber production and 48 percent of the country's electromechanical industry. The leading Soviet strategist during the 1920s, Alexander Svechin, compared the city's role in a future war to that of Sevastopol during the Crimean War. According to Svechin, it would have been more advantageous to the Russians in 1854 to give up this fortress and take up the fight further inland. However, as Sevastopol was also the main base of the Black Sea Fleet, the tsarist army had been forced to engage the enemy 'at the water's edge, under the most advantageous circumstances to the enemy's communications and under maximally disadvantageous circumstances to us'. Logistic conditions here were superior to those along the thinly populated border with Poland, as the sea-lanes of communications and the density of major population centers west of Leningrad would greatly facilitate the enemy's concentration.[19]

Through the outcome of World War I, Russia's coastal zone in the Baltic had shrunk to some 170 miles in the inner part of the Gulf of Finland. The main naval base remained in Kronstadt on the island of Kotlin, about 20 miles outside Petrograd. According to plans by General F. I. Todtleben, a circle of armored forts and battery positions had been erected in the late nineteenth century on the many islets and skerries surrounding Kotlin Island. Even before these fortifications were built, Kronstadt's position in the inner part of the Gulf of Finland had appeared safe and secluded (Peter the Great contemplated building Saint Petersburg here). However, the independence of Finland in 1917 suddenly relocated Kotlin strategically, situating it less than 13 miles from foreign territory and within range of hostile artillery. In the years 1919–20, when the Royal Navy held a squadron in the Baltic to support Balts and Finns in their struggle for independence, the dangers of this new environment were forcefully demonstrated. From bases on Finnish territory, Kronstadt was repeatedly bombarded from the air. One dark

August night in 1919, seven small British torpedo craft sneaked into the harbor and in a daring surprise attack slightly damaged battleship *Petropavlovsk*.[20]

The Baltic as a theater of operations

However, the Baltic's proven accessibility to Great power naval demonstrations is somewhat modified by the geographical conditions which characterize the region in operational and tactical terms—for example, in the way terrain, population density, communications, etc. influence the conduct of military operations in the area. From this perspective, local powers seem to have had an advantage in comparison with the great Western sea powers. The many narrow straits, the shallow archipelagos, the difficult ice conditions and the short distances from coast to coast make the Baltic a truly difficult environment for an ocean-going Great power fleet. The British gave up the idea of the Royal Navy entering the Baltic in wartime already before World War I, although romantics like Winston Churchill could still dream about it as late as 1939.[21]

The Gulf of Finland—which was the primary area of operations of the Soviet Baltic Fleet during the inter-war period—offers a particularly awkward environment. From December to April, ship movements are impeded by ice, and during the rest of the year the Gulf can easily be blocked where the waters are shallow and easy to mine (in the inner parts between the islands of Hogland/Suursaari and Kotlin); in the middle at the straits between Helsinki and Tallinn; at the exits at Hangö. Landing operations are also problematic. The eastern coast is lined by marshes, the northern coast by steep rocks and the many thousands islands and shoals that constitute the Finnish archipelago. Thus, the best area to land troops for an attack against Saint Petersburg is on the southern side of the Gulf, as the Swedes planned to do in 1788.[22] However, as the chief of the Soviet Naval Staff, Lev Galler, concluded in a special report in the summer of 1939, although there are no steep shores along the southern shore, difficult terrain conditions still make the landing of more than a company-sized force difficult. Only in the Kaporsky and Luzhky Bay areas at the city's southwestern approaches is there room to set ashore a larger force.[23]

However, as well as being difficult to enter from the outside, the Gulf of Finland can also be easily sealed off by outsiders. If the Soviets wanted to sail out of the Gulf northwards, into the Gulf of Bothnia, they would have to pass through the continuous archipelagos of Hangö, Turku and Åland. Here, all navigation outside marked sea lanes was hazardous, and there were also numerous hiding places for enemy submarines and torpedo boats. If the Baltic Fleet chose to sail southwards, into the southern Baltic Sea, it would have to pass the shallow Bay of Riga with the two major islands Hiiumaa (Dagö) and Saaremaa (Ösel), whose coastlines are perforated by numerous coves and skerries. Consequently, the approaches to the Bay of Riga (Muhu or Moon Sound in the north, Sõela Sound in the middle, Irben Sound in the south) could easily be barred with minefields. Thus, from a Soviet point of view the defensive advantages in the Baltic could just as easily become disadvantages. This is more or less what happened in 1941, when the Baltic Fleet was bottled up in port for most of the war.

Conclusion

From a strategic perspective, the way Soviet leaders perceived a naval war in the Baltic during the inter-war period is best explained by how they appreciated likely opponents and the international situation. As communication problems between the Soviet Union's different maritime theaters seemed insurmountable, they had to be regarded as separate arenas. This is what the Soviet strategists did, and for various reasons, they looked upon the Baltic Theater as the main region of naval interest.

Geographic factors did not decidedly recommend either an offensive or a defensive strategy in the theater. The threat from incursion by superior navies, and the risk of being bottled up in the Gulf of Finland in the initial stage of a war, suggested a preemptive strike against potential bases in neighboring countries and the blocking of the Sounds to outsiders. At the same time, the poor navigability in Soviet coastal waters would seriously hamper an attacking enemy and offered strong arguments to choose defense instead. As Posen claims with regard to Britain and France between the world wars, geography seldom recommends a clear choice between offensive and defensive doctrines. Instead, it is how the political landscape is evaluated that matters.

As we shall see, this would also be true of the Soviet assessments of the Baltic during the inter-war period.

Notes

1. Posen, *Explaining Military Doctrine*, pp. 69–73, quotation from pp. 72–3.
2. Ibid., passim.
3. Berezovsky *et al.*, *Boevaya letopis*, p. 604.
4. N. Yu. Berezovsky (ed.), 'Na borbu s limotrofami,' *Voenno-istorichesky zhurnal*, vol. 54(4) (1993), pp. 59–60.
5. Zonin, *Admiral L. M. Galler*, p. 237; Berezovsky *et al.*, *Boevaya letopis*, pp. 571–2.
6. Kuznetsov to Stalin, Molotov, Voroshilov and Zhdanov, 12 December 1940, f. r-1678, o. 1, d. 162, list 919–21.
7. Apart from the Soviet unwillingness to discuss military matters in public, this may explain why Isakov only mentioned the canal's role in strengthening the Soviet economy when evaluating its importance to national defense. Cf. I. S. Isakov, 'Belomorsko-baltiskaya vodnaya magistral: Naznachenie i mashtaby stroitelstva', in *Izbrannye trudy: Okeanologiya, geografiya i voennaya istoriya* (Moscow: Izdatelstvo Nauka, 1984), p. 511 (originally published in *Morskoy Sbornik*, vol. 86 [1933], pp. 11–12).
8. Berezovsky *et al.*, *Boevaya letopis*, pp. 587–8; Monakov, 'Sudba doktrin i teory. 8 [9, see p. 17, n. 11]', pp. 39–40.
9. The commander of the Baltic Fleet to the commander of the Naval Staff, 12 February 1938, f. r-1877, o.1, d. 41, list 1–2.
10. Kuznetsov to Stalin, Molotov and Voroshilov, 8 January 1940; Molotov to the People's Commissariat of River Transports, 8 January (draft); f. r-1678, o. 1, d. 162, list 9–12.

11 Berezovsky *et al.*, *Boevaya letopis*, pp. 603–4; cf. M. Mitchell, *The Maritime History of Russia, 848–1948* (London: Sidgwick & Jackson, 1949), pp. 306–9.
12 For the assessment of various naval theaters in Soviet strategy, see Gunnar Åselius, 'Naval Theaters in Soviet Grand Strategic Assessments, 1920–1940', *Journal of Slavic Military Studies*, vol. 13(1) (2000).
13 Alf W. Johansson, 'Östersjöproblematiken i ett historiskt perspektiv, sedd ur svensk synvinkel', *Gotlands roll i Östersjön i historiskt perspektiv och nutid*, appendix to *Kungl. krigsvetenskapsakademiens handlingar och tidskrift*, vol. 190 (1986), p. 5.
14 Cf. F. Askgaard, *Kampen om Östersjön på Carl X Gustafs tid*, Carl X Gustaf–studier 6 (Stockholm: Militärhistoriska förlaget, 1974), pp. 195–6.
15 Bo Johnson, 'Kolliderande suveränitet: Översikt över folkrättsliga problem i det nordiska närområdet', *Tidskrift i Sjöväsendet*, vol. 136(4) (1973), pp. 188–200.
16 On the strategic importance of the Baltic approaches, see Johan Engström and Ole L. Frantzén (eds), *Øresunds strategiske rolle i et historisk perspektiv: Föredrag hållna vid symposium på Revingehed i Skåne och på kastellet i København 3–7 juni 1996* (Stockholm: Armémuseum, 1998).
17 Göran Rystad, 'The Åland Question and the Balance of Power in the Baltic during the First World War', in Rystad *et al.* (eds), *In Quest of Trade and Security*, vol. II, p. 51; Bo Hugemark, 'The Swedish Navy – Auxiliary Force or Strategic Factor?', in ibid.
18 Mikhail Frunze, 'Nam nuzhen silny baltisky flot', *Krasnaya Zvezda*, 3 July 1925.
19 Alexander Svechin, *Strategiya* (Moscow: Gosvoenizdat, 1927), pp. 35, 98.
20 Berezovsky *et al.*, *Boevaya letopis*, p. 136; for many years, Western literature incorrectly stated that the British succeeded in putting two battleships and one depot ship out of action during their raid on 18 August: cf. R. H. Ullman, *Anglo-Soviet Relations, 1917–1921*, vol. II, *Britain and the Russian Civil War* (Princeton, NJ: Princeton University Press, 1968), p. 273; Olavi Hovi, *The Baltic Area in British Policy, 1918–1921*, vol. I, *From the Compiégne Armistice to the Implementation of the Versailles Treaty, 11.11.1918–20.1. 1920* (Helsinki: Studia Historica Helsinki, 1980), pp. 204–6.
21 David Sweet, 'The Baltic in British Diplomacy before the First World War', *Historical Journal*, vol. 13 (1970), pp. 482–4; Brian Bond, 'British War Planning for Operations in the Baltic before the First and Second World Wars', in Rystad *et al.* (eds), *In Quest of Trade and Security*, vol. II.
22 Jan Glete, 'Östersjön som maritimt operationsområde – ett historiskt perspektiv', *Tidskrift i Sjöväsendet*, vol. 162(3) (1999).
23 Memorandum by Galler to Kuznetsov, 28 July 1939, f. r-1877, o. 1, d. 39, list 152.

3

ORGANIZATIONAL RIVALRY

Chapters 6, 9 and 12 examine Soviet naval doctrine and the Baltic Fleet from the perspective of organizational rivalry. According to this perspective, inter-service competition is a more important factor in the formulation of doctrine than the influence of the external environment. In the real world, there is seldom a conscious choice between clearly defined alternatives. Various financial, domestic-political and bureaucratic constraints exercise their influence, pushing developments in a certain direction. To give professional legitimacy to the outcome, the military then formulates a doctrine in retrospect. The decision makers are not viewed primarily as experts dealing with problems within their sphere of professional competence, but as representatives of rival bureaucracies. In 1990, a US admiral publicly admitted that in 'peacetime I could just never, never bring myself to do anything to help the Air Force or Army'.[1]

It is often assumed that military organizations prefer offensive doctrines, as these provide a better basis for effective, long-time planning. Furthermore, offensive doctrines help to enhance the military's autonomy, influence and status in society in peacetime. A well-known example of this strand of research is Jack Snyder's study of the war planning of the European Great powers in 1914. Why did the three leading military powers on the European continent before World War I – France, Germany and Russia – all adopt offensive strategies, regardless of the fact that they only planned to go to war in self-defense, and that considerable evidence suggested that defensive strategies would be more cost-effective than offensive ones? According to Snyder, rational calculation is only one of the elements influencing the choice between an offensive and a defensive strategy. Just as important are motivational biases in the form of institutional interests, or the cognitive and organizational need to simplify large amounts of information into doctrine which can readily be translated into coherent field manuals, war plans and military college curricula. Rational calculation will only outweigh other determinants when the supporting evidence is clear and unambiguous. Otherwise, these motivational and doctrinal considerations will come into play.[2]

The Swedish historian Carl-Axel Gemzell offers another example of the role of organizational rivalry in his study of the German Navy in the period 1888–1940. Gemzell asserts that during the early twentieth century the influential 'Trafalgar

Ideal' in naval thinking, the Mahanian dream of winning the entire war by inflicting upon the enemy a single devastating blow, had in fact been taken over from ground-war theoreticians like Jomini, Clausewitz and Schlieffen. In order to compare favorably with armies and to justify the costly naval race, navies must prove themselves equally capable of winning wars in a short time. The notion of the decisive battle at sea satisfied the need to offer politicians a 'quick return' on defense investments. Gemzell has also studied the navy of the German Democratic Republic (GDR) during the Cold War, showing that for similar reasons the East German *Volksmarine* planned for offensive operations against Denmark, which it lacked the practical ability to carry out.[3]

In his study of the Swedish Navy during the inter-war period, Anders Berge also emphasizes the role of organizational considerations. Until the mid-1930s, the Swedish Navy argued for the procurement of a fourth armored coast defense battleship of the *Sverige* class. This ship was of pre-1914 design and could no longer be considered modern. From a strictly professional point of view, the navy should instead have been asking for something 'larger and faster'. Given the political circumstances at hand, however, such a proposal was deemed unrealistic. Hence the navy settled for what it believed to be best it could get, that is, more of what it already had.[4]

The Swedish naval officers thus reduced their appreciation of future naval threats in the Baltic, so that a role would be left for the *Sverige* ship. With the tight fiscal restrictions that governed public spending in most countries during the inter-war period, the military became more interested in preserving existing organizational structures than in developing new ones. When analyzing military doctrine from the perspective of organizational interests, one should therefore not necessarily ascribe to the military a constant urge to inflate possible threats or even to advocate offensive doctrines. Nor should doctrine always be understood as the result of conscious bureaucratic intrigue or conspiracy. Rather, a complex set of circumstances tend to coincide, narrowing the options of the decision makers. In this situation, the formula which seems possible to implement with the least pain is the one which is chosen. The Swedish peace researcher Håkan Wiberg has referred to the 'principle of the adjusted threat', according to which a military doctrine in most cases simply is a response to 'a threat perception which is not too difficult nor too easy, but adjusted to the existing organization and the current budget-proposals'.[5]

An illustrative example can be found in Wilhelm Agrell's study of Swedish military doctrine during the Cold War. During the 1950s, there was desire in the Swedish defense establishment to acquire tactical nuclear weapons. These plans were abandoned in the early 1960s – due to domestic opinion, but also due to fears that the development of nuclear weapons might be too costly and consume too large a proportion of the future defense budget. When it had become obvious that the Swedish military would possess no nuclear arsenal in the future, the major conflict scenario in defense planning was quickly rewritten. The risk of a nuclear war in Europe had to be played down. The idea of a full-scale European war was discreetly replaced by the prospect of a local conflict waged with limited, conventional means. Sweden's strategic position was also reassessed. The country was no longer said to constitute 'half the confrontation-line between the two military blocks in Europe', but ascribed a peripheral location, on the 'quiet northern flank'. As it were, NATO and Warsaw Pact military doctrines did change during the 1960s towards an increased emphasis on the possibility of conventional wars, but this only occurred some years later. Not until the end of the decade did the changed Swedish threat perception make real sense from a rational point of view.[6]

In short, Chapters 6, 9 and 12 deals with the question 'How?' How was the fleet to fight the war, and how was it to cooperate with forces on the ground and in the air? The competition between sailors and soldiers was not limited to discussions on the defense budget but also concerned the practical preparations for war. When we explain the shifts between various schools of naval thought, the navy's relationship to the Red Army and the Baltic Fleet's relationship to the Leningrad Military District (LVO = *Leningradsky Voenny Okrug*) will therefore play a central role.

To understand the problems of organizational rivalry better, we must first take a look at naval policy during the tsarist period, as well as at the international evolution of joint operations between the world wars.

The heritage of the 1912 naval construction program

Before the Russo-Japanese War in 1904–1905, Russia had no modern naval administration. In the wake of defeat, however, the antiquated office of 'General-Admiral' had been abolished (the last General-Admiral, Grand Duke Aleksey Aleksandrovich [1850–1908] was known for his idleness and love of 'slow ships and fast women'). In May 1906, a naval 'general staff' was created, for the first time providing the naval ministry with an efficient organ for long-term planning, analysis and intelligence collection, placing operational command firmly in professional hands. The naval staff chief was to be the Navy Minister's closest assistant, have a permanent seat in the newly created State Defense Council and a direct telephone line to the imperial palace. Simultaneously, voluntary organizations such as the League for Renewal of the Fleet and the Russian Naval Union began mobilizing public support in favor of a recreated battle fleet. There were, for the first time, efficient bureaucratic pressure groups within the administration as well as a lobby groups outside, dedicated to the furthering of Russian sea power. Paradoxically as it may seem, the sheer scale of the Far Eastern catastrophe had thus strengthened the navy's political position.[7]

On the other hand, after the setback in the Pacific the main task of the navy had to be sought in the Baltic, where the capital Saint Petersburg needed protection. Most likely, this protection was best secured through minefields, coastal artillery, submarines and torpedo boats. In fact, the few naval successes the Russians had registered during the war with Japan had all been related to the use of mines or torpedoes. During the conflict as many as 18 major warships – seven Russian and 11 Japanese – had been sunk by mines. Nonetheless, what the Russian naval establishment wanted – just like naval officers of any other Great power at the time – were battleships. As the navy had to be recreated from a shambles anyway, those ships could preferably be of the latest generation – similar to the *Dreadnought* type which the British had introduced in 1906.

Although the acquirement of these turbine-propelled warships with their ten 12-inch guns would secure Russia a prestigious position among the naval powers, dreadnoughts might not be ideal for waging a defensive struggle in shallow coastal waters. Navy Minister Biriliev offered a perceptive analysis of the navy's dilemma when he addressed his fellow officers at a conference in April 1906: 'Setting to work on these big multi-million ships we must ask ourselves, will they be suitable for the Baltic and the Gulf of Finland?' If the navy's principal justification was operations in the Baltic, its argumentation for capital ships must be plausible in this special maritime environment.[8]

The navy's initial strategy was to assign to the desired battleship squadron an independent, mobile role in 'upholding the Empire's interests in distant waters', separated from the main mission of defending the capital. Against angry opposition in the State Defense Council from the army and the foreign and finance ministries, this line of argument soon proved counter-productive. Then the need for heavy seaborne artillery to defend the mine barriers in the Gulf of Finland was put forward. Finance Minister Kokovtsov retorted that this could be done 'just as well from old ships; firing in defense of a position does not need fast ships; you just need gun platforms'. The Navy Minister vaguely replied that only battleships could defeat battleships.[9]

Discussions dragged on until 1912, when the navy finally won approval for a 'strengthened naval construction program' which by 1930 would supply Russia with a force of 24 battleships and 12 battle cruisers. A crucial role for the outcome was played by Navy Minister Admiral Ivan Grigorovich, a man who had a certain talent both as a speaker in the Duma and as a corridor lobbyist between sessions. Grigorovich also managed to convince some of his civilian colleagues of the advantages of strengthening the navy. Foreign Minister Izvolsky feared the consequences for Russia's Great power status if the country had no battleships. Finance Minister Kokovtsov changed his mind when he realized that huge defense contracts could benefit domestic industry.[10]

The discussion of the 1912 naval construction program has been described here in some detail as the same arguments were to reappear to a surprising degree during the 1920s, when the navy again sought to justify the need for capital ships and the fleet's operational area was again restricted to the Gulf of Finland. As was the case with the post-1905 debate, the discussion on naval policy during the 1920s largely dealt with conditions in the Baltic Theater. The greater part of Russia's remaining naval forces was stationed in these waters, as most ships of the Black Sea Fleet had joined the White side during the Civil War and been irretrievably lost abroad.[11]

Moreover, the 1912 navy construction program ensured that Russia at the end of World War I would be in possession of an embryo ocean fleet. There were three

23,000-ton battleships of the *Gangut* class in varying states of operational readiness, and a fourth *Gangut* ship (*Poltava*, renamed *Frunze* in 1926) under construction at the Petrograd shipyards. In addition, the keels of four 30,000-ton battle cruisers of the *Borodino* class lay rusting on the staple beds (in 1923 three of them were finally towed off to Germany and sold as scrap).[12]

Should Russia continue to build on its 'heritage from 1912', or should an entirely new naval structure be created? During the 1920s, this became a central issue in Soviet naval debate. Those skeptical of an ocean fleet could refer to Russia's poverty and industrial backwardness. However, the few warships Russia had were either capital ships or intended to operate around a core of such units, so a continuation of the 1912 heritage could also be rational.

Joint operations in the inter-war period

After World War I, the image of joint operations between fleets and armies was largely formed by the allied failure at Gallipoli in 1915. Although two years later in the Baltic Theater the Germans captured the island of Ösel (Saaremaa) in a successful joint attack with all three services participating, that episode gained considerably less attention in international debate. Few military analysts believed military power could be successfully projected from the sea to land. To the extent that amphibious operations did occur during the 1920s (American policing actions in Central America and the Caribbean, the French – Spanish expedition against Morocco in 1925) they were undertaken in a 'colonial' context against inferior opposition.

In 1939, Japan was the only Great power with a capacity for large-scale amphibious landings, the Japanese operation against Shanghai two years earlier being the largest of its kind since Gallipoli. However, the Japanese amphibious forces were divided between the army and the navy, each service preparing to solve its own strategic missions (on the Asian mainland for the army, in Southeast Asia and the Pacific for the navy) with little doctrinal coordination between them. In Britain, there was some serious theoretical thinking on the problems of amphibious warfare, but no firm institutional base for developing those ideas further. Before World War II, the US Marine Corps was alone in developing a coherent amphibious doctrine. The corps had as its wartime mission to seize advance bases for the navy and knew that its organizational survival depended on successful specialization. However, when it came to constructing efficient landing vessels, the United States lagged far behind both Japan and Britain.[13]

The Russian–Baltic perspective

Among the Baltic nations, the perspective on jointness differed somewhat from that of the leading naval powers. In a narrow sea, the projection of military power must always require close interaction between naval and ground forces, as well as a highly specialized amphibious capacity.[14] In older times, these functions were secured through the use of oared galley fleets, which closely followed the movements of armies along the coasts and in reality served as an offshore prolongation of the army's seaboard flank. In 1719–21, during the final stage of the Great Nordic War, the Russian Admiral Apraksin successfully ravished the Swedish eastern coast with his galleys. To some extent, Apraksin's success depended on the fact that Sweden had allowed its galley fleet to decline, having for several decades concentrated its naval spending on big ships of the line, as would be fitting for a European Great power. However, from 1756 to 1824 the Swedes maintained a 'fleet of the Army' (*Arméns flotta*), equipped with highly specialized shallow-going vessels, rowed gunboats and galleys but manned by ordinary infantry. Until Sweden had been finally reduced to small-power status through the Napoleonic wars, the archipelago fleet remained a crucial instrument in the country's planning for offensive operations. Along the island-clad coasts of the Baltic, only small vessels had the mobility and operational diversity required.[15] As the British naval historian Geoffrey Till points out, throughout history, the navies of the Baltic states have developed 'a different conception of maritime strategy and... a different maritime culture from those characteristic of nations facing the open oceans'.[16]

The Russian experience of World War I testifies further to this fact. In 1914, at the time of mobilization, the Baltic Fleet had been placed under the command of the Petersburg Military District with orders to support the defense of the capital. The Germans were expected to be superior (which in reality they were not), and so the strategy adopted in the theater was mainly defensive. In accordance with the operational plan of 1910, double minefields were laid out between Porkalla and Revel (Tallinn), that were covered by fire from heavy artillery ships and coastal batteries ashore. If intruders got through these barriers, submarines and fast torpedo craft were waiting in the archipelago behind. Further to the rear, an attacker would have to deal with the mighty fortifications of Kronstadt. The efficiency of these defenses was clearly demonstrated in November 1916, when a German attempt to force the mine barriers ended in catastrophe. Seven out of 11 German destroyers were sunk.[17]

During the war, the Baltic Fleet had also undertaken some minor offensive operations: submarines had attacked iron ore exports from Sweden to Germany and mines had been laid out off the Pomeranian coast. Sweden – a neutral neighbor whose honest intentions were in constant doubt – often featured as a target in Russian offensive planning. Already on 4 August 1914, the Baltic Fleet Staff had instructed all ships on patrol to look out for Swedish warships, as 'the appearance of the Swedish fleet off our coast would signify the beginning of operations against us'. Fleet Commander Admiral Essen prepared to sail to the port of Fårösund in the island of Gotland to present an ultimatum to the Swedes, requesting them to stay in port for the duration of the war. In spite of the friendly relations between the two countries, Essen explained in his draft of an ultimatum to his Swedish colleague that he could not disregard the repeated outbursts of anti-Russian sentiments in Sweden in recent years. To ensure the security of his forces, he was therefore obliged to regard any alien ships he would meet at sea as hostile. Luckily, a telegram from the commander in chief, Grand Duke Nikolay, canceled Essen's operation at the last moment. The Grand Duke reminded Essen that his main task was to protect the capital, and added that his proposed ultimatum would be an insult to a loyal neutral.[18]

However, fears that Sweden would enter the war on Germany's side remained. In the beginning of 1916, rumors were especially persistent. According to the Baltic Fleet Staff, the Swedes informed the Germans regularly on allied traffic in Swedish waters. There were also secret contacts between the Swedish and German general staffs, and in nationalist circles a continuous agitation for war. A German landing in Finland, followed by a popular uprising there, would probably increase the influence of this agitation on Swedish public opinion. The government in Stockholm had already allowed young Finns to pass through the country on their way to military training camps in Germany. If the Swedes also allowed German troops to pass across their territory in the opposite direction, the Russian capital Saint Petersburg would be in serious danger.[19]

In early May 1916, Captain Keller of the Baltic Fleet Staff department of operations presented a memorandum on how to react to such a contingency. His discussion of the problems of a Baltic campaign remained equally valid during the 1920s and 1930s, so his memorandum will be examined here in some detail.

Keller, who had served as naval attaché in Stockholm before the war, pointed out that if the Swedes were to invade Finland successfully, they first had to seize control over the Åland Islands. Hitherto, when neutral countries had entered the war there had always been some previous diplomatic bargaining, so the formal declaration of war had never come as a surprise to anyone. If Sweden's drift into the camp of the Central powers was to follow the same pattern, Russia would get a chance to seize the initiative itself and preclude the aggressor. Keller's successor as attaché in Stockholm, Lieutenant Petrov, had also realized the importance of preemptive action against Sweden and suggested a mine-laying operation in Swedish waters if the country was to abandon its neutrality.[20]

Keller went further than this and proposed a rather complicated and risky operation: a surprise attack with light naval and ground forces against the northern outskirts of the Stockholm archipelago, where Sweden's exits to the Åland archipelago were to be sealed off with minefields, coastal batteries, submarines and surface ships. The object would be to win control over the Granhamnsfjärden Bay. According to Keller, this area had been secretly designed as the wartime operational base of the Swedish Navy. Although there were no permanent installations here of any kind, the terrain offered many good anchoring sites and was easy to defend. The loss of Granhamnsfjärden Bay would impede a Swedish capture of Åland Islands, and thus eliminate any hopes for a successful Swedish – German landing on the Finnish mainland.

With regard to the risks, Keller stressed that one of the peculiarities of archipelago warfare was that major results could be achieved with small forces. Historical experience from previous wars between Swedes and Russians in the

Baltic testified to the fact that the display of initiative and the ability to operate in joint formations were of crucial importance. Absolute numbers, on the other hand, played a lesser role. At the same time, Keller observed, the ships of the Swedish Navy had for a long time been specially designed to operate in the archipelago and possessed a highly mobile logistic organization. Regrettably, the Baltic Fleet had no such advantages. However, he believed that an appropriate task force for the Granhamnsfjärden operation could be organized around gunboats, small destroyers, submarines and shallow-draft steamers.[21]

Seemingly, Keller's views won recognition. Only a few days later, the commander of the Baltic Fleet, Admiral Kanin, reported to Petrograd that he would be able to hold Åland and defend the Finnish mainland only if he was allowed to 'preclude the enemy in the execution of certain operations of decisive importance'. In his report, Admiral Kanin also emphasized the need to initiate preemptive operations at the proper time, 'immediately before the formal declaration of war', an idea which was sanctioned by the Tsar.[22]

Sweden stuck to her neutrality during World War I, so Keller's proposal never had to be put into practice. Nevertheless, he had identified some of the major problems which would occupy the Baltic Fleet Command during the following decades. Those of a strategic nature we have discussed in the previous chapter: the threat of being locked up in port in the initial phase of a war and the hope of escaping this threat through a preemptive strike. Those of an operational nature, which concern us here, pertained to the need for a joint approach before the challenges of archipelago warfare.

The influence of mechanized warfare

It could be argued that the problems concerning joint operations should not have come as a surprise to Soviet naval planners, keeping in mind the Russian experience of World War I and the common tradition of Baltic powers. However, during the Soviet period the problems of archipelago warfare were accentuated even further because of the Red Army's operational doctrine. From the mid-1920s, the Soviet Army prepared for a mechanized war based on highly mobile forces thrusting deep into enemy territory. Especially in the Baltic Theater, a forceful advance would be necessary to create a security zone around the vital city of Leningrad. This meant offensive operations against both Finland and Estonia, for example, along both the northern and southern shores of the Gulf of Finland. Securing control of the waters in between, the Baltic Fleet would constitute the strategic link between the two main thrusts of the ground campaign. As the ground forces advanced further and further into enemy country, the fleet must have considerable firepower and a capability to operate at an increasing distance from its own home bases. As it was to keep pace with the rapidly moving troops inland, it must possess sufficient mobility and the capacity to operate close to the shore.

If the Baltic Fleet was to invest in firepower, logistic capacity and operational range, it needed 'big ships'. If it were to remain mobile in the archipelago and keep pace with the swiftly advancing ground forces ashore, small ships would be preferred. As we will see, it proved quite difficult to strike a balance between these conflicting demands.

The influence of air power

A factor which further promoted the need for joint thinking during the inter-war period, in the Soviet Union as well as in other countries, was the rise of air power. This development did not follow from some natural law of technological progress. For many years after World War I the airplane's dependency on weather, its short operational range and the constraints of contemporary radio and navigation technology severely limited the effectiveness of air support, on land as well as at sea. Therefore, it is open to debate whether the early advocates of air power were really as perceptive and clear-sighted as they have often been depicted later.

From the viewpoint of organizational interest, however, the airmen certainly knew what they were doing. They realized the need to secure an independent position for their service in the peacetime military structure. In no country had military aviation enjoyed such a position before World War I, and in the early inter-war period – a time when the political climate in most countries was characterized by fiscal austerity and endeavors to reduce military spending – such ambitions had much opposition to overcome. To justify the continued existence of their arm and preferably assure its organizational autonomy, airmen in the 1920s therefore tended to exaggerate the military potential of the airplane, even proposing that it could replace most other forces. While Giulio Douhet in Italy suggested that future wars could be terminated within hours through strategic bombing, in the United States General William Mitchell staged a spectacular bombing experiment against a captured German battleship to prove that the era of capital ships was over. In Britain, the RAF (which had attained independent service status as early as 1918) made a more convincing demonstration of the unique capabilities of air power – but only in the highly specialized role of a colonial policing force.[23]

The main center of naval aviation during the inter-war period was the United States. Just as in the case of amphibious warfare, military progress was triggered by organizational rivalry. The challenge from General Mitchell and the army air force, which threatened the navy's traditional role in anti-invasion defense, inspired the US admirals to develop a powerful air arm of their own. From 1925, aircraft carriers participated regularly in fleet maneuvers, at first only in supportive roles, but soon as independent striking groups alongside the battle fleet. The other leading nation in carrier development was Japan, with a similar situation of service rivalry and with an interest to confront the US Navy in the future. Thus, while other navies continued to see the aircraft carrier as a support ship, in the United States and Japan they were increasingly regarded as capital ships with independent combat missions, and equipped with aircraft specially designed for service at sea.[24]

Russian naval aviation, which had come into existence in 1908, had developed rapidly during World War I. By 1917, the Baltic and Black Sea Fleets operated some 230 airplanes all together, primarily in a reconnaissance role but also in air defense, anti-submarine warfare (ASW) and bombing missions. The most celebrated feat of Russian naval aviators during the war occurred in the Black Sea Theater in January 1916, when a Turkish transport ship was sunk from the air. (The year before, in April, the Russian battleship *Slava* had been the first battleship ever to be hit by an aerial bomb.)

The Imperial Naval Air Service dissolved after the Russian revolution, and during the ensuing civil war only remnants of it came to join the Red side. In the autumn of 1918, the Baltic Fleet air arm consisted of merely 14 seaplanes. Even with such modest forces, however, the Reds were able to dominate the skies, using their naval aviators primarily inland in support of the ground forces. When British fliers appeared in the Baltic in 1919, the Baltic air arm proved unable to protect Kronstadt from aerial bombardment.[25]

During the first years of Soviet rule, military aviation was divided into ground and naval air arms. In 1924, a major reorganization began which aimed at strengthening the air force as an independent service with its own commander in chief and its own administrative structure. Although as late as October 1923 there had only been 36 naval aircraft in service, ambitious plans for a future naval air arm remained, consisting of interceptor, reconnaissance and minelaying squadrons. Thus, the Soviet Navy would not only have to face competition from the Red Army (RKKA), but also from the Air Force (VVS = *Voenno-Vozdushnye Sili*).[26]

Conclusion

From an organizational perspective, military doctrines are formulated in a struggle between competing bureaucracies within the military. The threat perceptions and the operational and tactical recommendations these contain reflect the power relationship between rival services more than they express any form of professional rationality.

The Soviet Navy in the inter-war period was the child of 'an ocean-going fleet to be', created from the remnants of the tsarist regime's grandiose naval construction program of 1912. The practical use of a 'Big Ship fleet' in a narrow inland sea theater like the Baltic could be called into question. Moreover, historical experience in this theater – not least Russian experience from World War I – suggested that any efficient doctrine must be based on the concept of joint operations. However, such a doctrine would be difficult to establish. Even if the intellectual heritage of 1912 could be overcome within the navy, there was little constructive thought on joint operations internationally. Also, in view of the growing operational range of ground and air forces and the navy's traditionally low standing in the Russian service hierarchy, it was highly unlikely that the Baltic Fleet would be allowed to plan and coordinate a joint campaign in the Baltic.

Notes

1. Admiral James Watkins as quoted in R. A. Beaumont, *Joint Military Operations: A Short History* (Westport. CT: Greenwood Press, 1993), p. 190.
2. Snyder, *Ideology of the Offensive*.
3. Gemzell, *Conflict, Organization and Innovation*, pp. 52–3; idem, 'Warszawapakten, DDR och Danmark. Kampen för en maritim operationsplan', *Historisk Tidsskrift* (Copenhagen), vol. 96(1) (1996).
4. Berge, *Sakkunskap och politisk rationalitet*; cf. Åselius, ' "The Unskilled Fencer" '; the three *Sverige* class coast defense battleships, *Sverige*, *Drottning Victoria* and *Gustav V*, were commissioned in 1917, 1921 and 1922 respectively. Their normal displacement was 7,600 tons, their top speed 23 knots and their main armament four 283 mm and eight 152 mm guns, Gustaf von Hofsten and Jan Waernberg, *Örlogsfartyg: Svenska maskindrivna fartyg under tretungad flagg* (Stockholm: Svenskt militärhistoriskt bibliotek, 2003), p. 124.
5. Quoted in Agrell, *Alliaspolitik och atombomber*, p. 182.
6. Agrell, *Alliaspolitik och atombomber*, passim.
7. Westwood, *Russian Naval Construction*, pp. 8–14.
8. Ibid., p. 44.
9. Ibid., p. 72.
10. Ibid., pp. 73–5; Mitchell, *A History of Russian and Soviet Sea Power*, p. 274.
11. The remnants of the Black Sea Fleet, known as the Wrangel fleet – two battleships, one cruiser, ten destroyers, four submarines and some minor vessels – fled with the Whites after the Civil War to the French colony in Tunisia. Until France's recognition of the Soviet Union in 1924, these ships continued to fly the tsarist naval colors (the blue and white cross of St Andrew). Its possible return for many years formed a basis for Soviet naval reconstruction programs. In 1936, the remnants of the fleet were finally scrapped cf. Mitchell, *A History of Russian and Soviet Sea Power*, pp. 333–4, 342–7. After the dissolution of the Soviet Union in 1991, the Black Sea Fleet experienced a second period of statelessness. For many years, the ships continued to fly the naval colors of the nonexistent Soviet state, while Russia and Ukraine were disputing how to divide them.
12. Siegfried Breyer, *Soviet Warship Development*, vol. I, *1917–1937* (London: Conway Maritime Press 1992), pp. 33–5, 114–15.
13. Beaumont, *Joint Military Operations*, chaps 2–3; A. R. Millet, 'Assault from the Sea: The Development of Amphibious Warfare between the Wars', in W. Murray and A. R. Millet (eds), *Military Innovation in the Interwar Period* (Cambridge: Cambridge University Press, 1995).
14. Cf. Milan N. Vego, *Naval Strategy and Operations in Narrow Seas* (London: Frank Cass, 1999).
15. This explains why the name of Svensksund (1790), the greatest victory at sea recorded in Swedish military history, is also inscribed on the colors of several Swedish army regiments. Cf. Hans Norman (ed.), *Skärgårdsflottan: Uppbyggnad, militär användning och förankring i det svenska samhället, 1700–1824* (Lund: Historiska Media, 2000); Jan Glete, 'Kriget till sjöss 1788–1790', in Gunnar Artéus (ed.), *Gustav III:s ryska krig* (Stockholm: Probus, 1992); idem, 'Bridge and Bulwark: The Swedish Navy and the Baltic, 1500–1809', in Göran Rystad et al. (eds), *In Quest of Trade and Security: The Baltic in Power Politics, 1500–1990*, vol. I, *1500–1890* (Stockholm: Probus 1994).
16. Till, 'Great Powers and the Baltic', p. 179.
17. Mitchell, *History of Russian and Soviet Sea Power*, chapter 14.
18. This fateful episode became known only several years after World War I; see E. Björklund, 'Det ryska anfallsföretaget mot Sverige 1914', *Svensk Tidskrift*, vol. 23 (1936). There are copies of most of the relevant documents in RGAVMF (historical section of the Naval

Staff, f. r-1529, o. 2, d. 184, list 2–7), including the order from the Baltic Fleet's chief of staff Kerber on 23 July 1914 (old style) on contingency measures against the Swedes, the draft of Essen's ultimatum and the telegram to Essen from Grand Duke Nikolay.
19 Cf. Cherkassky, 22 January 1916, 'Svodka nr 2: Svedeniya po voprosu o vozmozhnosti vystupleniya Svetsy na storone tsentralnikh derzhav vesnuyu 1916 goda', f. 479, o. 4, d. 65, list 7–10.
20 Petrov, 19 April 1916, f. 479, o. 4, d. 65, list 2–3.
21 Keller, 9 May 1916, 'Nekotoriye predpolozheniya o pervonatchalnikh nazhikh deystvyakh v slutchay vystupleniye protiv nas Shvetsii', f. 479, o. 4, d. 63, list 14–17.
22 Kanin to commander of the Supreme Command's Naval Staff Rusin, 12 May 1916, f. 479, o. 4, d. 65, list 14–16; Rusin to Emperor Nicholas II, 22 May 1916; ibid., list 26–8.
23 Robin Highham, *Airpower: A Concise History* (Yuma, KS: Sunflower University Press, 1972, 1988), pp. 21–4.
24 Highham, *Airpower*, pp. 28–31.
25 Jacob W. Kipp, 'The Development of Naval Aviation, 1908–1975', in R. Higham and J. W. Kipp (eds), *Soviet Aviation and Air Power: A Historical View* (London: Brassey's, 1977), pp. 137–44; Christopher C. Lovett, 'Russian and Soviet Naval Aviation 1908–1996', in R. Highham, J. T. Greenwood and V. Hardesty (eds), *Russian Aviation and Air Power in the Twentieth Century* (London: Frank Cass, 1998), pp. 108–13; Mitchell, *History of Russian and Soviet Sea Power*, p. 304.
26 Erickson, *Soviet High Command*, p. 176.

4

CULTURE

In Chapters 7, 10 and 13, we examine Soviet naval doctrine and the Baltic Fleet from a cultural perspective, viewing doctrine as an instrument for consolidating collective identity. Only in recent years has strategic culture attracted attention from military historians and students of international security. A basic assumption in this approach is that the notion of rational interest – whether that of a state in the context of the international system or of a military organization in the context of bureaucratic rivalry – does not offer a satisfactory explanation to human behavior. Norms – 'collective expectations of a proper behavior of an actor with a given identity' – are also important. In contrast to supposedly 'objective' rational interests, norms are subject to change. In the early twentieth century, the national self-image of countries like Germany and Japan was that of a heroic warrior state. Since 1945, it has been that of a peaceful merchant society. This sudden redefinition of national interest is likely to reflect a change in cultural norms.[1]

In a similar way, military doctrines reflect cultural norms as much as they do rational calculation. The decision to invest in certain weapon systems is not only a response to a perceived military threat, but also a way to signal identity and cultural belonging to the surrounding world. During the early twentieth century, the possession of an ocean-going battleship fleet was a typical sign of Great power status. Later, nuclear weapons gained a similar symbolic significance. To some extent, the militarization of the Third World reflects the ambitions of newly independent states to adhere to international norms. To have your own air force, even if the half-squadron of fighter planes you can afford will be of little military value, may be equally important to statehood as having your own flag or your own national anthem.[2]

A study of strategic culture is therefore something more than a study of the mentality and beliefs of generals and statesmen. According to Iver B. Neumann, Halvard Leira and Heinrikki Heikka, this is a problem with much of the existing literature on strategic culture, which concentrates on strategic thinking, operating 'with a reified concept of culture which is outdated elsewhere in the social sciences'. Inspired by anthropology and sociology, these authors instead argue for a concept of strategic culture which focuses on the interplay between discourse and practice, between 'potential grand strategy on the one hand, and specific practices such as doctrines, civil–military relations and procurement on the other'.[3] In my analysis of the cultural aspects of Soviet naval doctrine, I have tried to use a similar broad approach.

Obviously, military doctrines must be able to satisfy deep social and cultural needs in a society. The dividing lines between different military schools tend to coincide with social and cultural divisions in that same society. In the late nineteenth-century French Navy, the advocates of the *Jeune École* doctrine were anti-clerical republicans from a middle-class background, while their traditionalist opponents in the naval establishment were aristocrats with strong Catholic and monarchist sympathies.[4] Similar dividing lines could be observed in the early twentieth-century German Army, as Eric Dorn Brose has concluded in a recent study. According to Brose, Germany's military failure at the Marne in 1914 was less a consequence of operational dispositions than of 'backward looking prejudices that had accumulated over four decades of peacetime and could not be reformed in time'.[5]

According to Elisabeth Kier, who has studied the evolution of military doctrine in Britain and France between the world wars, a country's strategic culture also reflects what the civilian politicians expect of the military. What role do they want the military to play in society, and what degree of professional autonomy are they prepared to allow to the officer corps? How do the military leaders respond to these expectations? The relationship between the professional subculture of the military and the rest of society is often problematic. The ambitions of the military educational system to 'replace the family' by forging strong bonds between recruits and inculcating into them its own version of basic behavior makes the military comparable only to a religious sect. Such institutions, which want to teach adults how they should walk, salute and dress tend to evoke suspicion and fear in the surrounding world. Military leaders, for their part, will always suspect and fear that the demands for outside control will undermine their professional autonomy and the fighting efficiency of their forces. Even if this basic civil–military conflict looks the same in most modern societies, the way it is handled nonetheless differs greatly from culture to culture.[6]

Thus, the existing research suggests that a military doctrine is not only a product of rational strategic analysis or an excuse to further organizational interests. It also fulfills important sociocultural functions. By answering such questions as 'who are we?' and 'what are we fighting for?' the doctrine helps to boost national self-image, enhances the military's ésprit de corps and renders a wider meaning to military training. It may also reduce painful tensions within the services, as well as tensions between the military and civilian society.

The navy in Russia

How then, should Soviet strategic culture best be described, and what cultural role did the navy play? The former American intelligence analyst Robert B. Bathurst described Russia as a typical 'high context culture' where reasoning is inductive rather than deductive in character. According to Bathurst, who spent many years studying the Soviet Cold War Navy, the primary function of military doctrine in such a society is to manifest unity around certain ideals and confirm the truth and consistency of official dogma. When Admiral Gorshkov wrote about the Soviet Union as a global sea power in the 1970s his intention was not to describe the Soviet Navy as it 'really' was, nor to recommend certain concrete policies to his political masters in the Kremlin. Rather, Gorshkov wanted to contribute to the affirmation of official truth and underpin the Brezhnev Empire's claims for super power status. Bathurst is aware that Russian society is not unique in this respect. In the West, especially in the US Navy, quite a few observers were prepared to take Gorshkov seriously: 'They heard in Gorshkov's resonating Mahanian overtones... at last, a voice they could understand. The Admiral wrote little about class conflict and much about traditional blue-water navies.'[7] Thus, Gorshkov's claims that the Soviet Union aspired to become a global sea power were taken seriously in the US Navy because such ambitions made sense in the context of American strategic culture.

Since Peter the Great, Russian rulers have regarded their navy as a symbol of Great power status, a rate of measurement in relation to the West as much as a practical military instrument. Already in the 1830s, a British diplomat in Saint Petersburg complained that all official persons in the Russian capital regarded the navy

> as a very expensive toy, with which the Emperor delights to occupy himself, but not one of them... anticipates the possibility of its ever being made use of as a means of attack or defence, and all openly deplore the expense which it occasions, as weakening their financial resources, and withdrawing large sums annually from the more useful national purposes.[8]

During the last decades of Romanov rule, the navy's importance as a national symbol was emphasized by its special relationship to various members of the imperial family: grand dukes Konstantin Nikolaevich (1827–92) and Alexey Alexandrovich (1850–1908) both served as 'general-admirals', and heir to the throne Alexey Nikolaevich (1904–18), commanded the Naval Cadet Corps.[9] As we saw in Chapter 3, the naval construction program of 1912 also demonstrated the political significance attributed to naval power. The Russian Navy wanted modern dreadnought-type battleships, not because it could make use of them in the Baltic but because other Great power navies had them. Tsar Nicholas and Foreign Minister Izvolsky were prepared to second such demands because modern battleships would erase the shameful defeat by Japan and increase Russia's diplomatic weight in Europe.

Just as in the case of the German *Hochseeflotte*, the defensive posture taken by the Russian Baltic Fleet during World War I meant extended periods of inactivity, during which the personnel was exposed to radical agitation from civilians and discipline was undermined. Big ships with anonymous mass crews (each of the *Gangut* class battleships had a crew of some 1,125 men) proved especially fertile ground for revolutionary propaganda. During the course of 1917, the Baltic Fleet and its sailors' assembly TSENTROBALT became one of the main Bolshevik strongholds and was to play an active role during the Bolshevik coup in November. On 29 January 1918, the Council of People's Commissars announced the foundation of the Workers' and Peasants' Red Navy.[10]

When the Bolsheviks came to power, they filled the vacuum left by the fallen autocracy. Now, the Communist Party was to define national identity and 'our way of war', as well as confer upon certain institutions the privilege of a special relationship to power. Therefore, when in Chapters 7, 10 and 13 we explore the shifts between different schools of naval thought in the Soviet Union and how they coincided with shifts between different perceptions of collective identity, we will among other things study Soviet party–military relations.

Soviet Party–Military relations

For a long time, research on the political role of the Soviet military took place in the shadow of the Cold War and was limited to working with published Soviet sources. From the 1960s and onwards, at least four different schools can be discerned.[11]

The first of the four paradigms is often associated with sociologist Roman Kolkowicz's book *The Soviet Military and the Communist Party* from 1967, which stressed the element of conflict in the Soviet civil–military relationship. According to Kolkowicz, Soviet officers fought for professional autonomy and bigger budgets just like their colleagues in other industrialized countries. The distrustful civilian leadership kept an eye on them through its network of political officers.[12]

In the 1970s, Kolkowicz's model was challenged by William E. Odom, who stressed that the Soviet officers had their Marxist–Leninist ideology in common with the party elite, and probably saw themselves as an integral part of the state–party bureaucracy rather than as an autonomous profession or corporation.[13]

In 1979, Timothy J. Colton, questioned both these monocausal explanations and preferred to describe Soviet civil–military relations in terms of bargaining and interaction. The officer corps accepted the party's domination and in return was allowed to enjoy a privileged social position and assert influence within its own professional domain.[14]

So far, the scholarly debate on Soviet civil–military relations reflected the general divide in Western Sovietology between 'totalitarists' and 'pluralists' during the Cold War. To the 'totalitarists', Soviet politics represented various manifestations of a single, well-organized political will. Through a combination of massive repression and intensive propaganda, this will tried to subordinate society to its own centralized control, using the Communist Party and the Soviet state apparatus as instruments. To the pluralists, the Soviet experiment represented an alternative road to modernity. Soviet Communism was an essentially modernizing force, a successful – albeit brutal – strategy for rapid industrialization and popular mobilization. Consequently, Soviet politics must be analyzed in terms of competing interests and conflicts between rival social groups, much like the politics of any modern state. Related to the latter perspective was also an optimistic notion of the Soviet system's ability to reform, as well as a theory of convergence between the capitalist and socialist systems in the future.[15]

Needless to say, the sudden collapse of the Soviet Union and its east European satellites in 1989–91 made the pluralist approach somewhat problematic, as – in the words of American historian Martin Malia – 'genuinely modernized societies do not disintegrate as the result of a bout of mere reform'.[16] Although some of the prominent proponents of 'revisionist' pluralist positions have later revised their standing in light of new research, much of the earlier research on the Soviet inter-war period formulated its results in relation to the fundamental totalitarist–pluralist issue. Also, much of the debate among historians on the Soviet inter-war period must be analyzed along this divide.

After the end of the Cold War and the demise of the Soviet Union, Dale R. Herspring presented a fourth synthesis on Soviet civil–military relations. Herspring stressed the element of constant change in the situation of the Soviet military and rejected the notion that any of the earlier explanatory models could be valid for the entire Soviet history.[17] Until about this time, the debate on Soviet civil– military relations had been dominated by political scientists and sociologists. When access to Soviet archives and libraries improved after the Cold War, historians were also able to contribute. Between 1990 and 1998, studies by Mark von Hagen, Roger R. Reese and Oleg Suvenirov greatly increased the knowledge of the Soviet military during the inter-war period.[18] However, none of those authors dedicated any particular attention to the navy–party relationship, which will be in focus here.

When we study this relationship in the following, we will primarily use the assessments of the the Army Political Directorate (PUR = *Politicheskoe Upravlenie RKKA*) as sources. These documents provide interesting facts on the social and educational background of various categories of Soviet Navy personnel, but the judgments that they contain regarding the military skills, discipline and human and moral qualities of these people are not necessarily 'true'. Rather, they reflect the biased view that certain party officials had of navy personnel. To compensate for this and provide knowledge of what Elisabeth Kier refers to as the expectations of civilian politicians on the military and the military response to those expectations, Chapters 7, 10 and 13 begin with short characterizations of the domestic–political climate in the Soviet Union during the period in question, as well as of the generation of naval leaders in charge. The investigation itself is focused on three aspects of navy–party relations where the party's claim for a leading role was especially salient:

- political control
- ideological leadership
- modernization.

Political control

Although many officers in the imperial army and navy fell victim to revolutionary violence during 1917, many others were prepared to serve with the Reds. At the end of 1918, the RKKA employed over 22,295 former tsarist officers and 128,168 former NCOs. They constituted 75 percent of the commanding personnel, and without them victory in the Civil War would have been impossible.[19]

In the Baltic, for instance, the assistance of former imperial officers ensured that Bolsheviks secured a substantial naval force for the future. While in the Black Sea most warships joined the Whites and left Russia with the French interventionist forces, the Baltic Fleet supported the Reds and evacuated its bases in Revel and Helsinki in the beginning of 1918 in time to avoid foreign capture.[20]

The man who rendered this great service to the Soviet regime was the Baltic Fleet chief of staff, Rear-Admiral Alexey Mikhailovich Shchastny. When he agreed to lead the fleet's perilous retreat through ice and minefields back to Kronstadt, he did so on the explicit condition that no party representatives were to interfere with his orders. In reward, Trotsky first appointed Shchastny commander of the Baltic Fleet but later had him arrested and shot as a counterrevolutionary. Officially, he was rehabilitated only in 1995.[21]

Shchastny's fate demonstrated the dangers of questioning party control. During the Civil War, a system developed in the Red forces in which all commanders down to battalion level were supervised by commissars from PUR. Before an order from the 'military specialist' won formal authority, it had to be countersigned by the political commissar. This system of 'dual command' was not a Soviet invention but originated from the armies of revolutionary France, where just as in early Soviet Russia a large part of the officer corps could be suspected of sympathizing with the former regime. Also, it should be noticed that when commissars first appeared in early 1918, they did not take over authority from the military commanders – they no longer had any – but from the autonomous soldiers' and sailors' committees which had been formed in every unit since February 1917. The fact that chaos ended and a clear chain of command was established was probably something that many former imperial officers appreciated. Moreover, commissars were not supposed to interfere in tactical decisions. In 1918, the Baltic Fleet chief commissar Flerovsky explained to his subordinates that when they confirmed an order from their military commander, they did not take responsibility for the military contents of that order. They only certified that it did not contain any hidden counterrevolutionary objectives, would not damage people's property or reduce the fleet's fighting power. A special PUR administration for the navy was organized in March 1922, and in December the same year the political training courses, which had been held for navy personnel in the Baltic Fleet, were transformed into the Roshal Academy for Political Education (S. G. Roshal had been the chairman of the first Bolshevik party committee in Kronstadt in March 1917).[22]

However, the system of dual command was not well suited to the intensive pace of modern warfare. In combat, there would be no time to acquire the commissar's signature on every order. Also, in view of the changing social composition of the commanding personnel, there seemed to be little need for that kind of precaution in the future, when new 'red cadres' would have replaced the old imperial officer corps.

At the same time, the education of new commanders progressed much more slowly in the navy than in the army. As a consequence, the Bolsheviks had less trust for the naval officer corps with its persisting 'aristocratic culture' and purged it repeatedly. Apart from the great purge in 1937–38, there were waves of repression in the aftermath of the Kronstadt rebellion in 1921, as well as in 1926 and 1930. Longer than in the Red Army, surveillance of commanding personnel in the navy would remain a primary task for the PUR representative.

Ideological leadership

According to Marx and Engels, Carl von Clausewitz's classical description of war as a continuation of politics by other means should rather be phrased 'a continuation of *class politics* by other means', as class struggle was the ultimate source of international conflict. In 1916, Lenin correspondingly described the ongoing world war as 'a continuation by violent means of the politics waged by the ruling classes long before the war'. Consequently, the Bolsheviks saw little difference between the military and ideological dimensions of their coming struggle with the capitalist world, and so the Soviet armed forces could not settle with military instructors only. Lenin refused to talk of just and unjust wars. Wars were either revolutionary wars waged in the interest of progress (wars of national liberation, civil wars against class oppression), or imperialist wars waged in the interest of finance capital (wars for the exploitation of colonies and foreign territory). Questions about who had started the war or on whose territory it was waged were of minor importance. Although he never explicitly used the exact term, Lenin also noticed that some wars could be regarded as 'useful'. Wars between two imperialist powers, for instance, could further progress if they led to a general weakening of the imperialist camp. After the creation of the world's first socialist state, the difference between international wars and civil wars could no longer be maintained. In 1926, E. A. Korovin, a leading Soviet expert on international law, stated that any war in which the Soviet Union participated would by definition be a 'war of class defense'. In such a conflict, the distinction between foreign and domestic policy would be more or less irrelevant for the countries involved.[23]

As we shall see, the preparation and conduct of propaganda work was considered to be an integral part of any military campaign plan. PUR personnel were expected to participate in every staff exercise, and the background scenarios which guided these exercises as well as fleet maneuvers often contained detailed analyses of the political dimension of the conflict or the class character of the hostile forces, as such information seemed just as important as data on enemy ships, weaponry and tactics.

The future war had to be fought on many fronts, and there would be need for ideological as well as military leadership. Here lay the second great role of the political commissar.

Modernization

In his fascinating study *Revolutionary Dreams*, the American historian Richard Stites describes the cult of future and modernity in early Soviet society, emphasizing the strong utopian element in the Russian revolution during the 1920s. Stites detects a romantic passion for enlightenment and technical progress in all spheres of cultural life existing alongside a special form of carnival frenzy, with roots in traditional Russian popular culture as well as in the avant-garde art of the pre-war years. Under Stalin, however, the lust for experiment and emancipation from tradition was replaced by an authoritarian, traditionalist ideal. At the same time, much of the avant-garde rhetoric survived and became an important part of Soviet identity until the end.[24]

Another American historian, Stephen Kotkin, has questioned the proposition that Soviet utopianism 'ended' with Stalin. Rather, he claimed, Stalin revived the utopianism of the Civil War years, which had begun to fade under the New Economic Policy (NEP). Stalin's immense mobilization of the country would not have succeeded had he not articulated a vision of socialism which appealed to the dreams of ordinary people. In a detailed study of life in a Stalinist industrial city – Magnitogorsk – Kotkin finds that the Stalinist vision of paradise 'notwithstanding the rejection of capitalism, shared a great deal with other industrial countries'. In Magnitogorsk the capital of the American steel industry – Gary, Indiana – was often held up as a model.[25]

Both Stites and Kotkin draw attention to the ambiguous fascination with Western civilization in the Soviet Union. Although socialism was said to represent something entirely new and unsurpassed in the progress of human civilization, it was still admitted that Soviet Russia could not make the gigantic leap forward on its own, without first learning from the West.

Also, the Bolsheviks knew that for the foreseeable future their likely enemies would possess superior technical and material resources. The challenge was not only to acquire military technology at the same advanced level, but also to recruit and train people who could handle all the new equipment. It was highly unlikely that potential tank drivers, bomber pilots and submarine captains would rise automatically from the depths of the Russian peasantry. Soviet military training must not only familiarize young men with the ways of the military, but semi-illiterate peasants with the ways of industrial society. Although Western governments also used national service to indoctrinate their young male citizens, the educational task facing the Soviet military would be on an entirely different scale. During a short period of basic training, recruits from the Russian countryside were to be introduced to the rhythm and lifestyle of a wholly new civilization.

Apart from controlling the military commanders and inspiring the rank and file, here lay the third great task of the political instructors: preaching the gospel of modernization according to the Communist Party. Lenin had defined communism as 'Soviet power plus electrification of the whole country'. Propagating industrial civilization meant propagating communism, agitating against religion and traditional values meant agitating for a more 'rational' society founded on the 'scientific' principles of Marxism–Leninism. In consequence, the Soviet armed forces had little success in their educational efforts during the inter-war period. During basic training, conscripts could be sent away for months to build barracks, assist in harvest work or fill in as needed extra hands at civilian construction sites. Moreover, due to a chronic shortage of competent commanding personnel, military as well as political, drinking and other disciplinary infringements were frequent among the troops. The shortage of good leaders was further aggravated through the bloody purges in 1937–38 and the rapid organizational expansion that followed in the years thereafter. According to Roger R. Reese, the latter factor was of even greater significance than the purges in paving way for the disaster in 1941.[26]

In spite of material shortage and motivational problems, the army field regulation from June 1929 still depicted well-trained Soviet infantry, heavily supported by tanks, artillery and long-range aviation, outflanking and crushing the enemy in *Blitzkrieg*-style operations.[27] Here, the cultural dimension of Soviet military doctrine becomes visible. No doubt, the optimistic description of the future Soviet armed forces mirrored the high expectations placed in the recently initiated first five-year plan. Also, this depiction of the future war helped to immunize the obvious gap between Soviet rhetoric and Russian reality. The Soviet Union may be behind the West technologically, the need to 'catch up and overtake' the capitalist world obvious to all. However, as the world's first socialist country, the Soviet Union could not renounce its progressive identity. By definition, the Soviet way of war must be more advanced than that of any capitalist country. In that respect, the military sphere was no different from other parts of Soviet society.

In Chapters 7, 10 and 13, we will study how the Baltic Fleet's political organs assessed the results of its own 'enlightenment work', the political maturity of the Baltic Fleet's 'red navy men' and the prerequisites for turning them into modern combat fleet crews. In Chapter 13, our analysis focuses especially on the intelligence section of the Baltic Fleet Staff, its efficiency and professionalism, and how the struggle for modernization affected events during the 'Great Terror' in 1937–38 (additional details on the Great Terror can be found in the appendix).

It should be stated right away that the Baltic Fleet – and certainly its intelligence section – did not have as a primary function to civilize illiterate rural conscripts. The navy, which was small (less than 23,000 men in the autumn of 1924) and technically sophisticated (four-year service for conscripts according to the 1925 national service law, prolonged to five years in 1939), had a first choice among those conscripts who according to Bolshevik ideology belonged to the elite – the urban, working-class youth. These youngsters were as a rule allotted to the units of the line. The less educated and politically less 'mature' men from the countryside were sent to the second-rate territorial divisions – or, if they belonged to non-Slavic minorities, to any of the RKKA national units, which had a similar low status.

On the other hand, if the navy was a technically advanced service, which received the elite of each age class of Soviet conscripts, it is worth investigating for precisely that reason. Although the fleet staff intelligence section held very few conscript positions, educationally it represented an elite within the elite. The personnel employed there – whether they were enlisted men or had been drafted – needed analytical minds, knowledge of foreign languages and modern office work, had to be able to code and decipher and handle advanced communications and intelligence equipment. As we have seen, a trend in naval warfare between the world wars was a decreasing relative role for firepower and a growing role for scouting and command-and-control functions.[28] From this perspective, the standard and performance of the Soviet Navy's intelligence organs must be considered highly indicative of the service's capacity to change and adapt to modern developments.

Certainly, one could expect that a giant empire like the Soviet Union should have been able to recruit the few dozens of qualified people it needed for its naval intelligence without major problems. However, the supply of educated recruits was limited. Not only the massive emigration of families belonging the Russian intelligentsia ensured this, but also the socially discriminatory national service law of 1925 – which emphasized that the defense of the fatherland was a privilege of the toiling classes. Persons of 'bourgeois' origin were regularly exempted from call-up, as were people who had lived abroad, had relatives living abroad or relatives who had been sentenced as enemies of the people. During 1934–39 alone, more than 780,000 conscripts were exempted on those grounds.[29]

Thus, the best-educated strata of the population were not liable for recruitment to the armed forces. The Baltic Fleet simply had to manage with the people that were available. As we will see, Soviet military authorities were very conscious of this fact, considered it a major problem and invested considerable energy into ennobling their raw human material into good communist stock, turning the sons of peasants into able modern warriors.

Conclusion

The cultural dimension of a military doctrine pertains to the collective identity of the service that holds the doctrine, how the doctrine helps to define that organization's place in society and strengthens its internal cohesion. Consequently, in order to understand this aspect of a military doctrine, you also have to study the people who are the bearers of the doctrine and the society in which they live. You must also study the concrete, practical manifestations of the doctrine as well as the written texts in which it is formulated.

In Russian tradition, the navy symbolized the country's claim to Great power status. After the Bolshevik seizure of power in 1917, those claims became increasingly problematic. In any modern society, there is an element of distrust between politicians and military leaders, especially if the politicians have come to power through a revolution. The young Soviet state, which regarded the former tsarist officer corps with suspicion, had created a system of political commissars to supervise its armed forces during the Civil War. A few years into the 1920s, when an increasing number of military commanders had been educated in the Soviet system and become trusted party members, the PUR's original watchdog function seemed less necessary. In the navy, however, this change was less discernible than in the ground forces, as the naval officer corps seemed less reliable ideologically.

The second task of the PUR had to do with the perceived need for ideological leadership in the armed forces, which flowed from the Marxist–Leninist view of war. In a systemic struggle between socialist and capitalist countries there could be no fixed delimitations between war and peace, combatants and civilians, front and home front. While imperial Russia had settled as a protector of Slavs and Christians in neighboring empires, the Soviet state claimed to represent every proletarian in every country of the world. Against this background, the Soviet forces would have a need for political–moral commanders alongside their military commanders. This task was entrusted to the PUR instructors.

Finally, a cult of modernity was deeply embedded in Soviet culture, as Soviet society aspired to be the most progressive society in history and a model for all of mankind. At the same time, it was embarrassingly clear that the Soviet Union was far behind its potential enemies in the West. If it was to fight modern wars successfully, it had to modernize quickly and train millions of peasant conscripts in the ways of the twentieth century. The PUR was charged with this gigantic task as well.

Notes

1 For an introduction to the field, see Peter J. Katzenstein (ed.), *The Culture of National Security: Norms and Identity in World Politics* (New York: Columbia University Press, 1996); the definition of norm can be found in Peter Katzenstein, 'Introduction: Alternative Perspectives on National Security', ibid., p. 5.
2 See Dana P. Eyre and Mark C. Suchman, 'Status, Norms and Proliferation of Conventional Weapons: An institutional Theory Approach', in Peter Katzenstein (ed.), *The Culture of National Security: Norms and Identity in World Politics* (New York: Columbia University Press, 1996).
3 Iver B. Neumann, Halvard Leira and Henrikki Heikka, 'The Concept of Strategic Culture: The Social Roots of Nordic State Strategies', *Cooperation and Conflict*, vol. 40(1) (2005).
4 Bueb, *Die 'Junge Schule'*, pp. 157–8.
5 Eric Dorn Brose, *The Kaiser's Army: The Politics of Military Technology in Germany during the Machine Age, 1870–1918* (Oxford: Oxford University Press, 2001), quote from p. 240.
6 Elisabeth Kier, *Imagining War* (Princeton, NJ: Princeton University Press, 1997).
7 Robert B. Bathurst, *Intelligence and the Mirror* (London: Sage Publications, 1993), p. 87; cf. pp. 26–8, 61–2; for the reception of Gorshkov's writings in the US naval establishment, see Preston (ed.), *Red Star Rising at Sea*.

8 Quoted from G. Till, 'Luxury Fleet? The Sea Power of (Soviet) Russia', in N. A. M. Rodger (ed.), *Naval Power in the Twentieth Century* (Annapolis, MD: Naval Institute Press, 1996), p. 15.
9 Mitchell, *History of Russian and Soviet Sea Power*, p. 274.
10 The role of the sailors in the Russian revolution is treated in Evan B. Mawdsley, *The Russian Revolution and the Baltic Fleet: War and Politics, February 1917–April 1918* (London: Macmillan, 1978), and Norman E. Saul, *Sailors in Revolt: The Russian Baltic Fleet in 1917* (Lawrence: University Press of Kansas, 1978); on the founding of the Soviet Navy, see Berezovsky *et al.*, a *Boevaya letopis*, p. 3.
11 For an introduction to the early debate, see Timothy J. Colton, 'Perspectives on Civil Military Relations in the Soviet Union', in Timothy J. Colton and Thane Gustafson (eds), *Soldiers and the Soviet State: Civil Military Relations from Brezhnev and Gorbachev* (Princeton, MD: Princeton University Press, 1990).
12 Roman Kolkowicz, *The Soviet Military and the Communist Party* (Princeton, MD: Princeton University Press, 1967).
13 William E. Odom, 'The Party Military Connection. A Critique', in Dale R. Herspring and Ivan Volgyes (eds), *Civil Military Relations in Communist Systems* (Boulder: Westview Press, 1978).
14 Timothy J. Colton, *Commissars, Commanders and Civilian Authority* (Princeton, NJ: Princeton University Press, 1979).
15 For an introduction to Sovietology, see Frederic J. Fleron Jr. and Erik P. Hoffman (eds), *Post-Communist Studies and Political Science: Methodology and Empirical Theory in Sovietology* (Boulder, CO: Westview Press, 1993); a contribution particularly instructive on the perspective discussed here is Gabriel A. Almond and Laura Roselle, 'Model Fitting in Communism Studies', in ibid.
16 Martin Malia, *The Soviet Tragedy: A History of Socialism in Russia, 1917–1991* (New York: Free Press, 1994), p. 8; according to Malia, this 'modernist interpretation' of the Soviet system was closely linked to apologetic ambitions; for a similar critique see Kristian Gerner, Stefan Hedlund and Niclas Sundström, *Hjärnridån: Det europeiska projektet och det gåtfulla Ryssland* (Stockholm: Fischer, 1995), p. 205.
17 Dale R. Herspring, *Russian Civil–Military Relations* (Bloomington, IN: Indiana University Press, 1996).
18 Mark von Hagen, *Soldiers in the Proletarian Dictatorship: The Red Army and the Soviet Socialist State, 1917–1930* (Ithaca, NY: Cornell University Press, 1990); Roger R. Reese, *Stalin's Reluctant Soldiers: A Social History of the Red Army, 1925–1941* (Lawrence, MA: SunFlower Press, 1996); Oleg Suvenirov, *RKKA nakanune: Ocherki istorii politicheskogo vospitaniya lichnogo sostava krasnoy armii 1929 g.–yuon 1941 g.* (Moscow: institut voennoy istorii ministerstvo oborony, 1993); idem, *Tragediya RKKA, 1937–1938 gg.* (Moscow: Terra, 1998).
19 von Hagen, *Soldiers in the Proletarian Dictatorship*, pp. 36, 40.
20 Mitchell, *History of Russian and Soviet Sea Power*, pp. 333–5.
21 Dotsenko, *Morskoy biograficheskyy slovar*, pp. 454–5.
22 On the origins of the commissar system in the Soviet armed forces, see Erickson, *Soviet High Command*, pp. 41–5; von Hagen, *Soldiers in the Proletarian Dictatorship*, pp. 27–8; Flerovsky's instructions to the Baltic Fleet commissars have been published in *Rossiyisky Gosudarstvenny Arkhiv Voenno-Morskogo Flota v fondakh (1917–1940 gg.)* (St Petersburg: Russian State Archives fo the Navy, 1995), pp. 202–4; on Roshal and the navy PUR administration, N. A. Stupnikov (ed.), *Dvazdhi Krasnoznamenny baltiysky flot* (Moscow: Voenizdat, 1990), p. 105; Berezovsky *et al.*, *Boevaya letopis*, pp. 503, 506–7.
23 Edgar Tomson, *Kriegsbegriff und Kriegsrecht der Sowjetunion* (Berlin: Berlin Verlag, 1979), pp. 15–24, 44–9.

24 Richard Stites, *Revolutionary Dreams: Utopian Visions and Experimental Life in the Russian Revolution* (Oxford: Oxford University Press), 1988.
25 Stephen Kotkin, *Magnetic Mountain: Stalinism as Civilization* (Berkeley, CA: University of California Press, 1995), quote from p. 366.
26 Reese, *Stalin's Reluctant Soldiers*.
27 See the 1929 Field Regulation (on the role of maneuver operations, see sections 115–16, 157, 161, 169; on the role of tanks and artillery, see sections 33, 126–33, 152, 158, 164, 206–12, 227–31, 258–59, 261–3, 259, 288, 291, 301, 310, 322, 339; on the role of aviation and chemical weapons see sections 215–16), quoted from the Swedish translation *Från Röda Armén: Översättning av 1929 års fälttjänstreglemente jämte kort översikt av krigsorganisationen* (Stockholm: Militärlitteraturföreningens förlag, no. 156, 1930).
28 Hughes, *Fleet Tactics*, cf. introduction.
29 Yemelin, 'Sudba doktrin i teory, 3'.

Part II

THE OLD SCHOOL, 1921–1928

5

'MARE CLAUSUM' AND THE PROSPECTS OF WAR

In line with the traditions from tsarist Russia, the Soviets did what they could to limit the access of nonlittoral navies to the Baltic in the 1920s. In spite of their minimal trust in the surrounding world and their exclusion from the League of Nations, they tried to achieve this by way of international treaties. As early as June 1920, before they even had diplomatic relations with the West, the Soviet government proposed to the British that only littoral powers should be allowed to station warships in the Baltic and the Black Sea. The proposal was repeated during the Turkish peace conference in Lausanne in 1922, as well as during the League of Nations' naval disarmament conference in Rome in 1924. Provided that the Baltic and Black Seas were closed to the navies of nonlittoral powers, the Soviet representative Berendt declared, his country was willing to reduce its claims for battleship tonnage from 400,000 to 280,000 tons. In the Washington Treaty, the first-rank naval powers, Britain and the United States, had settled for 525,000 tons each and consequently could not take this offer seriously from a – momentarily – nonexistent naval power.[1]

Against this background, what would the reasons have been for the Soviet Navy to adopt an offensive doctrine like that recommended by the Old School?

Since Soviet diplomacy had failed to secure the exclusion of British and French naval forces from the region, it could be argued that Soviet naval forces must be made strong enough to seize the initiative in the initial stage of a war and block the exits of the Baltic or the Gulf of Finland. In his 1921 proposal for the navy's reconstruction, where we meet the Soviet Old School for the first time in the form of a policy recommendation, naval commander Alexander Nemits made this the main line of his argument. Nemits suggested that the republic's naval forces should be concentrated in the theater where they would weigh heaviest, be superior to those of potential enemies or make Russia a desirable ally. To him, that theater was the Baltic, where the collapse of Germany had created an opportunity for Russia to secure naval mastery. Even if Sweden, Denmark and the newly independent states combined their navies, he argued, these would be inferior to the 23,000-ton *Gangut* class battleships of the Baltic Fleet. In five years' time, a suitable strength of the fleet would be four battleships, two light cruisers, 22 destroyers and 35 submarines.

... it would be extremely inexpedient not to exploit fully the opportunities presented thanks to this. Furthermore, the geographical conditions in the Baltic Theater are especially advantageous to us, offering the possibility to create with small effort a number of positions in the Sounds leading into the Baltic Sea, which we could hold with comparatively small forces even against the first-rate navies of the strongest naval powers, gaining for ourselves complete command of the sea, security for our coasts and sea communications with all Baltic powers; this fact is especially important as those same geographic conditions make it virtually impossible to defend our coast in the immediate vicinity of our territorial waters, the fleet being easy to block in Kronstadt even by the weakest of enemies and to shell from the Finnish coast in its very base.

However, Nemits realized that Russia at present lacked the industrial capacity necessary to acquire sufficient naval forces. Until such a capacity had been created, the task of the Baltic Fleet would be limited to defense against invasion, but preferably as far west as possible, at the mouth of the Gulf of Finland.[2]

About a year later, when the Commission on the Resurrection of the Navy discussed the strategic objectives in various theaters, the head of the Naval Staff's operational section, Arkady Toshakov, returned to the creation of a defensive perimeter at the Baltic approaches. Apart from defending Leningrad and controlling the adjacent waterways, Toshakov stated, the Baltic Fleet could also be used to dominate the Baltic and block the Baltic approaches to external powers. He admitted, however, that the feasibility of this third option would very much depend on temporary circumstances.[3]

In 1925, when Toshakov's section outlined the strategic situation in the various theaters in an appendix to the Naval Staff's proposed construction program, self-confidence had grown. If the Baltic Fleet was to conduct its defensive battle at the Baltic approaches, it was argued, fewer ships might be needed than if a more retracted position was chosen.[4]

According to a balance of power interpretation, another reason for the Soviets to prefer an offensive doctrine in the 1920s would have been a desire to subvert the international status quo. As long as the dreams of world revolution remained, such a desire certainly existed.[5] In June 1924, the RVS passed a resolution which called for a navy capable not only of defending the Soviet Union, but of defending 'world revolution' as well.[6]

When Toshakov's section wrote the strategic chapter of the naval construction program, the revolutionary argument still featured. Toshakov and his co-authors discussed the prospects of supporting revolutionary unrest both in the Middle East and in the Pacific region and maintained that the Baltic was the main naval theater even from this viewpoint, not least because the capitalist world was particularly vulnerable in the region. A Soviet naval offensive to seize the Baltic approaches could be coordinated with a proletarian revolution in Weimar Germany. When German technology and German industrial might were placed at the disposal of the world proletariat, the Soviet Union's naval forces could be further reinforced and the flames of revolution spread to Asia as well. Control over the Baltic approaches could be attained without military operations against Denmark or Sweden, he believed. The Red Army only had to crush Poland as quickly as possible and secure ports along the Polish coast. Then, while the French and British navies were barred from entering the Baltic, strikes and revolutionary unrest would spread across Germany.[7]

In spite of its ideological militancy, the 1925 naval construction proposal did not meet with much support from the Politburo or the army. In Moscow, dreams of world revolution had begun to fade.

When trying to justify an offensive role for the Baltic Fleet during the RVS debate in May 1928, navy representative Petrov therefore turned back to the geostrategic argumentation used by Nemits in the beginning of the decade. For 400 years, Petrov asserted, the Baltic had been an area of primary interest to England. During the Great Northern War, during the Napoleonic wars and during the Crimean War, British warships had appeared in support of Sweden against Russian aspirations, and at present the 'Limotrophes' or 'Border States' (Poland, Finland and the newly independent Baltic states) could expect similar support against the Soviet Union. Even if a defensive strategy was adopted in the Black Sea, the fleet in the Baltic must be sufficiently strong to take to the offensive, at least strong enough to seal off the theater and support the RKKA's offensive operations ashore.[8]

Furthermore, even if the entire world was hostile to the Soviet Union, there was reason to believe that the enemy fleets in the Baltic Theater would not be overwhelmingly strong. At least, this is what Soviet intelligence estimates claimed.

In August 1922, when the head of operational section in the Baltic Fleet presented his draft proposal for the mine defenses outside Kronstadt, he discussed the need for such defenses in the event of a war with the 'Minor Entente' (Poland, Finland and the Baltic states). Echoing the optimism of Nemits's naval plan of 1921, he claimed that these small powers lacked sufficient naval resources to force the minefields, and that the Baltic Fleet even stood a good chance of defeating their combined fleets in a pitched battle. However, he concluded, for that very reason an isolated war with the Minor Entente was not very likely. By preparing for a worst-case scenario, he argued, the Baltic Fleet would simply increase its ability to handle less serious situations.[9]

In these years, both French and British naval squadrons made regular visits to Finnish and Estonian ports, the British almost every summer. According to the Soviet naval attaché in Helsinki in the mid-1920s, A. K. Petrov, the aim of these visits was to counter German influence in Finland, but above all 'to show the Finns that in pace with the growth and development of the Red Fleet, their protectors can easily stretch out a hand to the Baltic as well'. The fact that the same ships sometimes returned the following summer seemed to prove that these visits were not only political demonstrations, but concrete operational preparations.[10]

The limited western squadron

What, then, would a war in the Baltic Theater be like?

In the autumn of 1922, the Baltic Fleet held its first maneuvers since the revolution. The exercise was based on a scenario prepared by the Fleet's chief of staff, Lev Mikhailovich Galler, which was to be varied again and again over many years. A British squadron consisting of battle cruisers, destroyers and troop transporters was operating from Tallinn, and light British forces had been observed at the mouth of Luzhky Bay. The aim of the attacking force was to lock up the Baltic Fleet in Kronstadt and land troops in Luzhky Bay for an offensive against Petrograd. The task of the defenders was to prevent the enemy's operations, weaken him through active defense measures and eventually engage him in battle. If the landing in Luzhky succeeded, the Baltic Fleet was to cooperate with the RKKA in throwing the enemy back into the Gulf of Finland.[11]

The political background of the defensive maneuver scenario was further elaborated for the maneuver of 1924 when France was identified as the main enemy. After a conflict over trade, the scenario explained, the French government had decided to reestablish capitalism in Russia by force. A border conflict between the Soviet Union and Estonia offered a pretext for sending a French naval squadron to the Gulf of Finland. The task of the Baltic Fleet in the maneuever would be to prevent a landing in the rear of the RKKA as it advanced into Estonia. The scenario instructions emphasized that the enemy landing force consisted of Estonian troops, as the French government could not send French soldiers to the Baltic due to domestic opinion.[12] In 1927–28, joint war games were staged between the Naval War College and the Military-Political College. The background scenario described how Britain had exploited the Anglo-Soviet crisis to propagate for war among the European powers, driving both Italy and France to break off relations with the Soviet Union. After a border incident, Poland declared war on the Soviet Union. Declarations of war then followed from Rumania, Estonia, Latvia, Finland, Lithuania and finally Britain.[13]

Thus, a constant assumption during all exercises was that Britain and France would need more than access to local ports. Just as during the Civil War, they would also demand active military participation from their allies in the region.[14]

The scale of the Western support to the expected small-power coalition was not easy to foresee. The French expeditionary force portrayed in the 1924 scenario was expected to contain battleships, but the head of the Naval Staff's foreign section, Vladimir Belli, found that supposition unrealistic. In a special report a few months later he emphasized the need to remember the constant rivalry among the capitalist powers. France, for instance, had for a long time had its navy concentrated in the Mediterranean, and could not dispatch any major force without exposing her southern coast or its North African colonies to a British attack. A French squadron must be kept in reserve in the Channel as well. As the French Navy was limited in size, it seemed unlikely that it would risk any of its six modern battleships to help the Estonians, who were no important allies. Therefore, the most probable French expeditionary force would consist of submarines and destroyers, with the possible addition of some aircraft. The British, on the other hand, had no serious opponents in Europe since the disappearance of the German Navy. Therefore, the Royal Navy would always be able to concentrate forces at least twice as strong as those of the Baltic Fleet.[15]

As the Baltic Fleet at that time had two battleships, and the Royal Navy 24, Belli's estimate would still seem overly optimistic. In their desire to justify the need for new battleships for the Baltic Fleet, in its appendix to the 1925 naval construction program, Toshakov's section even exaggerated the number of British battleships to 32, claiming that a significant part of this force would appear in the Baltic Theater during an Anglo-Soviet war.[16]

Belli, however, seem to have counted on Britain's global commitment as a limiting factor. Mikhail Petrov certainly did so during his debate with Tukhachevsky in the RVS in May 1928. Although admitting that the enemy would be superior, he still insisted that the balance of power could not be calculated mechanically from naval calendars. The Royal Navy had several important missions in other parts of the world, he said, and would always have to reserve substantial forces for the protection of imports to the British Isles. The entire Royal Navy could not be concentrated in the Baltic without upsetting the global balance of power.[17] Toshakov seconded this opinion while Nikolay Vlasyev, head of the Naval Technical Directorate, asserted that more than two-thirds of the 50 battleships in the world were inferior to the *Gangut* class.[18]

Furthermore, although this was seldom explicitly stated, the difficulty of navigating in the Gulf of Finland was likely to reduce the number and size of enemy ships. In the 1927–28 war games, the British expeditionary force was limited to one battle cruiser, four light cruisers, 3–4 submarines, one squadron of destroyers and a large number of minesweepers and supply ships.[19]

Another difficulty for the British in the Baltic would be the lack of prepared bases. In the summer of 1925, the People's Commissariat for Foreign Affairs was worried by rumors that Estonia would lease out the islands of Hiiumaa and Saaremaa to the British for this purpose. From here, the Baltic Fleet could easily be blocked. When the British General Kirke was employed as an advisor in the organization of Finland's coastal defenses, similar suspicions arose about British intentions in Finland. According to Belli, the British planned to resurrect the Russian fortifications in the Turku–Åland archipelago to obtain a northern prolongation of their future base area in the Estonian archipelago. The diplomats wanted to launch a press campaign on the matter, but the naval attaché in London, although not questioning the substance of the rumors, still found it improbable that the Labour-influenced parliament would approve of any peacetime military preparations outside the British Empire.[20]

A similar, less alarmist view of the British engagement in the Baltic can be found in a report from the naval attaché in Helsinki, Petrov, in February 1925. Referring to Nikolay Gogol's famous theatrical play, he claimed that London was sending an 'Inspector General' (*Revizor*) to organize the Finnish Air Force. The outcome of this mission would reveal what role Britain had assigned to Finland in its Baltic schemes. In contrast to France, Petrov stated, the British were not arming openly. For financial reasons, they preferred forging regional alliances that would be dependent on British support but have no definite guarantees.[21]

To sum up, a fundamental principle of Soviet strategic estimates during the 1920s was that the active military contribution of the Great powers in the Baltic Theater would be limited. They would at most send one or two battleships, light naval and air units but hardly any ground forces. They would avoid formal defense commitments in the region or the permanent stationing of forces, and rely on local powers to execute their policies.

The weak 'Border States'

Although the Soviets had little success in their diplomatic efforts to reduce Western naval forces in the Baltic, there were still prospects for bilateral agreements with their immediate neighbors on the Gulf of Finland. In their peace treaties with the Soviet Union, both Finland and Estonia had pledged to work for regional disarmament. As they wished to prevent a future restoration of Soviet naval resources, during the early 1920s both countries presented proposals for an international neutralization of the Baltic Sea. However, as long as such initiatives did not meet with the approval of other Baltic powers or any of the major nonlittoral powers, Moscow was not particularly interested.[22]

In a strategic survey from March 1924, the head of the Naval Staff's foreign section S. Kholodovsky aired his concern over the 'future development of Russia's manifold interests in the Baltic', especially with regard to the *Limotrofi* – the former Border Lands of the Russian Empire, which now existed as independent neighbor states in the northwest: Finland, Estonia, Latvia, Lithuania and Poland. This report probably summarizes rather well the navy's strategic perception at the time. Kholodovsky complained that although the Soviet Union had been invited by the Border States to cooperate on matters of railway traffic, postal service and sea rescue, it was nonetheless kept out of all regional negotiations on major political and economic issues. As always, he continued, the Western powers were busy forging the Baltic states into a 'rifle in the hands of the Entente, aimed at the USSR', and possibly at Weimar Germany as well. Kholodovsky regarded Estonia and Latvia as likely enemies – or under all circumstances 'hostile neutrals'. The only state in the Baltic he expected to observe strict neutrality in a war against the USSR was Lithuania (which, moreover, had no navy until the late 1930s). However, he did not doubt that 'in a not too distant future they [the Baltic States] will join the USSR as a result of our political victory'. Poland and Finland, countries dominated by strong anti-Communist currents, would not be defeated as easily. As Finland had close relations to Sweden and to Germany, it might still preserve some independence in relation to the Western powers. Poland seemed totally obedient to France, but could for that very reason just as well turn its forces against German East Prussia as against Soviet Ukraine.[23]

Kholodovsky's successor as head of the Naval Staff's foreign section, Belli, portrayed the armaments of the 'Border States' somewhat differently. According to him, the governments of these small states were not so much instruments in the hands of the imperialist great powers as independent actors, driven by genuine fear of the Soviet Union's growing might. The close relations between Poland and its southern neighbor Rumania also meant that a conflict in the Baltic could spread easily to the Black Sea.[24] Later in the decade, the Main Directorate for [military] Intelligence (GRU = *Glavnoe Razvedyvatelnoe Upravlenie*) reported on plans to relocate the Polish Navy to the Black Sea, as the Poles counted on their own coast being protected by allied navies.[25]

Because of her incomparable size among the Border States, Poland was expected to play the leading role in a coalition against the USSR. As we have seen, the authors of the 1925 naval construction program indeed saw the crushing of Poland as the key to gaining control in the Baltic Theater. Similar assumptions were made in the 1927–28 joint war games by the naval and military-political colleges, which recommended the defeat of Poland and the installation of a worker–peasant government there as the quickest road to total victory.[26]

According to the GRU's strategic survey from October 1928 (which claimed that 'the preparations of the imperialists for a new intervention in the USSR continues with unvaried pace'), since 1923 the Border States had increased the number of their infantry divisions from 98 to 114, the number of their military aircraft from 200 to 520. During the same period, the membership of 'bourgeois-fascist military organizations' in the five countries had quadrupled and now counted well over a million people. Of course, the lion's share of these figures fell on Poland alone, as did the major part of the rapidly growing arms industry in the region. At the same time, the GRU believed, Poland's dominance would endanger the political unity of an enemy coalition. The Polish–Lithuanian conflict over Vilnius excluded Lithuanian participation, and until that dispute had been settled Latvia and Estonia were likely to restrict their participation to the letting of bases on their territory. Also, Poland had to reconcile itself with Germany before turning her forces eastwards. For these reasons, war in the immediate future did not seem likely.[27]

To the Baltic Fleet, another important aspect of Poland's leading role in the Border State coalition was the army's primacy in the Polish defense structure. In 1923, naval attaché Petrov in Helsinki had forecast that within four years, the Finnish, Latvian, Estonian and Polish navies would be strong enough to block the Baltic Fleet in the Gulf of Finland.[28]

As it was, in 1928 these navies together consisted of ten destroyers, ten gunboats and two submarines. The Baltic Fleet at the same time deployed three battleships, two cruisers, 12 destroyers and nine submarines.[29]

Denmark and Sweden – hostile neutrals

The naval contribution of the Border States to the Anglo-French expeditionary force would thus be relatively insignificant. However, Denmark and Sweden also had to be included among potential enemies in the Baltic – or at least among the 'hostile neutrals'. The Deputy People's Commissar for Foreign Affairs, Maxim Litvinov, told the newly appointed Soviet representative in Oslo in the spring of 1926 that Norway was the only Scandinavian country with which the Soviet Union could hope for friendly relations. The relationship with Denmark was poisoned by the royal family's kinship to the Tsar, while Sweden was traditionally Russophobic and had sentimental bonds to Finland.[30]

In 1925, Denmark and Sweden attracted special attention from Soviet naval authorities when dredging works were initiated on the Danish side of the Sound (the *Drogden*), works which would considerably facilitate the passage of British battleships into the Baltic. As Soviet naval strategists had emphasized the advantage of securing good defensive positions close to the Sounds, conditions during the early stage of a war could now become radically altered. Otherwise, the threat from Denmark was not primarily of a military nature. As Belli had stated in a strategic survey in the autumn of 1924, Denmark's turn down 'the path of total disarmament' merely implied that Danish territorial waters in the future would become more accessible to Western warships. Although the Soviet representative in Copenhagen asserted that no military alliance existed between Denmark and Britain – such foreign policy adventures being alien to the cautious social democratic government – the People's Commissar for Foreign Affairs, Chicherin, was seemingly concerned by the rumors:

> We have received official and unofficial assurances that this is completely innocent, and that under no circumstances will the digging in this area proceed so deep as to allow the passage of warships. But these reassurances do not reassure us, and we fear that under the cover of semi-secrecy, the way is opened for the most powerful British warships to sail all the way up to our coasts.[31]

On the Swedish side of the Sound (the *Flintrännan*) there were no excavation works taking place, although the Soviet representative in Stockholm, Dobrolevsky, was convinced that such works were being prepared in secret. According to him, representatives of a certain foreign power had been invited to the Ministry of Defense in Stockholm for discussions on the matter. Also, it seemed highly suspicious that the Swedish Minister for Defense, Per Albin Hansson, had avoided denying press allegations on the strategic implications of the planned excavation works. According to Dobrolevsky, the difficulties he had had in obtaining correct information on this subject demonstrated the need for a proper naval attaché at the Soviet Stockholm legation.[32]

Dobrolevsky was prepared to trace foreign policy adventurism in Sweden not only among the Conservatives or the officer corps, but also within the Social Democratic government. The Swedish parliament had recently decided on substantial defense cuts. The Soviet party organ *Pravda* had published an interview with Defense Minister Hansson on the matter entitled 'Sweden's Defense Minister thinks the threat from the USSR exaggerated'. According to Dobrolevsky, this heading was grossly misleading. Did Hansson, Prime Minister Sandler, Foreign Minister Undén or the Social Democratic press honestly think so? Why did they remain silent when the Swedish Conservatives asserted that Sweden as a member of the League of Nations had an obligation to prepare for military assistance to Finland and the Baltic states? In their basic hostility against the Soviet Union, Dobrolevsky claimed, the Social Democrats really did not differ from the Conservatives. They merely saw the threat as temporarily weakened or focused in other directions. Furthermore, in parliament the Social Democratic minority government depended on the support of the Liberals. Like the Swedish bourgeoisie in general, the Liberals were puppets in the hands of the banks, and these in turn were ruled by British capital.[33]

Dobrolevsky's fears of excavation works on the Swedish side of Öresund proved groundless. Moreover, the main fear from Sweden in Soviet strategic calculations was not connected to the Sounds, but to Finland. Because of the conflict over the Åland Islands after World War I, relations between Sweden and Finland had remained rather cold for a long time. As Martti Turtola has shown in his study on Swedish–Finnish military contacts between the world wars, a thaw sat in only by the mid-1920s. The Finns had by then abandoned their hopes of security cooperation with Poland and the Baltic republics. Encouraged by the British, they instead turned westwards across the Gulf of Bothnia.[34]

At the same time, a group of young officers in the Swedish General Staff (some of whom had served as volunteers on the White side during the Finnish Civil War in 1918) saw a future for Sweden's heavily reduced army through the country's membership in the League of Nations. Sweden's obligation to assist other member states against armed aggression (e.g. Finland against the Soviet Union) would scarcely be denied by the parliamentary majority of Social Democrats and Liberals, who based much of their foreign and defense policy on the principle of collective security. Sweden's obligations to the League of Nations could thus serve as argument for a modernization of the Swedish armed forces.[35] The Swedish politicians, however, although recognizing the value of Finland's orientation toward Scandinavia instead of toward the Border States, shunned the idea of taking on any military obligations toward the Finns.[36]

Soviet naval observers seem to have had a rather realistic view of Sweden's position: Swedish interest in Finland was merely dictated by self-interest. 'Sweden sees Finland as a shield against danger', Belli explained in a report from November 1924. Although Sweden did not wish to enter into a formal alliance, it would certainly adopt a benevolent attitude if the 'Finnish bourgeoisie' tried to realize its aggressive plans toward the USSR.[37]

The Soviets had registered the first signs of an approaching Finnish–Swedish rapprochement already in the summer of 1924, when the navies of the two countries together celebrated the 136th anniversary of a common victory over the Russians – the battle of Svensksund on 9 July 1790. The Soviet naval attaché in Helsinki saw the British minister in Finland as a discreet promoter of these celebrations, and duly noted how, in a small motor boat, he had accompanied the Swedish ships all the way through the Helsinki archipelago at their departure. According to the Soviet minister in Stockholm, Dobrolevsky, the pompous state visit by King Gustav V to Helsinki the following year – the king being escorted by two coastal battleships and four destroyers – clearly demonstrated how the Swedes wished to impress the Finns with their military might.[38]

In a Baltic context, the Swedish Navy was indeed impressive. According to Petrov, it was likely to appear off the Finnish coast in a Soviet–Finnish war, if only to protect the Swedish-speaking minority in Finland 'on a mandate from the League of Nations'. But even if Swedish support to Finland were to complicate matters to the Baltic Fleet, Sweden's *Sverige* class coast defense battleships (7,600 tons) were primarily designed for defensive operations outside the archipelago, and could hardly be compared to the capital ships of the Great powers.[39]

Weimar Germany

The only remaining power in the Baltic region, Weimar Germany, had naval resources superior to Sweden's but could not automatically be classified as an enemy of the Soviet Union. In spite of Germany's expected role as a powder keg of world revolution, official relations between the two countries were more than correct. The rapprochement between the Soviet Union and the other great power bordering on the Baltic, Weimar Germany was seemingly logical. Not only their status as international outcasts after Versailles formed a common bound between these two states, but also their enmity toward resurrected Poland. In addition, German industry needed Russian raw materials and markets, the German military secluded areas to develop military technology banned in the Versailles Treaty. To the Soviets, cooperation with Germany offered access to Western industrial and military expertise, as well as a way of disrupting the ring of 'Capitalist encirclement'.

Following the Treaty of Rapallo in 1922, a series of Soviet–German cooperation projects were initiated. In earlier research, the military dimension of these contacts has attracted much attention. It is usually emphasized that cooperation between the Soviet Navy and the *Reichsmarine* never developed as far as that between the Red Army and the *Reichswehr*. In 1926, the German Admiral Arno Spindler visited the Soviet Union to present designs for submarines, discuss the building of a joint submarine plant in the Black Sea and even the prospects for joint operations against the Poles. However, no binding agreements were made. Nor did the visit to Germany in 1930 by the Soviet Black Sea Fleet commander Orlov produce any lasting results. Unlike the *Reichswehr*, the German Navy had no technological advantages to gain from cooperation with the Russians, and did not wish to assist in the creation of a rival naval power in the Baltic.[40]

Soviet naval analysts during the 1920s usually described Germany as a friendly or neutral power. In his review of the strategic situation in the Baltic in the spring of 1924, Kholodovsky pointed out that a future restoration of Russia's and

Germany's naval forces in the theater would threaten any Anglo-French attempts to dominate Europe. In the event of a war, Kholodovsky concluded, Germany would be the USSR's only potential ally in the Baltic or at least a benevolent neutral.[41]

Only a few months later, Kholodovsky's successor Belli asserted that Germany could not be trusted because of unstable domestic conditions. Although the Germans would certainly support the USSR in a war against Poland, they could not be counted on as an active ally. In a conflict between the Soviet Union and the Baltic states, German hostile neutrality even had to expected.[42]

In December 1925, after Locarno, Belli was more certain of Germany's 'hostile neutral' status. However, he argued, the consequences of Locarno should not be exaggerated. As before, the Soviet Union could count on the internal strife in the imperialist camp, and Germany had recently expanded her trade with Moscow. This made German participation in an anti-Soviet coalition unlikely.[43]

The resolution of the RVS on 8 May 1928

Although there was an impressive list of possible enemies in the Baltic during the 1920s, the concrete military threat in the theater thus seemed quite manageable. The main enemies in Europe – Britain and France – were leading naval powers but would hardly dispatch any major forces to the area. The only other Great power in the Baltic, Weimar Germany, had several common interests with the USSR, and was even by some regarded as a friend and a potential ally. The hostile Border States were arming intensively, but their naval resources remained modest. The remaining naval power in the region – Sweden – would only reluctantly join a war and probably with inadequate strength to challenge the Soviets outside coastal waters. Against this background, the Old School could argue that command of the Baltic lay within Soviet reach.

During the debate before the RVS in May 1928, navy representative Mikhail Petrov tried to develop these arguments to the best of his ability. However, his opponent, chief of the RKKA General Staff Mikhail Tukhachevsky, was well prepared. During earlier debates, Tukhachevsky had argued that the navy could have no independent role apart from coastal defense and support for the Red Army.[44]

On this occasion, he even questioned the navy's value in general, quoting Friedrich Engels's pamphlet *Anti-Dühring*, which claimed that to a continental power like Russia naval armaments would be a complete waste of money. None of the Soviet Union's main enemies, neither Britain nor Japan, he said, could threaten the Soviet Union from the sea. Even if these powers could launch coastal invasions successfully, the outcome of those campaigns would still be decided on the ground. Only when it came to assisting a west European revolution might naval forces play an independent strategic role. That Tukhachevsky was prepared to give the navy that much recognition merely confirms that world revolution was no longer a major objective in Soviet strategic planning. Although in the spring of 1928 the RKKA staff's multi-volume report on 'The Future War' (*Budushchaya Voyna*) mentioned the intervention in support of social revolution abroad as a possible cause of war, only limited attention was paid to that scenario in subsequent discussions. As *Budushchaya Voyna* identified a deficit in the Soviet forces' offensive power compared to the defensive power of likely opponents in Europe, the lack of interest in exporting revolution is not surprising. Even for a campaign against Poland the RKKA would need at least half a year, and then only if the Poles were left to fight without support from other capitalist countries. The fact that Tukhachevsky in 1927 insisted on the building of fortifications along the western border is further proof that Soviet intentions were predominantly defensive at the time.[45]

In Chapter 7 of *Budushchaya Voyna*, the RKKA expressed its views on the role of naval forces. It emphasized that short of British participation, the naval threat would be negligible in the Black Sea as well as in the Baltic Theater. Therefore, the main mission of the navy in these theaters should be to defend coastal areas against invasion and to support the operations of the RKKA. In line with this view, Tukhachevsky's concluding recommendation during the debate with Petrov in the RVS was that the naval forces in the Baltic should only be made strong enough to fight the navies of the Border States. During the ensuing discussion, several army leaders seconded these opinions.[46]

The resolution of the RVS on 8 May 1928 ('on the importance and tasks of the naval forces in the country's system of armed forces'), went along with these views. Coastal defense and the support of ground operations were explicitly mentioned as the main missions of Soviet naval forces.[47]

Conclusion

Perceiving its strategic position in the Baltic as vulnerable during the 1920s, the Soviet Union made repeated diplomatic efforts to keep the navies of non-littoral powers out of the region. At the same time, the proponents of an offensive naval doctrine – the Old School – used this predicament to argue that Soviet naval forces must be made strong enough to seize the Baltic approaches in the initial stage of a war. This way, the superior fleets of the Western powers could be kept out of the theater and the Baltic Fleet allowed to deal with the weak regional powers undisturbed. An offensive navy could also support the spread of world revolution, which – at least officially – remained an objective of Soviet foreign policy until the mid-1920s.

To strengthen their case, the Old School could refer to the fact that Western expeditionary forces to the Baltic were expected to be limited in size. The brunt of the capitalist coalition's effort would instead be carried by the newly independent neighbor states on the Soviet Union's northwestern border. It was against the navies of those powers that the strength of the Baltic Fleet should be measured, and all such comparisons would turn out to the Soviet Union's favor. The only real Great power in the region was Weimar Germany, with whom relations were amicable.

In the end, however, the perception of strategic conditions in the Baltic as comparatively advantageous did not lead to the adoption of an offensive naval doctrine. Instead, the relatively modest proportions of the threat at sea came to serve as an additional argument for reducing the navy's role. An offensive navy had little rationale. The resolution of the RVS in May 1928 meant a decisive defeat for the Old School.

Notes

1 E. L. Woodward and R. Butler (eds), *Documents on British Foreign Policy 1919–1939*, series 1, vol. VIII (London: Her Majesty's Stationery Office, 1958), pp. 294, 305–6; Johnson, 'Kolliderande suveränitet', p. 197; E. W. Peyron, 'Årsberättelse av föredragande i sjökrigsvetenskap', *Krigsvetenskapsakademiens handlingar*, vol. 125 (1923), p. 13; 's', 'Några ord om Sveriges lant- och sjöförsvar', *Krigsvetenskapsakademiens Tidskrift*, vol. 127 (1925), p. 18; Patrick Salmon, 'British Security Interests in Scandinavia and the Baltic 1918–39', in Aleksander Loit (ed.), *The Baltic in International Relations between the Two World Wars* (Stockholm: Studia Baltica Stockholmiensa, 1988), p. 134 n. 67.
2 Nemits and Gaylis to the RVS, 15 February 1921, *RGVA*, f. 33988, o. 2, d. 314, list 26–7.
3 Monakov, 'Sudba doktrin i teory, 2', p. 21; Ye. F. Podsoblyayev, 'Kakoy flot nuzhen RSFSR? (po materialam diskussii, proshedshey posle pervoy mirovoy voyny)', *Novy Chasovoy* (5) (1997), pp. 138–9.
4 The report carries the signatures of Toshakov, his commissar Dranitsyn and his deputy Vasilyev. It has been published together with the main proposal signed by naval commander Zof and naval chief of staff Blinov in N. Yu. Berezovsky (ed.), ' "Dlya kakikh tseley stroit flot?" Proekt pyatletnego plana RKKF 1925 g.', *Istorichesky Arkhiv*, no. 4 (1996).
5 P. J. Salmon, 'Perceptions and Misperceptions: Great Britain and the Soviet Union in Scandinavia and the Baltic Region 1918–1939', in John Hiden and Alexander Loit (eds), *Contact or isolation? Soviet–Western Relations in the Interwar Period* (Stockholm: Studia Baltica Stockholmiensa, 1991), pp. 416–22; Hain Rebas, 'Probleme des kommunistischen Putschversuches in Tallinn am 1. Dezember 1924', *Annales Societatis Litterarum Estonicae in Svecia*, vol. 9 (1980–85).
6 Berezovsky *et al.*, *Boevaya letopis*, p. 535.
7 Berezovsky (ed.), ' "Dlya kakikh tseley stroit flot?" ', pp. 50–4.
8 Berezovsky (ed.), 'Na borbu s limotrofami', pp. 59–60.
9 'Plan minnogo oborony teatra balticheskogo flota,' 23 August 1922, f. r-1, o. 3, d. 1306, list 6b.
10 Petrov, 12 May 1924 (quote), f. r-1, f. 3, d. 2121, list 38; preparations for war – 'Politicheskaya obstanovka balticheskogo teatra', 30 December 1925, f. r-1, o. 3, d. 2884, list 2b; cf. f. r-1, o. 3, d. 2116, list 186; f. r-1 o. 3, d. 2878, list 36–42; f. r-1, o. 3, d. 2121, list 12, 29, 38–9, 54–6, 74; f. r-1483, o. 1, d. 120, list 5–7.
11 Zonin, *Admiral L. M. Galler*, pp. 198–99; Berezovsky *et al.*, *Boevaya letopis*, pp. 512–13.
12 Ordinsky, 21 June 1924, 'Polit. obstanovka k manevram B. F. v. t/g', f. r-1, o. 3, d. 2563, list 10–10b; cf. the account of the maneuver in Berezovsky *et al.*, *Boevaya letopis*, p. 539.
13 Documents on the 1927–28 war games, compiled and commented by Belli in 1929, can be found in f. r-92, o. 2, d. 57; on the political background scenario of the exercise see list 39–40.
14 On the rather passive British policy toward the Baltic states, see Salmon, 'British Security Interests'; French interests in the region were primarily directed against Germany, while the struggle against Bolshevism was a secondary objective; cf. K. Hovi,

'The French Alliance Policy 1917–1927: A Change of Mentality', in Hiden and Loit (eds), *Contact or Isolation?*; Suzanne Champonnois, 'The Baltic States as an Aspect of Franco-Soviet Relations 1919–1934: A Policy or Several Policies?', in ibid.

15 Belli, 20 September 1924, 'Spravka inostrannogo otdela', f. r-1, o. 3, list 11; V. Kachalev, assistant for the Baltic Theater to the head of the strategic section, 25 November 1924, 'sluzhebnaya zapiska', ibid., list 15; Belli, 26 November 1924 ibid., list 16–16b; 30 December 1925, 'Politicheskaya obstanovka na balticheskom teatre', f. r-1, o. 3, d. 2884, list 2–3.
16 Berezovsky (ed.), 'Dlya kakikh tseley stroit flot?', p. 53.
17 Berezovsky (ed.), 'Na borbu s limotrofami', p. 59.
18 Rohwer and Monakov, *Stalin's Ocean-going Fleet*, p. 26.
19 Documents on the 1927–28 wargames, compiled by Belli, f. r-92, o. 2, d. 57, list 40.
20 Aralov (NKID = *Narodny Kommissariat Innostranikh Del* [People's Commissariat for Foreign Affairs]) to Zof, 16 July 1925, f. r-1, o. 3, d. 2887, list 55; Vasilyev, Ladygich and Belli to Zof, 8 August 1925, ibid., list 60–60b; 'Politicheskaya obstanovka balticheskogo teatra', 30 December 1925, f. r-1, o. 3, d. 2884, list 2; on Kirke's mission see Martti Turtola, *Från Torne älv till Systerbäck: Hemligt försvarssamarbete mellan Finland och Sverige 1923–1940* (Stockholm: Militärhistoriska förlaget, 1987), pp. 57–60.
21 Petrov, 12 February 1925, 'Zakonoproekt finskogo pravitelstva po usilieniyu finskogo flota', f. r-1, o. 3, d. 2878, list 6.
22 Cf. Zinovyev, 2 April 1929, 'Tesis k dokladu o Finskom zalive', f. r-92, o. 12, d. 2, list 1–3.
23 Kholodovsky, 29 March 1924, 'Veroyatnaya mezhdunarodnaya obstanovka na balticheskom i chernomorskikh teatrakh v blizhashie gody', f. r-1, o. 3, d. 2563, list 6–7b.
24 Belli, 22 November 1924, 'Politicheskaya obstanovka ha balticheskom teatre', f. r-1, o. 3, d. 2563, list 13–14; cf. extract from intelligence bulletin no. 14, 20 December 1925, 'Polsha. Podgotovka konferentsii v Varshave', f. r-1, o. 3, d. 2116, list 80.
25 GRU to Muklevich, 13 December 1928, f. r-1483, o. 1, d. 51, list 74–9.
26 f. r-92, o. 2, d. 57, list 40.
27 Nikonov, October 1928, 'Voennaya podgotovka protiv SSSR i osnovnye voprosy usileniya oborony', f. r-1483, o. 1, d. 51, list 36–73b.
28 Petrov, 23 November 1923, f. r-1, o. 3, d. 2116, list 116–25.
29 The forces of the Border States from *Jane's Fighting Ships 1928* (London: Jane's Yearbooks, 1928); the Soviet Baltic Fleet from Berezovksy *et al.*, *Boevaya letopis*, p. 562.
30 Holtsmark, Sven G. (ed.), *Norge og Sovjetunionen, 1917–1955: En utenrikspolitisk dokumentation* (Oslo: Cappelen, 1995), p. 147.
31 Belli, 22 November 1924, 'Politicheskaya obstanovka ha balticheskom teatre', f. r-1, o. 3, d. 2563, list 14; Kobetsky to Chicherin, 2 July 1925 (copy), f. r-1, o. 3, d. 2887, list 51; Chicherin to Kobetsky, 20 July 1925 (extract–copy), ibid., list 81.
32 Dobrolevsky to Chicherin, 13 August 1925 (extract–copy), f. r-1, o. 3, d. 2887, list 82–3; Dobrolevsky to Litvinov, 20 August 1925 (extract–copy), ibid., list 79; Dobrolevsky to Litvinov, 10 December 1925 (extract–copy), ibid., list 132; a naval attaché was appointed in Stockholm in the following year. P. Yu. Oras's reports from 1926–28 can be found in f. r-910, o.1., d. 41, d. 113, d. 114.
33 Dobrolevsky to Litvinov, 13 August 1925 (extract–copy), f. r-1, o. 3, d. 2887, list 83–6 (quote from 86).
34 Turtola, *Från Torne älv*, pp. 36–73; cf. Jorma Kalela, *Grannar på skilda vägar. Svensk–finska relationer 1921–1923* (Helsinki: Historiallisia tutkimuksia, 1971).
35 Arvid Cronenberg, *Militär intressegrupp-politik: Kretsen kring Ny Militär Tidskrift och dess väg till inflytande i 1930 års försvarskommission* (Kristianstad: Militärhistoriska förlaget, 1977).

36 Turtola, *Från Torne älv*, pp. 207–17; cf. W. M. Carlgren, 'Svek Sverige Finland?', *Historisk Tidskrift*, vol. 105 (1985), pp. 266–8.
37 Belli, 22 November 1924, 'Politicheskaya obstanovka ha balticheskom teatre', f. r-1, o. 3, d. 2563, list 13–14.
38 Petrov, 29 July 1924, f. r-1, o.3, d. 2121, list 73–5; Dobrolevsky to Litvinov, 20 August 1925 (extract–copy), f. r-1, o. 3, d. 2887, list 79.
39 'Petrov, 23 November 1923, f. r-1, o. 3, d. 2116, list 116–25; Petrov, 12 February 1925, 'Zakonoproekt finskogo pravitelstva po usilieniyu finskogo flota', ibid., d. 2878, list 8.
40 A recent document publication on the subject is Yury Dyakov and Tatyana Bushuyeva (eds), *The Red Army and the Wehrmacht: How the Soviets Militarized Germany 1922–1933 and Paved the Way for Fascism. From the Secret Archives of the Soviet Union* (New York: Prometheus Books, 1995); special focus on naval contacts in Tobias R. Philbin III, *The Lure of Neptune: German–Soviet Naval Collaboration and Ambitions, 1919–1941* (Columbia: University of South Carolina Press, 1994); cf. Erickson, *Soviet High Command*, pp. 251–5, 274–7.
41 Kholodovsky, 29 March 1924, 'Veroyatnaya mezhdunarodnaya obstanovka na balticheskom i chernomorskikh teatrakh v blizhashie gody', f. r-1, o. 3, d. 2563, list 6–7b.
42 Belli, 22 November 1924, 'Politicheskaya obstanovka na balticheskom teatre', f. r-1, o. 3, d. 2563, list 13–14.
43 Belli, 30 December 1925, 'Politicheskaya obstanovka na balticheskom teatre', f. r-1, o. 3, d. 2889, list 2b; on German apprehensions about France in the anti-Soviet coalition see Nikonov, October 1928, 'Voennaya podgotovka protiv SSSR i osnovnye voprosy usileniya oborony', f. r-1483, o. 1, d. 51, list 36–73b; on the role of the Polish–German relationship, cf. the background scenario of the 1927–28 war-games, f. r-92, o. 2, d. 57, list 39b.
44 Monakov, 'Sudba doktrin i teory, 2', pp. 22–3.
45 On 'The Future War', see Lennart Samuelson, *Plans for Stalin's War Machine: Tukhachevskii and Soviet Defence Industry Planning, 1925–1941* (London: Macmillan 1999), pp. 22–8; a memorandum by Snitko, head of the military section of Gosplan's Defense Sector, in early 1930 likewise discusses the possibility of Soviet support to revolutionary movements in the West and the conduct of offensive operations in east and central Europe. However, Snitko mentions Soviet military preparedness and a sufficient economic basis as prerequisites. Furthermore, the status of this memorandum is uncertain: cf. Samuelson, *Plans for Stalin's War Machine* pp. 102–8; see also David M. Glantz, *The Military Strategy of the Soviet Union: A History* (London: Frank Cass, 1992), pp. 29–54.
46 Berezovsky (ed.), 'Na borbu s limotrofami', pp. 56–7; Lennart Samuelson, 'The Naval Dimension of Soviet Five Year Plans, 1925–1941', in W. M. McBride and E. P. Reed (eds), *New Interpretations in Naval History: Selected Papers from the Thirteenth Naval History Symposium* (Annapolis, MD: US Naval Institute Press, 1998), pp. 208–9; Monakov, 'Sudba doktrin i teory, 8 [9, see p. 17, n. 11]', p. 34; Rohwer and Monakov, *Stalin's Ocean-going Fleet*, pp. 24–6.
47 The resolution has been published by N. Yu. Berezovsky (ed.), 'Postanovlenie revvoensoveta SSSR ot 8 maya 1928 g. O znachenii i zadachakh morskikh sil v sisteme vooruzhennykh sil strany', *Voenno-Istorichesky Zhurnal*, vol. 49(5) (1988).

6

THE MEANING OF 'SMALL WARS'

On 1 January 1921, the naval delegates at the VIIth Congress of Soviets in Moscow convened for a separate session to discuss the navy's future. In view of Russia's economic plight, they found that the construction of new and modern ships had to be postponed until older units had been repaired and the country's naval infrastructure restored.[1]

In spite of this cautious resolution, only a few weeks later naval commander Alexander Nemits presented his ambitious program for the navy's restoration, the first open manifesto of the Soviet Old School. According to Nemits, a total of six battleships, four cruisers, 65 large destroyers and 56 submarines should be deployed in the European theaters by 1926. This impressive fleet was primarily to be created through the repair and completion of older ships, but some new units would also have to be constructed. As we saw in Chapter 5, Nemits wanted to use the navy offensively.[2]

About two weeks later, the Kronstadt mutiny broke out. Not only did the mutiny cause serious material and personal losses to the navy, it also deprived Nemits's program of any prospect of success. On 7 March 1921, Lenin wrote to the People's Commissar of the Army and Navy, Leon Trotsky:

> Should we not close down the Navy *completely* for a year? What is its purpose? And give the coal to the railways or textile factories, to provide the peasants with clothes? I think that here we should be prepared to take decisive measures. Let the Navy suffer. The Soviet regime will benefit.[3]

After Nemits's proposal had been rejected, the task of formulating Russia's future naval policy was entrusted to a special commission under the chairmanship of V. I. Gusev (head of PUR), containing representatives of the RVS, the navy and the Cheka (*Chrezvychaynaya Kommissiya* = special commission [for fighting counterrevolution and sabotage]). In late August 1921, Gusev's commission presented a report, stating that for the time being the navy's chief function must be to support civilian sea traffic, clear mines and provide sea-rescue services. Militarily, it would suffice if it could provide fire support to the ground forces in coastal areas. Already during the 1921 sailing season, fuel shortage had compelled the Baltic Fleet to mothball one of the two operational battleships, four of the 19 destroyers and eight of the 13 submarines. In view of the dire economic situation and the navy's limited defense responsibilities, the Gusev commission now proposed that the number of active ships should be kept at about this level during the coming years, suggesting further reductions in other theaters.[4]

If the navy's role in national defense was to be reduced, it could also be questioned whether all naval support functions should be preserved within the navy. Already in May 1921, the coastal artillery had been transferred to the Red Army. In January 1922, the main sea fortresses in Sevastopol and Kronstadt went the same way and were to be subjugated to the fleet commanders in operational matters only. In November, the naval air arms were taken over by the regular air force on similar conditions. In January 1923, the GPU (Gosudarstvennoe Politicheskoe Upravlenie = State Political Directorate, the former Cheka), which for more than a year had been using naval patrol vessels for border control purposes, was given sole responsibility for the Soviet border and consequently took over the navy ships and personnel involved.[5]

Finally, certain administrative reforms added to the navy's subjugation. In August 1921, the title 'Commander of the Navy' was replaced with 'Naval Assistant to the Commander in Chief', the navy's central administration was substantially reduced and the fleets in the Baltic and the Black Sea renamed as the 'Baltic' and 'Black Sea Naval Forces'. In May 1922, the Naval Staff was transferred from Petrograd to Moscow and on 12 November 1923, the independent People's Commissariat for the Navy dissolved to be replaced by a joint People's Commissariat for the Army and Navy.[6]

Furthermore, the navy had no intelligence organization of its own but depended on the Red Army for its analyses of strategic conditions or the fighting power of foreign navies. In fact, the main functions of the Naval Staff's foreign section were to study international law, handle foreign naval attachés and receive visiting warships. According to Vladimir Belli, head of section from 1924 to 1926, the absence of active intelligence collection evoked criticism from the Naval Staff's chief of operations, Arkady Toshakov.[7] In the autumn of 1925, naval commander Zof requested that the army should transfer parts of its trained intelligence personnel to the Baltic and Black Sea Fleet staffs, but was told that due to the meager resources of the GRU, this would be impossible. The fleet staffs would have to make do with studying press material on foreign navies. A permanent naval intelligence function was a thing that Zof dreamed of but which would remain missing for some years.[8] No doubt, this constituted a handicap for the navy in its discussions with the army.

Scenarios for war in the 1920s

When it came to operational planning, in the mid-1920s the naval command contemplated at least three different cases of war in the Baltic:

- Case 1 (most probable): War against Estonia and/or Finland, supported by an Anglo-French naval squadron.

- Case 2 (less probable): War against Poland.
- Case 3 (least probable): War against the Baltic states and/or Finland alone.[9]

Cases 1 and 3 were very much alike in that they were both to be fought in home waters in the Gulf of Finland, requiring close interaction with the ground forces in both defensive and offensive operations. Case 2, on the other hand, was a predominantly offensive alternative, containing operations as far away as Poland. As we are primarily interested in comparing the defensive and offensive alternatives in Soviet naval planning and how they interacted with organizational rivalry, and as the work with case 2 has left few archival remains, these three cases will below be analyzed as two: one defensive and one offensive scenario.

Just as had been the case in 1906, when the battleship supporters tried to find a role for capital ships in the Baltic, the first line of argument of the Old School was that Russia must have a mobile strike force at sea – in addition to the minelayers and torpedo craft needed for coastal defense. Their tsarist predecessors had formulated the mission of such a force as 'upholding the Empire's interests in distant waters'. In the early Soviet era this was formulated as giving 'support to the international proletariat'. However, the attempts to justify battleships as a strike force in distant waters proved no more successful now than they had been for Nemits before Kronstadt, or for the Imperial Naval Staff in 1906. If the young Soviet state was to retain these traditional instruments of sea power, their combat role must be harmonized with the prevailing doctrine. Just as in tsarist times, the best strategy would be to find a rationale for capital ships within the framework of defensive operations.

In an article in *Morskoy Sbornik* in December 1922, Boris Zherve, professor at the Naval War College, therefore publicly rejected the idea of developing a doctrine for war between big navies in the oceans. Instead, the Soviet Navy should formulate a theory about 'small war' (*malaya voyna*), with which a superior enemy could be confronted in home waters. At a conference with military commanders in late spring 1923, Zherve and his colleague at the Naval War College, Mikhail Petrov, elaborated the notion of 'small wars' as warfare on sea communications, warfare for the sea coast (the enemy's as well as one's own) and warfare in cooperation with the Red Army.[10]

When Zherve and Petrov followed the example of the French Navy in the late nineteenth century and rejected an ocean-going navy for the concept of 'small wars', they changed from a traditional offensive doctrine – aiming at destroying or disarming the enemy (also known as sea-control) – to a defensive doctrine, aiming at denying the enemy from reaching his goal (also known as sea-denial), at least until a certain equalization of forces had been accomplished. Although often identified with the idea of the offensive, the Old School doctrine was thus really defensive, at least after 1923.

However, 'small wars' meant weakening the enemy through a series of minor operations and then – when strengths were even – switching to the counteroffensive. It was a strategy similar to the one Russia had employed against Napoleon in

1812. More importantly, in World War I, it had been a long-term objective of German naval operations. Why had Germany failed? In 1926, Ivan Kozhanov, former commander of the naval forces in the Pacific, now a student at the Naval War College in Leningrad, published a special study in *Morskoy Sbornik* on the *Hochseeflotte*'s campaign in 1914. He concluded that to be successful in their 'small wars' strategy, the Germans should have committed their battleships alongside their light cruisers and submarines.[11] In short, you needed capital ships to wage 'small wars', at least in the final counterstrike. Also, it could be argued, the navy must be retained as an independent service.

At the same time, 'small wars' could also be taken literally, in the Spanish meaning of the word – 'guerilla warfare' – an attritional campaign to exhaust a superior enemy who was too strong to be confronted in the open but might still be broken morally through numerous and damaging raids. Such an interpretation would result in a force structure radically different from that of a fleet centered on capital ships. Aircraft, coastal artillery, mines and torpedoes could then be major instruments of combat and not just supporting weapon systems. This rival definition of 'small wars' suggested a doctrine closer to the ideal of deterrence – a struggle aiming at 'punishing the enemy'.

Hence, the future structure of the Soviet Navy and its position within the armed forces had not been decided through the adoption of the 'small wars' concept. The 'true' meaning of this term would remain a matter of dispute during the entire Old School era.

Defensive operations – in defense of the battleship

At the conference with the naval command in February in 1922, the head of the Baltic Fleet's operational section, Arkady Toshakov, had already identified the protection of Petrograd as a primary mission in the theater. In August that same year he presented a draft for an operational plan in the Baltic based on a defensive system consisting of mine barriers.[12]

Although experience from World War I recommended this solution, there was little chance of establishing a defensive system as effective as that of 1914. As a result of the territorial changes that had followed after the war, the struggle against an invading fleet must now be taken up in the immediate vicinity of the former capital. The Russian defense zone consisted mainly of the area east to the Stirsudden–Shepelev perimeter, a narrow stretch that could be covered by fire from the batteries of Kronstadt in any case.

Furthermore, there was a limited supply of mines in the Baltic Fleet. According to Toshakov's calculations, 2,500 mines could be deployed within two weeks, a figure which should be compared to the 2,100 mines laid out in the Baltic by the Imperial Navy in less than five hours in 1914! A minimum demand was a supply of 2,000 mines within 48 hours. As most of the Baltic Fleet's destroyers had to be used to protect the minelayers, there was also a considerable lack of suitable transport capacity. Only 500 mines could be laid out at a time. The shortage of minesweepers in the fleet seemed just as deplorable. Because of technical problems, half the minesweeper fleet was constantly out of service. Moreover, the fortifications of Kronstadt were poorly protected. To prevent a surprise attack – similar to the disastrous British raid in 1919 – they had to be reinforced with great quantities of underwater obstacles, searchlights and sweeping obstacles.[13]

Toshakov prepared two versions of his plan. Either 2,240 mines could be concentrated into one main defense zone situated about 7–9 miles from the outermost fortifications, to be defended mainly by the surface ships, or, alternately, the system with double mine zones protected by coastal artillery, which had proved so successful during the world war, could be repeated. A modified version of the latter alternative was finally chosen.[14]

The forward defense zone would consist of 1,300–1,400 mines, situated 9–11 miles from the outermost fortification, Fort Krasnoflotsky, whose 12-inch guns had a theoretical range of 13 miles. Seven miles further to the rear, the fallback position would be situated. Here, only some 240 mines were to be deployed, as there had to be ample space for the Soviet ships to maneuver, whether in counterstrokes against enemy ships or in support of the army's operations ashore. The rearward zone would be defended by the only operational battleship, *Marat* (ex-*Petropavlovsk*), and by the fire from the 10-inch batteries of Fort Krasnoarmeysky and Fort Rif. The principal landing sites for an attack on Petrograd, the Kaporsky and Luzhky Bays in the south, could not be covered by fire from the Kronstadt batteries. Here, additional minefields had to be laid out, with motor torpedo boats (MTBs) and aircraft ready to protect them.[15]

The defense plan was tested in September–October 1922, when the Baltic Fleet held its first maneuvers since the Civil War. As described in Chapter 5, the aim of this exercise was to repel a landing attempt in Luzhky Bay through the joint efforts of coastal artillery, naval, ground and air units.[16] The maneuvers demonstrated serious deficiencies in the preparedness of Kronstadt, so the mine defense plan was further elaborated during 1923. The Baltic Fleet requested additional resources for antisubmarine warfare (ASW), and the Naval Staff investigated the possibility of supplying some 5,000 fathoms of submarine nets and 5,000 fathoms of underwater obstacles. The overall capacity for ASW operations was reviewed, and mobilization regulations improved in order to strengthen the protection of the border during the initial stage of a conflict.[17]

In August 1923, naval commander Pantserzhansky ordered the Baltic Fleet Soviet to prepare a new, 'ideal' mine defense plan based on the assumption that there would be a supply of 5,000 mines in five years, as well as a plan which could be ready for use in the immediate future. Just as before, the aim was to prevent an attacker from reaching Kronstadt and the landing sites on the southern shores of the Gulf of Finland. If the enemy managed to break through the first defensive barrier, he was to be caught in the fire from ships and coastal artillery and prevented from escaping out of range of the heavy artillery of Fort Krasnoflotsky. At the same time, mines and obstacles should be positioned in a way that did not hamper the Soviet ability to conduct offensive operations.[18]

Toshakov realized that the targets of enemy air attacks would be concentrated in the area east of the intended main defense zone (which ended at the Stirsudden–Shepelev perimeter), where the major fortifications, supply depots and naval facilities were situated. In 1923, fighter planes, anti-air artillery and observation posts aboard the ships were therefore united into a joint air defense command. Although the initiative for this reform came from the Baltic Fleet Staff, the new organization was placed under the command of the Kronstadt fortress commander, who no longer belonged to the fleet administratively but to the Petrograd Military District. The Baltic Fleet's remaining fighter planes were few and old, so the batteries of Kronstadt would have to play the leading role in air defense anyway.[19]

Thus, in addition to the humiliation the navy had suffered after Kronstadt, the joint character of the defense plan forced further concessions upon the sailors. In an article in *Morskoy Sbornik* in November 1922 on the Baltic Fleet's recent maneuvers, Old School partisan Mikhail Petrov fought back. He underlined that the maneuvers had been a *naval* exercise, drawing parallels to the situation 15 years before when the Russian Navy had been reorganized after the defeat by the Japanese. Petrov seems to have expected a similar outcome this time – a new version of an expansive construction program rather than the formulation of a new, radical concept of naval warfare. At least, he drew no lessons from the exercise related to the value of joint operations. Instead, he thought it had demonstrated the need for modern battleships. A defensive struggle meant fighting a positional war, which relied on concentration of fire, which – in turn – relied on capital ships. To preclude any suggestions that battleships could be replaced by coastal artillery, Petrov took care to emphasize that in a positional war fixed positions ashore could never replace mobile units at sea. In fact, the mobility and speed of warships formed the very essence of naval warfare. It was therefore necessary to keep all naval support functions under naval control. The fleet air arm and the coastal artillery should remain wholly integrated in the navy, pilots and artillery men should train and be taught to operate according to naval principles.[20]

About this time, the Old School also launched a counteroffensive against the advocates of air power, starting a controversy which would fill the pages of *Morskoy Sbornik* for many years. Naval War College professor G. N. Pell claimed that the airplane was more expensive than the battleship, as at least 100 sorties would be needed to put one battleship out of action – given the accuracy of aerial bombing and the amount of bombs needed to sink one battleship. Furthermore, a battleship had a life expectancy of 20 years against three years for an aircraft. Also, a battleship consumed less fuel, service personnel and base area than 100 aircraft.

The Old School's main opponent in *Morskoy Sbornik* was naval aviator K. Veygelin, who questioned Pell's figures. Even if it was correct that 1,000 aircraft would be required to sink ten battleships, Veygelin wrote, the airplane would still be more economical as the cost of the ten battleships equaled not 1,000 but 20,000 bombers! The airplane had a leveling potential similar to that of David's stone against Goliath, according to Veygelin, and this was especially important to a militarily inferior state like the Soviet Union. Veygelin also referred to the 1921–22 naval conference in Washington, where the signatory powers had shunned all limitations on aircraft carriers, suggesting this would be the main weapons system of imperialist navies in the future. Moreover, in view of the many special tasks that had to be solved by military aviation, the air force must be organized as a regular service and kept independent of both army and navy.[21]

Part of the Old School's air power critique was directed against US General William Mitchell. It was pointed out that Mitchell was a controversial figure even in his own country, and that he had been court–martialed for insubordination and demoted to colonel. Moreover, the circumstances surrounding his famous bombing experiment in 1921 were called into question. According to naval historian Evgeny Shvede, the Russian Navy would therefore be wise not to lose its head over novelties, as had happened so often in the past: in the 1870s circular ironclads (the *Popovkas*), in the 1880s minelayers, in the 1890s protected cruisers and submarines. N. Gorsky, who was not afraid to argue in an openly conservative way, claimed that the composition of modern battle fleets was the result of centuries of historical development, which meant that no single category of ships – certainly not the battleship – could be removed without upsetting the entire balance between the different types of forces. Therefore, there must be no more talk of military units 'in the greatest possible number at the lowest possible cost', as Naval War College professor Nikolay Novikov characterized the agitation of the air power enthusiasts.[22]

In short, the Old School claimed that a naval force was the only thing capable of defeating another naval force. From this perspective, the aircraft carrier was just another capital ship, using bombers instead of artillery to deliver fire upon the enemy, although in a less cost-effective way. Two aircraft carriers with 50 planes each would theoretically equal one battleship in firepower, and would cost at least as much. However, the need to protect the fleet from air attack suggested that the majority of aircraft aboard the carriers would not be bombers with the capacity to damage the enemy's ships, but fighter planes effective only against other aircraft. Airplanes had an important role to play in coastal defense and in supporting the fleet at sea, but they must be organizationally integrated into the navy if they were to prepare for these missions in an effective way.[23]

The Old School's struggle for capital ships could not be limited to the pages of *Morskoy Sbornik*. By the mid-1920s, the battleship campaign started to have an impact on operational planning as well. The 1923 Baltic Fleet maneuvers, which had demonstrated that the defensive depth in the Gulf of Finland was too small, offered convenient arguments for such changes. As Kronstadt could not be moved further east, the only way to extend defenses was to move them further west. This meant the forward minefields could no longer be covered by fire from the heavy batteries at Fort Krasnoflotsky. Instead, this task must be entrusted to 'floating' artillery. While in the original version of the mine defense plan the battleships had been stationed behind the rear minefield, in 1924 they were therefore moved up to the forward zone. Also, the scenario of a classic Nelsonian encounter between battle lines reappeared in the planning directives – the enemy force only had to be worn down to a manageable size first.[24]

Thus, during the Baltic Fleet maneuvers in 1924 the forward mine zone was no longer situated about 15 miles outside Kronstadt, but in the vicinity of the Finnish islands of Seiskari and Hogland, about 30 miles further west. Also, during exercises the battleships were made use of in a more offensive way. During the 1925 maneuvers, before falling back to the main defense zone after the enemy's breakthrough of the forward line, they engaged the attackers in a protracted struggle. The same pattern was repeated during the 1926 exercise, when as many as three battleships were included in the defending squadron.[25]

Offensive operations: the Björkö batteries and the problems of jointness

Although the main mission of the fleet remained defensive, even during the Old School era considerable energy was spent on preparing for offensive operations as well.

As early as October 1921, the operational directives issued by the RVS had mentioned the possibility of offensive operations by the Baltic Fleet as far away as Vyborg and Tallinn, provided that the Red Army's advance into Estonia and Finland proceeded fast enough.[26] When supplementing the 1925 naval construction program with a strategic analysis (as was shown in Chapter 5), Arkady Toshakov's operations section described the crushing of Poland as a central element in Soviet strategy. Afterwards, a strong defensive position should be established at the Baltic approaches, Western navies prevented from entering the Sounds while Germany, one of the world's largest industrial economies, was revolutionized and put at the disposal of the international proletariat.[27]

Already in the summer of 1924, the Polish campaign was implemented as War Case 2 in Toshakov's operational directives for the Baltic Fleet. No doubt, this was the closest the fleet would ever come to an independent strategic mission: the small Polish Navy was to be destroyed in its bases in Gdynia and the Danzig area, and mines laid out at the accesses of the Polish ports and naval bases. There was no mention of landing operations or cooperation with ground forces (although it is reasonable to assume that the Red Army would have advanced across the Polish border at the time). Also, most of the Polish coast would be out of reach for the Soviet Air Force, and so this would be an exclusively naval operation, whose objective Toshakov with uncensored Mahanist terminology described as 'gaining naval mastery in the theater'.[28]

Although the battleship *Marat*, four destroyers and one tanker conducted exercises off the coast of Danzig in September 1924 (in order to evaluate the fleet's ability to operate 'in distant parts of the Baltic'), the southern Baltic nonetheless received limited attention in Soviet exercises. In spite of prevailing Old School rhetoric, the Baltic Fleet concentrated on preparing for War Cases 1 and 3 in the Gulf of Finland. However, these war cases included offensive operations in support of the ground forces. For instance, the maneuvers in 1924 and 1927–28 contained the landing of troops in the enemy's rear, artillery support to troops ashore and bombardment of enemy coastal fortifications. Also, according to Toshakov's 1924 directives, War Case 3 (a conflict with the Border States exclusively) had as its stated objective the attainment of 'naval mastery in the Gulf of Finland'.[29]

As a rule, offensive operations were usually practiced during the early phase of the Baltic Fleet maneuvers, after which the fleet usually fell back toward Seiskari and Kronstadt to train in the mine defense zones. During the first part of the 1925 maneuvers the area of operations included the Moon Sound archipelago off Estonia's west coast, outside the Gulf of Finland. Similar assumptions could be made with regard to the 1927 scenario, according to which the enemy was superior in the Baltic but equal in the Gulf of Finland, and the 1928 scenario, which counted on Soviet superiority in all areas except 'light forces'.[30]

The latter exception, however, was of some importance. Without small ships, the Baltic Fleet would be handicapped when fighting in the shallow Finnish archipelago. The Finns, on their part, could count on large numbers of civilian motorboats, which were easy to mobilize or already in peacetime enrolled in the voluntary militia flotillas (the naval *skyddskår* organization). The regular Finnish Navy would use mines, fast torpedo craft and – from the early 1930s – specially designed coastal defense battleships.[31]

Whether the Baltic Fleet would have command of the Gulf of Finland or not, whether it would confront solely the Border States or have to fight the Western powers as well, there were some offensive operations which had to be undertaken under all circumstances. The Stirsudden lighthouse was situated on the Finnish side of the border, so Soviet troops must cross into Finland in the initial stage of any conflict to secure this northern anchor point for the main mine defense zone. The eight small Finnish islands in the eastern part of the Gulf (Hogland, Great and Small Tootersaari, Lavansaari, Peninsaari, Seiskari, Someri and Narvi) must also be secured. They were needed as observation posts and as battery sites for the forward defense zone. The importance of the islands had been apparent already during the 1922 maneuvers. Shortly afterwards, a special naval infantry detachment in Kronstadt had been designated as landing force.[32]

As the Gulf islands had been declared demilitarized in the Tarttu Peace Treaty of 1920, it was unlikely that this landing operation would encounter much opposition. The two islands of Koivusaari and Tuurisaari, south of Vyborg, posed a far greater problem. To protect the approaches of Saint Petersburg, the tsarist regime had created a system of coastal fortifications along the shores of the Gulf of Finland ('the Sea Fortress of Peter the Great'), which played an important role in the Baltic Fleet's mine defense during World War I. Although the peace of Tarttu in 1920 ruled that the Finns had to demolish the easternmost installations at Fort Ino, they kept Fort Saarenpää in Koivusaari Island and Fort Tiuuri in Tuurisaari Island. In addition, there was a third battery on the mainland at Hummaljoki, close to Koivusaari Island. Together, these three fortified points

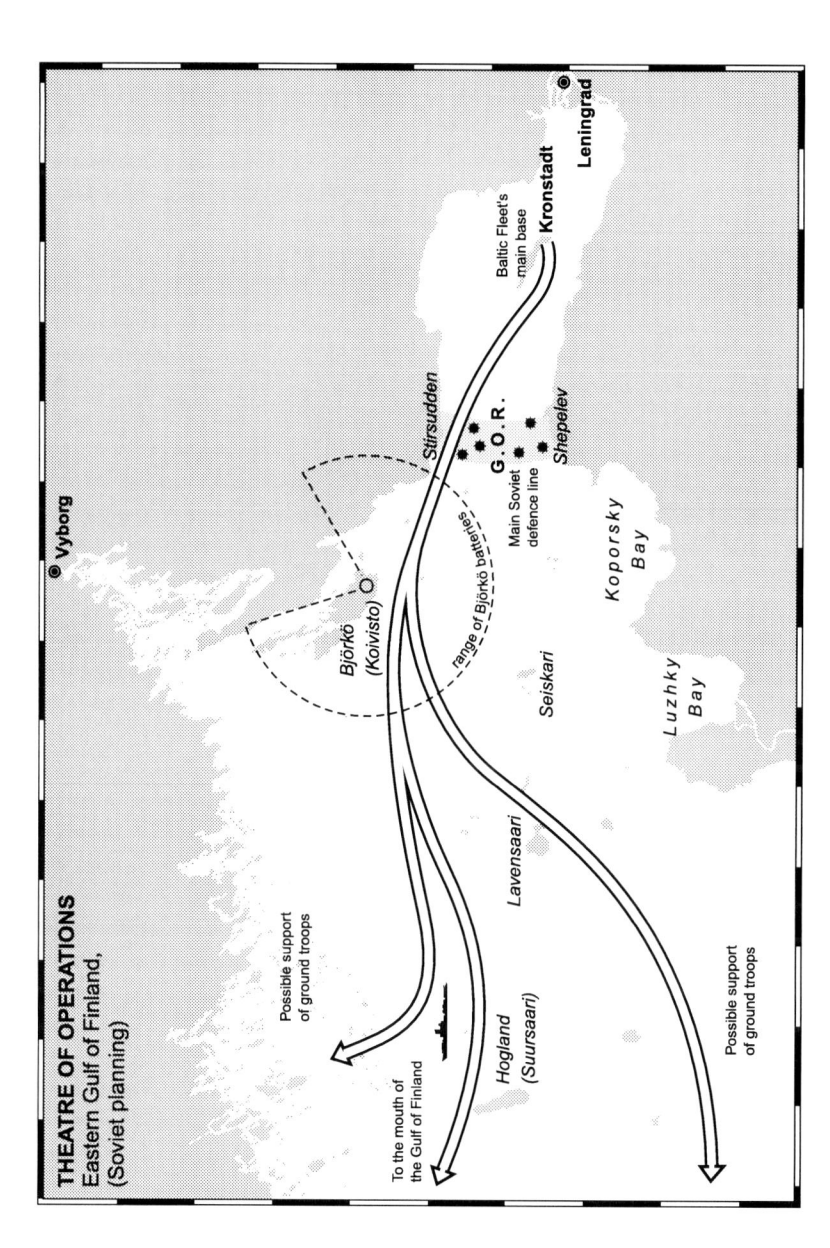

Map 2 Theater of operations.

formed the Koivisto batteries, better known under their Swedish name as the Björkö batteries.[33] Not only did the Finns rely on them for protection against the sea, but also to anchor their flank on the fortified Karelian Isthmus. During the 1930s, the Björkö batteries were thoroughly modernized and renovated. These fixed batteries could also be reinforced with mobile railroad guns, as from the mid-1920s the Vyborg–Helsinki railroad ran right beside the coast.[34]

The tsarist fortifications outside Vyborg would thus be a harder nut to crack than the undefended islands in the Gulf of Finland. Although the fire from the Björkö batteries could impede Soviet troop movements on the Karelian Isthmus, it was above all a threat to the Baltic Fleet. If the batteries were not silenced in the early phase of a war, the Baltic Fleet's entire campaign would be jeopardized, as the only navigable passage out of Kronstadt for the Soviet battleships ran within their range. No doubt, a joint effort by naval, air and ground units would be necessary. The Björkö operation was not only a militarily complicated undertaking, but also a rich source of organizational friction between services.

The dispute first surfaced in March 1925, when the Naval Staff in Moscow decreed that Björkö must be taken on the very first day of war. Only two months later, the Baltic Fleet deputy head of operations, Khvostchinsky, reported from a meeting with his counterpart in the LVO[35] staff that relations with the army had become somewhat strained and all joint planning work had ceased. Boris Shaposhnikov, soon to command the LVO, questioned the right of the Naval Staff in Moscow to issue any operational directives at all regarding the fleet, as in wartime it was to be subordinated to Leningrad anyhow. The LVO staff was at present busy preparing its own operational directives for the Baltic Fleet. Khvostchinsky did not know to what extent they would differ from the earlier ones issued by the Naval Staff, but it would probably be inappropriate if the Baltic Fleet changed its operational plan without permission from Moscow.[36]

The Baltic Fleet's awkward position between its two masters in Moscow and Leningrad is also apparent from a report by Khvostchinsky's superior, B. A. Sokolnikov, concerning a planned conference between the chiefs of staff of Soviet fleets and military districts at the time. Among subjects 'undesirable to include on the agenda' at the meeting, Sokolnikov listed rather central aspects of the operational planning process. How were the fleets to be subjugated to the military districts? Who was to be responsible for the mobilization of transport tonnage? Were the directives of the Naval Staff to the fleets or the directives of the RKKA General Staff to the military districts to be given preeminence? Were the military districts and the fleets even to participate in each other's maneuvers? If Sokolnikov's recommendations were followed, it is hard to see how that conference could have been particularly meaningful.[37]

The conflict between the LVO and the fleet over Björkö also pertained to the distribution of resources. In the event of War Case 1 (war against the Border States supported by the Western powers) the capture of Björkö was estimated to require a force of 9,100 men, 3,700 horses, 326 guns, 1,300 wagons and over 720 tons of supplies and equipment. Would these resources – almost an entire division – be operational on the first day of mobilization? According to the LVO, they would first be available after ten days, when the call-ups had been concluded. Even in the event of War Case 3 (war against the Border States only), when the Björkö assault force was estimated at a mere regiment, it could not be ready before the sixth day of mobilization. If the Baltic Fleet managed to conquer Björkö on its own, the LVO explained to the Fleet Staff in May 1925, it would not object. However, unless the ground operations proceeded more smoothly than expected and the Björkö fortifications could be captured from land, the navy should not expect any support from the RKKA before day 10 of the war.[38]

The organizational dispute about the Björkö batteries did not develop wholly along service lines. There were also tensions between the regional naval command in Kronstadt and the Naval Staff in Moscow. According to a critical report by the Baltic Fleet Soviet to the RVS, the Naval Staff had, without much knowledge of local conditions, prepared the plan for the Björkö operation. Even if the LVO could be made to supply the necessary infantry, how were these troops to get across to Björkö? Most of the civilian river sloops designated for requisition had to be unloaded and refurnished before they could take aboard the Björkö task force. Furthermore, as the Baltic Fleet Soviet acidly remarked, Moscow seemed to presuppose there would be nice weather at the time of the operation. Otherwise, how should one understand a plan that calculated on the landing troops being towed some 40 nautical miles across the sea in open sloops and barges? What if there was a storm? What if the task force had to wait in port until the weather improved? The Baltic Fleet Soviet concluded that 'the stay aboard non-sea-going transport vessels in rough weather, or the stay in harbor at anchors for two–three days, does not produce a military force but a crowd of tormented and exhausted people'.

Moreover, there were no escort vessels to protect the task force, nor any anti-aircraft artillery. The appearance of a single enemy airplane in the skies above would probably cause panic aboard the crowded boats. Luckily, there was a reserve of suitable ships, which could be drawn upon to reduce the dependency of non-sea-going transports. According to a preliminary estimate, the total transport tonnage available in the Leningrad area could take as many as 12,000 men and 2,000 horses. If the passenger ships trafficking the Leningrad–Kronstadt route were also included, perhaps another 3,000 men could be squeezed in.[39]

Although a copy of the Fleet Staff's report was sent to naval commander Zof, he refrained from comment.[40]

Even if the Baltic Fleet were to call off the complicated Björkö operation altogether, in any campaign scenario the shortage of minor warships would pose a serious problem for the Soviets. According to an assessment by Sokolnikov in the spring of 1925, the Fleet's 8–10 destroyers were too few to provide protection for the battleships outside Kronstadt, while the minesweepers were in such a poor state that up to 14 days of preparations would be needed before they could even put to sea. In addition, several of the MTBs operated by the GPU for border control purposes and intended to serve in the Baltic Fleet in wartime had been transferred to the GPU in the Black Sea without the navy's permission.[41]

The end of the navy in Russia?

In January 1925, Mikhail Frunze succeeded Lev Trotsky as People's Commissar for the Army and Navy. Compared with Trotsky, Frunze was a friend of the navy, who participated personally in the Baltic Fleet's maneuvers, allegedly writing his article 'We Need a Powerful Baltic Fleet' aboard the battleship *Marat*. At a meeting with the RVS in mid-July 1925, he also enforced the transfer of the coastal artillery back to the naval forces.[42]

The 1925 naval construction program (the strategic contents of which were discussed in the previous chapter) was presented by naval commander Zof and his chief of staff Blinov in March that year, calling for a total naval strength in 1931 of four battleships, four cruisers, one aircraft carrier (through conversion of the not yet completed *Borodino* class battle cruiser *Izmail*, to be used in the Black Sea), 40 submarines, 26 destroyers, 60 MTBs and some 76 other minor ships. That force was to be created through the completion of older units, through retrival of the lost 'Wrangel Fleet' from France and also through the construction of new ships.[43]

In October, Arkady Toshakov backed up earlier demands with a report on the 1925 naval maneuvers, casting doubt on the Baltic Fleet's ability to solve its combat missions at present. To exercise local command of the sea in the Gulf of Finland, he asserted, at least four battleships were needed. The coastal fortifications and the Baltic Fleet's weak air arm also needed strengthening. All in all, in 1928, the Soviet naval forces should consist of five battleships, five cruisers, 16 destroyers, 18 submarines, 60 MTBs and 186 aircraft.

Toshakov's report made the Red Army General Staff react. In a report of its own, it questioned the substance of his estimates, rejected such concepts as 'local command of the sea' and emphasized that the navy's missions should remain limited to supporting the ground forces and defending the coast. Two battleships would suffice in the Baltic instead of four, and in 1928, the total Soviet Navy should consist of three battleships, four cruisers, eight destroyers, six submarines, 12 patrol craft and 60 MTBs.[44]

At this stage, Frunze was dead and had been succeeded as People's Commissar by the rugged cavalryman Kliment Voroshilov, who was less friendly toward the navy. To decide its future role and composition, a special commission was appointed within the RVS, led by Deputy People's Commissar for Army and Navy I. S. Unshklikht and counting among its members both Tukhachevsky and Air Force Commander P. I. Baranov. As could be expected, service rivalry soon came to paralyze the work of this group, so in February 1926 the army presented its own naval proposal. That report allowed for a slightly larger force than the earlier army plan (one additional cruiser, four more destroyers, two more submarines but fewer MTBs). However, it also demanded the abolition of the regional fleet staffs. In spite of the navy's desperate protests, the Unshklikht Commission recommended similar changes, canceling both the restoration of the fourth *Gangut* class battleship (*Frunze*, former *Poltava*), and the conversion of the battle cruiser *Izmail* into an aircraft carrier.

In July, the RVS decided to reorganize the naval command in accordance with the army's proposal, bringing to an end the more than 200-year-long existence of the Russian Navy as an independent armed service. A special directorate, the UVMS, within the People's Commissariat for the Army and Navy replaced the Naval Staff. It would be responsible for training, maintenance, organizational, technical and hydrographical matters. However, operational planning, naval construction and the direction of coastal artillery was entrusted to the second section of the Red Army General Staff, which specialized in naval matters but was manned by army officers and was independent of the UMVS. On a regional level in the coastal areas, a similar transfer of responsibilities took place from fleet staffs to military district staffs. The regional fleet soviets were the only naval organs that continued to play an active role in operational planning. Vladimir Zof, who had fought stubbornly for service independence, was sacked as naval commander and replaced by Romuald Muklevich.[45]

The five-year naval construction program, which was approved in November 1926, was largely modeled on the Red Army naval plan, although the battleship *Frunze* was still to reinforce the Baltic Fleet. In addition, two cruisers, four destroyers, 12 submarines, 18 patrol craft and 30 MTBs were to be divided between the Baltic and the Black Sea Theaters. Only about a month later, the cruiser intended for the Baltic was removed from the plan.[46] The decision by the XVth Party Congress in late 1927 for a speedy industrialization of the Soviet Union meant that the naval construction program soon had to be revised again to adapt to the general five-year plan. Both the UVMS and the Red Army presented their proposals, which were discussed at a meeting with the RVS and the leading military commanders in May 1928. It was during this conference that the debate between Mikhail Petrov and Mikhail Tukhachevsky – cited in Chapters 2 and 5 – took place. As we have seen, the RVS on 8 May 1928 passed its resolution 'on the importance and tasks of the naval forces in the country's system of armed forces' as a result of these discussions, which, just like the earlier RVS resolution from 1926, went along with the views of the army. Although battleships were still acknowledged as the basic weapon system for providing a naval force with 'battle steadiness' and 'activity', the resolution also called for the development of lighter ship categories in the future. Furthermore, it was stated that the navy's active operations should be conducted in accordance with the methods of 'small wars'.[47]

But what exactly did this mean? The heavy reduction of the navy from 1926 onwards called for a revision of naval campaign planning, bringing matters to the critical point where the meaning of 'small wars' finally had to be defined. Was it to be a campaign to reduce the fighting strength of the enemy until he could be challenged on even terms, or a fight to exhaust him morally and break his will? When the Baltic Fleet Soviet and the naval section of the Red Army General Staff drafted their preliminary campaign plans, their different views became all too visible.

The meaning of 'small wars' finally decided

The Fleet Soviet thought the enemy's main objective would be to eliminate the Baltic Fleet. It regarded 'small wars' as a 'war for equalization', aiming to create favorable conditions for a final, decisive encounter between battleship formations, and warned the Red Army from expecting too much support from the sea. As soon as the enemy had been weakened through a series of minor engagements, the Soviet battleships would move west of the Stirsudden–Shepelev line and – as the Fleet Soviet emphasized through the use of capital letters – 'EXPLOIT THE VICTORY AND FINALLY ANNIHILATE THE ENEMY'. Provided there were no Great Powers taking part in the enemy coalition, some offensive actions with submarines and battleships could also be contemplated against the Polish coast.[48]

The naval section of the Red Army General Staff described the contents of 'small wars' more along the lines of a guerrilla campaign, being less confident of the navy's ability to operate west of the Stirsudden–Shepelev perimeter, whether against the shore or against enemy warships. This not only followed from the West's expected superiority at sea, but also from the belief that the Soviet ground forces' swift advance along the southern shore of the Gulf of Finland would make such operations unnecessary. Nor did the army believe there existed a real threat from the sea against Leningrad or Kronstadt. The enemy would be just as unwilling to operate east of the Stirsudden–Shepelev perimeter for fear of losses as the Soviets were to operate west of this area. Although there would still be a role for battleships in the future Baltic Fleet, the most important weapons systems at sea were bomber aircraft, coastal artillery, surface torpedo boats and submarines.[49]

In 1927–28, the Naval War College had staged a series of war games to examine the problems further. The Baltic Fleet's capability to solve various missions was tested: support to the ground forces ashore, capture of Björkö and the islands in the Gulf as well as delaying actions at the forward defense zone. As Vladimir Belli, now serving at the college's department of operational art, later concluded in his evaluation, the results had not been satisfactory. Although there had been no requirement in the games that the fleet should capture Björkö before the army had advanced far enough to support the attack from the rear, the outcome of the landing operations had been disastrous. In the first of two exercises, defeat had occurred almost immediately, the unescorted troop transports becoming easy targets for the enemy. In the second war game, the Soviets managed to land troops on the islands and even provide some artillery support to the Red Army down in Estonia. However, the Soviets failed to make proper use of their submarines, lost control of the air space and in the end suffered heavy losses. During the battle at the forward defense zone, they showed a complete negligence of the favorable Nordic light conditions and suffered far heavier losses than could be tolerated in an initial skirmish: one battleship (as well as substantial damage on the three remaining battleships), eight destroyers, two MTBs and 13 aircraft. Belli concluded that the commanders of the Red side had neglected a joint approach and proved unable to conduct their attacks according to the 'method of small wars'.[50]

What, then, was the correct interpretation of the term 'small wars'? By the time Belli wrote his evaluation in the spring of 1929, the matter had finally been settled. The 1928 campaign plan established that the mission of the Baltic Fleet was to defend the approaches of Leningrad, support the army's advance on the south side of the Gulf of Finland, defend occupied territory in the rear of the army and raid enemy communications. The main defensive struggle was to be fought in the Stirsudden–Shepelev defense zone, which was to be laid out at the time of mobilization with some 3,444 mines and 610 sweeping obstacles. Within 36 hours, most of the Baltic Fleet would be mobilized to engage the British expeditionary force when it arrived in the Baltic (it was estimated that the Royal Navy would need at least five days to reach Kronstadt from its home stations in Scotland).[51]

The suppression of the Björkö batteries outside Vyborg, which had been requested by the Naval Staff in Moscow in 1925 to enable the battleships to move freely out of Kronstadt, no longer figured among the Baltic Fleet's primary missions. The vulnerable battleships were not to move west of the minefields unless the enemy's main force was absent. Soviet light forces (cruisers, destroyers, MTBs) would be more active, conduct night raids against enemy bases with mines and torpedoes and occasionally support the advancing Red Army with flanking fire. As the ground forces advanced further into Estonia, parts of the torpedo flotilla could take up new positions in the Estonian archipelago. When Tallinn had been captured, the rest of the fleet was to follow. Soviet submarines would attack cargo traffic to and from Estonian and Latvian ports and keep watch against British warships in the Baltic. Whether an official state of war with Britain existed or not, British forces would be legitimate targets from the moment they appeared east of the Belts. If Britain stayed out of the conflict and there was Soviet superiority in the theater, an even more active stance could be taken. This did not mean sailing off to the Polish coast, however, but supporting the ground forces through landing operations.[52]

In short, the 1928 campaign plan signified that the struggle to define 'small wars' had been won by the army. The notion of the battleship's special status had been rejected, as had the 1912 naval construction program as a basis for the navy's restoration. With this, the resolution of the RVS from May 1928 on 'the importance and tasks of the naval forces in the country's system of armed forces' was translated into concrete operational directives.

Conclusion

After the Kronstadt mutiny in 1921, the Soviet Navy suffered a gradual curtailing of its service independence. The navy was not blind to this development and proclaimed at an early stage that defense against invasion and support for the army should be its main missions. The preparations for such operations necessarily contained a high degree of jointness, which could damage service integrity further. In response, the Old School representatives introduced the notion of 'small wars' – a concept sufficiently vague to warrant substantial offensive operations and allow for the preservation of heavy artillery ships. In addition, the specific conditions in the Gulf of Finland could be called upon to justify such elements in the doctrine.

Parallel to this positive development, however, the navy suffered several setbacks in the bureaucratic struggle in Moscow. It failed to win acceptance for its plans for warship construction, and in 1926 lost its status as a separate fighting service. The 1928 campaign plan in the Baltic Theater confirmed these developments. The Baltic Fleet was now deprived of all missions except supporting the ground forces. The heritage of the 1912 naval construction plan was finally liquidated.

From 1921 to 1928, the history of the Old School could thus be described as a continuous retreat from one position after another. First, the idea of a powerful thrust to the Baltic approaches had to be abandoned. Then, the traditional role of seaborne artillery was challenged by the new concept of joint operations, exposing the battleship to competition from coastal artillery and aircraft. Finally, the navy's organizational autonomy was curtailed, its wartime role limited to rendering support to the ground forces and the battleship reduced to a secondary role in the rear. In the future, the Soviet naval forces would probably have no core of heavy artillery ships at all. In the struggle ship against ship, the Baltic Fleet was to be a mere guerrilla force, fighting a war of psychological attrition. It had gone from an offensive to a defensive doctrine, and then finally reached something very similar to a deterrent doctrine – aimed at breaking the enemy's will rather than his material fighting power.

Notes

1. Berezovsky *et al.*, *Boevaya letopis*, pp. 476–7.
2. Nemits and Gaylis to the RVS, 15 February 1921, *RGVA*, f. 33988, o. 2, d. 314, list 23–4; cf. Berezovsky *et al.*, *Boevaya letopis*, pp. 478–9; Rohwer and Monakov, *Stalin's Ocean-going Fleet*, p. 14.
3. J. M. Meijer (ed.), *The Trotsky Papers*, vol. II, *1917–1922* (The Hague: Mouton, 1971), p. 414.
4. Protocol of RVSR (*Revolutsionny Voenny Soviet Respubliki* = Supreme Revolutionary-Military Council/Soviet of the Republic), 20 August 1921 (copy), f. r-1. o. 3, d. 916, list 62–4; Berezovsky *et al.*, *Boevaya letopis*, pp. 478–9; 'Boevoe raspisanie baltiskogo flota na 1921 god', f. r-1, o. 3, d. 916, list 66–70.
5. 'Vremmenoe polozhenie o vzaimotnozheniakh voenno-morskogo komandovaniya i osobykh organov V. Ch. K. po okhrane granits', revised 18 January 1922, f. r-1, o. 3, d. 916, list 242–3; Berezovsky *et al.*, *Boevaya letopis*, pp. 485, 489, 491, 502–4; 519; Erickson, *Soviet High Command*, p. 176.
6. Berezovsky *et al.*, *Boevaya letopis*, pp. 489, 492, 494–5, 508, 526.
7. Belli's memoirs, f. r-2224, o. 1, d. 4, list 124–5.
8. Zof to the Baltic Fleet Soviet, 12 November 1925, f. r-92, o. 1, d. 729, list 27.
9. Toshakov to Dombrovosky and Zof, 18 July 1924, 'Operatsii pervogo periody voyny', f. r-92, o. 2, d. 16, list 14–20; Toshakov to Dombrovosky and Zof, ibid., list 22–4; Baltic Fleet Soviet to RVS, April 1925, f. r-92, o. 1, d. 731, list 7–11.
10. Monakov, 'Sudba doktrin i teory, 2', p. 18–19; Herrick, *Soviet Naval Theory and Strategy*, pp. 2–3; Podsoblyayev, 'Kakoy flot nuzhen RFSR?', pp. 140–2.

11 I. Kozhanov, 'Sootvestvovali organisatsiya i metody maloy voyny strategicheskim zadacham nemtsev i obstanovke v protsesse razvitiya ot nachala do kontsa 1914 goda?', *Morskoy Sbornik*, no. 5 (1926).
12 Monakov, 'Sudba doktrin i teory, 1', p. 22; 'Plan minnoy oborony teatra balticheskogo flota', f. r-1, o. 3, d. 1306, list 2.
13 'Plan minnoy oborony teatra balticheskogo flota', f. r-1, o. 3, d. 1306, list 1–8b; on the minelaying action in 1914, see B. Shalagin, 'Sobiratel baltflota: K 130-letiyu so dnya rozhdeniya admirala N. O. Essena', *Morskoy Sbornik*, no. 12 (1990), p. 74.
14 Vayev to the head of the Baltic Fleet operational section, 10 September 1922; Pantserzhansky and Zof to the commander of the Baltic Fleet, 13 September 1922, f. r-1, o. 3, d. 1306, list 10–11; Vayev to the deputy commander of the Baltic Fleet operational section, 9 January 1923, ibid., list 17–18.
15 'Plan minnoy oborony teatra balticheskogo flota', f. r-1, o. 3, d. 1306, list 1–8b.
16 Zonin, *Admiral L. M. Galler*, pp. 198–201; Berezovsky *et al.*, *Boevaya letopis*, pp. 512–13.
17 Commander Baltic Fleet to Naval Commander, 2 February 1923, f. r-1, o. 3, d. 1306, list 62; head operational section Naval Staff Toshakov to chief of staff Baltic Fleet, 11 November 1922, ibid., list 68; head arms section Naval Staff Zagulyayev and head mine section Naval Staff Fedosov to Toshakov, 27 February 1923, ibid., list 29–30; protocol no. 0241 from meeting at the head of operational section, 16 April 1923, ibid., list 20–2; head of operational section, no date, ibid., list 56.
18 Pantserzhansky to Baltic Fleet Soviet, 16 August 1923, f. r-1, o. 3, d. 1306, list 38–9.
19 'Plan kampanii na 1923 god. Organisatsiya vozdukhnooboroni teatra voyni finskogo zaliva', f. r-1, o. 3, d. 1306, list 75–80; head of operations no date (1923), 'Obyansnitelnaya zapyska k planu vozdukhnooborony teatra voennykh deystvy baltiyskogo flota', f. r-92, o. 1, d. 631, list 11–14b.
20 M. Petrov, 'Po povodu manevrov balticheskogo flota', *Morskoy Sbornik*, vol. 75 (11) (1922).
21 K. Veygelin, 'Sili vozdushnie i morskie', *Morskoy Sbornik*, vol. 75 (11) (1922).
22 E. Shvede, 'Yeszhyo neskolko slov po povodu spora mezhdu lineynym korablem i vozdushnym apparatom', *Morskoy Sbornik*, vol. 75 (11) (1922); N. Gorsky, 'Flot i aviatsiya', *Morskoy Sbornik*, vol. 75 (11) (1922); N. V. Novikov, book review of *Problema oborony za rubezhom v 1925 godu*, *Morskoy Sbornik*, vol. 79 (5) (1926).
23 P. I. Smirnov, 'K itogam spora o morskom i vozdushnom flotakh', *Morskoy Sbornik*, vol. 79 (5) (1926); cf. Monakov, 'Sudba doktrin i teory, 2', pp. 17–18; Herrick, *Soviet Naval Theory*, pp. 3–7; Podsoblyayev, 'Kakoy flot nuzhen RSFR?', pp. 139–41.
24 Toshakov to Dombrovosky and Zof, 18 July 1924, 'Operatsii pervogo periody voyny', f. r-92, o. 2, d. 16, list 14–20.
25 Berezovsky *et al.*, *Boevaya letopis*, pp. 539, 548–9, 553. In 1926 the third battleship of the *Gangut* class, the *Parizhskaya Kommuna*, entered service after several years of repair. As noticed in Chapter 2, she was transferred to the Black Sea Fleet in 1929.
26 Yu. M. Kilin, 'Voenno-politicheskie aspekty sovetsko–finlandskikh otnosheny v 1920–1930-e gody', in S. B. Koreneva and A. V. Prochorenko (eds), *Rossiya i Finlandiya v XX veke* (St Petersburg: Evropeysky dom; Vaduz: Topos Verlag, 1997), pp. 84–5.
27 Berezovsky (ed.), ' "Dlya kakikh tseley stroit flot?" ', pp. 50–4.
28 Toshakov to Dombrosky, 24 July 1924, 'Operatsii pervogo periody voyny', f. r-92, o. 2, d. 16, list 22–4.
29 Berezovsky *et al.*, *Boevaya letopis*, pp. 537–8, 548–9; Toshakov to Dombrosky, 24 July 1924, 'Operatsii pervogo periody voyny', f. r-92, o. 2, d. 16, list 22–4.
30 Berezovsky *et al.*, *Boevaya letopis*, pp. 546–7, 555, 560; Zonin, *Admiral L. M. Galler*, pp. 211–12.
31 Head of Baltic Fleet intelligence section Zinovyev to squadron commanders, commander of Baltic Fleet air arm and commander of the Baltic Fleet PUR, 12 July

1929, 'Reorganitsatsiya finskoy beregovoj oborony i osuzhestvlenie finskoy sudostroitelnoy programmy', f. r-92, o. 12, d. 1, list 4–14; Baltic Fleet intelligence section, 'Informatsionnyj byulleten no 1', May 1929, 'Rol Finlandii v baltisheskom teatre', f. r-92, o. 12, d. 3, list 4–5.
32 Kilin, 'Voenno-politicheskie aspekti', p. 44.
33 The parish of Koivisto is better known under its Swedish name Björkö because of the treaty that the German Kaiser William II and the Russian emperor Nicholas II concluded when they met here in 1905 (the Treaty of Björkö). I have therefore chosen to refer to Koivisto as Björkö throughout this text. Björkö is also the name which was used in contemporary sources.
34 Martti Turtola, 'Aspects on Finnish–Estonian Military Relations in the 1920s and 1930s', in Hiden and Loit (eds), *the Baltic in International Relations*; P. O. Ekman, 'Sjöstridskrafterna', in Henrik Ekberg (ed.), *Finland i krig 1939–1945*, vol. I (Helsinki: Holger Schildts förlag, 1986), pp. 170–1, 178–9.
35 Abbreviation for Leningrad Military District = *Leningradsky Voenny Okrug*.
36 Khvostchinsky to head of Baltic Fleet section of operations Sokolnikov, 11 May 1925, f. r-92, o. 1, d. 731, list 11.
37 Sokolnikov, 19 May 1925, 'Voprosy, nezheleniyu v programmu syezda nachalnikov shtabov morskikh i Okrugov', ibid., list 16.
38 Baltic Fleet Soviet (Bekman, Kurkov and Galler) to RVS, April 1925, f. r-92, o. 1, d. 731, list 7–10.
39 Baltic Fleet Soviet (Bekman, Kurkov and Galler) to RVS, April 1925, f. r-92, o. 1, d. 731, list 7–10.
40 Khvostzhinsky to head of the Baltic Fleet section of operations Sokolnikov, 11 May 1925, f. r-92, o. 1, d. 731, list 11.
41 Sokolnikov, 17 May 1925, 'Spravka po voprosy nedostatki v melkikh yedintsakh', f. r-92, o. 1, d. 731, list 17.
42 Berezovsky *et al.*, *Boevaya letopis*, pp. 544–46; Zonin, *Admiral L. M. Galler*, pp. 218–20.
43 Berezovsky *et al.*, *Boevaya letopis*, p. 541; Berezovsky (ed.), ' "Dlya kakikh tseley stroit flot?" ', p. 47.
44 Monakov, 'Sudba doktrin i teory, 2', pp. 22–3.
45 Berezovsky *et al.*, *Boevaya letopis*, pp. 543–4, 552; Monakov and Berezovsky, 'Sudba doktrin i teory, 4', pp. 24–6, 28.
46 Berezovsky *et al., Boevaya letopis*, pp. 553–4; Monakov and Berezovsky, 'Sudba doktrin i teory, 4', p. 28; when the 1926 construction program was cancelled in February 1929, no more than six MTBs had been commissioned, while one patrol boat and one D-class submarine – *Dekabrist* – had been launched, Breyer, *Soviet Warship Development*, vol. 1, p. 192.
47 The resolution has been published in Berezovsky (ed.), 'Postanovlenie revvoensoveta SSSR'; cf. Monakov and Berezovsky, 'Sudba doktrin i teory, 5', p. 22; Westwood, *Russian Naval Construction*, pp. 140–1; L. Samuelson, 'Naval Dimension of Soviet Five Year Plans', pp. 208–10.
48 The operational plan of the Baltic Fleet Soviet, compiled by Viktorov, Smirnov and Galler ('Sobrazheniya po vypolneniyu zadach vydayostikh na morskie sili baltiskogo morya 1927 g'), f. r-2041, o. 1, d. 2, list 1–28, the Fleet Soviet's draft for an operational plan in ibid., d. 3 (quote from list 41).
49 Varagin and Zabolotsky (section 2 of RKKA General Staff), 5 February 1927, f. r-2041, o. 1, d. 2, list 29–48.
50 V. A. Belli, 'Otchet po voenno–morskim igram provedennym v voenno–morskoy i voenno–politicheskoy im t…akademiyakh RKKA v 1927–28 uchebn.godakh v vostochnoy chasti balticheskogo morya', f. r-92, o. 2, d. 57, list 37–42b (quotes from list 39, 42b). For some reason, the fourth, never completed *Gangut* ship *Frunze* must

have been included in the Baltic Fleet during the war game, although by this time its scuttling had been finally decided.
51 Cf. 'Sobrazheniya po vypolneniyu zadach vydayoshikh na morskie sili baltiskogo morya 1927 g', f. r-2041, o. 1, d. 2, list 1–28.
52 RKKA General Staff section 2, 'Operativnaya chast plana voyny na balticheskom more', f. r-2041, o. 1, d. 3, list 55–63.

7

THE NAVY OF THE MILITARY SPECIALISTS

Just as the capitalist world was forced to accept the existence of the Bolshevik regime, the Bolsheviks had to reconcile themselves with the fact that their state existed side by side with bourgeois states in the international system. After the Civil War, foreign capital and foreign experts were needed for Russia's reconstruction, and so was the domestic mobilization of private enterprise. To get the country going, the peasants were allowed to sell their surplus on the market and to hire labor; small-scale entrepreneurs were allowed to operate in the cities (above all in the service sector). It should be remembered that the overall impact of this economic deregulation – known as the New Economic Policy or NEP – was fairly limited. In retrospect, however, the NEP years would appear as a golden age, especially to the Soviet peasants.[1]

Nor did political oppression disappear during NEP. The constitution of 1924 promoted the Cheka from its Civil War status as an 'extraordinary committee' into an ordinary federal state agency, the GPU (renamed as the OGPU [*Obyedinyonnoe Gosudarstvennoe Politicheskoe Upravlenie* = United State Political Administration] in September 1923). Although its activities – at least formally – were subject to legal restrictions, its extensive powers, which had formerly been regarded as extraordinary, were now made permanent. The number of political arrests (for 'counter-revolutionary crimes') shrank from 76,820 in 1921 to 30,676 in 1926. However appalling these numbers are, they should nonetheless be compared to the situation in the 1930s when the number of repressed persons each year could be counted in six-digit numbers (1934 and 1936 were the only exceptions, when the number of political arrests was 'limited' to 90,417 and 91,217 respectively).[2]

In the same way, although cultural freedom had clearly defined limits during NEP, in light of later developments it would still seem a comparatively liberal period, as the party position on the relationship between proletarian culture and bourgeois tradition had not yet been decided. Against the notions of revolutionaries like Bogdanov, Anatoly Lunacharsky and the Proletkult movement of culture as a 'third front in the revolutionary struggle against the bourgeoisie' – a front equally important to those of state power and economic power – the view of Lenin, Gorky and others emphasized the need for mass education and urgent emancipation from the old, 'uncivilized' Russia. The revolution could not survive, they argued, much less could a genuine proletarian culture develop, if the proletariat did not first learn to appreciate – and critically evaluate – the heritage of previous civilizations. In this educational effort, the assistance of bourgeois specialists trained in the old society could not be avoided.[3]

The parallel to the doctrinal debates within the armed forces is striking. According to Trotsky, the concept of a distinct Marxian form of warfare was as peculiar as the notion of a 'distinct Marxian form of veterinary science'. Therefore, he had no objections to seeing former tsarist officers like Major-General Alexander Svechin serve in the ranks of the RKKA. In spite of Trotsky's advocacy of world revolution, he and his 'military specialists' also believed that Soviet security interests would be better served by a defensive strategy. A large conscript territorial militia seemed more adapted to Russia's geographical vastness, economic backwardness and educational level. It would also be in keeping with the experience from World War I, which suggested that defense was a superior form of strategy in modern wars of attrition.

However, 'angry young men' in the RKKA like Gusev and Tukhachevsky – who had earned their laurels during the Civil War – questioned these presumptions and envisaged an offensive doctrine. They too realized Russia's economic inferiority, but regarded it as a factor that made a quick decision even more desirable, as the country was unable to sustain the hardships of modern war for any long period. They also argued that the experience from the Western front during World War I was inapplicable to Russia. Instead, lessons should be drawn from the country's own recent civil war, in which victory had been secured through a series of offensive operations deep into enemy territory. Such an offensive strategy, they suggested, would also be more in keeping with the revolutionary spirit of the Russian proletariat. An offensive strategy, however, could not be executed with a hastily trained militia army but demanded some kind of cadre or professional volunteer force. With the support of Stalin, Mikhail Frunze replaced Trotsky as People's Commissar for Defense in January 1925, bent on realizing such a program.[4]

The proponents of offensive class warfare triumphed, but for financial reasons, in 1928 more than half of the RKKA's 88 divisions and brigades still consisted of territorial units. The conscripts in these units had less than 12 months of training, spread over a period of five years, as compared to the 2–3 years continuous time spent by conscripts in the cadre forces.[5] Furthermore, the dismal state of the Soviet Union's industry meant that not even the cadre forces could be adequately equipped. When reporting on the military aspects of the first five-year plan in 1928, Frunze's successor Voroshilov openly admitted a serious shortage of tanks and transport vehicles. Even such basic necessities as uniforms and heating fuel for the barracks were in short supply.[6]

In conclusion, the comparatively permissive cultural and political climate during the NEP period allowed for some pluralism of opinion, at least as long as the party had not made up its mind on a certain question. The debate within the armed forces on the use of bourgeois specialists reflected rather well the general discussion in Soviet society in the period on the role of traditional expertise and traditional education in the building of socialism. Ideological militancy clashed with practical considerations.

The navy and NEP

In the navy, the NEP period was synonymous with the Old School era. The Communist Party's indecision in the cultural field and its dependence on experts with a traditional education meant that that former imperial officers were allowed to propagate traditional concepts of sea power undisturbed. When Vladimir Belli came to the Naval War College as a strategy teacher in the autumn of 1926, authors like Anton Leer (a nineteenth-century Russian general of international repute) and Trotsky's former protégé Svechin dominated the reading list. The course in naval strategy relied on international authorities like Colomb, Mahan, Corbett and Otto Groos (author of a book on Germany's naval strategy during World War I). Tukhachevsky's work on class warfare was probably the only work that would not have appeared on the reading list of a Western naval war college at the time.[7]

A way for the party to balance the navy's imperial heritage, however, was to change the names of Russian warships in accordance with ideological directives. The three battleships of the *Gangut* class (*Gangut*, *Sevastopol* and *Petropavlovsk*) were renamed after the great revolutionary leader Marat, after the October Revolution (*Oktyabrskaya Revolutiya*) and the Paris Commune (*Parizhkaya Kommuna*) in 1921 and 1925. The cruiser *Svetlana* was first renamed after the German socialist heroine Klara Zetkin. Later, it carried the name 'Red Crimea' (*Krasny Krim*) and finally *Profintern* (abbreviation for the trade union international). The destroyers of the Imperial Navy, whose names had often been related to military, heroic and masculine adjectives (*Bdetelny* = watchful, *Storozhevoy* = guard-, *Voyskovoy* = troop-, *Vnushitelny* = impressive, *Vynoslivy* = endurable), were renamed after revolutionary leaders. Karl Marx, Friedrich Engels, Lenin, Stalin, Trotsky, Frunze, Zinovyev, Rykov and Kalinin were all honored in this way. The submarines in the Imperial Navy, which had carried the names of various predators (*Tigr*, *Leopard*, *Jaguar*, *Smeya* = snake) were given names that represented radical political or social positions: 'the Communard' (*Kommunar*), 'the Red Army Man' (*Krasnoarmets*), 'the Red Navy Man' (*Krasnoflotets*), 'The Proletarian' (*Proletary*), 'the Worker' (*Rabochy*) 'the Bolshevik' (*Bolshevik*), 'the Comrade' (*Tovarishch*). The British submarine *L 55*, which had been sunk by the Soviet destroyer *Azard* in July 1919 and then raised and repaired, joined the Soviet Navy as 'the Atheist' (*Bezbozhnik*).[8]

As can be gathered from these examples, the naming of Soviet warships was unique not only in the sense that it aimed at developing the service's revolutionary identity, but also in that the historical figures and events the new ship names alluded to were not exclusively national. By naming two of its three mightiest warships after a French eighteenth-century journalist and a short-lived nineteenth-century revolutionary regime in Paris, Soviet Russia emphasized its commitment to internationalism in a powerful way. As we recall from Chapter 5, this may also have been tactically wise on the part of the Navy's Old School lobby, which saw the support to revolutions abroad as an important argument for keeping and developing the Soviet Union's battleship fleet.

In February 1928, the Baltic Fleet was awarded the Order of the Red Banner. After 1935, when the fleet's official name had changed from the Naval Forces in the Baltic Sea (MSBM = *Morskikh Sil Balticheskogo Morya*) to the Baltic Fleet, it was always officially referred to as the Red Bannered Baltic Fleet or KBF (*Krasnoznamenny Baltiysky Flot*).[9]

The tsarist specialists

As a rule, the leading men of the Old School had a background as officers in the Imperial Navy.

Captain Nikolay Lavrentivich Klado (1862–1919) had been a prominent propagandist for Mahanist ideas before World War I, and introduced naval history as a subject in Russian military colleges in the 1890s. Klado realized that for geographical reasons, the navy in Russia could never play the same role as in Britain or the United States, but he was nonetheless critical of the lack of long-term thinking in the country's naval policy. Klado's writings had greatly annoyed the naval command, the General Staff and the Ministry of Finance. His public criticism of the management of the Russo-Japanese War (in which he served as a staff officer) even led to a temporary discharge from the Naval War College.

In May 1917, when the old order was falling to pieces, Klado's reputation as an angry oppositional instead turned into an asset. His colleagues hurriedly elected him commandant of the college, and together with a group of 'progressive' faculty members he later sided with the Bolsheviks. In September 1918, the new regime appointed him chairman of a history commission to study the naval lessons of the recent war. Only a few months later – in April 1919 – Klado died. The history commission, however, remained in existence until 1923, and Klado's spirit kept lingering over its work. The commission was mainly recruited from the faculty of the Naval War College and contained people like Admiral Ivan Grigorovich, Captain Boris Zherve and Captain Mikhail Petrov. While Grigorovich had been the father of the 1912 naval construction program and was the only tsarist minister to be retained by the Provisional Government after the February Revolution, Zherve and Petrov were soon to become the leading spokesmen of the Old School.[10]

Boris Borisovich Zherve (1879–1934) had graduated from the Naval Academy in 1898 and from the Naval War College in 1913. Having served in both the Russo-Japanese War and World War I, he was promoted to captain and commander of the Baltic coastal fortifications by the Provisional Government. In 1918, after the Bolshevik takeover, he was recruited to lecture at the Naval War College. He served as the college's commandant for a brief period in 1920–21, was again appointed to that position in 1923 and remained throughout the 1920s (becoming a full professor only in 1927). Under this period, the 'academic view' of naval warfare became synonymous with the views of the Old School. Before the Civil War had even been concluded, Zherve began publishing a work on the foundations of naval strategy (*Osnovy morskoy strategii*, 1919–21), based on lectures he had given at the college. Subsequently, he published a work on the importance of naval forces to the state (*Znachenie morskoy sily gosudarstva*, 1921), which appeared in several editions.

Although Zherve was a specialist in mines and coastal defense tactics, he still portrayed ship artillery as the principal weapon system, and naval warfare as synonymous with struggling for command of the oceans. Only the navy, Zherve argued, had the capacity to protect the sea lines of communications of the state and to interrupt those of the enemy. Only the navy could prevent seaborne invasions or launch invasions upon the enemy's coast. Only the navy, through its superior mobility and speed, could provide valuable assistance to the ground forces without being hampered by setbacks on the continental theaters. Zherve even drafted the ideal composition of a 'normal' navy, structuring it along the lines of the 1912 naval construction program: two squadrons of battleships (eight ships), one squadron of heavy cruisers (four ships), four squadrons of light cruisers (16 ships), eight squadrons of destroyers (32 ships). In addition, there should be submarines, gunboats for riverine operations, transports and support vessels of various kinds. As we saw in Chapter 6, from about 1923 Zherve seemingly abandoned the notion of a blue-water navy and instead propagated the doctrine of 'small wars'. In keeping with this thinking, he also asserted that a weaker fleet could prevail against a stronger one, as long as the difference in strength remained quantitative rather than qualitative.[11]

According to Belli, Zherve still lectured on naval reconnaissance in 1928 as if World War I had never taken place. When his students questioned the realism of sending cruisers (of which the Baltic Fleet had only one) off to the mouth of the Gulf of Finland to reconnoiter instead of aircraft or submarines, he looked disturbed and bewildered but did not change his view. In later years, he acquired some knowledge of Marxist philosophy, which added a revolutionary scent to the fairly traditional contents of his teaching. Although he could be mildly sarcastic about notions of a special Marxist–Leninist method in naval warfare, he still claimed that matters of defense and offense must be decided by ideology, and that the present 'revolutionary ideology' of the Russian people suggested an offensive navy.[12]

Although Mikhail Aleksandrovich Petrov (1885–1940) was younger and had graduated from the Naval Academy in 1905, he attended the Naval War College together with Zherve and reached the rank of captain in 1917, just like him. Petrov's Mahanist sympathies were perhaps less surprising than Zherve's. He was an artillery officer who had served as a senior officer aboard the battleship *Gangut* (later *Oktyabrskaya Revolutsiya*) during World War I. As a participant in the Baltic Fleet's dramatic evacuation from Estonia and Finland in the winter of 1918, he had also actively assisted in the securing of sea power for the Bolshevik regime. He was appointed the successor of Rear-Admiral Shchastny as the Baltic

Fleet's chief of staff, but was relieved in June 1918, allegedly after a conflict with Trotsky over the treatment of Shchastny. Due to the lack of experienced naval specialists, Petrov was able to return to service already the following year, first as head of operations in the Naval Staff and later as commandant of the Naval War College (before Zherve acquired this position permanently in 1923). Having had his draft for a new naval fighting regulation rejected in 1924 Petrov returned to the college to teach and write on Russia's war at sea 1914–1918. In 1927, he was appointed head of the UVMS Instruction Directorate.[13] In this capacity we met him in Chapters 5 and 6, debating the future role of the Soviet Navy before the RVS in May 1928 together with Mikhail Tukhachevsky.

Prominent Old School representatives outside Klado's history commission were Alexander Nemits and Arkady Toshakov. In that group it is also proper to include Eduard Samuilovich Pantserzhansky, Lev Mikhailovich Galler and Mikhail Vladimirovich Viktorov, although they made few known statements on doctrine.

Nemits (1879–1967) had written extensively on the Russo-Japanese War, held the rank of rear-admiral and commanded the Black Sea Fleet at the time of the Bolshevik takeover. In 1920, he was appointed naval commander. In his ambitious proposal to the RVS for a restoration of the navy from February 1921, he claimed that Russia's history as a Great power had been intimately linked to its history as a naval power. Conversely, he argued, its greatest military defeats – the Crimean War, the Russo-Japanese War – had followed after periods of naval reduction. From 1924, he served mainly as a teacher in the Naval and Air War Colleges. He retired in 1947.[14]

Eduard Samuilovich Pantserzhansky (1887–1937) was born the son of a Polish nobleman in Libau (Liepaya), the forward base of the imperial Baltic Fleet. He graduated from the Naval Junker School in 1909 and became an officer in 1911. At the time of the revolution he joined the Reds and during the Civil War served as commander in the Arctic, Caspian Sea and Black Sea Theaters. In December 1921, he succeeded Nemits as naval commander and remained in this position until December 1924 (from April 1924 under the title of 'naval assistant to the commander in chief'), when he was made commander of the Black Sea Fleet.

Toshakov (1887–?) had held the rank of second lieutenant at the time of the revolution. He served as chief of operations in the Baltic Fleet 1922–24 and in the Naval Staff in 1924–26. As we saw in Chapter 5, his appendix to the naval construction program of 1925 discussed the uses of Soviet sea power to advance class struggle in a global context. To spread revolutionary unrest and secure material resources for the coming liberation of Asia, Toshakov recommended strong naval offensives in the Black Sea and Baltic Theaters. He also regarded the Northern Theater as a suitable base area for Soviet submarine operations in the western hemisphere.[15]

Lev Mikhailovich Galler (1883–1950) had graduated as a naval artillery officer in 1912. During World War I, he served as a senior officer aboard battleships, participating in the battle of the Moonsund archipelago in 1917 aboard the *Slava*. At the time of the Bolshevik takeover, he commanded a destroyer, and he immediately joined sides with the new regime together with his crew and took part in the great evacuation in February 1918. In 1921, Galler became chief of staff of the Baltic Fleet and in 1927 commander of the Baltic battleship squadron. In the latter capacity, he was later to lead the *Parizhkaya Kommuna* and the *Profintern* on their famous voyage from the Baltic to the Black Sea in 1929. As the Baltic Fleet's chief of staff, it was Galler who worked out the maneuver scenarios during the 1920s in which the duel between capital ships always played an important role.[16]

Mikhail Vladimirovich Viktorov (1893–1938) had graduated from the Naval Junker School in Yaroslav in 1910 and later attended various classes at the Naval Academy. He joined sides with the Bolsheviks after their seizure of power in 1917, participated in the 1918 evacuation and in the suppression of the Kronstadt rebellion in 1921. After having served as commander of destroyers and battleships he was appointed commander of the Baltic Fleet in May 1921. After a short term as commander of the Black Sea Fleet and head of the Hydrographic Service in 1924–26, he then returned to Kronstadt as fleet commander.[17]

Finally, the Chief Commissar of the Navy in 1921–23, later naval commander (1924–26), Vyatcheslav Ivanovich Zof (1889–1937), was a professional revolutionary with no background in the tsarist officer corps. Nevertheless, for ideological reasons he supported the Old School's demands for an ocean-going fleet. Zof was born in Latvia. During the Civil War, he had served as division and army commissar on the Eastern Front in Siberia, and in 1919 he became a member of the Baltic Fleet Soviet. In 1922, during the naval command's conference on the future navy, he declared that for the past four years Soviet power had had no idea of how to use its naval forces outside rivers and lakes. The state needed a fleet not only to defend itself against the surrounding neighbors, but a workers' and peasants' fleet strong enough to confront any navy in the world, either defensively or offensively. It must also be able to protect the sea lanes of communication, the 'life-arteries' of the Soviet state from which it received two-thirds of its imports. Zof also propagated for the navy within the party, publishing several pamphlets.[18]

In conclusion, the Old School seems to have had its foremost supporters among former tsarist officers, many of whom were born in the latter half of the 1880s and had experienced Russia's humiliating defeat at Tsushima in their teens or early twenties. Later, their early careers had coincided with the era of the 1912 naval construction plan. In spite of their background in the old regime, they did not hesitate to argue from the standpoint of revolutionary ideology when they tried to convince their political masters of the need for an offensive 'Big Ship' navy.

Political control: from commissars to 'One-Man Command'

After the Kronstadt rebellion, subjugating the navy to firm political control became a matter of the utmost concern to the regime. Already on 16 March 1921, when Cheka and RKKA units were deploying on the ice outside Kotlin Island for the final assault against the rebellious sailors, the Xth Party Congress in Moscow passed a resolution on the restoration of the navy which strongly emphasized the Communist Party's role in this process.[19]

On 21 April, at the same meeting where the RVSR rejected Nemits's proposal to restore a 'Big Ship' navy, it was decided that a special political commissar should be appointed for the naval forces. This special commissar, I. D. Sladkov, began reviewing the reliability of naval personnel. By the end of August 1921, the screening process had led to Nemits's removal from the post as navy commander. Also, in spite of protests from fleet commander Viktorov, about half of the 977 commanders and officials in the Baltic Fleet had been arrested. According to Zonin, more than 200 of these were later deported. Although most were released within a year, only about a hundred were ever allowed to return to service.[20] Vladimir Belli, who had served as an officer in the Imperial Navy, would describe in his memoirs the '1921 filtration' as comparatively mild. At the time of the purges, he was stationed at the Directorate of Naval Educational Institutions (UVMUZ = *Upravlenie Voenno-Morskimi Uchebnimi Zavedeniyami*) in Petrograd, where one day he was called before a commission headed by a GPU official. When asked about his relationship to Soviet power, Belli simply replied that he was unable to oppose it since the revolution had deprived him of his property and his social position. Had he once taken on a job, however, he would consciously fulfill the duties that came with it. To the surprise of Belli's superiors, such an answer was deemed fully satisfactory. Belli himself explains his luck with good judgment on the part of the commission's GPU chairman, and also points out that he had made sure that all his answers during the interview were in accordance with his prior written statements. However, one should remember that the aim of political terror is to make physical control unnecessary through the instigation of fear. Later, when Belli served as naval attaché in Beijing (1922–24) and as head of the Naval Staff's foreign section (1924–25), there was little need to monitor him. Although he had frequent contacts with foreigners, he did his best to avoid any private relations with them.[21] In this respect, the filtration of 1921 obviously served its purpose.

Another way to make control less necessary in the future would be to increase the recruitment of reliable elements. In October 1922, the study at the Naval Academy was reorganized into a system with three three-year-long specialist courses, preceded by one year of general preparatory study. Later, this preparatory year was abolished and the regular course prolonged to four years.[22] Before this reform, however, the conclusion of the preparatory course offered an opportunity to get rid of students who had proven ideologically or socially unsound. Among 44 students who completed their preparatory year in the spring of 1924, 14 were barred from continuation at the academy for these reasons. Proletarian background was not an absolute prerequisite for admission. Two students who were loyal party members with a good working-class background were sent down for another year at the preparatory course – probably because of unsatisfactory academic results – while two others who had stated their social origins as 'bourgeois', were recommended for admission. They were both, however, members of the party and the

Komsomol (*Kommunistichesky Soyuz Molodezhi* = Communist Youth League). Another person with a favorable recommendation had suspiciously characterized his origins as 'bourgeois-proletarian' and spent much time in the Ukraine where many 'terrorist bands' had been operating in the past. He was recommended for further supervision. Yet another student of bourgeois origin was rejected in spite of his Komsomol credentials. The man had described his father as a simple rabbi when he in fact had taught religion at a Jewish school – a suspect occupation on social as well as ideological grounds. To have supplied misleading or insufficient information on one's family was apparently a worse crime than to come from the 'wrong' family.[23]

In November 1924, the Naval Educational Directorate evaluated the social and political status among the students at the various academies. Out of 941 students in the different specialist courses, four-fifths (754) were party, candidate or Komsomol members. About half (458) were workers, a third (284) peasants and about a fifth (189) 'others'. Among the 341 students in the preparatory class – of whom the youngest were but 15 years old – figures looked even more reassuring. Only about one in ten (36) had no affiliation to the party or the Komsomol, three-quarters came from a working-class family (251), about one-seventh (51) were peasants and only about one-tenth (39) 'others'.[24] In a few years' time, the social composition of the officer corps would have been markedly improved, from the party's point of view.

In January 1925, Mikhail Frunze succeeded Trotsky as People's Commissar for the Army and Navy (in practice, he had taken over already after Lenin's death in February 1924). Frunze's reign was short. After only ten months in office, he died while undergoing surgery. Nonetheless, he manage to initiate a thorough reorganization of the armed forces that was to influence the Soviet defense structure for decades to come. It was Frunze who finally settled the old dispute on whether the RKKA should consist of cadre or militia troops. He also restructured the Red Army General Staff, modernized its operational doctrine and began reviewing the country's industrial preparedness for total war. The most famous of Frunze's reforms was the system of 'one-man command' (*edinonachalie*), which concentrated authority in the hands of the unit's military commander and limited the commissar's responsibilities to political matters. With the exception of a few years around 1940 (1937–40, 1941–42) this system remained in force for the rest of the Soviet Union's existence. Through the introduction of a penal code for the armed forces, Frunze also strengthened discipline and the authority of military commanders.[25]

The new penal code evoked much opposition from party circles as it contained different punitive measures for the same offense for soldiers and commanding personnel, and thus ran against Soviet egalitarian ideals. Frunze challenged such sentiments in other ways as well. Officially, there had been no officers in the Soviet Union since December 1917, when a decree had abolished all ranks in the armed forces. Even the terms of 'officer' and 'soldier' had been regarded with suspicion, so commanding personnel were usually referred to as 'military specialists' (former imperial officers) or 'red commanders' (commanders trained in the Soviet era). Privates held the title 'Red Army man' (*krasnoarmets*) or 'Red Navy man' (*krasnoflotets*). Frunze abolished the distinction between 'military specialists' and 'red commanders' and instead introduced a system of four distinct groups of commanding personnel: the junior, middle, senior and superior groups, which were divided into 14 different categories. The junior group (*mladshaya gruppa*, categories 1–2) contained positions equivalent to squad-leader. The middle group (*srednyaya gruppa*, categories 3–6) contained positions from platoon commander to deputy battalion commander/deputy officer of the watch. The senior group (*starshaya gruppa*, categories 7–9) consisted of positions from battalion commander/commander of a third-class warship (ASW ship) to regimental commander/commander of a second-class warship (torpedo craft – MTBs, destroyers and submarines). The superior group (*vyshaya gruppa*, categories 10–14) consisted of positions from deputy division commander/commander of first-class warship (artillery ships – cruisers and battleships) to commander of an entire military district or a fleet. As commander in chief and People's Commissar, Frunze himself of course stood outside the system, holding the modest rank of 'Red Army man'. Likewise, the Deputy People's Commissar for the Navy/Naval Commander held the simple rank of 'Red Navy man'.[26]

For the one-man command system to work, however, the military commander had to be a party member himself. Former tsarist officers had seldom earned that kind of trust – at least, not in the navy. In reality, the one-man commander had to be a person whose loyalty was beyond question – not only a party member but also someone altogether uncontaminated by a career in the Imperial Navy. In this respect, the commissar system was probably easier to combine with the retention of former tsarist officers. The reports of PUR representatives during the early 1920s portrays a subdued officer corps with little interest in the daily service. In April 1923, the commissar in the Baltic Fleet's 2nd Minesweeper Group complained that work in his unit never started when it should, that the sailors were allowed to go ashore whenever they wanted and that commanding personnel left most of their tasks to unqualified NCOs. The commanders also tended to be absent during political lectures or to interrupt them with petty inspections.[27]

With such basic motivational problems among the commanding personnel, there seemed to be little need to fear mutiny. Nor would it be necessary to extend party control further, into the realm of doctrine or officers' education. In 1927, the required percentage of party members in the navy (10 percent) was markedly lower than in the Red Army.[28]

For better or for worse, the old officers were left alone, could write freely in *Morskoy Sbornik* and teach whatever they wanted at the Naval War College. As long as they did not conspire actively against the party, they were free to cultivate a strictly professional attitude to their work. However, if the commissar system was to be replaced by the system of one-man command, the demands for ideological orthodoxy would increase and there would be less room for eccentric bourgeois specialists, dreaming of new battleships.

Morale – the responsibility of the commissars

In the May issue of *Morskoy Sbornik* 1926, A. P. Alexandrov pointed out that in modern wars, the preparations for war were not limited to the armed forces or the industry. The coming war between the Soviet Union and the capitalist world would also contain a propaganda struggle. As could be expected, the enemy's propaganda against the Soviet Union would try to break up the unity between workers and peasants and between the country's various nationalities. The Soviets must not only strengthen the fighting morale of their own side, but also counter-attack the fighting morale of the enemy and transform their war of aggression against the USSR into a class war. Soviet propaganda intended for domestic consumption should emphasize that a capitalist victory would mean the return of slavery, exploitation and oppression. To spread this message effectively, the Soviet Union's 600 newspapers, its 30,000 wall newspapers and 900 journals must all contain a military column. The 3,500 cinemas and 10,000 traveling cinemas should all show military films. The Soviet broadcasting corporation should enlighten the country's 400,000 radio listeners through frequent lectures on military subjects. The 3,500 workers' clubs should form special study groups dealing with military problems, while the 25,000 village libraries in the countryside should offer special military leaflets and books, specially adapted for the peasantry. The village teacher could also contribute by giving a special military twist to all cultural activities in his school: theatrical performances, the celebration of revolutionary jubilees and even the recitation of poetry. A clear advantage to the Soviet side would be its firm belief in the triumph of socialism, and its superior ability for long-term planning, which followed from the extensive state regulation of production. Most important, however, was the fact that the RKKA fought for the interests of the workers and peasants, and thus could count on a genuine mass mobilization.[29]

In short, just as the industrial sector before it, the cultural sphere had to be organized in the country's preparations for war, be included in the general 'militarization' (*voennizatsiya*) of society (in Soviet parlance, *voennizatsiya* was a positive term, communicating resolve and readiness). The importance attributed to propaganda in Soviet visions of the coming war is further evident from the 1923 mobilization regulation for the naval forces. Here, a special section was dedicated to 'cultural enlightenment and agitation work during the period of mobilization'. As could be expected, these activities were to be handled by the political commissars. When the mobilized personnel arrived at their unit, the commissars were to organize special ceremonies to greet them and have them pledge the oath of allegiance. Through special lectures and meetings, they were also to inform the arriving personnel of the reasons for the present war. The commissars were to remind the conscripts of the importance of military secrecy, and that victory would depend on an effective and undisturbed effort behind the front by the 'forces of production'. They were also to keep a watchful eye on the behavior of party members among the personnel and not hesitate to use them as helping hands in their agitation work. To keep morale high, there must also be a rich supply of newspapers and books. Complaints – especially concerning food – should be taken seriously so that causes of discontent could be swiftly eliminated.[30]

In peacetime too, the commissars were expected to report continuously on the status of morale among the men. The assistant head of the Baltic Fleet PUR, Mikhail Dolya, issued a circular note in July 1924, criticizing the negligence of his subordinates in the Kronstadt naval base in keeping him informed. Recently, there had been cases of drunkenness among the personnel (including PUR functionaries), worrying frictions between PUR personnel and the rank and file as well as sloppy management aboard some of the ships, which had resulted in great quantities of food being destroyed. These events had not been properly reported.[31]

What, then, were the perceived inner threats to morale on the Soviet side in the event of war? According to directives from the Baltic Fleet PUR in March 1924, the present economic reforms would actively strengthen unity between the countryside and the city, the *smytka* between workers and the peasants and thus strengthen the country's ability to resist foreign enemies.[32] One should notice that even in optimistic forecasts such as these, the rural population was indirectly identified as a potential source of weakness and treacherous behavior. In the fall of 1927, the ideological background of a possible conflict was depicted in great detail in a war game conducted jointly by the Naval War College and the PUR College. The rupture of diplomatic relations between the Soviet Union and Britain, which had taken place earlier that year, was used as a pretext for organizing an anti-Soviet coalition in Europe in the scenario. Although the British Labour Party did not openly support the war, it helped the Tory government indirectly by attacking the British Communists, who remained loyal to the Soviet Union. The social and economic situation in the capitalist world seemed generally stable at the time, especially since unemployment had been more or less eliminated through hectic rearmament. Only in Latvia and in Poland – where the communist parties had registered a considerable growth lately – was there some dissatisfaction among the working classes. The Belorussian and Bessarabian (Moldavian) minorities in Poland and Rumania would probably also oppose the war, as would the peasantry in general in the Border States. This opposition could probably be exploited by the Soviets.

In the Soviet Union, morale among the proletariat was good and the country's mobilization had run smoothly. The Soviet industrialization was under way according to plan, although in some regions people were complaining about the shortage of goods. The prospects of a winter campaign might create further discontent. Several agents and provocateurs – sent out by anti-Soviet organizations abroad – had been caught along the western borders. Moreover, in Georgia and the Tatar Republic conscripts had refused to go to the front, claiming they were only obliged to defend their own republics. Around Leningrad, peasants had expressed their dissatisfaction with the fact that workers in the munitions industry were exempted from call-up. Against this background, a primary objective for the Soviet side would be to win a decisive victory as quickly as possible, preferably through an offensive against Poland, where a workers' and peasants' government was to be installed.[33]

This war game scenario reveals which groups were perceived to be unreliable inside the Soviet Union. The two regions that were singled out as problematic, Tatarstan and Georgia, had both been the scene of nationalist unrest in 1923–24. While in Tatarstan the purge of the party secretary-general had been sufficient, in Georgia the restoration of order had cost thousands of lives. Still, these two areas were now described in a way suggesting that poor political consciousness was the root of problems more than any ill will or genuine hostility on the part of the population. In a similar way, the envious peasants outside Leningrad seemed to be more in need of enlightenment than of any stern disciplinary measures. At this time, collectivization had not yet begun and the regime was still unaware of how weak the support was that it had in the countryside.

Soon, domestic threats to fighting morale would play a greater role in maneuver scenarios.

Modernization through 'Komsomol Patronage' and 'Political Hour'

In an article on the political work in the navy, published in *Morskoy Sbornik* in May 1926, A. Melenkovsky quoted Lenin's words about the quick pace of development in the capitalist countries compared to Russia. Therefore, the Bolsheviks had to muster their strength and modernize their country as quickly as possible so that they would be prepared when these powers turned upon Russia with all their might:

> We should put the emphasis in our work on re-educating the masses, on organizing, teaching and spreading knowledge, on combating that inheritance of darkness and lack of culture, of demoralization and coarseness which we have taken over from the old society.
>
> We should remember that an illiterate people, an uncivilized people, cannot win.

Melenkovsky also repeated what Trotsky had said on the task of the armed forces:

> We must learn how to work well: meticulously, neatly, and economically. We need culture in our work, culture in our life, culture in our existence. The prime factor in our international situation is national defense, above all the Red Army and the Red Navy. In this sphere, nine-tenths of our task consists of civilizing work: raising the level of the army, making it completely literate, teaching it how to use dictionaries, booklets, maps, accustoming it to modernity, thrift, attentiveness.[34]

What were the abilities of the Baltic Fleet to live up to these expectations? In December 1922, its mobilization strength had been calculated at 24,146 men. Some 9,126 of these were classified as 'voluntary' or enlisted personnel (about half of whom held 'commanding' or 'administrative' positions'). The remaining force was to be called up at mobilization. Ethnically, the overwhelming majority (20,603) were Russians. The largest minorities were Ukrainians (1,232) and Belorussians (859), the smallest Bashkirs (3!). Some 30 percent of the navy personnel were classified as 'workers'; 18 percent belonged to 'other' social groups while the majority (52 percent) were peasants. Thus, in the eyes of the party, the most conscious elements of the proletariat formed a minority among the conscripts. If the Baltic Fleet was to operate in a 'correct' and 'modern' way, there seemed to be a great demand for ideological leadership. Out of the 15,000 people who were to be called up at mobilization, no less than 1,000 were to serve in the PUR apparatus.[35]

Further progress could be made by urging members of the Komsomol to apply for military service in the navy. The first of these recruiting drives started shortly after the Kronstadt mutiny, when the navy was being demobilized after the Civil War (during the course of 1921, total personnel shrank from 86,580 to 41,244). In a few months, the percentage of communists in the Baltic Fleet swelled from 1.08 percent to 12.7 percent.[36]

In October 1922, at the Vth Congress of the Komsomol, the communist youth league officially took on 'patronage' (*shefstvo*) of the naval forces. During a ceremony at the Bolshoy Theatre in Moscow attended by People's Commissar for the Navy Zof and prominent party leaders like Trotsky, Radek and Lunacharsky, sailors and young communists swore to work together in the reconstruction of the naval forces. The Komsomol was to organize study groups on naval matters among its members, propagate for the navy among the population and support the families of naval personnel while the men were at sea. One of the first results of the Komsomol patronage was the national Red Fleet Week in January 1923, organized together with the Navy PUR. All over the country exhibitions, public lectures and fund-raising events were held. One popular activity was the special ceremony in which a Komsomol club solemnly presented its flag to a local naval unit to demonstrate the unity between the Communist Youth and the naval forces.

The stream of young communists who entered the navy following these campaigns did raise the level of education among the personnel. In July 1923, out of 250 men in the Baltic Fleet training squadron about 4 percent had studied at university, while 38 percent had a complete or incomplete secondary education (10 or 8 years of 'middle school', which gave entitlement to apply to university or professional college respectively). In the autumn of 1923, the Komsomol launched the third and last of its great recruitment drives. Out of 3,215 conscripts who were admitted the following year, 99.6 percent were full members or candidate members of either the party or the youth league, 76.2 percent were workers, 21.3 percent peasants and 2.5 percent students. The level of literacy among them was 99.9 percent, which should be compared to the average among Russian males between the ages of 9 and 49, which in 1926 was still 71.5 percent.[37]

According to a survey in 1924, out of 3,939 Baltic Fleet conscripts 69 percent could be classified as well educated, 30.5 percent as satisfactorily educated and only 0.5 percent as poorly educated or illiterate. According to the chief inspector of school propaganda, Yermolenko, the lack of books and suitable class-rooms still impeded the fleet's educational efforts.[38] In May 1926, PUR inspector Stepanov listed among such desirable 'equipment for political propaganda and enlightenment work' aboard a modern Soviet destroyer the following:

- Musical equipment (orchestra instruments, an accordion, a gramophone with 25 records – aboard cruisers there should be a piano as well)
- Games (including 10 chess sets and 10 checkers sets)
- Teaching equipment (maps, posters, blackboards, a globe, a slide projector, etc.)
- Sports equipment (dumbbells, barbell)
- Radio and cinema equipment (loudspeaker, movie projector, screen)
- Equipment for the Lenin corner and the library (desks, tables, showcases, bookshelves, 1,500 books, portraits and busts).[39]

In reality, ship libraries seem to have consisted of books remaining from before the revolution. In July 1925, the Baltic Fleet PUR ordered the immediate removal of a biography of Tsar Nicholas II, which had survived on the shelves since 1917.[40] Political agitation was also regarded as primitive. At least during 1923, several PUR assessments speak of absent or passive instructors, inactive study groups, irregular agitation meetings and a disturbing shortage of propaganda material.[41]

Toward the end of the year, the PUR organization in the Baltic Fleet counted a peacetime strength of 456 men. Less than a third (146) had at the time served more than a year in their present position and about a sixth (79) – administrators, librarians or leaders of study groups (*pol-lekchiks*) – were not even party members. Out of the 377 party or candidate members, only ten had been members before 1917. The majority (292) had joined up during the Civil War (more than half – 166 – in the year 1919 alone). Also, the average age of instructors was comparatively low – about 25, which was about the same age as the oldest navy conscripts.[42] In the naval air arm, moreover, political work was divided between the naval PUR and the VVS PUR. In a report to the naval air arm commissar in November 1924, base commissar Lakomsky recommended that political training should be placed entirely under the naval PUR to avoid further confusion.[43]

Twice a week, the political officer was to gather the men for the 'political hour' '*pol-chas*', during which a wide variety of subjects could be treated. The Baltic Fleet PUR decided themes monthly. During January–February 1924, for instance, the following topics were on the agenda:

- The political situation in England
- The armed forces of Poland
- A characterization of Polish society
- The Communist Party of Germany
- The fifth anniversary of the death of Karl Liebknecht and Rosa Luxemburg

- Volkhovstroi (the powerplant at Volkhov River) and its role for the Petrograd industry
- 9 January 1905 (the so-called 'Bloody Sunday' that started the 1905 revolution)
- Scissors – the price-gap between industrial and agricultural goods
- Lenin and the world proletariat (issued shortly after Lenin's death)
- Why have the bourgeois countries begun to talk about recognizing the Soviet Union?
- The armed forces of France
- Results of the IInd Congress of Soviets
- The Paris Commune
- The question of work among the youth at the XIIIth Congress of the Russian Communist Party.[44]

As can be seen from this sample, the political hour could deal with current affairs at home and abroad, the likely enemy's military organization or Marxist–Leninist ideology. As is apparent from instructions distributed before a *pol-chas* in July 1924 on relations between the USSR and the Scandinavian countries, more than one of these themes could be addressed on one and the same occasion. The material contained detailed statistics on trade between the Scandinavian countries and the Soviet Union, as well as an account of how their governments had come to recognize the Soviet regime a few months earlier. In the concluding paragraph the Bolshevik world-view was reaffirmed. Diplomatic relations between the Soviet Union and Scandinavia had been established only after a long and hard struggle, during which 'our friend had been the proletariat of these countries, guided by the communist parties, and our enemies – aligned with the Russian White Guard rabble – the Conservatives and the Social Democrats, acting on orders from France and America'.[45]

The struggle against the navy's tsarist legacy

Around 1926, at the height of NEP, several signs indicated that a cultural counter-offensive was under way in the navy, targeted at its tsarist legacy.

In a speech to the Moscow branch of the Society of Naval Science in the beginning of 1926, the former head of the Naval Academy Bzheshinsky posed the question if Soviet naval technology was to be developed in cooperation with the capitalist countries or independently. Even if the Soviet state was still industrially backwards in comparison to the West, Bzheshinsky argued, one could not expect that the capitalist countries would voluntarily share their advanced military technology with the Russians. Therefore, it would be better if the Soviet state pursued an independent course and refrained from slavishly imitating other Great powers in the way tsarist Russia had done.

Bzhezinsky's speech was later published as an article in *Morskoy Sbornik*. Nikolay Alyakrinsky, a graduate of the Imperial Naval Engineering Academy, soon published a reply entitled 'On Big Mistakes in a Short Lecture'. According to Alyakrinsky, the secrecy surrounding military projects could only temporarily delay the spread of new technology. Moreover, it did not affect the spread of civilian technology, which – contrary to Bzhezinsky's assertions – was of great importance for a society's ability to mobilize military power. In shipbuilding, for instance, there was little difference between the construction of warships and civilian vessels, and most navies also had to mobilize civilian ships in war. Nor was the production of artillery or poison gas anything but applications of civilian production techniques. In fact, Alyakrinsky claimed, Bzhezinsky's line of reasoning represented a non-Marxist way of thinking which denied the fundamental concepts of base and superstructure, suggesting the Soviets could develop a sophisticated military superstructure without first having a solid base in the civilian forces of production. Bzhezinsky's article also neglected the laws of dialectic, by suggesting that cultural progress could come about in some other way than through a synthesis between Soviet proletarian culture and Western bourgeois culture. Indeed, Bzhezinsky was close to that dangerous nationalist way of thinking recently condemned by the party as 'ethnic-cultural self-righteousness' (*svoeobraznoe narodnichestvo v otnoshenii kultury*). Only through a flow of new ideas and impulses from outside, combined with a gigantic mobilization of the masses inside the Red Navy, would further improvements in Soviet naval warfare be possible.[46]

Bzhezinsky's article expressed the typical criticism against NEP from orthodox groups in the Communist Party. Moreover, it was rather timely. Later that year, the German naval commander Admiral Arno Spindler would visit the Soviet Union for secret discussions on extending the Soviet–German military cooperation to the naval sector. One of the few Soviet naval engineers who were later invited to Germany as a result of these talks was Bzhezinsky's opponent Alyakrinsky, who studied a naval testing basin in Hamburg in 1930 and afterwards became director of a similar installation in Leningrad.[47]

Finally, the discussion on the Soviet Union's need for Western bourgeois culture had obvious implications for the need of the academically trained 'military specialists' with their background in the previous society. What would be their role? There was also a discussion on the role of naval history in officers' training. Could the experience of imperialist wars in the past be of any use to future commanders in the Red Navy? In an article in *Morskoy Sbornik*, P. Bykov – history professor at the Naval Academy – claimed that naval history was still indispensable for the education in tactics and strategy, especially for students who were later to continue to Naval War College. The age of oars and sail was covered rather quickly in Bykov's course, and the only conflicts treated in any depth were the Russo-Japanese War, World War I and the Civil War. Bykov could testify that interest among his students used to grow when they were studying conflicts in their own century.[48]

However, the mere fact that Bykov needed to motivate the study of history at a military school suggests that the cultural heritage of the old navy was under fire. Already in January 1926, the head of the Kronstadt base PUR administration, Vasilyev, had issued a circular note to his subordinates, instructing them to report to him personally – outside their official correspondence – on how the struggle against old traditions was proceeding in their units. Judging from the replies, there was much left to do, not only among the former tsarist officers but also among the rank and file. The commissar of the gunboat *Krasnaya Zvezda*, K. Davidovich, even criticized the former tsarist officers' custom of kissing ladies on the hand. As it did not promote the proletarian revolution, he argued, it must by definition be considered unethical. When defending this habit, the old officers used to say that it offered them an opportunity to satisfy their lower impulses while showing respect to the opposite sex. Davidovich found such answers truly repulsive and typical of 'vile bourgeois ethic'.[49]

During the latter half of 1926, the head of the Baltic Fleet PUR administration Peter Smirnov made use of Vasilyev's survey to write a special memorandum on the problem of political incorrectness in the Red Navy. At that time, the position of the old officer corps had been further weakened. The year 1926 saw the last of the post-civil-war demobilization reductions of the armed forces, when some 16,000 commanders and political commissars were dismissed from the RKKA. In the words of Roger Reese, this measure 'heralded the beginning of the Red Army's continual shortage of leaders'.[50] At the same time, about 60 former tsarist officers in the navy were either dismissed or arrested on political grounds.[51] Most of them, it seems, had in various ways demonstrated their opposition to the abolition of the Naval Staff.

Although nine years had passed since the revolution, Smirnov wrote in his report, many aristocratic traditions still lived on in the navy. Some traditions – love of the sea and of the ships, the sense of comradeship, etc. – were indeed valuable and must be further cultivated in the future. Most of the old heritage, however, was clearly detrimental to the fleet's fighting capability. Contrary to what one would expect, the old naval culture had not been weakened through the influx of new red commanders into the navy. Instead, the newcomers had come under the influence of their senior colleagues and adopted their ways. This was perhaps no surprise, Smirnov argued, as Muklevich's predecessor Zof had actively encouraged the preservation of the navy's old traditions and sadly neglected its revolutionary heritage. Naval commanders had been allowed to continue cultivating that same arrogant attitude toward the other armed services which had been so typical of the old, aristocratic navy. Their hostility toward the recent reorganization of the naval command offered an example, as did chauvinist demonstrations against the army, which had surfaced during the Baltic Fleet's recent sports games. Unfortunately, such attitudes easily spread among the crews. Regular fistfights had been reported between sailors and soldiers in the streets of Leningrad, after navy personnel had shouted *kasha* (porridge) at their army comrades (presumably in reference to the color of their uniforms).

Aristocratic arrogance also characterized the way in which navy commanders handled their subordinates. Smirnov pointed out a number of primitive customs which seemed virtually unchanged since before the revolution:

- The ceremony of hoisting the flag at sunset, while sounding a signal and ordering the crew to stand at attention.

- The exchange of salutes between passing ships at sea.
- The use of separate gangways for crew and commanding personnel when ships were in port.
- The ridiculous, hierarchic dining ceremonial in the commanders' mess.
- The exaggerated, tiresome polishing of the ship's tender – which commanding personnel claimed must look good as it constituted the 'face of the ship'.
- The prohibition of sailors to stroll on the ship's afterdeck when off duty.
- The introduction of the rank 'commander' (*komandir*, which had taken place in January 1926); the daily use of such traditional expressions as 'captain' when talking about the commander of a ship and 'admiral' when talking about the commander of the navy. (The navy signals book still contained such standard phrase messages as 'the admiral expresses his discontent that...' and 'the admiral brings attention to...')
- The use of old Cyrillic letters when writing the ship's name on the hull side, originating in the belief that a warship was as a 'church on water', clearly inappropriate when Russian warships carried revolutionary names.
- The deceitful polishing and dressing up of units before inspection by superiors (*ochkovtiratelstvo*). Even commissars and political officers accepted that several days of valuable training time were wasted for such purposes.
- Superstitious customs, such as throwing a coin in the sea outside the island of Hogland as an offering to Neptune, or the refusal to go to sea on Mondays or to allow women aboard for fear of bad luck.
- The tracing of ship genealogies back to tsarist times; the battleship *Marat* had been named *Sevastopol* before 1921 so the ship's commander – when addressing his crew on celebrations – talked of the 1828 frigate *Sevastopol* as the first ship in the Russian Navy carrying *Marat*'s name! Equally disturbing was the fact that the journal *Morskoy Sbornik* – published since 1848 – appeared as volume 79 on the cover.
- The use of gold stripes and badges as marks of distinction between groups of personnel, similar to the practice in foreign navies.
- The obligatory haircut, which was frequently mentioned among sailors' complaints, increased discontent and prepared the ground for anarchist agitation.
- The tolerance of rowdy behavior among the sailors – drinking, swearing, gambling, tattooing, bullying of fresh recruits, anti-Semitism and disrespectful talk about women.

According to Smirnov, this strange prevalence of a tsarist legacy in the navy created distrust among 'the Red Navy mass' (*krasnoflotskaya massa*). In the long run, it would undermine the authority of the commanding personnel. Not only must the navy's service and uniform regulations be modernized, but the political agitation work be increased and the old officers gradually replaced by young, red commanders.[52]

In October 1926, at a meeting between naval commander Muklevich and the leaders of the navy PUR, several changes were made in the service regulation in accordance with Smirnov's proposals. The only point that caused controversy was the request to adopt the RKKA standard uniform in the navy. Muklevich, the head of the Black Sea Fleet Matskevich, and the senior inspector of the PUR Rodionov opposed the replacing of gold stripes on the sleeve with the discreet red signs used in the army to distinguish between the four groups of commanding personnel (triangles, quadrates, oblongs and rhombs). In the end, the navy was allowed to keep its uniform. More importantly, the same meeting also decided to slow down the implementation of Frunze's one-man command reform. Although commanders in the RKKA above a certain rank were automatically promoted to *edinonachalniki*, there would be individual examinations of naval commanders. Obviously, this was a clear sign of distrust of the old officer corps. The matter was settled with seven votes against four. Who voted how is not registered in the protocol, but the PUR had seven representatives at the meeting and the naval forces four.[53]

At the time (1 October 1926), no less than 105 one-man commanders had already been appointed in the naval forces, 40 of them in the Baltic.[54] Most of them, however, served in the coastal artillery. The sailing fleet had only six *edinonachalniki* promoted during 1926 – no more than 15 before 1930. Apparently, former tsarist officers were not among the favorite candidates. In the senior category of commanding personnel, there were 11 *edinonachalniki* in 1929. Not one had had a military career before 1917.[55]

Conclusion

From a cultural perspective, the Old School was significant for the general situation in Russian society during the 1920s. The NEP period marked a temporary halt in the march toward socialism. The country's economy lay in ruins, and the regime's dependence on experts trained under the old society was all too apparent. For the time being, former tsarist officers could be left in charge of the military sector. Until a new generation of 'red commanders' had made their way through the military academies, political commissars were to supervise these 'military specialists' and ensure their loyalty.

In spite of ambitions to the contrary, this lack of trust in the 'military specialists' guaranteed them a certain level of professional autonomy, especially in the navy, whose concrete role in national defense was somewhat vague. Memories of the 1912 naval construction program and the concepts of sea power that came with it influenced the group of ex-imperial officers who were identified with the Old School. As long as they did not challenge Bolshevik power, they remained free to cling on to those doctrines. Although the party gave new names to the battleships, the principles taught at the Naval War College for using the *Marat* and the *Oktyabrskaya revolutsiya* were the same as when they had been called *Gangut* and *Petropavlovsk*.

Until the mid-1920s, the steady influx of communist conscripts, the constant agitation of political commissars and the healthy patronage of the Komsomol were expected to maintain the navy's fighting morale. This way, the level of civilization among recruits was also to be improved gradually. In 1925, however, Mikhail Frunze's reforms strengthened the position of commanders by introducing hierarchic ranks and stricter discipline. The abolition of the dual command system also increased the demands on their ideological orthodoxy. There was no longer time to gradually replace the 'bourgeois expertise' with Soviet-trained specialists. The navy needed to redefine itself quickly, and from that perspective the service's old aristocratic culture appeared a greater problem than it had before. In 1926, the Navy Service Regulation was thoroughly reformed and cleansed of ideologically suspect traditions. At the same time, the one-man command reform was slowed down. At the end of the decade, the number of authorized one-man commanders – especially in the sailing fleet – was quite limited compared to the Red Army.

Notes

1 Manfred Hildermeier, *Geschichte der Sowjetunion, 1917–1991: Entstehung und Entwicklung der ersten sozialistischen Staates* (Göttingen: Verlag C. H. Beck, 1998), pp. 233–62.
2 Ibid., pp. 231–3; figures from J. Arch Getty, Gábor Rittersporn and N. N. Zemskov, 'Victims of the Soviet Penal System in the Prewar Years: A First Approach on the Basis of Archival Evidence', *American Historical Review*, vol. 98(4) (October 1993).
3 Ibid., pp. 302–52.
4 Roger R. Reese, *The Soviet Military Experience: A History of the Soviet Army, 1917–1991* (London: Routledge, 2000), pp. 52–6; Condoleezza Rice, 'The Making of Soviet Strategy', in Peter Paret (ed.), *Makers of Modern Strategy: Military Thought from Machiavelli to the Nuclear Age* (Princeton, NJ: Princeton University Press, 1986), pp. 648–9f; Erickson, *Soviet High Command*, chap. 5; Edward. M. Earle, 'Lenin, Trotsky, Stalin: Soviet Concepts of War', in Edward M. Earle (ed.), *Makers of Modern Strategy: Military Thought from Machiavelli to Hitler* (Princeton, NJ, Princeton University Press, 1944), p. 343.
5 Glantz, *Military Strategy of the Soviet Union*, pp. 52–3.
6 J. M. Mackintosh, 'The Red Army, 1920–1936', in B. H. Liddell-Hart (ed.), *The Soviet Army* (London: Weidenfeld & Nicolson, 1954).
7 Belli, f. r-2224, o. 1, d. 4, list 149.
8 Names of imperial and Soviet warships can be studied in Breyer, *Soviet Warship Development*, pp. 33–5, 49–50, 150–4).
9 Stupnikov (ed.), *Dvazhdi*, p. 154.
10 Ponikarovsky *et al.* (eds), *Voenno-morskaya akademiya*, p. 40; Monakov, 'Sudba doktrin i teory, 1', p. 15.
11 Dotsenko, *Morskoy biograficheskiy slovar*, pp. 164–5; M. V. Zakharov (ed.), *Voprosy strategii i operativnogo isskustva v sovetskikh voennikh trudakh (1917–1940 gg.)* (Moscow: Voenizdat, 1965), pp. 686–7; extracts from the third edition of Zherve's *Znachenie morskoy sily gosudarstva* (1925) reprinted in A. E. Savinkin *et al.* (eds), *Voenno-morskaya ideya Rossii: Dukhovnoe nasledie Imperatorskogo flota* (Moscow: Russky put, 1999), pp. 392–413.
12 Belli, f. r-2224, o. 1, d. 4, list 148–50; Monakov, 'Sudba doktrin i teory, 1', pp. 19–22; Podsoblyayev, 'Kakoy flot nuzhen RSFR?', pp. 137–8.
13 Dotsenko, *Morskoy biograficheskiy slovar*, pp. 323–4.
14 Nemits and Gaylis to the RVS, 15 February 1921, *RGVA*, f. 33988, o. 2, d. 314, list 3; Dotsenko, *Morskoy biograficheskiy slovar*, pp. 394–5.

15 Toshakov's appendix has been published in Berezovsky, '"Dlya kakikh tseley stroit flot"', pp. 46–65.
16 Dotsenko, *Morskoy biograficheskv slovar*, pp. 111–12; Zonin, *Admiral L. M. Galler*, pp. 198–201.
17 Dotsenko, *Morskoy biograficheskv slovar*, p. 94.
18 Ibid., p. 176; Monakov, 'Sudba doktrin i teory, 1', pp. 20–3.
19 Berezovsky *et al.*, *Boevaya letopis*, pp. 483–4.
20 Zonin, *Admiral L. M Galler*, pp. 192–3; Westwood, *Russian Naval Construction*, p. 126; Berezovsky *et al.*, *Boevaya letopis*, pp. 474, 485, 487, 519.
21 Belli, f. r-2224, o. 1, d. 4, list 72–3, 129–34.
22 Berezovsky *et al.*, *Boevaya letopis*, p. 515.
23 'Protokol 1–3 zasedaniya polit-proverochnoy komissii voenno-morskogo podgotovitelnogo uchilishcha', 1–3 July 1924, f. r-34, o. 2, d. 917, list 239–41b.
24 Makarov and Rudny, 'Svedenie o nalichii slushateley voenno-morskikh uchebnykh zavedeniy', r-34, o. 2, d. 917, list 396–7.
25 On Frunze's reform, see Erickson, *Soviet High* Command, pp. 189–99; von Hagen, *Soldiers in the Proletarian Dictatorship*, pp. 206–30.
26 Suvenirov, *RKKA nakanune*, p. 179; Dotsenko, *Morskoy bibliograficheskv slovar*, p. 467.
27 Dolya to PUR Baltic Fleet, 23 April 1923, f. r-34, o. 2, d. 975, list 30.
28 Suvenirov, *RKKA nakanune*, p. 40.
29 A. P. Aleksandrov, 'Oborona sovetskoy strany', *Morskoy Sbornik*, vol. 79(5) (1926).
30 Commander Baltic Fleet to Commander PUR Baltic Fleet, 22 July 1923, with extract from the naval mobilization regulation, f. r-34, o. 2, d. 908, list 1–3.
31 Circular, 14 July 1924, Dolya, f. r-34, o. 2, d. 917, list 254.
32 'Orientirovochnaya politdirektiva'; 'Prikaz politupravleniya revvoensoveta baltflota', draft, March 1924, f. r-34, o. 2, d. 917, list 65–72.
33 V. A. Belli, 'Otchet po voenno-morskim igram provedennym v voenno-morskoy i voenno-politicheskoy im t...akademiyakh RKKA v 1927–28 uchebn.godakh v vostochnoy chasti balticheskogo morya', f. r-92, o. 2, d. 57, list 39–40.
34 A. Melenkovsky, 'Poltirabota v flote', *Morskoy Sbornik*, vol. 79(5) (1926), pp. 18–19.
35 'Otchet o lichnom sostave v baltflote, za dekabr 1922', r-34, o. 2, d. 857, list 656.
36 Berezovsky *et al.*, *Boevaya letopis*, p. 474.
37 Ibid., pp. 483–6, 498, 501–2, 510–11, 514–15, 525, 539–40; on the level of education in the Soviet Union, see Hildermeier, *Geschichte der Sowjetunion*, p. 1179.
38 Yermolenko, 'Obshschie resultaty proverki', no date, r-34, o. 2, d. 917, list 390.
39 Stepanov, 21 May 1926, 'Perechen politoprosvetimushchestva dlya dostravaivayushchikhsya sudov', f. r-34, o. 2, d. 1304, list 176–176b.
40 Circular by acting commander for agitation and propaganda, 9 July 1925, f. r-34, o. 2, d. 1265, list 13.
41 Cf. reports from 1923 in f. r-34, o. 2, d. 975.
42 'Spisok politrabotnikov balticheskogo flota po sostayaniyu na 15 dekabrya 1923 goda', f. r-34, o. 2, d. 917, list 6–17b.
43 Lakomsky to the Baltic Fleet air arm commissar, 27 November 1924, f. r-34, o. 2, d. 917, list 389.
44 Cf. PUR directives in r-34, o. 2, d. 1017.
45 'Vzaimootnesheniya SSSR so skandinavskimi stranami (Materialy k Politchasu po tekushchemu momentu)', appendix to the paper *Krasny Baltisky Flot*, no. 152, 12 July 1924, f. r-34, o. 2, d. 1017, list 120–2b.
46 N. Alyakrinsky, 'O bolshikh oshibkakh v korotkom doklade', *Morskoy Sbornik*, vol. 79(5) (1926).
47 Dotsenko, *Morskoy biograficheskv slovar*, p. 27.
48 P. Bykov, 'K voprosy o prepodavanii v.-m. istoricheskikh predmetov', *Morskoy Sbornik*, vol. 79(5) (1926).

49 K. Davidovich to Vasilyev, 26 January 1926, f. r-34, o. 2, d. 1304, list 88; cf. reports from other commissars to Vasilyev on this matter, ibid., list 89–99.
50 Reese, *Stalin's Reluctant Soldiers*, p. 109.
51 Berezinsky *et al.*, *Boevaya letopis*, p. 553.
52 P. A. Smirnov to Muklevich, 'Dokladnaya zapiska. O traditisiakh', f. r-34, o. 2, d. 1304, list 101–4.
53 M. M. Khrenov *et al.*, *Voennaya odezhda Vooruzhennikh Sil SSSR i Rossii (1917–1990-e gody)* (Moscow: Voenizdat, 1999), pp. 66–71, 102–5; protocol draft from a meeting at the commander of the Naval Forces Muklevich, 26 October 1926, f.-34, o. 2, d. 1304, list 108–108b.
54 Berezinsky *et al.*, *Boevaya letopis*, p. 553.
55 Lyubich and Schakhov, memorandum, 15 December 1931, f. r-34, o. 1, d. 1460, list 1.

Plate I Sailors relaxing in the ship's 'Lenin Corner' Swedish Military Archives.

Plate II This poster from the mid-1920s offers a subtle illustration to the relationship between the Red Navy and Army. The RKKA soldier is the main author of the defense plan in the Baltic Theater, his sailor-comrade a mere advisor. Swedish Military Archives.

Plate III Sailors eating soup. Swedish Military Archives.

Plate IV Navy personnel enjoying grammophone music. The Bolsheviks regarded the armed forces as an important instrument in their struggle to bring 'culture' to the masses. According to Trotsky, 'nine tenths' of the Soviet military effort must consist of 'civilizing work'. Swedish Military Archives.

Plate V Few soldier – orchestras were probably as well equipped as this coastal artillery–band, portrayed on an official photo. Courtesy of the Swedish Military Archives.

Plate VI Poster from the early 1920s, illustrating the Komsomol campaign for naval revival. Swedish Military Archives.

Plate VII The anchor of the 25,000 ton *Gangut*-class battleship was manouvered from this huge steering wheel. Swedish Military Archives.

Plate VIII A seminar in operational art at the Naval War College in the mid-1920s. If students' recollections are to be believed, lectures in the subject had not yet been influenced by the experience of World War I. Swedish Military Archives.

Plate IX Naval officers attending a specialist course. The need for additional training remained great at all levels in the Soviet Navy. Swedish Military Archives.

Plate X The crew of the *Marat* gathered to listen to a representative of the Leningrad Soviet. As a rule, the chairman of the Leningrad party branch was also a member of the Baltic Fleet Soviet. Swedish Military Archives.

Plate XI The *Gangut* – battleships were of pre-World War I design and had mixed boilers for coal and oil. Although the *Oktyabrskaya Revolutsiya* was refitted with oil-fired boilers in the early 1930s, the *Marat* kept her original machinery. Swedish Military Archives.

Plate XII Provisions being carried aboard the *Marat*. In wartime, the ship's ordinary crew of 66 officers, 192 NCOs and 842 sailors would be increased by another 186 men. Considerable amounts of food would be needed. Swedish Military Archives.

Plate XIII Engine personnel under instruction. Swedish Military Archives.

Plate XIV When weather allowed, political hour could take place on deck. Swedish Military Archives.

Plate XV Fresh recruits receiving their first instruction about the Navy's organization. Swedish Military Archives.

Plate XVI 'Does our cook deserve a prize? Let us write to the paper!' The bolsheviks knew from their own experience that minor discontent among naval personnel could be exploited in order to undermine discipline. All complaints concerning food were therefore taken seriously. Swedish Military Archives.

Plate XVII In spite of the uneven level of education among her crew, the battleship *Marat* sponsored a school outside Leningrad. Here, crewmembers are seen together with local inhabitants at the opening ceremony of the 'Battleship Marat Working School' in 1925. Swedish Military Archives.

Part III

THE YOUNG SCHOOL, 1929–1935

8

THE ERA OF COLLECTIVE SECURITY – AND OF COASTAL DEFENSE

The defensive naval doctrine of the Young School period corresponded with a new course in Soviet foreign policy, when the Soviet Union supported status quo in the international system and the principle of collective security. The new course was confirmed when the country was admitted as a member to the League of Nations in 1934.

In reality, the road toward détente with the West had been initiated as early as after the Locarno Treaty in 1925, when the Soviet government started to suspect that its newfound German partner was drifting westwards.[1] The danger of renewed isolation forced the Soviet Union to rethink its external relations thoroughly. People's Commissar for Foreign Affairs Chicherin's report to the XIVth Party Congress in 1925, which suggested that peaceful coexistence with the West could be more than transitory, demonstrates that already at this early stage an alternative, pragmatic and less ideological view of the international situation existed within the Soviet leadership.[2]

Another powerful argument for improved relations with the capitalist world could be found in the approaching world depression, which meant problems for Soviet grain exports. These exports (which contributed considerably to the great famine in the early 1930s) were of vital importance as a source of finance for the Soviet Union's rapid industrialization. Finally, the rising threat from Japan in the Far East made some kind of détente in Europe desirable.[3]

Already in 1926–27, bilateral nonaggression pacts had been signed with Afghanistan, Persia, Turkey and Lithuania. In 1928, the Kellogg–Briand Pact – initiated by the French and American foreign ministers to prohibit war as an instrument for conflict resolution – made further progress possible. After having joined the Kellogg–Briand Pact, the Soviet Union offered its western neighbors bilateral security treaties in a similar spirit. During 1932, agreements were concluded with Estonia, Latvia, Finland and Poland. One by one, the territories of the western neighbor states were to be immunized from the presence of future aggressors.

The architect of the new foreign policy was Maxim Litvinov – People's Commissar for Foreign Affairs from 1930. In Litvinov's security system, the final step would probably have been the conclusion of a regional agreement modeled after Locarno, with all the Great powers concerned guaranteeing the existing borders in east and central Europe. However, through Hitler's coming to power in Germany in 1933 the strategic situation started to deteriorate. When Poland in 1934 refused to renew the existing nonaggression pact with the Soviet Union and concluded a similar treaty with Germany instead, Moscow became seriously alarmed. Attempts were made to form a common front with the former enemies Britain and France against German revisionism, but these were only partly successful. A French–Soviet nonaggression pact had been signed in 1932, and was now followed by formal alliances with France and Czechoslovakia in May 1935. However, these treaties did not contain any details on military cooperation. In addition, the British gave up naval mastery in the Baltic to Germany through the Anglo-German naval agreement of June 1935, allowing for an increase of the German Navy up to 35 percent of the Royal Navy's surface tonnage and up to 45 percent of its submarine tonnage.[4]

Around 1935, strategic predicaments in the Baltic were thus about to change again, and Soviet naval policy had to change accordingly.

Prospects of war

The planned employment of Soviet naval forces in the Baltic was soon revised in accordance with the 1928 resolution of the RVS. In April 1930, the naval commander Romuald Muklevich received a special report on the future role of naval forces in the Baltic Theater from a group of 'Young School' professors at the Naval War College which listed as the main missions protecting Leningrad, supporting the RKKA and raiding enemy communications. In order to solve such missions, the fleet must be concentrated east of the line Shepelev–Stirsudden, in the immediate vicinity of Leningrad.[5] The capture of the Baltic approaches to gain command of the entire theater was no longer desirable.

According to the new operational directives issued in January 1932, only two cases of war deserved further attention, depending on whether Finland and the Baltic states would stay neutral in the conflict.[6] That the mere possibility of the northwestern Border States staying neutral was considered, and that their neutrality was seen to be in the Soviet Union's own interest, seems conjectural in view of the new, status quo–oriented foreign policy. In March 1933, however, the distinction between the two war cases was abolished. If Finland and the Baltic states decided to stay neutral in a conflict between the West and the Soviet Union, Soviet forces would nevertheless deploy as if they were not.[7]

The expected enemy would still be some kind of Border State coalition, backed up by the Western powers. This assumption was also preserved as the basis for war games and staff exercises.

In the scenario presented at the joint war games between the LVO and the Baltic Fleet in March 1930, Britain and France conspired together with the United States to launch a crusade against the Soviet Union, using as main themes in their propaganda alleged domestic oppression and the 'bloody dictatorship of the Comintern'. As usual, Poland was expected to be the main supplier of ground forces to the campaign. While 'White Guard organizations' all over Europe were busy recruiting volunteers to the Polish Army, British and Finnish warships would form the backbone of the enemy's naval forces.[8]

In the scenario of the 1933 war games (conducted by the Baltic Fleet together with the Naval War College), the aggressors were Britain and France. As the capitalist world was experiencing its worst economic crisis ever, the Soviet Union's miraculous economic progress had provoked anger and fear among the ruling circles in London and Paris. Furthermore, not only fascists and White Guardsmen assisted in the anti-Soviet propaganda campaign this time, but also the Social Democrats ('social fascists'), who had managed to seduce a large part of the European proletariat. Luckily, Western Communist parties did what they could to agitate against the war and to sabotage war preparations. Having organized a coalition consisting of Poland, Rumania, Finland, Estonia and Latvia, the Western powers sent a naval task force into the Baltic (one aircraft carrier, five cruisers, 14 destroyers and five submarines). Just like before, the objective of the enemy's operations would be to bottle up the Baltic Fleet, destroy its heavy units and support army operations ashore.[9]

Consequently, while the official doctrine had changed, the concrete military threat in the region remained the same as under the Old School. The choice of defense instead of offense reflected new objectives in security policy, but also an adjustment to the relatively modest threat perceptions which had been in sway since the mid–1920s.

The Border States and Sweden

If the Young School's image of a naval war in the Baltic remained basically unchanged from the 1920s, so did the expected behavior of the minor states in the region.

As Soviet ships would have to pass through Finnish territorial waters to confront the enemy, from a naval perspective Finland was undoubtedly a key country in the Baltic. The presence of British military advisers in Finland, the construction of the strategic Ladoga Canal as well as numerous articles in the Finnish press served to illustrate the country's role as a 'forward outpost of the imperialists on the Baltic in the struggle against the USSR'.[10] Furthermore, in 1930 the Finnish and Estonian navies initiated their secret cooperation to close the Gulf of Finland to the Soviets in the event of war. During the following years, the localization of coastal batteries and permanent minefields in the two countries was closely coordinated, and a series of joint naval maneuvers were held. The last one took place in August 1939, only weeks before Estonia was drawn into the Soviet sphere of influence through the forced security pact with Moscow. As Jari Leskinen has shown, the existence of this partnership was no secret to the Soviets. Through well-placed agents in Tallinn, they had detailed knowledge of Estonia's defense planning and of the military exchange with the Finns.[11]

The League of Nations' long-expected conference on disarmament convened in Geneva in 1932. The Finnish and Polish general staffs had worked out a common position in advance, hoping to win support from other countries in the Baltic region. Although the Swedes declined, the Balts joined in. Through the conference preparations, Finnish–Estonian military cooperation was to develop even further.[12]

The Soviets followed these developments with great interest. In a report on the conference preparations, Telegina of the Baltic Fleet Intelligence Section predicted that a greater coordination of naval policies between the Border States should be expected in the future. Aiming to secure a leading role for the Polish Navy in this context, France was certain to endorse such a development. Only Lithuania, which was too poor to have a navy and too hostile to Poland to join a Border State coalition, could be counted out.

The reason for France's influence at the conference, it was argued, was that the Border States lacked naval traditions and would be completely in the hands of their Great power protectors. Although the Finnish and Estonian navies had been trained and equipped in Britain, Britain's insistence on an international moratorium on naval budgets was likely to estrange those countries. The French, on the other hand, would welcome an increase in defense spending among the Border States as they wanted Germany's neighbors to be as militarily strong as possible. Furthermore, both Finland and Estonia wanted to expand their submarine fleets (in 1933, Estonia exchanged two newly acquired destroyers for two French submarines), and were consequently annoyed by Britain's insistence that submarine orders must be placed with British shipyards. According to Telegina, only Sweden could detach Finland from the group of French client states. In her usual fashion, Sweden was expected to endorse the British disarmament stance at the Geneva Conference. However, Sweden's position was not all together clear. The Swedes also wished to preserve friendly relations with the other Border States and secretly longed for a strengthening of the German Navy, as Germany could act as a counterbalance against Soviet influence in the Baltic.[13]

In June 1933, the Baltic Fleet held war games according to a scenario in which the Soviet Union had been at war with the Border States for three weeks. The enemy was supported by Sweden and the Western powers. The game started with the Red Army advancing into Estonia and Swedish active intervention seeming imminent. When Swedish troops concentrated in the ports of Stockholm, Oskarshamn and Karlskrona, a British naval squadron entered the Baltic, prepared to ship them across.[14]

In reality, the notion of Swedish armed assistance to Estonia was highly theoretical.[15] Finland appeared the main receiver of assistance in Swedish military planning, and Swedish–Finnish relations remained in the focus of Soviet attention. Suspicions were that in the event of a Soviet–Finnish war causing revolution in Finland, the Swedes would occupy parts of western Finland.[16] Indeed, during the Finnish Civil War in 1918 Sweden had briefly occupied the Åland Islands, and at least the 1927 operational plan of the Swedish Army made provisions for a seizure of these islands again. From 1933 onwards, the Swedish and Finnish general staffs carried on detailed discussions on how Åland could be defended. The Finns feared the Soviets would capture the island group in the initial stage of a conflict, cutting communications across the Gulf of Bothnia. Hence, they wanted to change the 1921 convention on Åland's demilitarized status. The Swedes, who were less convinced of this danger, objected to alterations in the existing treaty that would increase tension around their capital.[17]

In 1931–1933, the Baltic Fleet Intelligence Section claimed that the Swedish Navy now regarded the Gulf of Finland and the Turkku–Åland archipelago as a part of its theater of operations.[18] The Soviet military attaché in Helsinki knew that Åland had been a topic during the Finnish–Swedish staff talks, but could not supply any additional information. In the autumn of 1934, the attaché also reported of the Swedish General Henri de Champs, who in the Stockholm daily *Aftonbladet* had publicly advocated a revision of the Åland treaty. Ten years before, de Champs had been one of the initiators of Finnish–Swedish staff talks.[19] However, just as before Soviet observers were skeptical of Sweden's willingness to go to war for Finland, or even to spend money or technical advisors to reinforce Finnish border fortifications.[20]

Moreover, the *Sverige* class coast defense battleships, considered relatively modern during the 1920s, were now aging rapidly. In the autumn of 1933, the Stockholm naval attaché reported that the strength of the Swedish Navy was really insufficient to solve the missions it had been assigned, and that for the next five years coastal defense would be its main concern.[21]

The rise of the German menace

During the first years of the Young School era, the scenario for war in the Baltic remained much the same, as did the appreciation of the Border States and Sweden. The challenge from these countries, even with the expected assistance from the Western powers, would not call for a revision of the Soviet Navy's defensive doctrine. Weimar Germany was looked upon as a benevolent neutral or even potential ally. During war games held a few weeks after Adolf Hitler's coming to power in January 1933, Germany was still expected to stay neutral in a war against the Soviet Union. In exchange for its neutrality, the scenario instruction stated, the newly installed fascist government in Germany was likely to demand concessions from the Western powers regarding the borders of Poland.[22]

Soon, however, the new regime in Berlin began to play a more prominent role in Soviet threat perceptions. Already in the spring of 1933, German naval visits to Finland, Estonia and Sweden seemed to reveal a new constellation of powers in the Baltic.[23] In early April 1934, RKKA chief of staff Yegorov informed the LVO and the Baltic Fleet that recent political developments called for a revision of operational planning in the theater (the loss of certain secret documents to hostile powers also contributed).[24]

In March 1935, People's Commissar for Defense Voroshilov ordered a revision of the Baltic Fleet's operational planning, identifying Germany as the main aggressor in the Baltic Theater, supported by Poland and Finland. Until the summer of 1939, most threat scenarios and war games calculated with these three countries in a powerful coalition, and with the Baltic states likely to join. In December 1935, naval commander Orlov made a special request to the GRU, asking that information on the German and Japanese navies from now on should become a top priority in intelligence collection.[25]

In light of the new situation, even the military preparations of minor countries in the region took on a threatening image. The proposal of a Swedish naval committee in November 1934 to build a fourth coast defense battleship, Swedish naval visits to Latvia and Estonia and the construction of airports and coastal highways in eastern Sweden seemed to indicate that this country was preparing to join the German-led Border State coalition. Even Denmark appeared more aggressive in its naval strategy, responding to German and Swedish pressure. In its summary of developments during the first half of 1935, the Baltic Fleet Intelligence Section concluded that Germany was striving for hegemony in the Baltic. British naval visits to the region had virtually ceased.[26]

The Nikonov–Shteynbryuk report

In June 1935, the Anglo-German naval agreement was signed, and in August the GRU analyzed the new strategic situation in a special report signed by the directorate's deputy head Nikonov and the head of its first section, Steynbryuk. Nikonov and Steynbryuk interpreted the agreement as a part of Britain's strategy to dominate Europe. When the German Navy was reinforced, the Soviet Union's nominal ally France would have to transfer naval forces from the Mediterranean to northern Europe, which would benefit the Royal Navy. Although the British were likely to support a German attack on the Soviet Union, they would still not allow the Germans to dominate Scandinavia.[27]

Most likely, German troops would be deployed in Estonia and Latvia for the invasion of the Soviet Union, and they would get there by sea transport. Their concentration would take about two weeks, so enemy naval forces would do their utmost to block the Baltic Fleet in its bases during the initial stage of a war. In its present shipbuilding program, Germany had given priority to destroyers, submarines and other vessels that would be useful in the shallow waters of the Gulf of Finland. To be able to seal off the Gulf in an early stage of a conflict, Germany needed bases in the northern part of the Baltic. Here, the best harbors for operating major warships were to be found in Stockholm and Fårösund in Sweden.[28]

The Åland Archipelago could serve as a base for the enemy's light forces (destroyers and submarines), as could the Hiiumaa–Saaremaa area and the island of Gotland. Estonian and Finnish coastal batteries along the shores of the Gulf of Finland would play an important role in sealing off Soviet exits, as would the German Air Force. From bases in northern Estonia and southern Finland, it could easily dominate the skies and impede all Soviet ship movements.[29]

Together with Poland, Finland and Sweden, the Germans could concentrate a force of seven small battleships (the *Deutschland* class being the only modern ones), five coast defense battleships, nine cruisers, 18 destroyers, 28 submarines and 950 aircraft. Substantial German naval resources would have to remain in reserve west of the Kiel Canal against a possible French intervention. But even if the French appeared off the German North Sea coast and cut the influx of goods from the west, Sweden could offer ample supplies of strategic resources and alternative import routes.[30] Nikonov and Shteynbryuk admitted that the German Navy was not yet strong enough to dominate the Baltic on its own. It would have to be reinforced by a British squadron, although the British – just as before – would try to limit their contribution as much as possible. If construction programs rolled along at the present pace, however, in a few years Germany could control the Baltic alone.[31]

When the defense against invasion had to commence out on the open sea, the coast defense doctrine of the Young School seemed increasingly obsolete.

Conclusion

Victory for the notion of 'Socialism in One Country' in the late 1920s led to a shift in Soviet security policy. Now, the goal was integration into the international system, nonaggression pacts with neighboring states and the preservation of the status quo through active diplomacy. As a logical consequence, all thoughts of an independent strategic role for the Baltic Fleet were dismissed. Although the threat perceptions in the theater remained the same as before – a limited Western squadron supporting the navies of local powers in an attack on Leningrad – the main idea of the so-called Young School was to concentrate on defense in the eastern part of the Gulf of Finland.

With Hitler's coming to power in Germany in 1933, however, things began to change. From March 1935, Germany was considered to be the most likely opponent in the theater, and a few months later the Anglo-German naval agreement removed all bans against Germany's naval rearmament. As was pointed out in a GRU analysis by Shtenbryuk and Nikonov, it was now necessary for the Baltic Fleet to have the capability to operate outside the Gulf of Finland. The special geographic conditions in the region – narrow straits, shallow archipelagos, short flying distances – which for many years had served to prove the soundness of the Young School's doctrine, now suddenly pointed in the opposite direction. In the new strategic landscape, these factors would only serve to paralyze the Baltic Fleet and allow German troops to be safely shipped on the very borders of the Soviet Union.

Notes

1 Gabriel Gorodetsky, *The Precarious Truce: Anglo-Soviet Relations 1924–27* (Cambridge: Cambridge University Press, 1977), pp. 73–80; Adam B. Ulam, *Expansion and Coexistence: Soviet Foreign Policy, 1917–73* (New York: Holt, Rinehart & Winston, 1974; 1968), pp. 158–60.

2 J. Jacobson, 'Essay and Reflection: On the Historiography of Soviet Foreign Relations in the 1920s', *International History Review*, vol. 18(2) (May 1996), pp. 343–4.
3 Jonathan Haslam, *Soviet Foreign Policy, 1930–33: The Impact of the Depression* (Cambridge; Macmillan, 1983), pp. 4–9.
4 Hildermeier, *Geschichte der Sowjetunion*, pp. 587–9; on the 1935 naval agreement see Claire Scammel, 'The Royal Navy and the Strategic Origins of the Anglo-German Naval Agreement 1935', *Journal of Strategic Studies*, vol. 20(2) (June 1997).
5 Monakov, 'Sudba doktrin i teory, 7', p. 37; Rohwer and Monakov, *Stalin's Ocean-going Fleet*, pp. 29–30.
6 RKKA General Staff to Baltic Fleet Soviet and LVO, 21 January 1932, f. r-92, o. 2, d. 181, list 2–3; Chief of Staff LVO to Baltic Fleet Soviet, 9 February 1932, ibid., list 6–7; head of operations LVO (no date), ibid., list 9.
7 RKKA General Staff to Baltic Fleet Soviet and LVO, 21 January 1933, f. r-92, o. 2, d. 181, list 10–11; LVO to commander Baltic Fleet, 23 March 1933, ibid., list 14–17; cf. V. N. Baryshnikov, 'K voprosu o planirovanii Sovetskim baltiyskim flotom voennikh deystvy protiv Finlandii v, 1930-e gg. (raschety i realnost)', in Koreneva and Prochorenko (eds), *Rossiya i Finlandiya*, pp. 102–3.
8 'Voennaya igra LVO i MSBM 1930 g.', f. r-92, o. 2, d. 142, list 131–2.
9 The background scenario is presented in f. r-92, o. 2, d. 178, list 8–17.
10 Information bulletin no. 1 (of the Baltic Fleet intelligence section), May 1929, f. r-92, o. 12, d. 3, list 4–5.
11 Leskinen, *Vaiettu Suomen Silta*, pp. 454–6, 459; cf. the Baltic Fleet's archives, f. r-92, o. 2, d. 121, which contains translations of the Estonian Navy's operational planning for the period 1930–40; Zinovyev and Petrovsky, 3 December 1931, f. r-92, o. 12, d. 6, list 32–5; Jalkanen, 27 June 1933, f. r-92, o. 12, d. 8, list 11; Petrovsky, 8 July 1933, ibid., list 14–15, Petrovsky, 2 August 1933, ibid., list 20–1, Petrovsky, 25 August 1933, ibid., list 28–9.
12 Leskinen, *Vaiettu Suomen Silta*, pp. 450–1.
13 Telegina, 9 December 1931, 'Podgotovka pribaltiskikh stran k konferentsii po razoruzhenii', f. r-92, o. 12, d. 7, list 41; on France and the Baltic states, see also GRU to Naval Commander Muklevich, 16 February 1931, f. r-1483, o. 1, d. 120, list 5–7; on the Estonian exchange of destroyers for submarines, see Leskinen, *Vaiettu Suomen Silta*, p. 456.
14 Background of the war game on 13 June 1933 in f. r-92, o. 2, d. 234, list 32–4.
15 Berge, *Sakkunskap och politisk rationalitet*, pp. 54–5, 78–9.
16 Petrov, 29 July 1924, f. r-1, o. 3, d. 2121, list 74.
17 Arvid Cronenberg, 'Säkerhetspolitik och krigsplanering: Huvudlinjer i arméns operativa planering 1906–1945', in Bo Hugemark (ed.), *Neutralitet och försvar: Perspektiv på svensk säkerhetspolitik 1809–1985* (Stockholm: Probus, 1986), pp. 104–6; Turtola, *Från Torne älv till Systerbäck*, pp. 87–90, 150–65.
18 Zinovyev and Petrovsky, 3 December 1931, f. r-92, o. 12, d. 6, list 12–13; Petrovsky, 2 July 1933, f. r-92, o. 12, d. 8, list 14–15; Petrovsky, 13 July 1933, ibid., list 16–17; Petrovsky, 21 July 1933, ibid., list 18–19; Petrovsky, 28 June 1933, f. r-92, o. 12, d. 9, list 5–6.
19 Ivanov, 10 October 1934, f. r-1483, o. 1, d. 224, list 145–7; on the role of de Champs, see Turtola, *Från Torne älv till Systerbäck*, pp. 98–9; Henri de Champs, *Från svunnen tid* (Stockholm: Fritzes, 1948), pp. 125–7.
20 Ivanov, 10 October 1934, f. r-1483, o. 1, d. 224, list 145b.
21 Kossov, 10 October 1933, f. 1483, o. 1, d. 185, list 93.
22 The background scenario of the 1933 war games in f. r-92, o. 2, d. 178, list 8–17.
23 Cf. the surveys of the Baltic Fleet Intelligence section, 14 May, 25 May 1933, f. r-92, o. 12, d. 5, list 4–8; see also surveys 15 August, 19 September 1933, f. r-92, o. 12, d. 8, list 24–35, 34–5.

24 Yegorov to the Baltic Fleet Soviet and LVO, 2 April 1934, f. r-92, o. 2, d. 181, list 20–1; Baltic Fleet head of operations to Fleet Commander Galler, 9 April 1934, ibid., list 22–4.
25 Voroshilov to the commanders of the Baltic Fleet and LVO, 9 March 1935, f. r-92, o. 2, d. 260, list 1–2; Captain 1st rank N. Zuykov and Regimental Commissar S. Molodtsov, 'Obshaya obstanovka 15.5 1939', f. r-1877, o. 1, d. 98, list 127; Galler to the Baltic Fleet Soviet, 26 June 1939, ibid., list 130; Orlov to Uritsky, 28 December 1935, f. r-1483, o. 1, d. 300, list 105–6.
26 Surveys from the Baltic Fleet intelligence section, January–February, April, June–October 1935, f. r-1883, o. 2, d. 62 (the summary of the first half of 1935 in August survey, list 115).
27 Nikonov and Shteynbryuk, 20 August 1935, 'Kratky obzor strategitcheskogo polozheniya na balticheskom teatre v svyazi s anglo-germanskim morskim soglasheniem', f. r-1483, o. 1, d. 329, list 195–6, 204.
28 Ibid., list 198, 203, 206–9, 215, 217–18.
29 Ibid., list 199–203.
30 Ibid., list 197, 205, 210.
31 Ibid., list 205, 209–10.

9

SUPPORT FOR THE RED ARMY

The 1928 RVS resolution on 'the importance and tasks of the naval forces' had defined coastal defense and support to the Red Army as their main missions. In consequence with this decision, a revised naval shipbuilding program was adopted in February 1929, containing one light cruiser, six destroyers, 18 patrol craft, 23 submarines, five ASW ships, three river gunboats, 63 MTBs and one submarine depot ship. In addition, the three operational *Gangut* class battleships were to be modernized (the *Frunze* was quietly left to rust at the Leningrad Shipyard, used only as a source of spare parts). Shortly afterwards, when 85 million rubles in the defense budget were redirected from shipbuilding to tank construction, this more modest program was also threatened. Although funds were restored after UVMS commander Romuald Muklevich had protested personally to Stalin, the incident demonstrated the navy's difficult situation. As could be expected, only a few of the ships in the 1929 program were ever completed.[1]

In view of the limited number of large Soviet warships and the naval rearmament of other Baltic countries at the time (Poland, Germany, Finland), Muklevich complained to the Soviet government, as did a group of Leningrad construction engineers. In their letter of October 1931, the latter quoted Lenin's words on external aggression being best countered abroad, demanding the acquisition of cruisers and battleships. Apart from these instances, there was little explicit opposition from the navy during the Young School era, especially after the service had been purged in 1930–31. We will study these purges more closely in the next chapter. Suffice it here to say that they offered the army another opportunity to humiliate the navy. In June 1930, about a month after the first trials against arrested naval men, the Red Army chief of staff Shaposhnikov demanded that the RVS should strengthen Soviet coastal artillery, claiming that it had been severely neglected in the past because of an exaggerated interest in big ships in naval circles.[2] When a People's Commissariat for Defense replaced the RVS in 1934, the naval forces received only eight of the 85 seats in the People's Commissariat's Supreme Soviet.[3]

Although the army attracted the lion's share of defense investments under the second five-year plan, a modest expansion of Soviet naval forces did occur.

The growing threat from Japan led to the creation of special naval flotillas in the Northern and Pacific Theaters. In the summer of 1931, Voroshilov had taken Muklevich with him on an inspection trip to the Far East. Although a certain chill had existed between the two men before, personal relations seem to have improved during that trip. In a letter to his deputy, Yan Borisovich Gamarnik, Voroshilov described how Muklevich used to come to have tea with him in his compartment aboard the train.[4]

In response to the new strategic situation, the 1933 naval program contained eight cruisers, 32 destroyer leaders and destroyers, 355 submarines of various sizes, 194 MTBs, four monitors and six minelayers, all to be produced during the term of the second five-year plan. When the program was later revised the number of cruisers, destroyer leaders and submarines was reduced, the number of destroyers and MTBs increased. In the Baltic there were to be two cruisers, 18 destroyer leaders and destroyers with some 43 large and medium-size submarines. Less than half of the ships commissioned were ever delivered. Moreover, the warships that were eventually completed had fundamental flaws with regard to weaponry, protection, maneuverability and operational range.[5]

Otherwise, in view of the navy's subjugated status and even 'nonexistence' as an independent service, organizational rivalry at the national level is not easy to detect during the Young School era. If we are to discuss doctrinal developments from this perspective, we should rather direct our attention to the regional level and the relationship between the Baltic Fleet and the LVO.

The central apparatus, the UVMS, was reorganized in the summer of 1929. The head of the directorate for training and personnel would at the same time be 'inspector of the naval forces', while the position of the commander of the RKKA naval forces (the UVMS commander) was somewhat strengthened.[6] According to the Fleet Staff Regulation of 1929, the fleet staffs were to be subordinated to the local military district, but at the same time execute many of the functions previously handled by the abolished Naval Staff in Moscow. They were to be responsible for training and combat preparations, for the maintenance of operational and technical efficiency as well as for war planning and mobilization. To this end, the fleet staffs were expected to collect information on the operational environment and on the likely enemy. Each staff was to contain three sections: operations, organization-tactics and intelligence.[7]

When the navy had been abolished at the center, it resurrected in the regions. Suddenly it was allowed to develop an intelligence function, for instance. The main sources of knowledge for the fleet staff intelligence sections seem to have been foreign press, radio intelligence and observations made by Soviet ships at sea. In May 1930, the chief of the Baltic Fleet Staff (who was Arkady Toshakov at the time) and the head of the intelligence section, Zinovyev, urged subordinate commanders to collect intelligence about neighboring coastal areas on a routine basis, without instructions. In addition to military installations, they were to register landmarks along enemy shores, landing sites, roads and railways.[8]

Scenarios for war in the early 1930s

Just as before, during the early 1930s the Baltic Fleet prepared for a war against the Border States, supported by the Western powers. War Case 'A' from December 1930 calculated with a British squadron in Finland and a French squadron in Poland. The Red Army would concentrate its forces against Poland and did not expect any support from the sea in this theater. In the Gulf of Finland, however, support was needed to protect the industries of Leningrad, secure the RKKA's flank and attack the enemy's lines of communications.[9]

In January 1932, instructions were renewed with only two war cases attributed any real probability:

- Case V: War against Romania and Poland, supported by Britain and France. The Baltic states and Finland were believed to remain neutral at least in the beginning of the conflict. It would be in the interest of the Soviet Union to respect that neutrality.
- Case V-1: War against the same Rumanian–Polish–Anglo-French alliance, in which the Baltic states and Finland participated from the outbreak of hostilities on the side of the enemy.

Under case V the task of the Baltic Fleet was still to protect the approaches to Leningrad and raid enemy communications, with the object of destroying Poland's trade. In Case V-1, Leningrad was to be defended 'actively', through the occupation of the islands in the Gulf. At the same time, the Red Army's campaign against Estonia and Finland was to be supported.[10]

In January 1933 the two war cases were renamed 'S' and 'S-1', and a few months later the distinction between them was abolished altogether. If Finland and the Baltic states decided to stay neutral in a conflict between the West and the Soviet Union, it was stated, Soviet forces would nevertheless deploy as if not. Alternative S meant a ground offensive into Estonia, S-1 meant a preparedness to attack into Finland as well. In both situations, the task of the fleet was to defend Leningrad, support the Red Army and raid enemy communications.[11]

Although the emphasis on defensive operations in coastal waters was even stronger than before, the mission to support operations ashore remained. The 1931 maneuvers, for instance, involved the landing of a platoon of tanks in the enemy's rear.[12] Soon, the dissonance between the defensive orientation of the Soviet naval forces and their offensive mission to support the advance of the Red Army would become disturbingly apparent.

Defensive operations – Rodionov's vision

When it came to defensive operations, the idea was still to create an impenetrable mine-defense zone between Stirsudden and Shepelev ('the main defense area' or GOR, *Glavny Oboronitelny Rayon*). Konstantin Rodionov, deputy head of the

Baltic Fleet operational section, further elaborated these plans. In February 1935, Rodionov presented his graduation thesis at the Naval War College. The concerted attacks of air, submarine and surface units which Rodionov envisioned demonstrated how the latest improvements in radio communications had been exploited in practice.[13] His thesis could be described as an apogee of Young School theory, and will therefore be discussed here in some detail.[14]

In the existing war plans, the general idea was to confront the enemy in a preliminary skirmish somewhere in the Lavensaari–Hogland area, after which the fleet fell back to the GOR for the final battle. As we saw, the tendency during maneuvers and war games in the late 1920s had been that this initial skirmish became increasingly prolonged and costly, as the Old School sought to assert an active role for the battleship squadron without openly challenging the general defensive role assigned to the naval forces. In Rodionov's version of the mine-defense plan, however, the only Soviet units operating west of the GOR were to be submarines and aircraft, their main mission reconnaissance and not combat. Any attempt to lure the Soviet main fleet out into the forward battle zone was to be strongly resisted. Rodionov calculated with a British–Finnish–Latvian enemy force consisting of three battleships, one aircraft carrier, four cruisers, some 20 destroyers and 15 submarines. The Soviet forces, which were to be concentrated in the GOR with a minor reserve in the rear, were estimated as two battleships, three cruisers, eight destroyers, four submarines, 21 MTBs, three minelayers, three minesweepers, 22 reconnaissance aircraft and 36 torpedo bombers. In addition, supportive fire from the Kronstadt and Izhorsky fortifications could be counted on.

The British would probably divide their forces into two echelons. The forward echelon, consisting of cruisers and minesweepers, would clear a path through the minefields close to the northern shore, while the rear echelon – containing the enemy's battleships – kept Soviet ships and coastal fortifications under fire and prepared for the final thrust.

Rodionov recommended that the Soviets should try to upset and disorganize the enemy formations by opening fire themselves, as soon as the forward echelon approached the mine barriers. These attacks were to be executed by submarines, MTBs and long-range coastal artillery. When the main focus of the enemy thrust had been established, the real counterattack could be unleashed. The Soviet battleships, cruisers and 12-inch coastal batteries were to engage the enemy rear echelon from afar, while two other strike groups consisting of destroyers, MTBs, submarines and torpedo bombers dealt with the forward echelon. Rodionov admitted that the depth of the enemy's formation constituted a problem, and that it could be difficult to strike against the battleships in the rear echelon with artillery fire from a distance. To finish off the opponent, a mobile strike group with aircraft and MTBs was kept in reserve.[15]

The 1935 operational plan, which was presented in May that year, a few months after Rodionov's graduation, calculated with some 550 mines and 50 sweeping obstacles in the forward defense zone and 2,381 mines, 902 sweeping obstacles and three miles of submarine net in the GOR. There was, however, an important deviation in the plan from Rodionov's recommendations: destroyers and battleships were supposed to participate in the initial skirmish at the forward defense zone.[16]

Offensive operations – preferably close to home

As we have seen, the conduct of offensive operations was intimately linked to the war on land. In December 1930, when Moscow's issued instructions to prepare for 'War Case A', Mikhail Tukhachevsky was commander of the LVO, which in wartime would organize the Northwestern Front. Apart from the Baltic Fleet, the Northwestern Front would consist of the troops manning the border fortifications on the Karelian Isthmus, the Seventh Army operating north of the Gulf of Finland and the Tenth Army operating south of the Gulf. While the troops north of the Gulf were to defend Leningrad, the Tenth Army was to strike from Pskov against Narva and Tallinn, supported by the Baltic Fleet. Although its main mission was defensive, the Seventh Army on the northern shore also expected an active naval presence on its flank and on Lake Ladoga. Just as before, the islands in the Gulf of Finland must be captured at the outbreak of hostilities. Tukhachevsky also invigorated the old plan to capture the Björkö fortifications, designating two infantry regiments of the Karelian garrison troops as landing force. He also emphasized the need for modern landing vessels and mechanized transport.[17]

When the system with two alternative war cases (V and V-1) was introduced about a year later, the Baltic Fleet's operational plan was revised again. The mission of the Baltic Fleet was to stay on the defensive in the event of case V, and to perform its former missions (supporting the defense of the Karelian Isthmus and the advance into Estonia) in the event of V-1. In addition, the fleet was to secure an ability to operate west of the Stirsudden–Shepelev perimeter in a later stage of the conflict. To this end, Hogland, Great and Small Tootersaari, Lavensaari, Seiskari and Björkö must be taken. Although the main ground offensive into Estonia was to start only about three weeks after mobilization, troop landings could already become necessary in the Narva area close to the border on the fifth day. In that operation the battleships might come to use, although they were not to operate independently but jointly with other forces.[18]

Lev Michailovich Galler – commander of the Baltic Fleet from March 1932 – had serious doubts about his ability to fulfill these expectations. Since the 1930 maneuvers, the need for modern minesweepers in the Baltic Fleet had been all too apparent. Galler tried to have such vessels included in the 1933 naval construction program but without success.[19] In the autumn of 1933, he openly admitted that the Baltic Fleet could no longer solve its missions. The fleet had severe problems with wireless communication with its ships at sea. Several ships were constantly undergoing repairs and the infantry units assigned as landing troops were probably too weak for the objectives they had been assigned. Furthermore, Galler doubted that Soviet ships could operate against enemy communications as far away as the mouth of the Gulf, where they would be out of range of their shore-based air cover. Such operations had to be performed by submarines and not by surface units.[20] Having visited the Baltic Fleet's 1932 maneuvers, even Tukhachevsky, a former opponent of big ships, saw the need for aircraft carriers in the Baltic.[21]

In addition to other problems, the likely enemies seemed to know all that was worth knowing about the Soviet Navy. According to agents abroad, German, French and Finnish intelligence had become well aware of the Baltic Fleet's difficulties in communicating with ships at sea merely by studying reports on naval exercises published in *Morskoy Sbornik* and *Krasny Flot*.[22] Furthermore, through signals intelligence and visual observation, Finns and Estonians had acquired a detailed picture of the Baltic Fleet's operational plans and the deployment areas. Even French intelligence surveys, compiled far away from the shores of the Gulf of Finland, could pinpoint with great accuracy the patrol stations of Soviet submarines and the location of the mine-defense zones.[23]

The 1933 operational plan, which only a few days before had been prolonged for another year, was now hastily abolished.[24] According to the fleet's chief of staff, Isakov, the question was not to find out what the enemy knew about Soviet war preparations, but what he did not know.[25] In a special memorandum, the head of the intelligence section, Petrovsky, suggested various deception measures. Ship movements should take place at night or when sight was limited, and ships should change place when they passed in file in or out of Kronstadt. Wireless communication should be restricted and numbers used instead of names as call signs, as numbers could be changed more easily. Press reports on Soviet naval maneuvers must also be made less descriptive in character. Finally, exercises should be staged in areas where no forces were to be deployed, simulating an incorrect tactical conduct.[26]

What were the Baltic Fleet's own personnel expected to know about the enemy? Already in May 1929, the fleet's intelligence section had distributed its first intelligence survey to inform on 'the naval forces of our likely and possible enemies'. From the autumn of 1931, the ambition was to publish these surveys monthly.[27] In the beginning of 1934, Chief of Staff Isakov reported that the other Baltic navies, as well as the navies of France and Britain, were in the focus of interest. Whereas junior commanding personnel were trained in the practical recognition of silhouettes of enemy ships and aircraft, middle-level commanders were expected to know about the composition, organization and tactics of enemy forces. The senior commanding personnel should also be informed about the organization of enemy units at an operational level, their peacetime localization, the training and morale of enemy personnel, their ethnicity and class background, the organization of enemy ground forces, their training for amphibious operations and the geography of the theater of operations. Finally, commanders at the highest level were expected to be well informed on conditions in the Pacific Theater too. There were, however, no books or leaflets available for the study of foreign navies, so the Baltic Fleet staff had to produce its own teaching material.[28]

Another weak spot was the supply of modern sea charts. Already in the spring of 1934, the Baltic Fleet's chief of staff had pointed out the lack of a modern geographical description of the Baltic Theater, proposing that a four-volume work should be produced in cooperation with the Naval War College. Work began that summer when Yevgeny Shvede of the college's department of military geography sailed aboard the training ship *Leningradsoviet* on its annual Baltic cruise.[29]

As has already been mentioned, new operational directives were issued for the Baltic Theater in March 1935, pointing out Germany as the main enemy. In addition to defending Leningrad and supporting the advance into Estonia, the Baltic Fleet was now also to eliminate the Finnish Navy and cut off communications between Germany, Finland and the Baltic states. Dimitry Rechister of the fleet staff's section of operations believed the fleet's air arm was too weak to solve all its new missions simultaneously: reconnoitering, bombing enemy bases, hunting submarines and protecting its own bases. To reinforce the air campaign, preparations had already been made to detach three wings of heavy bombers from the RKKA Western Front to the Baltic Fleet during the first two weeks of the war. However, Rechister observed, the Soviet air bases were not well located to attack targets outside the Gulf of Finland, nor would the stock of aircraft spare parts be sufficient for an extended campaign.

In addition, the surface fleet was expected to support the Red Army's invasion of Estonia from the very first week of the war. Rechister believed it would take at least three weeks from mobilization before the ships would be operational. Even the Ladoga Flotilla needed 14 days to get ready. Moreover, the 1935 campaign plan estimated that 4–5 days would be needed to deploy the mine-fields of the GOR, and about a week to deploy the distant forward defense zone. The plan also envisaged the capture of Great and Small Tootersaari, Lavansaari, Peninsaari and Seiskari on the second day of the war. After the Finnish inhabitants had been evacuated and artillery, supplies and building materials brought ashore, these five islands were to be fortified. Someri and Narvi would be captured on the third day, but only used as listening posts and anchoring sites for Soviet MTBs. The most distant island, Hogland, would be shelled but left unoccupied. Only if the enemy air forces had been destroyed and there were no German battleships operating in the Gulf would a landing attempt be undertaken. Of course, the Björkö batteries must also be dealt with, but hopefully they could be silenced from the air, after which a regiment-sized force was to be set ashore. However, as amphibious resources would hardly suffice, Rechister thought landing operations in southern Finland must be given lower priority than the islands in the Gulf. Efforts to organize a special amphibious squadron had begun only a year before, and there were still virtually no landing craft in the fleet. There were enough resources to transport one battalion, but only if horses and vehicles were left behind.[30]

Furthermore, apart from the battleships there were no units in the Baltic Fleet with sufficient firepower to support ground operations. In June 1935, Galler wrote to Voroshilov and proposed that two cruisers should be transferred from the Black

Sea to the Baltic for this purpose. In addition, a special amphibious brigade must be created with appropriate vessels and engineering equipment, as well as a squadron for archipelago warfare with gunboats and MTBs. Even if the Gulf islands could be captured successfully, Rechister added, there was also a need for anti-air artillery to defend them. Although the second five-year plan promised additional submarines for the Baltic Fleet, the serious shortage of minesweepers remained (Galler believed at least another four squadrons would be necessary).[31]

In short, the Baltic Fleet command was not confident in its capability. The following year, although the war plan remained largely unaltered, demands increased even further. According to directives from the Red Army chief of staff, Yegorov, enemy ports outside the Gulf of Finland (Pärnu, Riga) should be included on the list of objectives for the fleet's submarine operations. Also, there could be need to execute minor tactical landings east of Vyborg before the big push against Björkö. For instance, it would be convenient if during the first few days of the war the demolished Finnish fortifications at Ino (immediately west of the border) were seized and secured as a strong flank position for the ground forces.[32]

Toward a resurrection of the navy

Evidence suggests that in the course of 1935, the decision was made to build an ocean-going fleet during the third five-year plan. About this time, the Soviet government began to reestablish the navy as an autonomous fighting service and restore its former structures of command and control. In view of the rapid expansion that lay ahead and the growing operational demands on the naval forces, there was certainly good reason to increase their organizational independence.

Already in January 1935, the naval forces in the Baltic, the Black Sea and the Pacific theaters were elevated to the status of independent fleets. Fleet staffs were expanded to consist of an independent intelligence section (directly subordinated to the fleet commander) and eight special sections for operations, training, military communications, organization and mobilization, material and planning, personnel and signals and ciphers.[33]

At the central level, in May the office of commander of UVMS was changed into commander of the naval forces, to whom the fleets and flotillas were to be directly subordinate. Also, naval aviation, which since 1924 had been a part of the VVS, was transferred back to the naval commander's immediate control. In July, the UVMS was renamed UMS (*Upravlenie Morskikh Sil* = Directorate of the Naval Forces), and was equipped with a special section for operations and tactics, which the naval forces had lacked at the central level since the abolition of the Naval Staff in 1926.[34]

With this, the navy had regained a commander in chief of its own, an air arm of its own and something very similar to a central, executive operational command of its own. The last step in this process came on 23 September 1935, when the Soviet government reintroduced the system of personal ranks in the armed forces. Now, for the first time since 1918, there was also a naval officer corps.

Conclusion

During the Young School era, the navy had coastal defense and support of the Red army as its primary missions. The Baltic Fleet's ability to conduct joint operations in the main defense zone (GOR) in the Gulf of Finland seemed to have improved greatly, but the capacity to support the ground forces was less certain. As Soviet army doctrine was characterized by an aspiration for high mobility and offensive operations in depth, the fleet must possess a real capability for offensive operations and be able to operate at an increasing distance from its own home bases. Between 1930 and 1935, the Baltic Fleet's operational focus shifted gradually westwards. Defending Leningrad and supporting the ground forces' advance along the shores of the Gulf of Finland (which seemed a difficult task in itself) was no longer sufficient. If Finland and the Baltic states were to be denied reinforcements and supplies in a future war, the mouth of the Gulf must be the fleet's initial deployment area rather than the far end of its theater of operations. That the Baltic Fleet Staff doubted its capacity to solve its new missions is clear. Complaints were numerous about the lack of suitable ships, the training of personnel, the amphibious capacity, etc.

Organizationally, the Soviet Navy underwent a strange metamorphosis during the Young School era. Although central service functions such as the Naval Staff had been abolished some years before, special sections for operations, organization-tactics and intelligence were instead added to the regional fleet staffs as compensation. Then, in 1935, when the ocean-going fleet program was under way, the reestablishment of the old order could proceed smoothly.

Notes

1 Breyer, *Soviet Warship Development*, vol. I, pp. 35, 179–213, 224–31; Rohwer and Monakov, *Stalin's Ocean-going Fleet*, pp. 27–30, 35–38, 236–7, 243–4; cf. Berezovsky et al., *Boevaya letopis*, p. 566; Samuelson, 'Naval Dimension of Soviet Five Year Plans', p. 212; Monakov, 'Sudba doktrin i teory, 6', pp. 37–9.
2 Monakov, 'Sudba doktrin i teory, 8 [9, see p. 17, n. 11]', pp. 36–8.
3 The naval representatives were naval commander Orlov and his deputy Ludri, the commanders of the Baltic, Black Sea and Pacific Fleets Galler, Dushenov and Viktorov, their respective PUR commanders Grishin, Gutin and Okunev – Suvenirov, *RKKA nakanune*, pp. 321–7.
4 A. V. Kvasonkin (ed.), *Sovetskoe rukovodstvo: Perepiska, 1928–1941* (Moscow: Rosspen 1999), pp. 154–5.
5 Breyer, *Soviet War Ship Development*, vol. I, pp. 192–242; Rohwer and Monakov, *Stalin's Ocean-going Fleet*, pp. 42–55, 232–40; V. N. Burev, *Otechestvennoe korablostroenie v tretyem stoletii svoey istorii* (St Petersburg: Sudostroenie, 1995), pp. 129–56, 160–4, 166–8; cf. Monakov, 'Sudba doktrin i teory, 8 [9, see p. 17, n. 11]', pp. 37–8; Samuelson, 'Soviet Naval Five Year Plans', pp. 214–15.

6 Berezovsky et al., Boevaya letopis, p. 567.
7 Cf. introduction by A. M. Blinov to the catalogue of f. r-92, o. 1, RGAVMF.
8 Toshakov and Zinovyev to the commander of the destroyer flotilla et al., 22 May 1930, f. r-92, o. 12, d. 1, list 1–2.
9 RKKA Staff to Baltic Fleet and LVO Staffs, 30 December 1930, f. r-2041, o. 1, d. 7, list 1–2; cf. LVO (Tukhachevsky and Feldtman) to Baltic Fleet, 7 January 1931, ibid., list 3–7.
10 RKKA Staff to Baltic Fleet Soviet and LVO, 21 January 1932, f. r-92, o. 2, d. 181, list 2–3; chief of staff LVO to Baltic Fleet Soviet, 9 February 1932, ibid., list 6–7; head of operations LVO (no date), ibid., list 9.
11 RKKA Staff to Baltic Fleet Soviet and LVO, 21 January 1933, f. r-92, o. 2, d. 181, list 10–11; LVO to commander Baltic Fleet, 22 February 1933, ibid., list 14–17.
12 Berezovsky et al., Boevaya letopis, pp. 592–3.
13 In August 1931, the Baltic Fleet had began experimenting with fire control from the air, Berezovsky et al., Boevaya letopis, p. 582.
14 Cf. Baltic Fleet chief of staff Rechister to the commander of IUR (*Ikhursky Ukreplenny Rayon* = Ikhorsky Fortified Area), 19 February 1935, f. r-92, o. 1, d. 984, list 2–3.
15 The development of the mine defense doctrine can be followed in Berezovsky et al., *Boevaya letopis*, pp. 527, 538–9, 546, 548–9, 553, 555, 560; Rodionov's thesis dated 19 February 1935, 'Boy na glavnom oboronitelnom rubezhe pro popytke proryva ego protivnikom s morya; s prikluchenyami', f. r-92, o. 1, d. 984, list 6–21.
16 The 1935 operational plan can be found in f. r-2041, o. 1, d. 52, list 1–33.
17 Tukhachevsky and Feldtman to Baltic Fleet, 7 January 1931, f. r-2041, o. 1, d. 7, list 3-7.
18 The 1932 operational plan is dated 26 April and can be found in f. r-2041, o. 1, d. 20, list 1–24.
19 Berezovsky et al., Boevaya letopis, pp. 575–6; Zonin, *Admiral L. M. Galler*, pp. 259, 264–5.
20 Memorandum by commander Baltic Fleet, 31 October 1933, f. r-92, o. 2, d. 181, list 31–3; Zonin, *Admiral L. M. Galler*, pp. 259, 265–6; on Western estimates of Soviet performance see Petrovsky, 5 April 1933, 'Vyvody po materialam germanskoy, frantsuskoy i finskoy razvedki za 1932–33 g.', f. r-92, o. 12, d. 15, list 12.
21 Herrick, *Soviet Naval Theory and Strategy*, p. 52.
22 Petrovsky, 5 April 1933, 'Vyvody po materialam germanskoy, frantsuskoy i finskoy razvedki za 1932–33 g.', f. r-92, o. 12, d. 15, list 12.
23 Petrovsky, 5 April 1934, f. r-92, o. 12, d. 15, list 35–6, 74.
24 Yegorov to the Baltic Fleet Soviet and LVO, 2 April 1934, f. r-92, o. 2, d. 181, list 20–1; head of operations to Galler, 9 April 1934, ibid., list 22–4.
25 Isakov, 14 May 1934, f. r-92, o. 12, d. 15, list 78.
26 Petrovsky, 5 April 1934, 'Vozmozhnost maskiruyustikh i desorientiruyustikh meropriyatiy', f. r-92, o. 12, d. 15, list 76–7.
27 Baltic Fleet intelligence section, May 1929, 'Informatsionny bullentin no. 1', f. r-92, o. 12, d. 3, list 3–18; Zinovyev, 23 October 1931, f. r-92, o. 12, d. 7, list 22.
28 Isakov to UVMS, 13 February 1934, f. r-92, o. 2, d. 242, list 1–3.
29 Isakov to Aleksandrov, 10 April 1934, f. r-92, o. 12, d. 243, list 1; Shvede's report from *Leningradsoviet* dated 4 July 1934, ibid., list 25–7.
30 The 1935 operational plan from 25 May 1935, in f. r-2041, o.1, d. 52, list 1–33; Rechister's comments on operational directives in memorandum to commander of LVO, 4 April 1935, f. r-92, o. 2, d. 260, list 18–26; on transferring heavy bombers from the Western Front to the Baltic Fleet, see memorandum by RKKA head of operations, February 1934, f. r-2041, o. 1, d. 19, list 7; documents on the island squadron in f. r-2041, o. 1, d. 34.

31 Galler to Voroshilov, 7 June 1935, r-2041, o. 1, d. 76, list 1–7; on the fleet's mobilization and early warning procedures, see memorandum by Isakov and Rechister, 30 May 1935, r-2041, o. 1, d. 55.
32 Yegorov to Baltic Fleet, 15 March 1936, f. r-2041, o. 1, d. 19, list 12; the operational plan of 1936, signed by Galler and Chief of Staff Sivkov, 31 May, in f. r-2041, o. 1, d. 77.
33 Cf. introduction by A. M. Blinov to the catalogue of f. r-92, o. 1, RGAVMF.
34 Berezovsky *et al., Boevaya letopis*, pp. 598–600.

10

THE NAVY OF THE RED COMMANDERS

In spite of the new spirit of détente and cooperation in Soviet foreign policy in the late 1920s, the perception of the West remained hostile. In July 1927, Joseph Stalin proclaimed that peaceful coexistence between the Soviet Union and the West was now a thing of the past. He based his conclusion on certain recent events – the rupture of diplomatic relations with Britain, the expulsion of the Soviet diplomatic representative from Paris, the murder of the Soviet diplomatic representative in Warsaw. These allegations were repeated in a speech to the XVth Party Congress that same autumn. This so-called 'War Scare of 1927' has attracted much attention, as it helped to promote Stalin's rise to power. Most historians see it as a consequence of the internal power struggle within the ruling elite. As Adam B. Ulam has stated, it is highly unlikely that the Soviet government would have dared to launch the brutal policy of collectivization against the rural population the following year, had it earnestly believed that aggression from outside was imminent. Nor do the military archives from the period contain any evidence of genuine invasion fears. On the contrary, the notion of a general war during the next few years was regularly dismissed.[1]

But even if the 1927 crisis and the outbreak of collective hysteria that it fomented was a product of conspiracy and domestic tension, on a more profound level the feelings of vulnerability and impending crisis it revealed reflected the genuine mentality among Soviet leaders at the time. If the Soviet state was not be overtaken by the West, the country must acquire the proper means to defend itself. In a famous speech to the congress of all-union managers in February 1931, Stalin emphasized that unless Russia modernized rapidly, she would be beaten by the imperialist powers just as she been beaten by her enemies in the past – the Mongols and the Turks, the Poles and the Lithuanians, the Swedes and the Japanese, the British and the French: 'We are fifty to a hundred years behind the advanced countries. We must make good this distance in ten years. Either we do it or they crush us.'[2] As Stalin had stated two years before in a speech on Revolution Day 1929, Russia's long-felt sense of inferiority would turn into pride as soon as modernization had been accomplished:

> And when we have put the USSR in an automobile, and the *muzhik* on a tractor, let the esteemed capitalists, who boast of their 'civilization,' try

to overtake us. We shall see which countries may then be 'classified' as backward and which as advanced.[3]

Historians writing from a 'totalitarist' perspective have often pointed out the tragic consequences for the Russian peasantry of Stalin's radical policy. Through mass deportations and organized starvation, the opposition of the peasants was broken. Through forced collectivization, the Bolsheviks finally gained control over the countryside. Until the dissolution of the Soviet state in the early 1990s, dark memories of these events would loom over the rural population and contribute to its alienation from society.[4]

Those historians who represented a 'revisionist' or 'pluralist' perspective used to make a somewhat different interpretation of Soviet history in the early 1930s. Many of them had a background in the new social history of the 1970s, or in the Marxist tradition emanating from Stalin's contemporary rivals – Nikolay Bukharin and Leon Trotsky. They saw the Communist Party less as a monolithic structure, forcing itself upon society, than as an arena for competing societal interests, Stalin less as an almighty dictator than as a broker between rival fractions. Stalin labeled his policy 'a revolution from above'. Sheila Fitzpatrick, regarded as the foremost representative of the 'revisionist interpretation', also talked of Stalin's 'cultural revolution' – an expression pointing out parallels between events in the Soviet Union in 1928–32 and in Mao Zedong's China some 40 years later. The attack on the traditional intelligentsia was said to have had widespread support from below, especially among workers who had received administrative or technical education after the revolution and now found their careers blocked by bureaucrats and industrial managers trained in the old society. Collectivization was regarded as inevitable in view of the Soviet Union's international situation, or was analyzed in the perspective of the century-long struggle between city and countryside in Russia.[5]

There is no doubt that the party regarded collectivization as a prerequisite for the creation of an industrial economy in the Soviet Union. This economy was a war economy, primarily suited to producing armaments and ammunition in great quantities. This was not only because of the country's perceived vulnerability. Also, the production demands of a militarized economy were the kind of demands that could be most easily satisfied through a system of central planning. It was not in the works of Marx and Engels that the Bolsheviks had found the prototype for their economic planning model, but in the German war effort of 1914–18. Moreover, as Lennart Samuelson has demonstrated, they assumed that all the leading capitalist economies were directed by secret plans for industrial mobilization that would become functional in the event of war. In short, they saw the five-year plans as an instrument for Russia's westernization. By putting the *muzhik* on a tractor, the Soviet Union would catch up with and overtake the capitalist countries. Although the society that the Bolsheviks were about to create represented something entirely new and unsurpassed in the progress of human civilization, this gigantic leap could not be made without first learning from the West.[6]

The actual increase in Soviet GNP during the two first five-years plans (1928–37) is difficult to assess, especially if it is to be compared to the production increases of other European countries during their industrialization. According to some estimates, Soviet growth may have been as high as 50–60 percent per capita. What is important in this context is not the actual figures, but the fact that most ordinary people only saw their living conditions deteriorate. The five-year plans meant rationing of basic foodstuffs (famine in the countryside), a shortage of most goods, declining real wages, unspeakable housing conditions, frequent accidents in the factories and an intensified working pace. To control the movements of labor, draconian disciplinary measures were introduced against employees. Workbooks (in the Russian Republic) and domestic passports (in the entire USSR) appeared in 1930 and 1932 respectively. According to a statute from November 1932, unauthorized absence could result in discharge, which in turn led to eviction from the company-owned apartment and the suspension of ration cards. In 1935, the introduction of a cult around elite 'shock workers', like Donbas mineworker Alexander Stakhanov, added inflated work norms and increasing wage-differences to the picture.[7]

However, despite all the suffering created by Russia's forced industrialization, for many it also meant increased opportunities and an exciting acquaintance with urban life. Living in a city like Magnitogorsk could still be a fascinating experience compared to living in the countryside. As has been demonstrated through recent research, working conditions may also have been less severe in practice. The chronic shortage of manpower and the desperate need to meet centrally fixed plan goals meant that factories had to compete for trained labor and could not implement harsh regulations to the letter. Instead, locally workers could have a rather strong bargaining position against management.[8]

Apart from the *kulaks*, engineers and technicians with academic training – bourgeois specialists of the old society – were the real victims of Stalin's revolution. The first Stalinist show trial was staged in the Urals in the spring of 1928. It was no coincidence that the defendants were mining engineers, who were accused of wrecking and espionage on the behalf of Western intelligence services. In 1929, purges hit the People's Commissariat for Agriculture and in 1930, the so-called 'Industrial Party' was disclosed among officials and technical experts in the Gosplan (*Gosudarstvennaya planovaya Komissiya* = State Planning Commission).[9]

The navy and Stalin's Cultural Revolution

It is in this perspective that we should see the shift between the Old School and the Young School, the demise of the military specialists of the old society and the coming of the 'young red commanders'. The new Soviet Navy had to be oriented toward 'reality' and concrete goals, and had to do away with formalist, bourgeois theory. In the Naval War College, the leading role of the 'practical' faculty of naval warfare over the other three 'theoretical' faculties (naval weaponry, hydrography and ship construction) was established in 1930. In February 1931, the college was also named after Kliment Voroshilov, the People's Commissar for the Army and Navy, a staunch Bolshevik and Army man.[10]

The ideological principles which had directed the naming of warships since the 1920s lived on during the Young School period. Now, for the first time in Soviet history there was also a domestic production of warships. The first submarines launched in 1928–32 were named after revolutionary archetypes: the Revolutionary (*Revolutsioner*), the Komsomol Member (*Komsomolets*) and the Red Guard Man (*Krasnogvardets*) were honored, as were the disciples of various Soviet leaders: the Leninist (*Leninets*), the Stalinist (*Stalinets*) and even the Frunzeist (*Frunzovets*). Warships were also named after revolutionary activists dating back to the pre-1917 period: the Decembrist (*Dekabrist*), the member of the People's Will (*Narodvolets*). Nor was the Soviet Union's responsibility as leader of the world revolutionary movement forgotten. Submarines were named after the German Spartakist (*Spartakovets*), the French Jacobin (*Yacobinets*), the British Chartist (*Khartist*) as well as after the Italian Carbonari (*Karbonary*) and Garibaldi supporter (*Garibaldisets*).

Warships that were built later in the 1930s, however, were given fairly conventional names. The long series of submarines that went into production during 1932 and was later abbreviated as the Shch-class, was named after a fish, the pike (*Shchuka*). Other submarines were named after perches (*Okun, Yorzh*) or the burbot (*Nalim*). The class of midget submarines which was launched in 1933 were called M-submarines, simply due to the fact that they were small (*Malyutka* = baby). The famous class of submarines that went into production in 1936 and became the Soviet standard submarine in the Baltic during World War II was designated as the 'S'–class, simply because of its middle size (*sredny* = middle). The series of flotilla leaders which began appearing in 1933 were named after major Soviet cities: *Leningrad, Moskva, Kharkov, Minsk, Baku*.[11]

Concrete realism gradually pushed out revolutionary romanticism as a cultural ideal in Soviet society, even when it came to naming warships.

The red commanders

Robert W. Herrick has described in great detail the campaign in *Morskoy Sbornik* in 1928–32 against the so-called Old School of naval thinking.[12] The professors at the Naval War College, Boris Zherve and Mikhail Petrov, were the main targets of criticism, but who were the oppositionists? Just like Pavka Kortyagin, the famous social realist hero of Nikolay Ostrovsky's novel *How the Steel Was Tempered* (1932–34), the leaders of the Young School were children of the October Revolution, and consequently convinced that their relationship to life and reality was immediate and direct. They had served in the Civil War as political commissars. Later, they had been sent to study at the Naval War College, where many graduated in the class of 1927.

Ivan Martynovich Ludri (1895–1937) was the son of an Estonian peasant. He had entered the navy in 1911 as an NCO and joined the revolution at an early stage. In 1918, Ludri became deputy commissar and then chief commissar of the Kronstadt Naval Base. In 1920–21, he served as chief commissar for the Black Sea Fleet, and later as commander of the Caspian Flotilla. In 1923–27, Ludri attended the Naval War College and then served as commander of the coastal defences and as chief of staff of the Black Sea Fleet. In 1932, he became deputy commander of the Soviet naval forces and in 1936 commandant of the Naval War College. Ludri's article in the October 1927 issue of *Morskoy Sbornik* has been regarded as the first battle cry of the Young School. Here, Ludri stated that there could be no independent missions for the navy outside the common mission of the armed forces – to defend the country. He also labeled his opponents in the naval establishment as 'the Old School'. In a follow-up article 'On the Tactics of a Small-war Navy' (*O taktike malogo flota*) in March 1928, Ludri openly identified Professor Zherve with the Old School.[13]

Alexander Petrovich Alexandrov (1900–46) was a merchant sailor from Odessa who had been active during the Civil War in the military tribunals of the Black Sea Fleet. He is often portrayed as the cruelest and most fanatical of the Young School supporters. Because of his Jewish–proletarian background, Belli claimed, Alexandrov was full of hatred for the old regime, despised the tsarist specialists and did his best to humiliate them whenever he could.[14]

Alexandrov belonged to the class of 1927 at the Naval War College. Having served for a year in the Baltic Fleet aboard battleships and destroyers, he was appointed political commissar to the department of strategy at the Naval War College in October 1928. From this position, he launched a public campaign against his former teachers, who were now his colleagues. His first attack came in a series of articles in *Morskoy Sbornik* in 1929–30, in which he criticized the theory of command of the sea. New weapon systems such as aircraft and submarines, the present material conditions in the Soviet Union, the German failure during World War I with a 'small-wars' strategy aimed at force equalization – all these factors suggested that the teachings of Zherve and Petrov were wrong. Later, Alexandrov went even further and accused Zherve and Petrov of having 'propagated defeatism and sowed distrust in the force and power of our naval forces of the Red Army'. They had deliberately promoted the spread of reactionary theories on war, conspiring to this end with like-minded people in the RKKA, such as Alexander Svechin. Alexandrov served as head of the department of strategy in 1930–36 and later went to Spain as a military advisor during the Civil War. During World War II, he saw active service in the Azov Sea and Lake Ladoga. He served on the allied control commission in Finland in 1944 and was later appointed chief of staff of the Baltic Fleet. In January 1946, he was killed in a plane crash.[15]

Konstantin Ivanovich Dushenov (1895–1940) spelled his name Dushinov until 1925. He had entered the Baltic Fleet in 1915, had served as a clerk aboard the famous ship *Aurora* and in 1917 been elected secretary of the ship's committee. He participated in the storming of the Winter Palace and afterwards commanded the patrol that brought the imprisoned ministers of the Provisional Government to the Peter and Paul Fortress. In 1919, Dushenov joined the Communist Party and in the following years served as port commander, ship commander and chief of staff of the battleship squadron in the Black Sea. Later, he held various assignments in the Sea of Azov and in the Baltic. He also studied at the Naval War College in 1923–27 but did not graduate from there until 1928. After a tour as naval attaché in Japan he returned to the college as commissar and commandant in 1930, and was then reassigned to the Black Sea Fleet as chief of staff. Here, he remained until 1935, when he was appointed commander of the Northern Fleet in Murmansk. In an article in *Morskoy Sbornik* in March 1928, Dushenov was the first to point out the ideological dimension of the opposition against the Old School. Civil War veterans like himself, he claimed, found the traditional, bourgeois concepts of sea power one-sided, nondialectic and essentially non–Marxist.[16]

Alexander Yakimychev (1897–?), had been trained as a naval aviator during World War I. He had graduated from the Naval War College in 1926 and served on the college faculty until 1931, when he was promoted to chief of staff of the college. In 1934, he was appointed as deputy naval attaché to the United States and later commander of the foreign section of the reestablished Naval Staff. In September 1928, Yakimychev was the first to label the opposition against the Old School the 'Young School', which he did in an article entitled 'War of a "Small (Weak) Navy" and "Small Wars" in the Era of the Steam Navy' (*Voyna 'malym (slabym) flotom' i 'malaya voyna' v epokhu parovoga flota*).[17]

The Soviet naval commanders during the Young School era – Romuald Adamovich Muklevich and Vladimir Mitrofanovich Orlov – were less impressive in their academic achievements. Nonetheless, they must also be included among the figureheads of the Young School.

Muklevich (1890–1938) was the son of a Polish textile worker. He had joined the Bolshevik Party in 1906 at the age of 16. He was called up to the navy in 1912 and remained in service after the outbreak of war in 1914. At the time of the 1917 revolution, Muklevich served as an NCO at the Navy Motorist School in Kronstadt. As a reliable party veteran, he received important assignments from the PUR RKKA during the Civil War. He served as commissar of the Sixteenth Army, and later as chief commissar on the Western Front. In 1922–25 he was commissar of the RKKA Academy and deputy commander of the Soviet Air Force. After a short term as deputy chairman of civil aviation, Muklevich returned to the navy in 1926 to succeed Zof as commander in chief. In this capacity, he served until 1931, loyally administering the extensive purges of 1930–31. In a speech to the students of the Naval War College in Leningrad around 1930, reported by Admiral Kuznetsov in his memoirs, Muklevich chose to formulate the dilemma of the Soviet Union's naval policy as a choice between 'the Gulfs or the Sounds'. Should the Soviet state build a navy suitable for littoral warfare, capable of operating in the Gulf of Finland but not beyond? Should the tradition from the tsarist era be continued, Russia advance through the sounds in the Baltic and the Black Seas and become an oceanic power? According to Muklevich, the Soviet Navy should above all be a strong navy. As the Soviet Union had no ambitions for global domination, it would need no battleships or heavy cruisers. But a fleet with many different types of ships, capable of solving various tasks, would still be needed.[18]

Vladimir Mitrofanovich Orlov (1895–1938) had been called up to the navy in 1916. He underwent training as an NCO, participated in the evacuation of the Baltic Fleet in 1918, joined the communist Party and was subsequently sent on an officer's crack training course. His next assignment had been as chief commissar of the Baltic Fleet in 1920–21. After a short interlude in the civilian water transport administration he returned to the navy as deputy chief commissar. In 1923–26, he served as chief commissar of the naval schools and in 1926 replaced Eduard Pantserzhansky as commander of the Black Sea Fleet. As the most high-ranking Soviet naval functionary going abroad on an official visit during the inter-war period, Orlov visited Germany in 1930. In 1931, he was chosen to replace Zof as Soviet naval commander. He is credited with having rehabilitated many of the victims of the 1930–31 purges.[19]

In conclusion, most of the red commanders came from a proletarian background. They had joined the party or the military during the Civil War and had been formed by this conflict, in which naval forces had played their main role in supporting the RKKA, operating close to shore or along the rivers. Some of them had first-hand experience of the struggle against the British in the Baltic in 1919, when airplanes, torpedo craft and submarines had proved more efficient weapons than battleships. Few of them had seen active command at sea. Instead, the primary military experience of the Young School advocates came from service in the political apparatus.

Political control: building a proletarian navy

The Soviet Navy was not immune to the general trends of the first five-year plan period. Through increased recruitment among working-class youth, the party decided, the military forces were to be rejuvenated and the political-ideological standards of their commanding personnel improved. According to a resolution by the Central Committee in February 1928, 50 percent of the students at military schools should be workers. About a year later, the number was raised to 60 percent.[20]

Not only must the admission to military schools change, but also the teaching itself. Bourgeois theorizing should be replaced with preparations for 'real life'. At the Naval War College, Zherve was forced to leave his position as commandant and take over the department of strategy instead. His former student Dushenov replaced him and started to revise curricula to make them better suited to the naval forces' practical needs. Greater emphasis should also be put on the study of the Marxist–Leninist theory, so that graduates of the main three-year staff course could serve as one-man commanders when they returned to service. The number of study hours dedicated to 'the Marxist–Leninist study of war and the army' soon outdistanced those spent on operational art.[21]

Another facet of the politicization of Soviet society at the time was the *spez-edstvo* campaigns, 'specialist bashing' directed against academically trained specialists of the old society. This movement also took its toll of the Navy. In 1930–31, about 100 former tsarist officers were arrested as saboteurs and counterrevolutionaries, accused of having links to the Gosplan 'Industrial Party'. It was perhaps no surprise that the first arrests were made in at the UVMS's technical administration, as engineers were popular targets for specialist bashing.[22] Mikhail Petrov was also arrested, but most other victims were serving in the Baltic Fleet. Already in January 1930, the head of the Baltic Fleet PUR, Grigory Kireyev, had received a secret report from OGPU which warned of widespread discontent among the commanding personnel in his force, especially among those with a past as tsarist officers.[23] In mid-October, professors Zherve, Belli, Pell and Goncharov were arrested at the Naval War College. In Kronstadt, Chief of Staff Arkady Toshakov fell victim and so did eight out of five squadron commanders, one out of two battleship commanders, ten out of 12 destroyer commanders and five out of nine submarine commanders. Most of those arrested were sentenced to ten years in a labor camp.[24]

Already by the end of 1933, the majority had been released. Zherve, who was arrested in February 1931, was liberated after only a few months. As a part of his rehabilitation, he had to send a letter to the editorial board of *Morskoy Sbornik* (published in the March 1932 edition) recanting his former beliefs. Zherve admitted that the theory on command of the sea had been a 'bourgeois-reactionary theory completely inapplicable to Soviet conditions'. After that, he was able to move to Moscow were he was employed as professor at the RKKA academies for engineers and PUR personnel. He died in 1934.[25]

Belli, who was a professor in Zherve's department, was also arrested on the night of the 15 October 1930. After a night at the local OGPU in Leningrad, he was brought to Lubyanka Prison in Moscow where he spent the next four months in a cell with 14 others, most of them former naval officers. In February 1931, he was shipped off to Butyrsky Prison, where conditions were much worse than in Lubyanka. Here, up to a hundred prisoners had to share one cell, and ordinary criminals sat together with the members of the repressed 'intelligensia'.

Belli did not yet know why he had been arrested, and only in June did he learn that he – like all other former naval officers – had been given a ten-year sentence. Together with three colleagues, he was sent to a prison camp in Krasnovechersk in Siberia, on the River Visher. Luckily, the director of the local steamship company was a former sailor who had served under Belli before the revolution, so he was assigned to light office work instead of hard outdoor labor. After about two months in the camp, Belli and his colleagues were suddenly told that they would be released and were transferred back to Butyrsky Prison in Moscow. Among the prisoners who had been brought here they recognized Mikhail Petrov and the famous strategist of the Red Army, Alexander Svechin. Then, however, several months passed without anything happening. Only in December did prisoners begin to be released. Belli was freed on New Year's Eve and spent the first night of 1932 alone on the street, outside a railway station. The next day, the newly appointed deputy commander of the naval forces, Ivan Ludri, received him at the

UVMS headquarters. Ludri supplied him with a new ID, money and instructions to return home to Leningrad and the Naval War College. Here, he was reinstated as professor in his old department, which had now been renamed the department of strategy and operational art to emphasize its concern with the practical aspects of warfare, and was headed by Alexandrov. Alexandrov forced Belli to renounce the theory of command of the sea and to promise to break off all relations with Zherve. This, Belli readily accepted. After all, less than 48 hours before, he had still been in prison. For many years, he suspected that Alexandrov was the person who had denounced him. Only later, after his full rehabilitation in 1953, Belli learnt that he had become a victim simply because he had served in the Naval Staff in the early 1920s.[26]

Like Belli, most of the former tsarist officers who returned from captivity were employed as teachers in military schools or in staff work, but not in active command.[27] Miracuolously, both the Baltic Fleet commander, Viktorov, and his battleship squadron commander, Galler, were spared. Galler's biographer Zonin attributes this to the fleet PUR commander, Kireyev, who belonged to the influential class of 1927 at the Naval War College and who recommended both Viktorov and Galler for admission as party members (they were accepted in 1932).[28]

When the former tsarist officers had been removed, the vacancies could be filled up with loyal party men. Finally, Frunze's one-man command reform could be effectively implemented. During the course of 1931, almost three times as many one-man commanders were appointed as during the preceeding four years combined.

In December 1931, the superior, senior and middle groups of commanders (from fleet commander down to commanders of minor ships/company size units) in the Baltic Fleet numbered altogether 166 men. Out of these, 63 served aboard ships, 66 commanded coastal batteries and infantry units ashore, 25 were commanders of schools, bases and other ground facilities and 12 served in the air arm. Out of these 166 commanders, 103 were party members and almost half (79) had been approved as one-man commanders.[29]

Most of these 79 belonged to the 'generation of tempered steel'. Only nine of them had been party members before 1918, and not one had been in the military before 1917. Their proletarian background was also typical of Civil War upstarts: 41 were sons of workers, 23 sons of peasants and only 15 sons of officials.

The number of one-man commanders appointed in the Baltic Fleet, 1926–31[30]

Year	Number
1926	6
1927	2
1928	1
1929	6
1930	7
1931	57

A few months later, in May 1932, the number of party members was even somewhat lower among commanding personnel – 98 compared to 103 in December. The number of one-man commanders had also gone down from 79 to 71. On the other hand, another 18 commanders were soon to be promoted to one-man commander status, raising the total number of one-man commanders in the Baltic Fleet to 88, or 94.8 percent of all party members among the commanding personnel.[31]

As could be expected, in the superior category of commanding personnel the concentration of one-man commanders was the highest – 25 out of 33. Among the seven squadron commanders the only one not to be a one-man commander was Galler, who had not yet been admitted as party member. In the senior and middle groups of commanding personnel, 25 out of 65 and 29 out of 68 were one-man commanders. All in all, among the 63 commanders of ships and ship squadrons, no more than 26 had been trusted with the status of one-man commander. None of the two battleship commanders was a one-man commander, only nine out of 12 destroyer commanders and no more than three out of 15 submarine commanders.[32]

A possible reason for the slow influx of proletarian submarine commanders was that this was a technically advanced weapon system. The proportion of commanders with a complete secondary education in the submarine force even exceeded that among personnel serving in the fleet staff (27 out of the 30 submarine officers compared to 26 out of 36 staff officers). In the summer of 1935, out of 30 command posts in the submarine force (squadron commanders and political officers included), as many as six (one squadron commander and five ship commanders) were filled with former noblemen. Out of the remaining 24 commanders, 16 were sons of workers, two sons of peasants and six sons of officials. Of those 16 'working-class commanders', only six commanded ships while the majority served as political officers.[33]

Thus, after the 1930–31 purges, establishing the one-man command system no longer seemed to be a major problem in the Baltic Fleet. However, in the mid-1930s, the PUR personal files still had special columns for noting if an individual had served with the enemy, been an enemy prisoner or stayed in enemy territory during the Civil War. If he had relatives or contacts abroad, if he had relatives who were *lishensy* (belonged to social groups which had been the deprived of their citizens' rights after the revolution: priests, merchants or bourgeois) or had a criminal record, this was also to be registered.[34]

In the Baltic Fleet intelligence section, the six commanders were all party members. However, the educational requirements of intelligence work meant that most of them – from a Bolshevik point of view – had a problematic social background.

The head of the section, Alexander Yevseyev, was born in 1902 as the son of a musician. Yevseyev had some higher education and knew English. He had been in the armed forces since 1922, had graduated from the Naval Academy in 1925, become a party member in 1927 and graduated from the Naval War College in 1931.

I. A. Babenko, born in 1905 as the son of an official and a peasant woman, had a secondary education, knew English and possessed a reading ability in French and German. He had entered the military in 1927 and become a party member that same year.

Evgeny Vostrykh was born in 1902 as the son of an official, and had served in the military since 1924. Vostrykh's brother had emigrated to Norway in 1919, but after having denounced him Vostrykh had been allowed as a party member and later into the Naval Academy, from which he graduated in 1932.

Mikhail Karpyshev was born in 1906 as the son of a petit bourgeois. He had entered the RKKA as volunteer in 1925 and had graduated from the Naval Academy in 1928.

Nikolay Tulmets was also the son of an official and had graduated from the Naval Academy in 1930.

The only person with a genuine working-class background was Nikolay Petrovich Timofeyev, born in 1897. In addition, Timofeyev was also the only one apart from the section head, Yevseyev, who had a degree from the Naval War College.[35]

The introduction of personal ranks in 1935

On 23 September 1935, the People's Commissariat for Defense announced the introduction of personal titles of ranks in the Soviet armed forces. Whereas before the titles of Soviet military personnel had been dependent on their assignment, from now on each individual would keep his title until he was either promoted or sentenced to degradation by a court-martial (the verdict of which had to be affirmed by the People's Commissariat for Defense). The formal training and the time of service required for each rank were officially regulated. Also, a clear distinction was made between commanders who had risen through the ranks and those who had been awarded their commission after having attended a regular military academy. Although the traditional title 'officer' was not yet used (it was introduced only in 1943), the names of most ranks roughly corresponded to those used in other countries or in imperial Russia. Among the five persons who in November 1935 were awarded the highest rank of Marshal of the Soviet Union was People's Commissar Voroshilov, who had previously made do with the humble status of Red Army man (*krasnoarmets*).

No doubt the party saw the introduction of rank as a cheap way to raise the status of the military profession and improve recruitment to the armed forces. About the same time, a judicial reform was introduced which allowed for military personnel to be tried separately by military courts, even for civil crimes. The official justification for personal ranks spoke of the need to 'enhance the prestige of commanders and strengthen discipline'.[36]

In the naval forces, the former 14 main categories of personnel were replaced with 14 ranks (15 in the coastal artillery and naval air force): Red Navy man (*krasnoflotets*), Squad-Leader, Sergeant, Junior Lieutenant, Lieutenant, Senior Lieutenant, Captain-Lieutenant (Captain in the coastal artillery and naval air force), Captain 3rd rank (Major), Captain 2nd rank (Colonel, the rank of Lieutenant-Colonel in the coastal artillery and naval air force having no equivalent in the fleet), Captain 1st rank (Brigadier), Flagman 2nd Rank (Division-Commander), Flagman 1st rank (Corps Commander), Flagman of the Fleet 2nd rank (Army Commander 2nd rank), Flagman of the Fleet 1st rank (Army Commander 1st rank). There were special titles for PUR and technical personnel, whose ranks were organized according to a similar hierarchy.

When the first ranks were awarded in November 1935, the highest rank – Flagman of the Fleet 1st rank – was awarded to Orlov and Viktorov, naval commander and commander of the Pacific Fleet respectively. The fleet commanders in the Baltic and the Black Sea (Galler and Kozhanov) were appointed Flagman of the Fleet 2nd rank. Another five men were appointed Flagman 1st rank (Northern Fleet Commander Dushenov, Kadatskiy-Rudnev – commander in the Azov Sea – Deputy Pacific Fleet Commander Kireyev, Deputy Naval Commander Ludri and Head of Naval Training Pantserzhansky).[37]

Only a few weeks before these appointments were made, mineworker Alexander Stakhanov had set his miraculous coal-cutting record, and in February 1936 the naval forces assembled their own 'Stakhanovite workers' for a four-day conference in Leningrad.[38]

In distancing itself from programatic egalitarianism, the navy was in pace with general developments in the Soviet Union. New elites, having ousted the old ones, were consolidating their positions.

Ideological leadership – with growing instability on the home front

When the one-man command reform began to change the political officer's role from party watchdog to chief agitator, there were different opinions on what he was to do during combat. In his article in *Morskoy Sbornik* in 1926, which was cited in Chapter 7, A. Melenkovsky concluded that political work must continue even during combat, as political work in the navy was not waged for its own sake but for the sake of victory. Even if there was no time to hold meetings or give lectures if in the midst of battle, political officers could inspire courage in weaker comrades, calm panic during gas attacks or take command of enemy ships whose crews had hoisted the red flag and deserted to the Soviet side.[39]

The newly appointed naval commander, Romuald Muklevich, who had spent most of his military career in the PUR, favored a more active military use of political officers. Provided their personal ability allowed, he thought PUR personnel should serve in ordinary commanding positions during combat. In a special directive from 1927, he stated that while the ship's commissar and his deputy were to stay close to the ship's commander, the remaining PUR personnel aboard could command artillery turrets, guard posts or fire brigade units.[40] According to a resolution by the RVS in 1930, naval PUR personnel should have a military competence at least equivalent to that below their own rank, so that a senior political officer could serve as watch officer, a political officer in the middle group as deputy watch officer.[41]

At this time, collectivization and industrialization were affecting military discipline in such a negative way that other tasks seemed more urgent for the PUR than discussing the combat role of its personnel. In 1933, the security organs registered some 346,711 'negative statements' among RKKA personnel, which was more than a 10 percent increase compared to 1932. Especially frequent were complaints about taxes and fees (31,564), and complaints about shortage of food and goods (79,194).[42] However, given the exclusive workers' recruitment to the navy, this was probably a lesser problem in the Baltic Fleet than in the Red Army.

When trying to describe the domestic forces that threatened an effective war effort, during the 1920s the war game scenarios of the Baltic Fleet had pointed to narrow-minded Caucasian nationalists or less enlightened peasants and workers worrying about rationing. Around 1930, when Russia was experiencing conditions close to civil war under the turmoil of collectivization, the portrayal of domestic enemies in war game scenarios took on a more alarmist tone. In exercises staged in March 1930 and February 1933 together with the LVO and the Naval War College respectively, flaws in the home front were no longer explained as the result of ignorance among the masses. Instead, saboteurs and enemies of the people were portrayed as deliberate conspirators. It was stated that the working class and the *majority* of the peasantry supported the Soviet war effort, but kulaks and urban NEP elements (bourgeois circles, intellectuals) were sympathizing with the enemy. Among these groups the secret police, OGPU, was said to have disclosed unreliable persons. The slogans that would be used to mobilize the masses identified kulaks and NEP men as enemies and urged the rest of the citizens to gather firmly around the party and its traditions. While in the 1930 exercise the slogans only mentioned Lenin as a great inspiration and leader of the party, in the 1933 exercise Stalin had been added. The war game instructions also contained directives for the propaganda campaign which was to boast morale among Soviet soldiers and sailors. The coming struggle should be described as the final battle against capitalism. All over the world, the poor and oppressed would look with sympathy upon the Soviet Union. The external capitalist enemies were no longer depicted as overwhelmingly superior in strength. Rather, their aggressiveness stemmed from despair over the Soviet Union's successful industrialization. Also, the Western communist parties were attributed a more active role as supporters of the Soviet war effort compared to the scenarios of the 1920s. They were said to agitate among the enemy soldiers, organize strikes and sabotage actions in arms factories and ports, spurring the proletariat of their home countries with slogans like 'The country of socialism is in danger – all working people rally to its defense!'[43]

The concern for the moral-ideological aspects of a future conflict also tainted the appreciation of the fighting value of foreign navies. This is especially apparent from the 1930 war game, which had as its main purpose to examine the 'political securing of operations' during a campaign against Finland in which the Finns were supported by a British expeditionary squadron.[44] To this end, the war game instructions contained rather detailed descriptions of the enemy's morale.

With regard to the Royal Navy, it was pointed out that class consciousness among the sailors was low, in spite of the fact that 70 percent of the recruits came from a working-class background. Discipline was strict and officers and NCOs enjoyed great authority. In recent years, however, there had been some signs of unrest. During the naval visits to the Baltic in 1927, the distribution of communist propaganda leaflets among the crews had led to shore leave being restricted. Although the commanding admiral had offered a reward to anyone who could help to identify the perpetrators, no informers had come forward.[45]

In the Finnish Navy, fighting morale was believed to be worse. As a rule, navy conscripts came from fishermen's or farmers' homes. The sons of workers and rural poor were sent to the army. The severe discipline (which included flogging) had caused suicides among servicemen, and in spite of the prohibition in Finland at the time, drinking was widespread. Living conditions in the barracks and aboard ships constituted another source of discontent.[46]

Although the furthering of world revolution was no longer a mission of the Soviet Navy, the tendency to interpret relations with the surrounding world in the light of ideology still influenced the analysis of Soviet prospects in a future war. The Western communist parties were expected to undermine the enemy's preparations for war. Any major Soviet military success could initiate a popular rising in the enemy camp. That the enemy's fighting morale would be inferior to that of the Soviets was more or less taken for granted.

Modernization – through OsoAviaKhim

In order to make Soviet conscripts better prepared for military service, according to the 1924 national service law youngsters had to undergo some 200 hours of preparatory soldier training before call-up. When they later arrived at their unit, they were expected to know some elementary drill, how to handle their rifle and to move in the terrain. This way, a greater portion of the regular service time could be dedicated to specialist training. The system of pre-conscription training was an example of how the Soviet regime tried to come to terms with Russia's perceived backwardness in relation to the surrounding world. However, due to the lack of competent instructors and the high level of absenteeism, these courses were never particularly efficient.[47]

The naval preparatory training organization was formed in 1925 as a joint project between the Navy, the PUR RKKA and the Komsomol. Training centers were set up in coastal and riverine regional metropolises. The navy and the induction boards (*voenkomnaty*) supplied the installations, the training equipment and the instructors. According to plan, training was to be organized for one month during each of the two summers preceding the recruit's call-up. In the period of 1926–28, a total of 10,577 people passed through the naval pre-conscription program. After its formation in 1927, the voluntary Society for Defense, Aviation and Chemistry (OsoAviaKhim) become increasingly involved.[48]

In the autumn of 1932, the RVS decided to transfer the whole responsibility for preparatory military training – including training facilities and equipment – to the

OsoAviaKhim. According to a directive from the LVO staff in November 1932, the contingent subject to naval preparatory training in the coming year counted some 23,300 men, all born in 1911–12. In addition, each training center was expected to call up some extra 15–20 percent to their regular quotas, in order to compensate for possible absentees, people liberated from their service obligations because of marriage etc.

For the class of 1911, the basic training program was to be organized as a 30-day continuous course at the OsoAviaKhim centers or aboard the organization's training ships. However, some 7,680 of the 10,700 naval draftees born this year – the two-thirds who were physically most fit and best educated – were to undergo specialist training, which meant evening classes without 'absence from production', presumably in the workplace. For the class of 1912, the entire pre-conscription training was to take place without 'absence from production'. Apparently, the pressure of the five-year plan admitted no other solution.

No conscripts from the Pri–Volga Military District, which included the rebellious Tatarstan Republic, nor any conscripts from the rural 'Kulak-infested' Ukrainian Military District, were deemed suitable to become specialists. In order to keep 'alien elements' out of the ranks, the training centers were to investigate the social class of draftees, if necessary by contacting their workplaces. It was suspected that people who had been deprived of their citizen's rights due to social background would try to sneak their way back into the voting register by turning up for military service. Commanding personnel from the navy or RKKA reserves were to serve as instructors. There was to be about one junior instructor for each 15 conscripts, one middle-level instructor for each 50, one senior instructor for each 200 conscripts and one political instructor for each 400.[49]

As can well be imagined, the standards of training must have been low with this limited number of instructors. In a report to the OsoAviaKhim in February 1933, the head of the Baltic Fleet Personnel Section, Yagunov, described drill and discipline during the past year's training as insufficient. Recruits did not know how to stand or turn at different commands, or how to chose a suitable firing position in the terrain. They were good at shooting but did not know how to clean their rifles. Training aboard the ships was good but not the training in tactics or the pre-conscript specialist training, in which the distribution of recruits to various programs did not correspond with their civilian education. Conscripts sent to become wireless operators had proven barely literate, conscripts selected to become mechanics ignorant of mathematics. Training centers were described as understaffed and ill-equipped, instructors as ill-prepared and lacking in authority. Moreover, due to lax supervision, the level of absence among recruits was high.[50]

Apparently, the pre-conscription training and the privileged selection of conscripts did not prevent the navy from winding up with hundreds of poorly educated sailors anyway. After their call-up there were neither time nor resources to fill in the gaps in their education. These problems would only increase as the children of the chaotic Civil War era grew old enough for military service.

Conclusion

In various sectors of Soviet society, Stalin's revolution from above signified a major attack against professional cadres and academically trained expertise. In the navy, the 'military specialists' of the old regime had to give way to 'red commanders', brought up during the Civil War in the ranks of the PUR. This shift was made possible largely through to the massive purge of 1930–31, which swept away about a hundred former imperial officers. Most of those arrested were later released and some even returned to service, although seldom to active command. The cleansing of the ranks allowed for a more thorough implementation of Frunze's reforms. In 1931 alone, three times as many one-man commanders were appointed in the Baltic Fleet as during the preceeding four years combined. In some positions, however, where the demands for experience and specialist skills were high, such as in the submarine force, a large portion of commanding personnel with bourgeois or aristocratic origins remained.

That the Old School gave way to the Young School was not only a result of commanders from a proletarian background taking over the navy from the elites of the previous society. The cult in Stalinist society dedicated to concreteness also contributed to the shifts between the two schools. According to Stalinist self-perception, the naval doctrine of the proletarian state must be derived from 'reality' and from the naval forces' actual missions, not from abstract books by foreign authors on the 'command of the sea'. Abstraction gave way to concretion in other fields as well under the Young School. Most of the new Soviet warships that were constructed in the 1930s were given simple names that alluded to their size – even when they were named after fish – or named after Soviet cities.

The introduction of personal ranks for military personnel in 1935 marked the culmination of a process to integrate the officer corps with the ruling elite in Soviet society, initiated by Frunze's one-man command reform some ten years earlier. At the same time, the function of political commissars became increasingly vague when more and more naval commanders were trusted party members. Although commissars were required to have a certain minimum of military competence, the interest in their role as ideological leaders grew. The concern with the psychological dimensions of warfare may well have reflected an increased awareness of the instability of the Soviet home front after collectivization. Nonetheless, a basic assumption on the part of the Soviets was still that the enemy's fighting morale and discipline would be inferior. This may have been a way to compensate for feelings of inferiority with regard to other factors, such as general education. OsoAviaKhim's experience from preparatory conscription training indicated that the 'level of civilization' among Soviet navy recruits – in spite of a rigorous selection of conscripts – was quite modest.

Notes

1 Robert C. Tucker, *Stalin in Power: The Revolution from Above, 1928–1941* (New York: Norton, 1990), pp. 69–80; Hildermeier, *Geschichte der Sowjetunion*, pp. 357–8; Ulam,

Expansion and Coexistence, pp. 165–7, 181–2; Samuelson, *Plans for Stalin's War Machine*, pp. 34–7, 69–70.
2 Quoted from Richard Overy, *Russia's War* (London: Penguin, 1997), p. 19.
3 Quoted from Kotkin, *Magnetic Mountain*, p. 29.
4 Robert Conquest, *The Harvest of Sorrow: Soviet Collectivization and the Terror-Famine* (London: Hutchinson, 1986); Martin Malia, *The Soviet Tragedy: A History of Socialism in Russia, 1917–1991* (New York: Free Press, 1994); Tucker, *Stalin in Power*.
5 Sheila Fitzpatrick presented her interpretation in 'New Perspectives on Stalinism', *Russian Review*, vol. 45 (1986); cf. also her works *Cultural Revolution in Russia, 1928–1932* (Bloomington, IN: Indiana University Press, 1978); *Education and Social Mobility in the Soviet Union, 1921–1934* (Cambridge: Cambridge University Press, 1979); *The Cultural Front: Power and Culture in Revolutionary Russia* (Ithaca, NY: Cornell University Press, 1992); a Marxism-inspired social historian, who was critical of Stalin's revolution and collectivization while sympathetic of the regime's impatience with the 'backwardness' of the countryside, was Moshe Lewin, author of *The Making of the Soviet System: Essays in the Social History of Inter-War Russia* (New York: Pantheon, 1985).
6 Samuelson, *Plans for Stalin's War Machine*, passim.
7 Hildermeier, *Geschichte der Sowjetunion*, pp. 368–77, 415–23, 483–7, 521–3.
8 Ibid., pp 515–21; Kotkin, *Magnetic Mountain*, pp. 157–280; cf. also Robert W. Thurston, *Life and Terror in Stalin's Russia, 1934–1941* (New Haven, CT: Yale University Press, 1996), pp. 164–98.
9 Hildermeier, *Geschichte der Sowjetunion*, pp. 409–10.
10 Ponikarovsky *et al.* (eds), *Voenno-morskaya akademiya*, p. 75.
11 Breyer, *Soviet Warship Development*, vol. I, pp. 183–206.
12 Herrick, *Soviet Naval Theory and Policy*, pp. 19–64.
13 Dotsenko, *Morskoy biograficheskiy slovar*, p. 256; E. N. Shoshkov, *Repressirovannoe OSTEKHBYURO* (St Petersburg: Nauchnoinformatsionnoe tsentr Memorial 3, 1995), p. 161; Herrick, *Soviet Naval Theory*, pp. 19, 59–60 n. 1; Monakov and Berezovsky, 'Sudba doktrin i teory', 5, p. 16.
14 Belli, f. r-2224, o. 1, d. 4, list 152.
15 Herrick, *Soviet Naval Theory*, pp. 29–36, 38–46; biographical information, Dotsenko, *Morskoy biograficheskiy slovar*, p. 21; Barsukov and Zolotarev (eds), *Russky arkhiv*, vol. I.2, pp. 383–4.
16 Herrick, *Soviet Naval Theory*, pp.19–20; Monakov and Berezovsky, 'Sudba doktrin i teory, 5', p. 18; Dotsenko, *Morskoy biograficheskiy slovar*, p. 154; Shoshkov, *Repressirovannoe OSTEKHBYURO*, pp. 155–7.
17 Herrick, *Soviet Naval Theory*, pp. 22–6, 36–8, 60 n. 8; Ponikarovsky *et al.* (eds), *Voennoya-morskaya akademiya*, p. 64; Monakov, 'Sudba doktrin i teory, 6', p. 34.
18 Dotsenko, *Morskoy biograficheskiy slovar*, p. 286; Shoshkov, *Repressirovannoe OSTEKHBYURO*, pp. 161–2; Kuznetsov, *Nakanune*, pp. 52–3.
19 Dotsenko, *Morskoy biograficheskiy slovar*, pp. 308–9; Shoshkov, *Repressirovannoe OSTEKHBYURO*, p. 163.
20 Reese, *Stalin's Reluctant Soldiers*, p. 105.
21 Ponikarovsky *et al.*, *Voenno-morskaya akademiya*, pp. 71–9.
22 Shoshkov, *Repressirovannoe OSTEKHBYURO*, pp. 91–2, 154, 157; Dotsenko, *Morskoy biograficheskiy slovar*, p. 120.
23 Zonin, *Admiral L. M. Galler*, pp. 251–2.
24 Ibid., pp. 253–5; Shoshkov, *Repressirovannoe OSTEKHBYURO* , pp. 161–2.
25 Zherve's letter quoted from Herrick, *Soviet Naval Theory*, p. 48; Dotsenko, *Morskoy biograficheskiy slovar*, p. 165.
26 Belli, f. r-2224, o. 1, d. 4, list 177–80.
27 Zonin, *Admiral L. M. Galler*, pp. 260–2.

28 Ibid., p. 252; on the time of their admission to the Party, see Suvenirov, *RKKA nakanune*, p. 50.
29 Lyubich and Shakhov, 15 December 1931, f. r-34, o. 2, d. 1460, list 1–2; the numbers are given as 26 ship commanders, 33 ground unit commanders, 16 commanders of schools and bases and seven commanders of air units. However, the total sum of one-man commanders in that case would have been 82 instead of 79. One sometimes comes across counting errors in PUR documents.
30 Lyubich and Shakhov, 15 December 1931, f. r-34, o. 2, d. 1460, list 1–2.
31 Lyubich and Shakhov, 25 May 1932, f. r-34, o. 2, d. 1460, list 15.
32 Lyubich and Shakhov, 15 December 1931, f. r-34, o. 2, d. 1460, list 1–2.
33 'Neskolko svediniy na kommandirov shtaba KBF, sostavlennye na osnovanii ikh avtobiografiy', f. r-2185, o. 2, d. 1549, list 10–17, 28–30.
34 Ibid., list 10–17.
35 Ibid., list 11; 'razvedatlny otdel 1935 1.7', ibid., list 20.
36 Suvenirov, *RKKA nakanune*, p. 180.
37 Berezovsky *et al.*, *Boevaya letopis*, pp. 600–1.
38 Ibid., p. 602.
39 Melenkovsky, 'Poltirabota v flote'.
40 Commander of the naval forces, no date 1927 (draft), f. r-34, o. 2, d. 1304, list 472.
41 Suvenirov, *RKKA nakanune*, p. 164.
42 Ibid., p. 167; von Hagen, *Soldiers in the Proletarian Dictatorship*, pp. 308–25; Reese, *Stalin's Reluctant Soldiers*, pp. 84–92.
43 'Voennaya igra LVO i MSBM 1930 g.', f. r-92, o. 2, d. 142, list 131–2; on the 1933 games, f. r-92, o.2, d.142, list 8–17.
44 Viktorov and Kireyev, 11 March 1930, 'prikaz 50/22 "Ob organisatsii voennoy igri nachalstvyushchego sostava morskikh sil Baltmorya i Leningradskogo Voennogo Okruga', f. r-92, o. 2, d. 142, list 116–16b.
45 'Politiko-moralnoe sostayanie lichnogo sostava baltiskogo otryada britanskogo flota', f. r-92, o. 2, d. 142, list 121–2.
46 Ibid., list 123–4; 'Politiko-moralnoe sostayanie voenno-vozdushnikh sil Finlandii 3. gydro-eskadrilya (v Turki–Saari)', ibid., list 125; 'Politiko-moralnoe sostayanie beregovoy oborony Finlandii', ibid., list 126.
47 Reese, *Stalin's Reluctant Soldiers*, pp. 15–17; *idem*, *Soviet Military Experience*, pp. 57–8.
48 Berezovsky *et al.*, *Boevaya letopis*, p. 540.
49 Semenov and Starikov, LVO Staff, to Leningrad induction board *et al.*, 5 November 1932, f. r-1543, o. 2, d. 13, list 21–2; Lukashevich and Kurkov, no date, 'Vypiska iz naryada', to Leningrad induction board *et al.*, list 94–6.
50 Yakunov to the head of the naval section of Leningrad OsoAviaKhim, 25 February 1933, f. r-1543, o. 2, d. 13, list 98–103.

Part IV

THE SOVIET SCHOOL, 1936–1941

11

TOWARD THE GREAT OCEANIC NAVY

Western literature offers various explanations for the sudden change in the Soviet naval doctrine in the mid-1930s. The rising threat from Germany and Japan is usually mentioned. It is also stated that the building of capital ships formed a strong trend in the naval programs of other powers at the time, which is why the same tendency came to prevail in Soviet naval procurements. Moreover, as a result of the first two five-year plans, the Soviet Union finally possessed the necessary industrial basis to produce an ocean-going navy. Finally, the civil war in Spain had demonstrated that the Soviet Navy was unable to protect overseas shipping. After 86 attacks on Soviet transports and seven ships lost, seaborne supply to the Republicans had to be canceled in late 1937. 'The Spanish thesis' seems further substantiated by the fact that several officers who served as naval advisors or volunteers in Spain were later promoted to senior rank.[1] Parallels are drawn to the similar experience from the Cuban Missile Crisis in 1962, which supported Gorshkov in his struggle for an ocean-going navy in the 1960s and 1970s.[2]

However, Mikhail Monakov has refuted most of these explanations. According to him, the need to construct an ocean-going fleet had really been more pressing in the 1920s when the most likely enemies were major naval powers like Britain and France. In the case of Germany and Japan, it should have been obvious to the Soviet leadership that those states could only threaten the Soviet Union overland. Nor could it be asserted that a sufficient material basis for warship construction existed in the country in the late 1930s. In fact, the first two five-year plans had not noticeably increased the necessary industrial structure, although the rapid developments of other industrial sectors may well have led to that belief. Gigantic steel mills and machine tool factories had been created, but no shipyards or specialized manufacturing plants for the production of naval guns and optical equipment. More than half of the ships commissioned in the modest naval program of 1933 had never been delivered. In order to complete their oceanic naval program, the Soviets therefore had to turn to firms in Germany, Italy and the United States, in spite of the status of these countries as potential enemies. Monakov also dismisses the 'Spanish explanation' by pointing out the simple fact that the decision to create an ocean-going fleet was made months before General Franco's mutiny had even started! Although the experience from Spain inspired the revision of the Soviet naval plan in 1937, with its increased emphasis on escort vessels, it cannot have been an initiating factor.[3]

The explanation Monakov offers for the change of doctrine in 1936 still adheres to balance-of-power theory. He is unable to cite any particular documents, but argues that Stalin's wish to have the Soviet Union accepted as an international Great power was a decisive factor. To the Soviet dictator, the fact that his country had not been invited to sign the London Naval Treaty in March 1936 demonstrated the need for a powerful ocean-going fleet. Monakov believes that Stalin made up his mind no later than late 1935.[4] The revised naval construction plan of 1937 spelled out the political importance of a strong Soviet Navy explicitly. In the Baltic, this factor could help to 'influence not only the political orientation of the Border States, but also that of the Scandinavian states and especially the military conduct of those states'.[5]

However, by the mid-1930s there had also been dramatic changes in the perceived strategic balance in the Baltic Theater, which had troubling implications for the defensive doctrine of the Young School. The mission of the Baltic Fleet could no longer be limited to resisting a landing attempt against Leningrad. Instead, the fleet must be ready to attack the enemy's troop transports outside the Gulf of Finland. The new mission seemed to call for a radically different force structure.

Moreover, the force of the expected opponent continued to grow. In 1935, Nikonov and Steynbryuk had predicted the strength of the *Kriegsmarine* in 1938 as five modern battleships (of which two would be 26,000 tons, compared to the 23,000 tons of the Soviet *Gangut* class), two heavy and six light cruisers, 44 destroyers and 56 submarines. Already in 1937, its actual strength was stated as six battleships, six cruisers, 40 destroyers, 55 submarines, 40 torpedo boats and 900 aircraft (1,181 aircraft if the Polish, Finnish and Baltic air forces were included). The revised naval plan of 1937 suggested that in 1941–42, the German Navy would have ten battleships, five heavy and ten light cruisers, two aircraft carriers, 50 destroyers and 50 submarines.[6] The Soviet Navy had to match future German forces in the theater, and the continuous swelling of tonnage figures in Soviet naval plans during the late 1930s must be seen in relation to upgraded estimates of Germany's strength.

The prospects of common action against Axis aggression seemed gloomy, and only in the summer of 1939 were there military talks in Moscow with the Western powers. At that time, the Soviets also negotiated for a nonaggression pact with Germany, and these negotiations in the end proved more successful. On 23 August 1939, the signing of the Molotov–Ribbentrop Pact turned the European balance of power upside down. According to one interpretation, cooperation with Germany had been Stalin's long-term objective for many years. Another, generally more accepted view, claims that the Soviet Union was earnest in its endeavors for collective security during the 1930s, and that the agreement with Nazi Germany was resorted to only when an acceptable settlement with the Western powers seemed out of reach.[7] The treaty of 1939 meant a short revival of the economic and military cooperation between the two countries from the 1920s. On the naval side, the Soviet Union bought artillery, armor and even ships from Germany (the cruiser *Lützow*, renamed *Petropavlovsk*), while the *Reichsmarine* received vital oil deliveries, as well as a secret base in the Arctic Sea for its operations in the Atlantic (at the mouth of the Zapadnaya Litsa river). Later, through the German occupation of Norway in the spring of 1940, this port lost most of its strategic importance.[8]

If the search for an alliance with Germany did not constitute a constant motive in Soviet security policy between the wars, fears of encirclement certainly did. After sharing Poland with Germany, the Soviet government hurriedly cashed in the rests of its gains. Through force, Finland was made to surrender territory. The Baltic republics had to provide military bases, and were then liquidated as independent states. When the onslaught came in the summer of 1941, the strategic situation of the Baltic Fleet had been markedly improved compared to only two years before.

Germany as the main threat

In 1936, the strength of a probable German force in the Gulf of Finland was calculated at five battleships, six cruisers and 16 destroyers.[9] In May 1937, the GRU presented an updated version of Steynbryuk's and Nikonov's threat scenario from 1935, a report entitled 'Preparations for war against the USSR in the Baltic' signed by Nikonov and the head of the GRU, Berzin, containing enlarged strategic perspectives as well as more elaborate estimates of Germany's offensive power. The authors claimed that during the last two years, Germany had continued to expand its influence among the Soviet Union's western neighbors. The visit of the chief of the German General Staff, Werner von Blomberg, to Estonia, together with Japanese offers of technical aid to the Estonian coastal artillery, indicated that a fascist bridgehead was being prepared in the vicinity of Leningrad. It was only a matter of time before Germany would have air and naval bases in Finland and Scandinavia too.

The transport of troops was still seen as the primary mission of German naval forces in the Baltic. The transport of one German division would require 28 transport ships of about 3,000 tons each. If the Germans planned to send six divisions to Estonia and Latvia (Riga, Ventspils, Liepaya) and two divisions to Finland (Turkku, Raumo) they would need about 250 transport ships, provided some of those went for a second trip. In addition, some 200 minor vessels would have to be mobilized as escorts. With 900 ships in the German commercial fleet, this would pose no major problem. The entire operation could be completed in ten days, the GRU figured, although the head of the Baltic Fleet intelligence section, Captain 3rd rank Nikolay Timofeyev, believed it would take longer.

The Germans also had to block the mouth of the Gulf of Finland. Heavy coastal artillery was already in place in Finland and Estonia, and in less than one day some 8,000 mines could be laid out in the narrow waters. In view of the awkward navigation conditions, Nikonov and Berzin believed operations against Soviet naval forces in the area would be entrusted to aircraft, submarines and torpedo vessels.

The threat was not limited to the Baltic Theater. In later years, the Germans had demonstrated a clear interest in northern Scandinavia because of its strategic and economic importance. To protect their imports from Soviet submarines, they had an interest in preventing the Northern Fleet from leaving port. Here, German resources would be scarce, but submarines, hydroplanes and armed fishing boats could always be organized into a suitable task force, operating from the Norwegian archipelago or from bases in northern Finland.

Finally, the Germans had to protect their sea communications. A steady flow of supplies would go to their troops in Estonia, Latvia and Finland from Danzig and Stettin. Also, iron ore and victuals must be imported from Sweden and across the North Sea. To minimize losses, the Germans could be expected to send their convoys by night or try to transit goods across neutral countries.[10] In the beginning of 1939, the commanders of the Baltic, Black Sea and Northern Fleets were assembled for a conference at the Naval War College in Leningrad. At the conference, the Baltic Fleet Intelligence Section presented yet another report on 'Germany's preparations for war at sea and her likely allies'.[11]

The uncertainty of Britain's position

As always, the position of the leading European naval power, Britain, would be crucial in a Baltic war. In Voroshilov's planning directives from March 1935, the country's position was described as undecided.[12] Nikonov's and Berzin's report from 1937 asserted that Germany would need British support for a war against the Soviet Union. Even if reactionary circles in the British bourgeoisie would welcome an understanding with Germany, Berzin and Nikonov said, more influential elements were afraid of Hitler. However, these groups at the same time realized that German expansionism would weaken France and Italy, and that it could be directed eastwards against the Soviet Union. After the signing of the Anglo-German naval agreement in 1935, British naval visits to the Baltic had ceased. However, the head of the Baltic Fleet intelligence section, Timofeyev, viewed the Anglo-German relationship differently. In his comments on the backside of Berzin's and Nikonov's report, he pointed out that German naval rearmament, containing the procurement of battleships and oceanic submarines, could not have war against the Soviet Union as its long-term goal. The British knew they were the enemy. Only a few weeks after Nikonov's and Berzin's report had been submitted on 31 May, visiting British squadrons had also reappeared in the Baltic. Timofeyev also believed that Britain would object to German penetration in northern Scandinavia. That Germany and Britain were rivals was a major advantage to the Soviet Union.[13]

Denmark, Sweden and other neutrals

The neutral countries in the Baltic region posed a special problem, as their neutrality was not believed to be genuine. Timofeyev recalled how Sweden's so-called neutrality during the 1914–18 war had obstructed the operations of the

Russian Navy. Next time, he thought, the necessity to observe international law would be less binding through Scandinavian 'participation in the war under the cover of neutrality'.[14]

The Danish Sounds were vital to German supplies and communications, and according to Nikonov and Berzin an agreement existed which would give Germany access to Danish waters during a war against the Soviet Union.[15]

Sweden, although not mentioned as a potential enemy in Voroshilov's planning directives to the Baltic Fleet from March 1935, nonetheless appeared as such in mobilization directives and intelligence briefings. When Fleet Commander Galler and his deputy chief of staff, Dimitry Rechister, brought this to the attention of the RKKA General Staff, they were instructed to proceed with their planning in accordance with Voroshilov's directives. Nonetheless, when war approached, the Baltic Fleet must direct some of its intelligence resources to Swedish waters.[16]

Already in the summer of 1935, Galler had pointed out that trade with Sweden would be vital to the German war effort. The Baltic Fleet's war games in March 1938 described a situation in which the 'Red' (Soviet) forces were fighting the Great power 'Brown' and its loyal ally 'Blue.' Consideration also had to be taken to a neutral power called 'Green', which sympathized with the anti-'Red' coalition and supplied it with great quantities of iron ore, timber and food. 'Blue' received substantial deliveries from its neighbor 'Green' across the Gulf of Bothnia, where shipping could take place under the cover of 'Green's' vast archipelago. During the exercise, a central task for 'Red' was to interdict traffic from 'Green's' ports. Here, we see the origins of the Soviet submarine campaign along the Swedish coast in the summer of 1942, when an undeclared war was fought between Soviet submarines and the Swedish Navy, resulting in the sinking of five Swedish cargo ships.[17]

Even Estonia, Latvia and Lithuania, usually to be found on the list of likely enemies, could stay neutral in the initial stage of a conflict. Freedom of action against these countries could be secured through an official declaration at the outbreak of hostilities that neutral ports were to be attacked if they hosted enemy ships.[18]

The Åland problem

As we saw, in 1935 Steynbryuk and Nikonov had warned of the enemy coalition acquiring bases in the Åland Islands. In their report, they had also referred to preparations in Sweden and Finland for a revision of Åland's demilitarized status, which they believed to be directed against the Soviet Union. In their report from 1937, they again emphasized Åland's role as a lock to the Gulf of Finland.[19]

In the autumn of 1938, the Swedish and Finnish governments prepared a joint demarche to the Great powers, proposing that the Åland Convention of 1921 should be abrogated and the two countries allowed to fortify the islands together, assuring that all other powers were to be kept out in the future. The Swedish foreign minister, Rickard Sandler, regarded this proposal – the so-called 'Stockholm Plan' – as a way to reduce German influence in Finland and enhance peace and stability in the Nordic area. To the Finnish government, which was under Soviet pressure to give up territory for the protection of Leningrad, the prospect of engaging Sweden in the defense of Finnish territory was at least worth exploring.

However, Soviet opposition to the proposal forced it to be withdrawn. According to an official statement by the newly appointed People's Commissar for Foreign Affairs, Molotov – made in a speech to the Supreme Soviet on 31 May 1939 – the Soviet government feared that fortifications in Åland could be used to blockade the exits from the Gulf of Finland.[20] Soviet fears about Åland were probably genuine, and Molotov seemingly based his argumentation on a secret report by the Soviet general and naval staffs from November 1938. The chiefs of staff pointed out how the island group's strategic importance had been realized already by the tsarist regime, which had fortified it during World War I, and later by the Germans who had made frequent naval visits there. Through the advent of air power and long-range coastal artillery, it had become possible to block the Gulf of Finland from Åland, and to protect iron ore transports from Sweden to Germany. The chief of staffs were not optimistic of the legal possibilities to protest an abrogation of the demilitarization treaty. However, as the chief of the RKKA General Staff, Shaposhnikov, repeated in a letter to Voroshilov in June 1939, fortifications in Åland would simply be intolerable to the Soviet Union.[21]

In the summer of 1939, after Sweden and Finland had withdrawn the Stockholm Plan, the maritime journal *Morskoy Sbornik* published articles on Åland's status in international law, and on the island group's geography and navigation conditions. In the same issue, a series of articles began to appear treating the battle of Gangut in 1714, the first victory of the Russian Navy and its greatest triumph ever in Baltic waters. Quite appropriately, it was a victory won against Swedes in the Finnish archipelago.[22]

Expanding the base area

As we have seen, the Baltic Fleet's limited base area around Kronstadt had been acknowledged as a serious problem already in the early 1920s. With the adoption of a more offensive strategy and an expansion of the theater of operations to the west, the situation was further aggravated, and in 1938–39, naval authorities repeatedly demonstrated their irritation with the narrow territorial waters surrounding Kronstadt. For instance, the mine barriers planned to protect the base in times of war could not be laid out without violating Finnish territory. Before entering Finnish waters, the Baltic Fleet would need permission from the People's Commissar for the Navy or from his deputy.[23] When the Finns proposed a clearer demarcation of the borderline at sea, People's Commissar for the Navy Frinovsky protested to Foreign Commissar Litvinov. If the Finnish–Soviet border became visible, he argued, the Finns would notice when Soviet warships sailed into Finnish inner waters. They had already shown tendencies to object to Soviet ships sailing through their outer waters, although such traffic was permitted by international law. Frinovsky had his way. In January 1939, the Soviet government rejected the Finnish proposal. The costs of maintaining border signs at sea all the year round, it was said, would be too high. Instead, the respective parties should establish clearer demarcation signs on their own territory to prevent incidents.[24]

About the same time, Estonia's widening of its territorial waters to four nautical miles worried the chief of the Naval Staff, Lev Galler. An extension of Estonian inner territorial waters risked blocking a large part of the Gulf of Finland to Soviet warships. Also, the country's new neutrality regulations contained generous rights for foreign warships to enter Estonian territory, seek refuge in Estonian ports and replenish fuel and supplies. It would be good if Estonia revised her neutrality regulations in accordance with Soviet wishes, Galler wrote to the head of the law department in the People's Commissariat for Foreign Affairs, Plotkin. Plotkin replied that there was no lawful ground for a Soviet protest, especially in view of the Soviet claim of a 12-mile border in some parts of the Baltic. Furthermore, restricted mobility for foreign warships on Estonian territory would primarily harm the Soviets themselves. As long as they abstained from firing or minelaying, Soviet ships could move around rather freely in the Estonian archipelago. In addition, the peace treaty with Estonia from 1920 contained a clause which forbade the parties to let their territories be used for military preparations against one another, an obligation which would not cease through unilateral changes in the Estonian neutrality law.[25] Therefore, when Estonia somewhat later restricted the rights of foreign warships to use the country's waterways, the navy reacted differently. Now, it instead urged the Foreign Commissariat to press the principle of free passage for warships in the Baltic in peacetime.[26]

Since 1923, Finnish and Soviet representatives had met annually to discuss the maintenance of order in international waters in the Gulf of Finland. In late September 1939, a few weeks after the outbreak of World War II, an invitation for such talks was forwarded to the People's Commissariat for Foreign Affairs by the Finnish legation in Moscow. However, the Deputy People's Commissar for the Navy, Ivan Isakov, suggested that the conference should be postponed. First, a solution must be found to a number 'of more pressing issues that have come up in the Gulf of Finland and are linked to the present situation'.[27] No doubt Isakov was referring to the negotiations for base treaties with the northwestern neighbor states, talks which had just begun in Moscow and were to change the strategic situation in northern Europe in a profound way.

It seems as if the Soviets originally hoped to gain access to Finnish and Baltic territory through an agreement with the Western powers. In August 1939, during the talks in Moscow for a pact against Germany, Marshal Shaposhnikov, chief of the RKKA General Staff, asked for Britain and France to send naval squadrons into the Baltic.[28] The real motive for this plea seems to have been the belief that if the Soviet warships arrived together with British and French warships, Finns and Balts could not refuse them entry to their ports. When it came to specifying what concrete naval assistance the Soviets needed from the Western powers in the Baltic, Shaposhnikov had been unable to answer. He merely described three different scenarios for conflict with Germany, all three containing the arrival of a strong Anglo-French squadron in the Baltic. In spite of his vague picture of the coming war, he was certain what bases the Anglo-French squadron and its Soviet ally would need: Åland and Hangö in Finland, Haapsalu, Pärnu and Hiiumaa–Saaremaa in Estonia, Liepaya and Ainazi in Latvia. The types of missions he presented for the combined French–British–Soviet fleets in the Baltic were similar to those formulated for the Soviet naval forces already in 1935: minelaying off the coasts of East Prussia, attacking German shipping, blocking iron ore imports from Sweden.[29]

However, the British and French delegations were reluctant to promise the arrival of a squadron, at least during the early stage of a conflict. The head of the British delegation, Admiral Drax, proposed a rather limited force of destroyers and submarines 'for the purpose of stiffening and helping the Russian Navy'. He regarded the Soviet demand for bases in Finland and the Baltic states as opportunistic and not to be taken seriously, suggesting it had been inspired by a recent article in *RUSI Journal* (Royal United Services Institute) by a British admiral. When Drax had tried to press the Soviet Navy Commissar, Kuznetsov, on the desired composition of a Western expeditionary force, he had been just as vague as Shaposhnikov. He only said that the absence of Anglo-French naval forces in the Baltic would make it harder to fight the enemy, adding that Drax himself probably knew better the number and types of ships that would be needed![30] Thus, there seemed to be grounds for the conclusion drawn by General Heywood, the army representative in Drax's delegation:

> ...what the Soviets really want is the cover of our flags and our consent to the utilization of these ports. Token Naval Anglo-French forces would probably meet their requirements, even if it was only an Allied Port Commission in each place![31]

Whether Western fleets would enter the Baltic or not, the interest in expanding the Soviet naval base area remained. When an agreement with the Western powers proved unattainable, the Soviet government turned to Germany to obtain the freedom of action which Britain and France had been unable to provide. After the Molotov–Rippentrop Pact had been concluded, the Estonians were the first to be approached. On 24 September 1939, during trade negotiations in Moscow, the Estonian Foreign Minister, Selter, was suddenly confronted with demands for a security pact, which was to include Soviet naval and air bases on Estonian territory. According to the Soviets, the recent escape by the Polish submarine *Orzel* from internment in Estonia had demonstrated Estonia's inability to control its territory. Although Soviet warships were allowed to search for *Orzel* in Estonian waters, the Soviet press soon reported (incorrectly) that a Soviet submarine had been sunk outside Narva, and that Soviet cargo ships had been attacked in the area. The final settlement on 12 October ensured the Russians bases in Paldiski, Haapsalu, Saaremaa and Hiiumaa islands. Until facilities in Paldiski had been completed in two years, they had the right to use the port of Tallinn. Had the Estonians not been willing to budge, the Soviets would have used force. In late September, planning directives had been issued for naval operations against Estonia. Negotiations with Latvia were initiated on 30 September, the final treaty being signed on 5 October. Here, the Soviets acquired naval bases in Ventspils and Liepaya, as well as coastal artillery positions in Pitrags.[32]

As we can see from the list of base sites, most of the positions desired in Estonia and Latvia during the negotiations with the Western powers had thus been secured. Almost immediately, the flotilla leader *Minsk*, two destroyers and a squadron of submarines were deployed to the new ports in Estonia, the cruiser *Kirov* and a squadron of destroyers to those in Latvia. On 15 October, additional ships followed. In Sweden, this second echelon of Soviet naval forces released a series of nervous contingency measures. Already the following day, the Naval Staff in Moscow was able to present a detailed plan for coastal fortifications around the new bases.[33]

On 5 October, the same day the base agreement with Latvia was signed, negotiations with Finland began. Shortly before, the Social Democratic foreign minister in Sweden, Rickard Sandler, had been confident that the Soviets, as soon as they had had their demands in Estonia satisfied, would have no reason to trouble Finland. 'With a grip on Ösel[Saaremaa]–Baltischport, the Kremlin should have no more fears of Finland lending itself as a German area of deployment,' Sandler wrote in a memorandum. When he prepared a second draft of his text a few weeks later, he knew better and left this sentence out.[34]

Finland had been approached already in 1938 when Boris Yartsev, secretary at the Soviet legation in Helsinki, had tried to obtain a few of the small islands in the Gulf of Finland. To these earlier demands were now added requests for territory on the Karelian Isthmus and for the Hangö Peninsula at the southwestern tip of Finland. Together with Paldiski in Estonia on the opposite shore, Hangö would offer complete control of the mouth of the Gulf of Finland. When the Finns questioned that a modern battle fleet would risk forcing these narrow straits, Stalin dismissed their objections as mere theoretical speculation, fit for academic debate in some military journal but not for serious negotiations between two governments. The British had sailed this way during the Civil War, he said, and the victor in the present war between Germany and Britain would sooner or later send warships against Leningrad. As far as Stalin knew, both Germans and British were already pressing Sweden for bases, and the Soviet Union must therefore take appropriate countermeasures. According to the head of the Finnish delegation, Juho Paasikivi, later president of Finland, the Soviet desire for a foothold at the mouth of the Gulf was not to be mistaken. At one stage of the talks, Stalin was even prepared to drop the request for Hangö in exchange for three small islands east of the peninsula. However, this unexpected retreat only served to strengthen the Finns in their conviction that the Soviets were driven by opportunism. If a firm stand was made against the voracious great power, concessions could be avoided.[35]

During the negotiations with the Latvians in early October, Stalin repeated the view that Britain was pressing Sweden for naval bases, so the Soviet Union must take precautionary measures.[36] The Soviet dictator may have genuinely believed this, or he may not. What matters is that at least from the mid-1930s, Sweden had been present in Soviet strategic calculations as an enemy bridgehead. Bases at Paldiski and Hangö would not only secure control over the mouth of the Gulf of Finland, but also create a strong defensive position midway between Leningrad and Stockholm.

The war against Finland

In April 1939, a mighty coalition consisting of Germany, Poland, Finland, Latvia and Estonia still featured as a possible opponent in the Baltic.[37] Six months later, the strategic situation had been drastically improved. Germany was now the Soviet Union's alliance partner and preoccupied with a major war in the west, Poland had ceased to exist while Estonia and Latvia were under firm Soviet military control.

Finland, however, the only remaining opponent in the theater, had to be subdued by force. In October 1939, preparations for war began. Just as before when Finland was concerned, a Swedish intervention could not be excluded. In a draft memorandum dated 23 October, Captain 1st rank A. Shedshov of the Naval Staff claimed that although the Finnish and Swedish navies posed no threat to the Baltic Fleet in the open sea, they certainly did if they chose to operate from the archipelago. Also, a surprise minelaying action outside the ports of Liepaya and Paldiski, which the Swedes could perform at a few hours' notice, would effectively neutralize the new bases in Latvia and Estonia. Therefore, Shedshov concluded, Soviet submarines must be deployed outside Swedish ports at an early stage of a conflict, and the fleet air arm must be ready to destroy the Swedish Navy.[38] About a week later, Kuznetsov requested that in the event that Sweden or any other power tried to support Finland, unlimited submarine warfare must be declared in a 30-mile zone off the Finnish mainland.[39]

Although worries about a Swedish intervention later diminished, two submarine squadrons were detached to patrol the Gulf of Bothnia. During the first days of the war, five Soviet submarines lay outside Stockholm, Fårösund and Karlskrona, anxiously watching the Swedish Navy. To the relief of the Soviet Naval Staff, they could soon confirm that Sweden would stay out of the conflict.[40]

On 6 December 1939, however, the Swedes laid mines in their part of the South Kvarken Sound, opposite the Åland archipelago, cutting off the Gulf of Bothnia from the rest of the Baltic. According to the Swedish view, these minefields were situated entirely in Swedish territorial waters. Nevertheless, it could be claimed they violated international law as they blocked traffic between two zones of international waters. While Germany delivered a diplomatic protest, the Soviets never raised the matter officially with Sweden, although they were annoyed to see the movements of their submarines restricted. Only two days after the Swedish minelaying, Belli, now at the Naval War College, authored a memorandum on the matter. The Swedes claimed a four-mile border in the Baltic, Belli said, but during World War I they had only asserted a three-mile border against submarines. Although the Swedish and

Finnish sea borders were adjacent they did not overlap, but the present Swedish minefields in the South Kvarken Sound seemingly overlapped with Finnish minefields on the other side. Consequently, the Swedes had exceeded their rights as neutrals and committed a hostile act against the USSR and the people of Finland. According to Belli, Sweden could be expected to justify its actions by asserting the Finnish–Soviet War to be a civil war between the Helsinki government and the Soviet-backed regime in Terijoki. In analogy with how Germany and Italy had acted during the civil war in Spain, Sweden had taken sides in that conflict.[41]

In spite of Swedish aid, Finland's resistance was finally overcome. The Moscow Treaty of March 1940 not only secured the Soviets control over the six Finnish islands in the inner part of the Gulf, but also a steady foothold at Hangö at the mouth. Together with the bases in Estonia and Latvia, these positions would open most of the Baltic Theater to the Soviet Navy. At last, after 20 years of confinement in the Gulf of Finland, the Baltic Fleet had finally been liberated.

'An extremely awkward situation in the Baltic Theater'

On 5 April 1940, Kuznetsov reported to Stalin, Molotov and Zhdanov that in the future the Baltic Fleet would conduct its operations around the mouth of the Gulf and beyond.[42] Prospects of countering an enemy blockade had been markedly improved. At present there was no serious challenge to Soviet security in the theater, at least not as long as Germany was occupied with the war in the west. In the beginning of April 1940, when Molotov briefed the Baltic Fleet Soviet on possible security threats, the only possible aggressor was Britain, likely to try to organize the Scandinavian countries into an anti-Soviet alliance. Also, there was the threat of unrest by hostile elements in Latvia and Estonia.[43]

This threat perception signified a return to the situation of the 1920s, when the main preoccupation in the Baltic Theater had been a limited British expeditionary force, aimed at 'stiffening up' a Border State coalition. However, the group of hostile Border States had been substantially reduced compared to the 1920s. No longer did it contain a prominent military power such as Poland, nor did it possess the same advantageous geo-strategic position as before. Furthermore, although plans to send a naval squadron into the Baltic had existed in the British Admiralty during the autumn of 1939 (Churchill's famous plan 'Catherine'), after the German occupation of Denmark on 9 April 1940, these plans were no longer even a theoretical option.[44]

Soon, Germany's swift conquest of western Europe changed this pleasant situation. The likely opponents were no longer the Scandinavians supported by a British task force, but just as before the mighty German war machine supported by the Scandinavians. In view of this threatening development, it seemed advisable to tighten the grip over the newly acquired base area and annex the Baltic republics permanently. On 5 June, 1940, Defense Commissar Timoshenko took direct command of the Soviet armed forces stationed there.[45] Four days later, he ordered naval units in Estonia and Latvia into a state of alert for the coming 48 hours. A seizure of Estonian and Latvian naval and commercial vessels was to be prepared, the sea lanes of these countries blockaded. Government ministers, as well as military personnel, must be prevented from escaping abroad. Also, caution must be taken against a possible Swedish or Finnish intervention. Just as had been the case during the war against Finland, reconnaissance patrols were dispatched outside Swedish naval bases. In his final instructions for the operation – aimed at 'securing the freedom of movement for the RKKA on the territories of Estonia, Latvia and Lithuania' – Fleet Commander Tributs also mentioned the need to watch for the movements of an unmentionable 'third power' (Germany).[46]

The annexation of the Baltic republics proceeded comparatively smoothly and Tributs's instruction to his forces to be prepared to 'annihilate' fleeing Baltic vessels, military or civilian, never had to be implemented. However, the nervous atmosphere among Soviet decision makers during these fateful summer days is telling. The Soviet Union seemed to be engaged in a geo-strategic race against a powerful opponent, and although Soviet military forces controlled the territory of the Baltic States these could in no way be regarded as secured. In September, the Estonian islands of Hiiumaa, Saaremaa and Moon were declared restricted areas, and all islanders regarded as 'unreliable' or 'reactionary' were forced to resettle on the mainland.[47]

The crisis atmosphere is also present in a report by the Baltic Fleet's chief of staff, Rear-Admiral Panteleyev, to Kuznetsov in the beginning of July 1940. Although the recent war with Finland had created security on the northwestern border, Pantaleyev wrote, Finland still had a hostile government and could easily turn into a menacing bridgehead for an aggressor. Just as before, the Finns could count on a steady flow of supplies and troops from Sweden, and the Soviets lacked the capability to cut communications between the two countries. Sweden, being in no position to act independently against Germany at present, could as usual hide behind neutrality, even if the unmentionable 'third power' was allowed to use its territory. In addition, anti-Soviet forces in the newly incorporated Baltic republics would support the Germans. Germany's objective in a war against the USSR would be to capture the Ukraine. By conquering the Soviet Baltic coast – most likely through an assault across the sea from Sweden and Finland – they wanted to secure the northern flank of their Ukrainian operation. Germany's recent triumph in the west was from this perspective most regrettable.[48]

In response to the perceived threat, Kuznetsov shortly afterwards ordered a revision of the Baltic Fleet's operational planning. German superiority in the southern part of the Baltic Sea must be taken for granted. So must support to Germany from Sweden, Finland and anti-Soviet elements in Estonia and Latvia: 'The quickly changed situation in the west complicates the possibility of making exact calculations...Therefore, it is unavoidable to presuppose an extremely awkward situation and difficult circumstances in the Baltic theater.'[49]

'We have to prepare not for *Blitzkrieg* but for a long war...'

On 20–21 August, the Baltic Fleet conducted its first war games in the new geographical setting, training defense against the navies of countries 'G' (Germany),

'Sh' (Sweden) and 'F' (Finland). The Soviets hoped to be able to strike first, fighting the war far away from their own shores in the way Nemits and Toshakov had envisioned some 20 years before. As fleet commander Tributs reminded the participants before the exercise, the successes of Soviet foreign policy had truly improved the strategic situation in the theater.[50]

Against this background, the sudden cuts that the Soviet shipbuilding plans went through towards the end of 1940 may seem surprising. These changes have been explained as a result of material shortages, or as a reaction to the impending threat of German invasion. The technical problems that the Soviets faced were indeed great, but the notion of a growing fear of Germany seems less credible. Instead, it seems as if Hitler's inability to defeat Britain, the fact that Germany's final victory in the West failed to materialize, calmed the nervous atmosphere that had been prevalent during the summer months. 'If the English are defeated, why are we sitting here?' Soviet Foreign Commissar Molotov reportedly asked his German hosts during his visit to Berlin in November, when a RAF raid had forced him to seek shelter. During the ensuing negotiations, Molotov saw little reason to compromise regarding spheres of influence in Europe. Indeed, his demands for access to Finland and the Turkish Straits may well have been aimed at improving the conditions for future Soviet battleship deployment.[51]

It seems clear that the Soviet Navy drew similar conclusions regarding Germany's strength. At the Naval War College conference in Leningrad on 7–14 October 1940, Rear-Admiral Isakov admitted that the German triumphs in 1939–40 had been impressive. Nonetheless, the British had slipped away at Dunkirk, and could probably not be defeated without an invasion. *Blitzkrieg* (*molnienosnaya voyna*) was a form of warfare, Isakov claimed, that had been specially developed by states like Germany, Italy and Japan, which unlike the Soviet Union lacked the necessary prerequisites for autarchy. The object of their quick offensive campaigns was to conquer territory and secure resources and raw materials so that they could fight a protracted war. Like the conflict between Japan and China, the present world war would be a drawn-out struggle. The reason for this, Isakov explained, was that just like any other phenomenon, war was subject to the law of dialectics: every force would bring to life its own counterforce. The growth in offensive power, which made *Blitzkrieg* possible, had in turn caused a similar growth in defensive power. Industrial mobilization and the training of cadres would be crucial, and – as they all knew – the Soviet Union had for a long time prepared for war along such lines. Isakov asked his audience:

> Why do we have to talk about this? Because, Comrades, we have to prepare not for Blitzkrieg but for a long war, which will develop in a series of violent operations with pauses in between... Quick operations in a war do not mean a quick end to that war, when it is [a war] to overcome mighty enemies.[52]

As may be suggested by the above, the last shift in Soviet naval doctrine during the inter-war period – the sudden decision in October 1940 to halt the oceanic

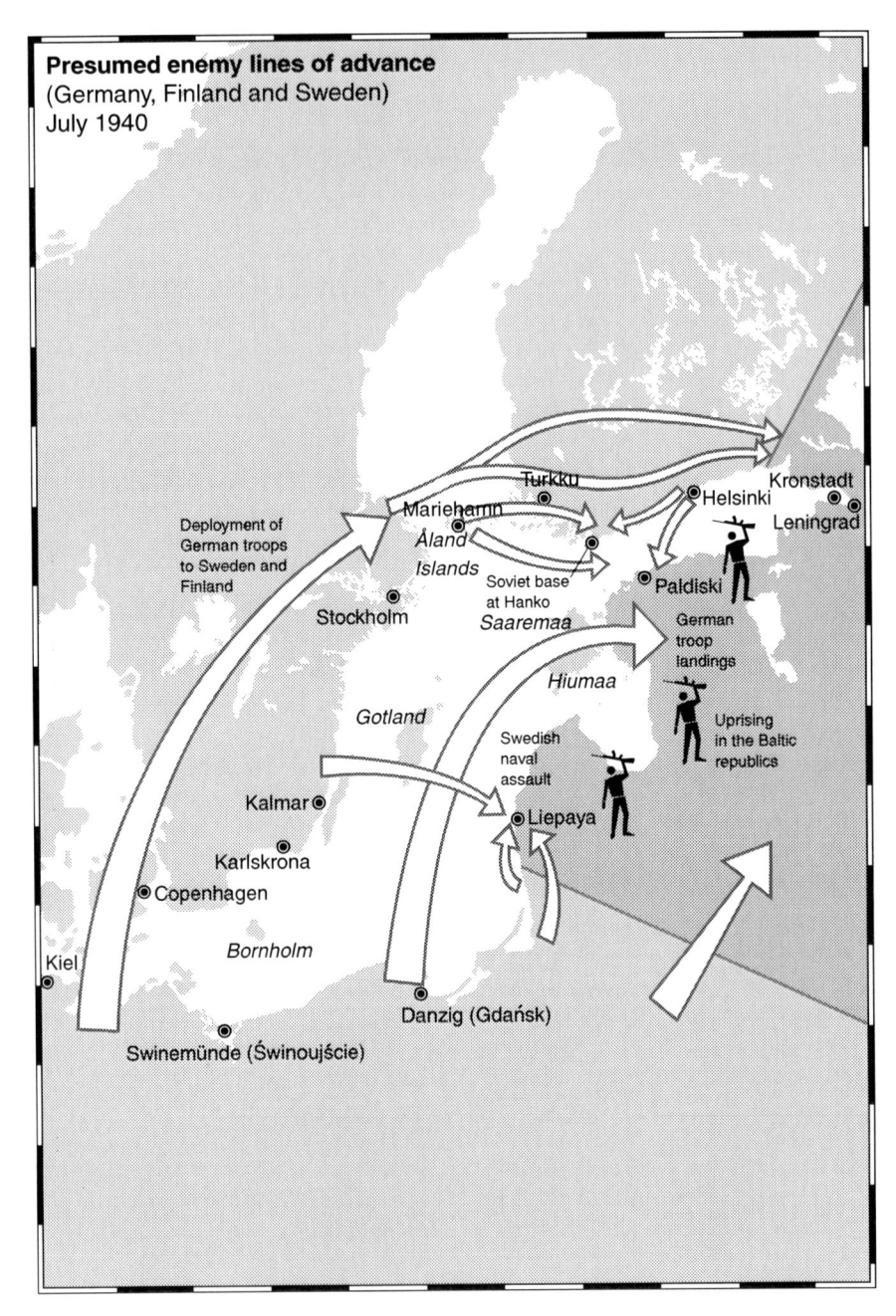

Map 3 Presumed enemy lines of advance, 1940.

naval program – was not only a practical measure, a consequence of the growing threat from Germany or shortages in construction materials. When German *Blitzkrieg* strategy had proved ineffective, the need for a Soviet (counter) offensive capability at sea also seemed less certain. Obviously, modern wars would be protracted affairs, and a navy centered around a core of heavy battleships would be of little value if there were to be no decisive naval battles.

Conclusion

Numerous explanations have been offered for the sudden shift in Soviet naval policy in the late 1930s. Although the grandiose plans for an ocean-going navy are often described as a reaction to humiliating experiences during the Spanish Civil War or as a response to the Japanese challenge in the Pacific, the German plans for naval rearmament in the Baltic must also be taken into account. Not only was there a certain conjuncture between increases in the Soviet naval construction plans and increases in the estimates of the future German tonnage figures. There was also a hope to impress the minor powers in the Baltic through a navy capable of offensive operations. If these countries were allowed to stay undecided vis-à-vis the Soviet Union, strategic planning in the Baltic Theater would become truly problematic. In the case of Sweden and Finland, matters were further complicated due to the suspicious-looking plans of these countries for a common defense of the Åland Islands.

Naval strategic considerations also contributed to the rapprochement with Germany and the territorial expansion in 1939–40. Although the Soviet Union's defensive depth increased through the subjugation of the Baltic states and Finland, there was still a genuine sense of insecurity and fear. Only in the autumn of 1940, as Germany remained unsuccessful in its attempts to defeat England, did a certain relaxation appear. Then, the oceanic naval program could also be called into question. If World War II was to be a protracted affair, there would be less need for a Soviet battle fleet.

Notes

1 Soviet losses in Spain – Gribovsky, 'Na puti k "bolshomu morskomu i okeanskomu flotu"', pp. 18–19; cf. Rohwer and Monakov, *Stalin's Ocean-going Fleet*, pp. 64–7; apart from Kuznetsov, other Spanish veterans with impressive careers were N. O. Abramov, rear-admiral, commander of the Danube Flotilla in 1940 and the Polish Navy in 1945; the former Young School theoretician Alexander Alexandrov, vice-admiral, member of the Allied Control Commission in Finland in 1944, chief of staff of the Baltic Fleet in 1945, killed in a plane crash in Germany in 1946; A. Alafusov, admiral, chief of the Naval Staff in 1944–45, commandant of the Naval War College in 1945–48, repressed but rehabilitated in 1953; V. P. Drozd, commander of the Northern Fleet in 1938, of the light forces of the Baltic Fleet in 1941, drowned on the ice outside Kronstadt in 1943; I. Yumashev, admiral, commander of the Black Sea Fleet in 1938–39, of the Pacific Fleet in 1939–47, supreme commander of the Naval Forces in 1947–50, People's Commissar of the Navy in 1950–51 and then commandant of the Naval War College;

and A. Golovko, admiral, commander of the Northern Fleet in 1940–46 – cf. their respective entries in Dotsenko, *Morskoy biograficheskiy slovar*.
2 Cf. Gorshkov, *Sea Power of the State*, pp. 281–3; I. V. Kasatonov, *Flot vyshyol v okean* (Moscow: Andreyevskiy flag, 1996), p. 360.
3 Monakov, 'Sudba doktrin i teory, 8', p. 37.
4 Ibid., p. 37; cf. Rohwer and Monakov, *Stalin's Ocean-going Fleet*, pp. 58–67, 221–3.
5 Voroshilov to Stalin and Molotov, September 1937, f. r-1877, o. 1, d. 435, list 28.
6 Nikonov and Berzin, 31 May 1937, 'Podgotovka voyni protiv SSSR na Balticheskom teatre', f. r-92, o. 2, d. 352, list 24–5; Voroshilov to Stalin and Molotov, September 1937, f. r-1877, o. 1, d. 435, list 27; Smirnov and Galler to Stalin and Molotov, 27 February 1938, f. r-1877, o. 1, d. 435, list 40.
7 The former interpretation can be found in Tucker's *Stalin in Power*, while Haslam, *Soviet Foreign Policy*, is an example of the latter interpretation. For an introduction to the debate – although heavily polemical against the 'German camp' – see Geoffrey Roberts, *The Soviet Union and the Origins of the Second World War: Russo-German Relations and the Road to War, 1933–1941* (London: Macmillan, 1993), pp. 1–9. Roberts sees A. J. P. Taylor's *The Origins of the Second World War* (1961) as an important source of inspiration for his own standpoint.
8 A thorough study on naval contacts during the period of the Nonaggression Pact in Philbin III, *The Lure of Neptune*; on 'Bas Nord' cf. A. B. Beznosov, 'Sekret Basis Nord,' *Voenno-istoricheskiy Zhurnal*, no. 7 (1990).
9 Commander LVO to commander Baltic Fleet, 15 May 1936, f. r-92, o. 2, d. 260, list 43–6.
10 Nikonov and Berzin, 31 May 1937, 'Podgotovka voyni protiv SSSR na Balticheskom teatre', f. r-92, o. 2, d. 352, list 4–25; for Timofeyev's views, see his written comments on back of this report, which was originally prepared for Mikhail Uritsky to sign, as he had been the acting head of the GRU during Berzin's assignment to Spain.
11 Galler to the head of Baltic Fleet Intelligence, 9 February 1939, f. r-1877, o. 1, d. 36, list 5–7; unfortunately, I have not been able to locate this report in the files of the RGAVMF.
12 Voroshilov to the commanders of Baltic Fleet and LVO, 9 March 1935, f. r-92, o. 2, d. 260, list 1–2.
13 Nikonov and Berzin, 31 May 1937, 'Podgotovka voyni protiv SSSR na Balticheskom teatre', f. r-92, o. 2, d. 352, list 6b–7, 21b.
14 Ibid., list 6b.
15 Ibid., list 6.
16 Rechister, 4 April 1935, f. r-92, o. 2, d. 260, list 18–26; Isakov and Rechister to commander Baltic Fleet Intelligence Yevseyev, 20 May 1935, ibid., list 11–15.
17 Galler to Voroshilov, 7 June 1935, f. r-2041, o.1, d. 76, list 1–7; tributes to Commander of the Baltic Fleet Levchenko, 14 April 1938 ('otchet po operativnoy igre KBF provedennoy 25–26 marta 1938g.'), f. r-92, o. 2, d. 432, list 276–96; on Soviet submarine operations in Swedish waters see Lars Ulfving, 'Sjökriget Sverige–Sovjetunionen: Det inofficiella kriget i Östersjön mellan Sovjetunionens ubåtsvapen och Sveriges flotta sommaren och hösten 1942', in Bo Hugemark (ed.), *Vindkantring: 1942 – politisk kursändring* (Stockholm: Probus, 1992).
18 Chief of staff of the Baltic Fleet to commander of LVO 4 April 1935, f. r-92, o. 2, d. 260, list 18–26; commander of LVO to commander of Baltic Fleet, 15 May 1936, ibid., list 43–6; Yegorov to commanders of Baltic Fleet and LVO, 30 December 1936, f. r-92, o. 2, d. 297, list 1–3; Shaposhnikov to commander of Baltic Fleet, 13 January 1937, ibid., list 4–7.
19 Nikonov and Steynbryuk, 20 August 1935, 'Kratky obzor strategicheskogo polozheniya na balticheskom teatre v svyazi s anglo-germanskim morskim soglasheniem', f. r-1483, o. 1, d. 329, list 203; Nikonov and Berzin, 31 May 1937, 'Podgotovka voyni protiv SSSR na Balticheskom teatre', f. r-92, o. 2, d. 352, list 18, 20.

20 On the Stockholm Plan, see Wilhelm M. Carlgren, *Varken – eller: Reflektioner kring Sveriges Ålandspolitik 1938–1939* (Stockholm: Militärhistoriska förlaget, 1977); cf. also Krister Wahlbäck, *Finlandsfrågan i svensk politik, 1937–1940* (Stockholm: Norstedts, 1964), pp. 137–62; Alf W. Johansson, *Finlands sak: Svensk politik och opinion under vinterkriget 1939–1940* (Stockholm: Allmänna förlaget, 1973), pp. 19–31.

21 Shaposhnikov, Gusev and Gavrilov, 3 November 1938, 'spravka po voprosu ob okruplenii Abo–Alandskogo arkhipelaga', draft, f. r-1877, o. 1, d. 132, list 3–5; V. N. Baryshnikov, *Ot prokhladnogo mira k zimney voyne: Vostochnaya politika Finlandii v 1930-e gody* (St Petersburg: Izdatelstvo Sankt Peterburgskogo universiteta, 1997), pp. 202–3; cf. directive by Voroshilov, 27 April 1939, on the subjugation of the various fleets and flotillas under the military districts in time of war, f. r-1877, o. 1, d. 77, list 1–3; Gunnar Åselius, 'Östersjöområdet i sovjetisk marindoktrin, 1920–1940', *Tidskrift i Sjöväsendet*, no. 1 (1997), pp. 53–4.

22 L. Ivanov, 'Problema Alandskikh ostrovov', *Morskoy sbornik*, vol. 92(12) (1939); Anonymous, 'Alandskie ostrova (geograficheskaya spravka)', *Morskoy Sbornik*, vol. 92(12) (1939); N. Novikov, 'Gangutskaya pobeda: Kampanii 1713 i 1714 gg. na finlandskom teatre i Gangutskaya operatsiya', *Morskoy Sbornik*, vol. 92(12) (1939).

23 Chief of Naval Staff Galler to Baltic Fleet Soviet, 13 May 1938, f. r-1877, o. 1, d. 39, list 7.

24 People's Commissar for the Navy Frinovsky to People's Commissar for Foreign Affairs Litvinov, 4 January 1939, f. r-1877, o. 1, d. 132, list 2; head of the department of law, People's Commissariat for Foreign Affairs, to Minister Yrjö-Koskinen, 15 January 1939 (copy), ibid., list 7–8.

25 Galler to Plotkin, 14 April 1939, f. r-1877, o.1, d. 132, list 15; Plotkin to Galler, 10 April, 25 April 1939, ibid., list 17, 21.

26 Kuznetsov to Deputy People's Commissar for Foreign Affairs Potemkin, 10 June 1939, f. r-1877, o.1, d. 132, list 27.

27 General Secretary Bogomilov, People's Commissariat for Foreign Affairs to Isakov, 28 September 1939, f. r-1877, o. 1, d. 132, list 31; Isakov to Bogomilov, ibid., 28 September 1939, ibid., list 32.

28 Cf. Herrick, *Soviet Naval Strategy*, p. 27.

29 E. L. Woodward and R. Butler (eds), *Documents on British Foreign Policy, 1919–1939*, series 3, vol. VII (London: Her Majesty's Stationery Office, 1954), pp. 576–7.

30 Ibid., pp. 33 (quote), 587, 597; there is no mention of this conversation in Kuznetsov's memoirs, but his image of Drax was clearly unsympathetic; cf. Kuznetsov, *Nakanune*, pp. 232–6.

31 Ibid., p. 601; cf. the final report of the military mission, p. 609.

32 For Soviet documents on these negotiations, including the texts of relevant treaties, see V. G. Komplektov *et al.* (eds), *Polpredy soobschayut…Sbornik dokumentov ob otnosheniyakh SSSR s Latviey, Litvoy i Estoniey: avgust 1939 g.–avgust 1940 g.* (Moscow: Ministerstvo Innostranikh del, 1990), pp. 57–88, 101–13, 135, 141–42, 220–7; cf. David M. Crowe, *The Baltic States and the Great Power: Foreign Relations, 1938–40* (Boulder, CO: Westview Press, 1993), pp. 88–98; on the military planning against Estonia, see Pavel Petrov, 'Osvoenie Pribaltiki: KBF v Estonii i Latvii (oktybabr 1939–febral 1940 gg.)', *Tayfun*, no. 3 (2000), pp. 14–15.

33 On the Swedish Navy's reaction, see Åke Holmquist, *Flottans beredskap, 1938–1940* (Stockholm: Allmänna förlaget, 1972), pp. 139–48; Stavitsky *et al.*, 16 October 1939, 'Artilleriskaya sistema oborony poberezha baltiskogo morya i vynesennogo vpered bazirovaniya KBF', f. r-1877, o. 1, d. 40, list 251–61; cf. order by Kuznetsov, 19 November 1939, ibid., list 317; on the Baltic Fleet's move into Estonia and Latvia in 1939–40, see part II of Pavel Petrov's article 'Osvoenie Pribaltiki: KBF v Estonii i Latvii (oktybabr 1939–febral 1940 gg.)', *Tayfun*, no. 4 (2000).

34 Wilhelm M. Carlgren, 'Den stora överraskningen. Regeringen och Moskvapakten', in Bo Hugemark (ed.), *Stormvarning: Sverige inför andra världskriget* (Stockholm: Probus, 1989), pp.152–3; idem, *Svensk utrikespolitik 1939–1945* (Stockholm: Allmänna förlaget, 1973), p. 38; Johansson, *Finlands sak*, pp. 54–6: Wahlbäck, *Finlandsfrågan*, p. 169.
35 Max Jakobson, *The Diplomacy of the Winter War: An Account of the Russo-Finnish War 1939–1940* (Cambridge, MA: Harvard University Press, 1965), pp. 114–18, 135–7.
36 Komplektov *et al.* (eds), *Polpredy soobschayut...*, p. 76.
37 People's Commissariat for Defense, directive on the subordination in wartime of various fleets and flotillas under military districts and armies, 27 April 1939, f. r-1877, o. 1, d. 77, list 2–3.
38 Shedshov, 23 October 1939, f. r-1877, o. 1, d. 80, list 12–20.
39 Baltic Fleet commander Tributs (signed A. Shedshov), 23 November 1939, draft memorandum, f. r-1877, o. 1, d. 80, list 12–20; Kuznetsov to Stalin and Molotov, 3 November 1939, ibid., list 21.
40 Kuznetsov to the Baltic Fleet Soviet, 23 November 1939, f. r-1877, o. 1, d. 91, list 115–21; Carl van Dyke, *Soviet Invasion of Finland*, pp. 52–3.
41 Holmquist, *Flottans beredskap*, pp. 148–92; Belli, 8 December 1939, 'Spravka o territorialnikh vodakh Shvetsii i olandskogo arkhipelaga', f. r-1678, o. 1, d. 125, list 122–6.
42 Kuznetsov to Stalin, Molotov and Zhdanov, 5 April 1940, f. r-1678, o. 1, d. 162, list 362.
43 Molotov to Baltic Fleet Soviet, 4 April 1940, f. r-1877, o. 2, d. 97, list 164; cf. Kuznetsov to Baltic Fleet Soviet, 4 April 1940, f. r-1877, o. 1, d. 164, list 164–6.
44 Bond, 'British War Planning', pp. 123–35.
45 Ilga Grava-Kreituse *et al.* (eds), *The Occupation and Annexation of Latvia 1939–1940: Documents and Materials* (Riga: Latvijas Vestures fonds, 1995), p.184.
46 Timoshenko to Baltic Fleet, 9 June 1940, f. r-1877, o. 1, d. 97, list 179–80; Tributs, 10 June 1940, ibid., list 174–8.
47 Soviet documents on the annexation in 1940 – including intelligence assessments of the situation and the text of the military treaties – can be found in Komplektov *et al.* (eds), *Polpredy soobschayut...*, pp. 339–40, 355–60, 397–8, 406–7, 412–13, 429–31, 443–5, 455–9, 462–3, 468–70; on the resettlement of the Estonian islanders, see Kuznetsov to Molotov, 9 September 1940, with draft for a regulation, f. r-1678, o. 1, d. 162, list 828–9.
48 Pantaleyev to Kuznetsov, 5 July 1940, 'Soobrazheniya o veroyatnikh boevikh deystviakh na Baltike', f. r-1877, o. 1, d. 146, list 108–11.
49 Kuznetsov to Baltic Fleet Soviet, 24 July 1940, f. r-1877, o. 2, d. 80, list 22–4.
50 Material on the 1940 war games in f. r-92, o. 2, d. 756.
51 Rohwer and Monakov, *Stalin's Ocean-going Fleet*, pp. 117–21.
52 Barsukov and Zolotarev (eds), *Russkiy arkhiv*, vol. I. 2, p. 33; cf. his statements during the December conference in Moscow, pp. 250–3.

12

READY FOR OFFENSIVE OPERATIONS?

In January 1936, together with his colleague Flagman Orlov at UVMS, the chief of the RKKA General Staff, Marshal Alexander Yegorov, presented a new naval construction program which signified the beginning of the Soviet School. All in all, the program contained 676 ships (among them 24 battleships, 20 cruisers, 199 destroyers and 344 submarines), with a total tonnage of 1.727 million tons. The marshal and the flagman had seemingly overcome traditional service rivalry, as Yegorov's original proposal had even been more ambitious than Orlov's, containing six aircraft carriers and a total tonnage of 1.868 million tons. In June the same year, the Soviet government approved a modified version of their joint proposal, containing 533 ships at 1.307 million tons. Orlov first made the great oceanic naval program public to the world in a speech at the extra-congress of Soviets, which had convened in Moscow in late November 1936 to approve the new Soviet Constitution. The Baltic Fleet was to have eight of the 24 new battleships. Four of these were to be of type A on 41,500 tons – to comply with the regulations of the Washington treaty their displacement was officially stated as 35,000 tons – and four of type B on 26,000 tons. In addition came six light cruisers, 44 flotilla leaders and destroyers and 78 submarines of various sizes.[1]

Orlov justified the new policy with a growing threat from the surrounding world, but most Soviet naval leaders were taken by surprise. According to Kuznetsov's memoirs, Galler – then commander of the Baltic Fleet – asserted that there had been a meeting between Stalin and the Soviet fleet commanders in late 1935, at which Stalin had asked what types of ships they needed in the future. They had all asked for submarines. The Pacific commander, Viktorov, also wanted big ships, the commander in the Black Sea, Kozhanov, cruisers, destroyers and MTBs. 'You don't know what you want,' Stalin commented and dissolved the meeting. Then, the fleet commanders heard little until Orlov's speech at the Congress of Soviets in November 1936. The details of the proposal had been worked out in secrecy by Orlov, the commandant of the Naval War College, Ivan Ludri, and representatives of the People's Commissariat for Armaments. In 1930, the naval branch of the RKKA had received less than 10 percent of defense spending. Nine years later, the proportion had risen to 18.5 percent or nearly 5 percent of total government expenditure.[2]

In keeping with the naval policy, the UMS was transformed into a regular naval staff on 17 January 1937. The new organization, which was created by Lev Galler, was to execute overall control of the naval forces, while the naval commander's responsibilities were extended to encompass all aspects of naval activities, including armaments and construction works (the Bureau of Coastal Construction Works was transferred to the new Naval Staff from the RKKA Engineering Directorate). In March, the office as naval commander was made synonymous with Deputy People's Commissar for Defense. Also, the fleet soviets, which until then had been reporting to the RKKA General Staff, were to answer directly to the People's Commissariat for Defense. On 30 December, the navy was finally endowed with its own People's Commissariat, and through the division of the People's Commissariat for Military Industry into four separate commissariats in January 1939, a special People's Commissariat for Naval Armaments was also created (the other three military industrial commissariats dealt with aircraft, ammunition and arms).[3]

The tightening of links between the naval command and the shipbuilding industry was necessitated by the repeated changes in the construction program. In the autumn of 1937, the number of planned battleships and submarines had been cut down and the number of cruisers and destroyers increased. As the tonnage of each of the two battleship types had grown heavily and two new categories of ships were added – heavy cruisers and aircraft carriers – the total tonnage of the future Soviet fleet had risen all the same, now approaching 1.99 million tons. According to this version of the program, the Baltic Fleet was to consist of six *B*-type battleships (48,000 tons), two *M*-type battleships (modernized *Gangut* class, 23,000 tons), two heavy cruisers (also 23,000 tons), six light cruisers, 44 destroyers and 78 submarines of various sizes.[4]

In the next version of the program, authored in early 1938 by Chief of Staff Galler and the newly appointed People's Commissar, Smirnov, the number of battleships had been further reduced (from 20 to 15) but their size again increased, so that the total naval tonnage was now close to 2.3 million tons – more than that of any other navy in the world! The *B*-type battleship had been scrapped but the *A*-type – the *Sovetsky Soyuz* class – somewhat enlarged (from 57,000 to 59,000 tons). At the same time, the number of battleships in the Baltic Fleet had been reduced from six to four. As compensation, the number of heavy cruisers was increased from two to three.[5]

Before the end of 1939, the naval construction plan had been revised a fourth time. The number of battleships in the Baltic Fleet was further reduced, the number of cruisers, destroyers and submarines expanded. According to a memorandum by Kuznetsov from October 1939, the scheduled force in 1947 was two battleships of type *A* (*Sovetsky Soyuz*), two battleships of type *M* (ex-*Gangut*), six heavy cruisers, eight light cruisers, 56 flotilla leaders and destroyers and 89 submarines.[6] Furthermore, the tonnage of the heavy cruisers had been increased from 23,000 to 35,000 tons to make them compatible with the German *Scharnhorst* class battleships.[7]

According to the program, the Soviet Union would possess a tremendous naval force in the narrow Baltic theater by the late 1940s. But how was it to be used effectively?

Scenarios for war, 1936–40

From the mid-1930s, one single scenario dominated all war planning in the Baltic Theater: war against Germany, supported by Poland, Finland, Estonia and Latvia. The two latter states might enter the war in a later stage, when the threat of immediate Soviet retaliation had been reduced. In 1938–39, the following missions were identified for the Baltic Fleet:

- Secure the area of deployment (= capture the islands in the Gulf of Finland) and defend the approaches to Leningrad.
- Support the Red Army's operations against Finland, Estonia and Latvia.
- Expand the fleet's base area westwards toward the mouth of the Gulf.
- Operate against enemy communications in the Baltic.
- Prevent the enemy from taking up positions along the coasts by attacking his naval forces and bases.[8]

The first of these tasks will be examined below in the context of defensive operations, the four others lumped together as 'offensive operations'. It is important to notice that all five missions had to be solved with the resources available at the time. None of the battleships envisaged in the oceanic naval program would be operational before 1942. Considering how questionable the Baltic Fleet's ability to operate outside the Gulf of Finland had seemed already in 1935, additional demands on operational range were likely to be critical. Nonetheless, such demands were now made, as the area of operations was extended all the way across the Baltic to the shores of Sweden and Germany. Before any of the new warships had been delivered, the only weapon systems in the fleet that could operate at such distances were submarines and aircraft. Although the fleet's submarine force was growing its air arm remained comparatively weak, and the question of how to divide the resources of air power between the fleet and the Red Army became an increasingly important aspect of organizational rivalry. In addition, the recreation of a naval staff and a people's commissariat meant that much of the fleet's operational planning was moved away from Kronstadt to Moscow. The conflict which had existed within the navy during the 1920s, between the regional and central levels of command, now reemerged.

Finally, the planned growth of the Baltic Fleet made certain that in a few years' time the existing base facilities would be inadequate. Although from a strategic perspective the expansion of the fleet's base area into Estonian, Latvian and Finnish territory in 1939–40 meant an improvement, it also put a heavy strain on the Baltic Fleet's resources.

Defensive operations

In April 1938, the newly appointed People's Commissar, Smirnov, reviewed the Baltic Fleet's plans for the initial stage of war. Just as before, the defense of Leningrad was to rely on minefields. Within 72 hours, about a third of the 4,754 mines and 1,926 sweeping obstacles in stock were to be dispersed along the GOR, between Shepelev and Stirsudden. Most of these mines would be of pre-World War I vintage, while the more modern material (model 1926 and later) was saved for later use. However, as Baltic Fleet Commander Levchenko made sure to notify the People's Commissar, he had received no information on the general campaign plan from the Naval Staff in Moscow. Levchenko assumed that some kind of forward defensive mine barrier would be necessary in the Hogland–Tootersaari area. However, unless he knew exactly where the fleet was to operate during the latter stages of the war, his staff could not prepare in advance the necessary instructions regarding ship movements in mined waters.[9]

The Naval Staff in Moscow imagined that the very first move in a defensive campaign would be to send out aircraft, submarines and destroyers to reconnoiter toward Tallinn, Helsinki and the mouth of the Gulf. If any enemy units appeared before the mine defenses had been completed, they were to be attacked. In the meantime, an infantry battalion was to storm ashore on Seskar and Lavensaari and erect two 6-inch batteries on these islands to stiffen up the forward mine defense zone, stretching from the Luzhky Bay area in the south to the waters off Björkö in the north with some 2,200 mines and 500 sweeping obstacles. When the enemy fleet had entered the Gulf and started its advance toward Leningrad, it was to be delayed in the forward zone by submarines and MTBs, patroling in the waters east of Hogland. However, no battleships were to engage the enemy at this position. In spite of the big-ship rhetoric of the day, this in fact signified a more cautious attitude compared to the 1935 operational plan.

The oblong-shaped main defense zone, the GOR, stretched out from the Stirsudden–Shepelev perimeter toward the southeast, sealing off Kaporsky Bay from landing attempts. However, the calculated number of mines to be used – some 15,000 – much exceeded the amount available in the Baltic Fleet's supplies. The defense of the GOR was to be conducted along the lines suggested by Rodionov in 1935. Three strike groups – one consisting of battleships, cruisers and destroyers, the two others of destroyers, MTBs and submarines, and all three supported by bombers and torpedo planes – were to take turns against the enemy when he approached the minefields. Along the shores in the north and south coastal artillery, gunboats, submarines and MTBs were prepared to fight off landing attempts and prevent escape. To protect Kronstadt, should the enemy advance that far, the remaining resources were kept in reserve together with units from the Red Army. In wintertime, should the enemy attack Kronstadt across the ice with ground troops the way Tukhachevsky had done during the 1921 mutiny, a special plan existed. A rather ambitious defense system would be erected around Kotlin Island, complete with anti-tank mines, explosive charges, barbed wire and an electric fence more than 15 miles long.[10]

Smirnov's short reign as Naval Commissar (in June 1938, after less than six months in the job, he fell victim to the 'Great Terror') was also characterized by efforts for increased preparedness. The risk of the fleet being locked up in port during mobilization must be avoided at all costs. Therefore, a part of the fleet was always to be ready to set sail within six hours: one battleship (later specified as *Oktyabrskaya Revolutsiya*), three patrol boats, three destroyers, four submarine squadrons (one with large, two with middle-sized and one with small submarines), one squadron of MTBs, one minelayer and three minesweepers. In addition (with two to six hours' readiness) came the normal contingency crew in the coastal fortifications, two squadrons of heavy bombers, one squadron of long-range reconnaissance aircraft and 12 squadrons of fighter planes. The level of readiness was to be tested in monthly exercises.[11] Finally, in the summer of 1939, the Soviet Navy introduced a three-level system of combat readiness. According to Sergey Zonin, this reform was inspired by Galler's memories of the successful mobilization in 1914 and by Kuznetsov's experience from Spain of the threat from the air. Normal peacetime conditions would be equivalent to level 3, level 2 meant readiness to go to sea within 4–6 hours, level 1 readiness to go to sea within 1–4 hours.[12] With this system, the Soviet naval forces entered World War II.

Clearly, the defense of the naval base area also pertained to the cooperation with the RKKA. To what extent could the army be relied on? A conference between the fleet staff and the LVO in May 1939 illustrated the lack of cooperative spirit between the two services. The RKKA representatives revealed that, according to their present plan, the area east of the old imperial summer palace at Peterhof would be left virtually undefended all the way to Kronstadt. It was decided that LVO would set up an additional infantry brigade and a unit of DB-3 bombers for this purpose, but that the money would be taken out of the fleet's budget. The Fleet Soviet made a reservation against paying for the aircraft, as these could be used for other purposes than defending naval installations.[13]

Offensive operations – and the question of air support

The growing role of air power and the increased competition for scarce aircraft primarily affected the planning for offensive operations. In 1937, Yegorov stated that any German battleships sighted at the mouth of the Gulf of Finland must be eliminated immediately, by submarines or from the air. For this purpose, he said, additional bomber units could be transferred to the Baltic Fleet air arm by the commander of the Northwestern Front.[14]

As we have seen, the notion of subordinating the front's air resources to the fleet was not entirely new. However, in 1937 the designated commander of the Northwestern Front was Boris Shaposhnikov, who had returned as commander of the LVO after a term as chief of the RKKA General Staff. Rather than transferring his own bomber regiments to the fleet, Shaposhnikov preferred to transfer those of the Baltic Fleet to his own command. During the first two weeks of the war, they were to participate in the Northwestern Front air campaign against Finland and the Baltic countries. Among the targets were the capitals of these countries, their airfields, ports and military bases, the city of Vyborg and the power station in Imatra.

Shaposhnikov also expected the Baltic Fleet to set ashore a division-sized landing force in the area of Hamina–Kotka–Lovisa during the third week of the war.[15] No later than 20 April, Shaposhnikov told the fleet staff in Kronstadt in January 1937, the plans for the landing operation must be ready. Toward the end of May, Fleet Commander Sivkov reported that due to shortage of personnel, planning had merely begun. One officer on Sivkov's staff, Captain 3rd rank Golubchev, was alone on the job, working 16–17 hours a day including weekends.[16] Although a division-sized landing at Hamina–Kotka–Lovisa seemed possible to execute, it was an undertaking which would be both difficult and risky. Just like his successor Galler before him, Sivkov complained about the shortage of large surface ships in the fleet. For want of cruisers and destroyers, he would have to send his vulnerable battleships into action on the very first day of war. Nor were there enough minesweepers, no amphibious brigade, no landing craft, no anti-air artillery, not enough ammunition. For certain types of artillery – the 1.8-inch (45 mm) ship gun and the 3-inch (76 mm) anti-air gun – the stock was limited to some 300 shells. There was also a shortage of fortification material. The field works that were planned on the islands in the Gulf of Finland and at Fort Ino during the first month of war would alone require some 600 tons more material than was available. Finally, as Galler had already noticed, the reinforced infantry battalion which was to capture Björkö was likely to prove too small.[17]

Because of the Terror, which engulfed both Sivkov and several of his close subordinates, it seems as if the 1937 operational plan was never completed. As alleged 'enemy agents' had been disclosed in the fleet staff, Shaposhnikov (who had now returned back to Moscow and the job as chief of the RKKA General Staff) shortly afterwards ordered a new version of the Baltic Fleet's operational plan. It was to be ready before the end of September, but Isakov, who had replaced the unfortunate Sivkov as fleet commander, asked for additional time.[18]

The RKKA General Staff was not the only organ issuing planning directives to the Baltic Fleet Staff. The Naval Staff in Moscow also had a list of requirements. In the spring of 1938, it mentioned among the fleet's offensive missions support for the RKKA, extension of the base area toward the mouth of the Gulf, operations against enemy communications, naval forces and bases in the Baltic. The mission to support the RKKA consisted of enlarging the base area westwards, giving fire support to the troops fighting ashore, protecting the RKKA's flank in the archipelago with mines and floating burners and executing minor landing operations on the enemy's flank. To this end, special coastal support forces (BOS = *Beregovoy Otryad Soprovozhdeniya*) were to be formed along the northern and southern shores of the Gulf, equipped with landing craft, amphibious tanks, midget submarines and MTBs. The widening of the base area to the mouth of the

Gulf was to be coordinated with the RKKA's advance ashore. A series of landing operations – from both the sea and the air – was to be followed by the establishment of fortified strong points along the Estonian coast and in the Finnish archipelago. To disturb enemy communications in the Baltic, submarines and aircraft were to operate against Tallinn, Helsinki, the mouth of the Gulf of Finland, the Gulf of Bothnia, the Gulf of Riga, Danzig Bay and the Baltic ports of Germany. The same combination of forces was also to strike against enemy naval forces and bases in Finland, Estonia, Latvia and Lithuania.[19]

Thus, the Naval Staff regarded aircraft and submarines as the only weapon systems with a sufficient range to operate outside the Gulf of Finland. In spite of the big-ship rhetoric of the period, the *Gangut* class battleships were reserved for fire support against the coast. Therefore, the Baltic Fleet's chief of staff, Vladimir Tributs, was probably disappointed when he evaluated the fleet's war games in March 1938. Although the air arm commanders had displayed tactical initiative, coordination between navy and air units had been slack or nonexistent. Landing operations had been attempted against the enemy coast without previous reconnaissance or sufficient fire preparation. When maneuvering through the archipelago, commanders had shown little awareness of the threat from torpedoes and mines. Had it not been for the many serious blunders of the defending 'blue side' during the exercise, the 'reds' would probably have been defeated.[20]

In order to facilitate the conduct of joint operations in accordance with the 1937 combat regulation (BU 37), in June 1939 surface combatants in both the Baltic and Black Sea Fleets were reorganized. The main body of the fleet was to form the *eskadra*, later defined by People's Commissar Kuznetsov as 'units able to carry out operations independently within the entire theater, separated from their bases'.[21] In the Baltic *eskadra*, the two battleships and four of the destroyers were to support ground operations and engage the enemy's heavy units. The two cruisers and the remaining eight destroyers formed the OLS (*Otryad Legikh Sil* = Group of Light Forces), which was to operate against enemy communications together with submarines and aircraft. In the rear, patrol escorts, minesweepers, depot ships and netlayers were to form a special force for base defense: the OVR (*Okhrana Vodnoga Rayona* = Aquatic Area Defense).[22]

Expanding the base area

As we have seen, the requirements put on the fleet were gradually increased during 1937 and 1938, the area of operations constantly extended westwards. In the 1939 operational plan (which had to be revised in August, when Poland no longer seemed a likely Germany ally), the Baltic Fleet was even expected to operate against the Åland Islands.[23]

In light of this, the location of the fleet's bases appeared even more awkward than before. Already in 1937, Marshal Yegorov had warned the government that a new naval base would be needed in the theater, pointing out Luzhky Bay as a suitable site.[24] In June 1939, Chief of the Naval Staff Galler reported that in 1947 the

Baltic Fleet would consist of eight battleships, two heavy and six light cruisers, 44 destroyers and 78 submarines. Only about two-thirds of that force could be accommodated within the present base facilities, even if these were to be enlarged. Consequently, additional ports must be secured, preferably ports that were closer to the expected area of operations out in the Baltic – and less vulnerable to enemy blockade – than the present ones in Kronstadt and Oranienbaum. According to Galler's proposal, three separate ports were to be constructed in Luzhky Bay, complete with docks, repair and supply facilities, an electrical power plant and a water reservoir, protecting fortifications, connecting roads and a railway network for internal transport. Furthermore, to house navy personnel and their families, an entire community was to be erected on the premises with schools, shops, a post office, a cinema and a sports arena with room for 2,000 spectators.[25] Needless to say, the existing bases in Kronstadt and Oranienbaum also had to be modernized and expanded.[26]

This, of course, was an enormous project that would bind the fleet's resources for many years. Had Galler known that the navy would soon have better base sites on foreign territory at its disposal, he would hardly have made such extensive long-term plans. The Molotov–Ribbentrop Pact came as a surprise to him just as much as to the rest of the world. When Soviet troops marched into Poland in mid-September, even Kuznetsov was uninformed, although the Pinsk flotilla was expected to support the operation. Nor had the desired locations for naval bases in the Baltic countries been specified when the first proposal for a base treaty was presented to the Estonians on 24 September 1939. According to Galler's biographer, Sergey Zonin, naval commanders knew nothing. One day, Galler was simply told that talks were going on about a deployment of Soviet military forces in the Baltic countries, so the navy must prepare a list of its 'maximum and minimum demands'. On the evening of 29 September, when a draft agreement had already been signed with the Estonians, Galler presented his proposal to Stalin personally. Present at this meeting were also Kuznetsov and his deputy Isakov.[27]

Zonin's account is difficult to harmonize with the list of Stalin's visitors in the Kremlin during September–October 1939. Galler's name appears only on 5 October, when he was received between 8.45 and 11.50 p.m. together with Kuznetsov. From the same source it is also clear that Stalin had met with Kuznetsov and Isakov before this date (on 15, 18 and 19 September).[28] The Baltic Fleet's future redeployment may well have been discussed on these occasions. Trying to establish the sequence of events in detail would bring us too far. What matters is that although naval considerations were the main motive behind the Soviet Union's propositions to the Baltic countries and Finland, the navy still played a secondary role during the following negotiations. When Kuznetsov informed Galler about the talks with the Estonians, he in turn had learnt it from the chief of the RKKA General Staff, Shaposhnikov. Although seven of the military treaties that were signed with the Estonians on 11 October concerned naval matters and were signed by Isakov, Deputy People's Commissar for the Navy, the Soviet military delegation was still led by an army general, LVO commander Meretskov. In a similar way, during the talks that followed with the Latvians shortly afterwards Isakov had to share chairmanship of the Soviet delegation with the commander of the Kalinin Military District, General Boldin.[29]

Although the Baltic Fleet's forward deployment to Estonia and Latvia was strategically advantageous to the navy, it would also require huge investments. In October 1939, Kuznetsov addressed the government on the matter, identifying four future base areas for the fleet. The former base complex in Kronstadt–Oranienbaum–Luzhky Bay would be maintained as rearward position with docks, repair and supply facilities. The new main base for large battleships and cruisers was to be Paldiski–Hanko at the mouth of the Gulf (Hanko was at the time still Finnish territory). To protect Paldiski–Hanko and operate against enemy communications in the Baltic, a support position for light cruisers, destroyers and submarines had to be created at Keygust in the Moonsund archipelago. Finally, a minor maneuver base was to be built at Liepaya–Vindava, close to the German border, where the tsarist government had tried to establish a naval base already in the 1890s.[30]

In order to defend these ports, some 30 new coastal battery positions had to be erected, together with 16 sites for anti-air artillery and ammunition depots. Not only the construction material and most of the artillery pieces had to be added to the navy's previous requests in the five-year plan, but also ammunition, range-finding and communications equipment (including several miles of cable), amphibious cranes, etc. Moreover, 10,000 local workers had to be hired in Estonia and Latvia, some 15,000 laborers called in from different parts of the Soviet Union, four new engineering battalions formed within the navy and two such battalions borrowed from the RKKA. In 1939–1940 alone, these works would run at some 220 million rubles, a sum roughly equivalent to the cost of operating the entire Pacific Fleet. Merely to man the new installations in the Baltic, navy personnel had to be increased by some 12,600 men during the next two years. While the navy's sailing personnel increased by some 31 percent during 1940, the coastal artillery and ground forces personnel grew by some 45 and 49 percent respectively.[31]

Meanwhile, Galler examined the need for new naval air bases, as the existing airstrips in the Baltic were no longer situated in the front line but some 250 miles away from the likely area of operations. In the future, these bases could only serve as areas for training and rest. However, if the air arm was to operate effectively over the mouth of the Gulf or as far away as the Kiel Canal or the Belts, at least ten new airstrips had to be built in Estonia and Latvia.[32] These additional construction works constituted a massive undertaking, and had not yet been included in the bill.

Even if the resources necessary to construct all these new installations could be found, air power would still be in short supply. According to optimistic calculations by the Moscow Naval Staff in November 1939, the Baltic Fleet could deploy 320 bombers and torpedo planes by 1943. Given a monthly operational time for each aircraft of 60 hours, there would be some 19,200 hours to spend on offensive missions in the theater.

There were four major ports for enemy warships – Danzig, Kiel, Karlskrona and Stockholm. Against these targets four attacks a month would be required, using four bomber squadrons each time. Enemy air bases in these cities and in Lübeck added another five targets to the list, each which would be attacked eight times a month with three squadrons. Three other cities – Pillau, Schweinemünde and Fårösund – constituted excellent forward bases for the enemy's light naval units and should be attacked six times each month with three squadrons each. In addition, enemy communications in the Gulf of Bothnia, along the coast of Sweden, in the southern Baltic and in the Sounds were to be raided at least ten times a month. Even if only one squad were sent on patrol in each direction, this operation would keep an entire squadron constantly occupied. Finally, some resources had to be reserved for support to the RKKA along the shores of the Gulf of Finland. When a deduction was made for the 10 percent losses expected, 92 percent (17,772 hours) of the available flying time for bombers and torpedo planes was already mortgaged. Thus, even if the Baltic Fleet air arm were substantially reinforced in the future, the margins would be truly narrow.[33]

Fakel

At 00.58 hours on 30 November 1939, the Fleet Staff in Kronstadt radioed the codeword *Fakel* (Torch) to all Soviet warships in the Baltic. This was the order to commence operations against Finland. After nearly two decades of preparations, the Baltic Fleet finally went into action. Fleet Commander Tributs disposed the surface warships in the *eskadra* and the OLS (two battleships, one cruiser, two flotilla leaders and 11 destroyers), three squadrons of submarines with 29 submarines and a number of smaller ships (62 MTBs, four gunboats, 12 patrol ships, 28 minesweepers, 33 patrol craft, three minelayers). In addition came the coastal artillery, organized into three fortified regions with 22 fixed batteries (93 heavy artillery pieces), and the fleet air arm, divided into one bomber, one fighter and one mixed wing, three reconnaissance squadrons and three special units – altogether 469 aircraft (246 fighter planes, 111 bombers, 102 reconnaissance planes and 10 fire-control planes).

The much weaker opponent, the Finnish Navy, consisted of two coast defense battleships (3,900 tons), four gunboats, five submarines, six minelayers, 18 minesweepers, seven MTBs and about 25 coastguard vessels of various types. The Finnish coastal artillery was organized into three regiments and two sections, deployed on Lake Ladoga and along the Gulf of Finland, with 410 pieces of artillery of various calibers. The Finnish naval air arm consisted of eight old hydroplanes, organized into two squadrons.[34]

In spite of this overwhelming Soviet superiority, the results of the campaign were not entirely satisfactory, as Kuznetsov admitted in his memoirs.[35] As the Kremlin had expected the Finns to surrender at the negotiation table, no serious war preparations had been made, especially not for a winter campaign. As late as 3 November, Kuznetsov issued the preliminary instructions to the Baltic Fleet, and an operational plan was prepared in great haste in the following days.[36] The final campaign orders appeared on 23 November, only a week before the beginning of operations.

The fleet air arm was to protect Leningrad, support naval operations and attack enemy fortifications in Helsinki, Hanko and Björkö. Attacks against population centers were to be avoided unless they contained significant troop concentrations (a few days after the initial bombing of Helsinki on 30 November, the bombing of civilian targets was forbidden altogether).[37] The fleet was to

- Destroy the Finnish naval forces and prevent their escape to Sweden
- Block the Finnish coast and the Åland Islands
- Support the ground offensive on the Karelian Isthmus
- Capture the islands in the Gulf of Finland
- Secure Soviet sea lines of communications and the naval forces' forward deployment.

How did the fleet perform these various missions?

In spite of an intensive search by submarines and aircraft, it proved impossible to sink any Finnish warships. The only ship lost to the Finnish Navy was the coastguard vessel *Aurora*, which sank when one of her own depth charges detonated aboard. The two coast defense battleships *Väinömöinen* and *Ilmarinen*, which were highly prioritized targets, were attacked repeatedly from the air without success. The Soviets dropped 63 tons of bombs against them without a single hit, losing at least three – perhaps as many as eight – aircraft in the attacks. The most effective weapon from the air against ships – torpedoes – could not be used because of the ice.[38]

The blockade of the Finnish coast, which was not proclaimed until 10 December, was initially entrusted to the submarine force. The main Finnish sea line of communication went from Sweden across the Gulf of Bothnia to the port of Turku. On the first day of the blockade, Soviet submarines sunk three ships (two German ships and one Estonian freighter) and during the following four weeks another two (one Finnish and one Swedish ship). One Soviet submarine was lost, probably to mines. After 20 January 1940, Soviet submarine operations ceased altogether. According to official Soviet historiography, this was a consequence of difficult weather conditions and thickening ice.[39] However, the Gulf of Bothnia was not completely covered by ice until about a week later, so the weather was only partly to blame. Mistakes committed by Soviet submariners seem to have played a more immediate role in halting the campaign. A report from Isakov to Kuznetsov reveals how the Finnish air reconnaissance's spotting of the *S-1* on 20 January – when she sailed through the minefields above the surface in full daylight, in clear violation of all instructions – contributed to the decision to withdraw the submarines from the Baltic. Now, the secret route that Soviet submarines had used during their expeditions in and out of the Gulf of Bothnia, had been revealed to the enemy. In spite of this mistake, *S-1* was decorated with the Order of the Red Banner for its achievements, its commander Captain-Lieutenant A. V. Tripolsky awarded the prestigious 'Hero of the Soviet Union'.[40]

To avoid unacceptable submarine losses, Isakov urged that the campaign against enemy shipping should from now on be taken over by the fleet's air arm, which had hitherto concentrated its attacks on stationary targets like ports and railways. Now it would switch the emphasis to moveable targets at sea. As the period of daylight grew day by day, Isakov hoped the enemy ship movements would become increasingly vulnerable. Also, mines were to be dropped outside enemy ports. Stalin wanted to send submarines to mine the port of Turku, but this Kuznetsov and Galler managed to turn down.[41]

In mid-February, Isakov suggested that the air campaign was to be concentrated against the Finnish ice-breakers. If these were eliminated, traffic between Sweden and Finland would cease.[42] However, the ice-breakers proved just as difficult to destroy from the air as the coast defense battleships. Nor did heavy bombing of the Turku docks or the dropping of 45 mines in the waters outside the port sever communications to Sweden. After 10 February 1940, when the entire Baltic was covered with ice, shipping to and from Finnish ports decreased. The air campaign registered another four ships sunk (three Finnish and one Swedish), making the total number of sunken vessels nine. This figure should be compared to the total number of ships cleared in or out of Finnish ports during the war – 425.[43]

When it came to supporting the ground forces on the Karelian Isthmus, this task was entrusted to the shallow-going gunboats and to the coastal artillery, which could fire across the water into Finnish territory. In addition, isolated raids were made by the cruiser *Kirov* and some destroyers in early December against Finnish coastal batteries. One objective for these operations was to reconnoiter for a division-sized landing in the Björkö area, an undertaking which was postponed in view of the hard Finnish resistance. Instead, the battleships were sent forward against the Björkö batteries, the *Oktyabrskaya Revolutsiya* on 10 December and the *Marat* on 18–19 December (led by Isakov personally). The *Oktyabrskaya Revolutsiya* sailed off for a third battleship raid against Björkö on New Year's Day, but was called back because of the weather. After this, the *eskadra* remained in port for the rest of the war. On 30 December, Kuznetsov ordered that the air arm should take over the task of crushing Björkö as well, supported by railway batteries from the coastal artillery. In late February 1940, after the Finns had evacuated them, Red Army units advanced across the ice against the Björkö batteries and finally captured them.[44]

The capture of the islands in the Gulf of Finland was an operation that had worried the Baltic Fleet staff for at least a decade and a half. To operate in the difficult archipelago terrain, the so-called OON (*Otryad Osobennogo Naznacheniya* = Special Mission Squadron), had been formed, consisting of mobilized transport vessels, tug-boats and barges. For support, the OON could count on seven destroyers, specially detached from the OLS, a great number of escort patrol vessels and MTBs as well as some 136 bomber, fighter and reconnaissance aircraft. In the preparatory bombardments, the air arm flew 387 missions and dropped over 58 tons of bombs. When the troops stormed ashore, they found the islands

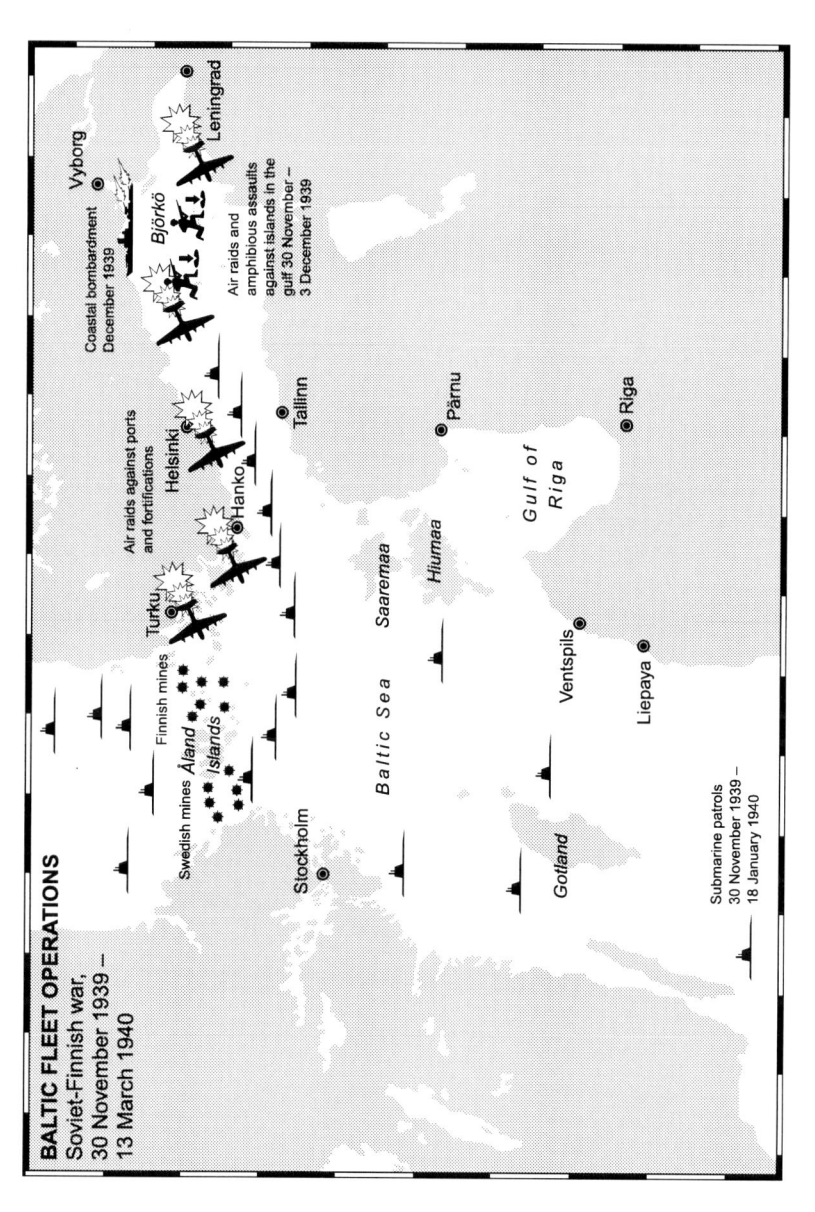

Map 4 Baltic Fleet operations, 1939–1940.

deserted. By 3 December 1939, all eight had been captured without losses.[45] In his report on joint operations during the conference of the Naval War College in October 1940, Vladimir Belli acidly remarked that the preparation of Soviet transport ships before the attack on the Gulf islands had taken considerable time, 'in spite of the fact that they had been preparing for this operation for 20 years and expected to meet strong opposition'.[46]

In late December 1939, the fleet organized its naval infantry into a rifle brigade consisting of five battalions, supported by an amphibious force consisting of small boats, artillery and tanks. This Baltic Fleet BOS did most of its fighting as regular infantry on the main front ashore at the Karelian Isthmus, rushing in alongside fresh recruits from the training squadron during the final days. Apart from the unopposed landing on the islands and some minor reconnaissance raids in the Björkö area in February, the Baltic Fleet's capacity for amphibious operations was never put to any real test during the war with Finland.[47]

The Baltic Fleet's last mission was to secure the Soviet sea lines of communication and expand the base area. The threat against the sea lines of communication was manageable. Finnish submarines mined the route between Leningrad and Tallinn/Paldiski (a German steamer was sunk) but never encountered any Soviet ships at sea. Kuznetsov's order to the Baltic Fleet Soviet on 14 February 1940 to prepare for a division-size landing east and west of Helsinki (at Hanko and Lovisa), could be described as an effort to expand the base area. This first echelon was later to be followed up by yet another division. Plans were also to be made for an invasion of the Åland Islands. However, none of these plans were to be ready before mid-April, and thus never acquired any real actuality.[48]

The Baltic Fleet lost submarine *S-2*, 12 aircraft, 309 dead and 1,291 wounded, sick and frostbitten (out of a total force of 62,780). The fleet air arm flew 16,663 missions (891 of them at night) and dropped some 2,600 tons of bombs. As there had been no missions against distant targets in Germany or Sweden, the flying time consumed was below the limits. However, as Deputy People's Commissar Isakov told the commanders of the Baltic Fleet at a meeting in Kronstadt on the day after the ceasefire, the next time the opponent would be harder to handle than the Finns.[49]

Apart from securing the islands in the Gulf, the Baltic Fleet thus hardly solved any of the tasks it had been assigned. As Pavel Petrov has demonstrated, not only did the campaign plan of 1939 contain too many missions, it also contained missions for which the fleet had not trained properly in peacetime. The blockade operation, for instance, presupposed a much closer cooperation between submarines and aircraft than really existed. In view of 20 years of preparations, intelligence on the Finnish naval forces and the geography of the Gulf of Bothnia had proven surprisingly weak.[50]

Out into the Baltic?

The Moscow Peace Treaty in March 1940 not only secured the Soviets control over the islands in inner part of the Gulf. It also gave them a foothold at Hanko

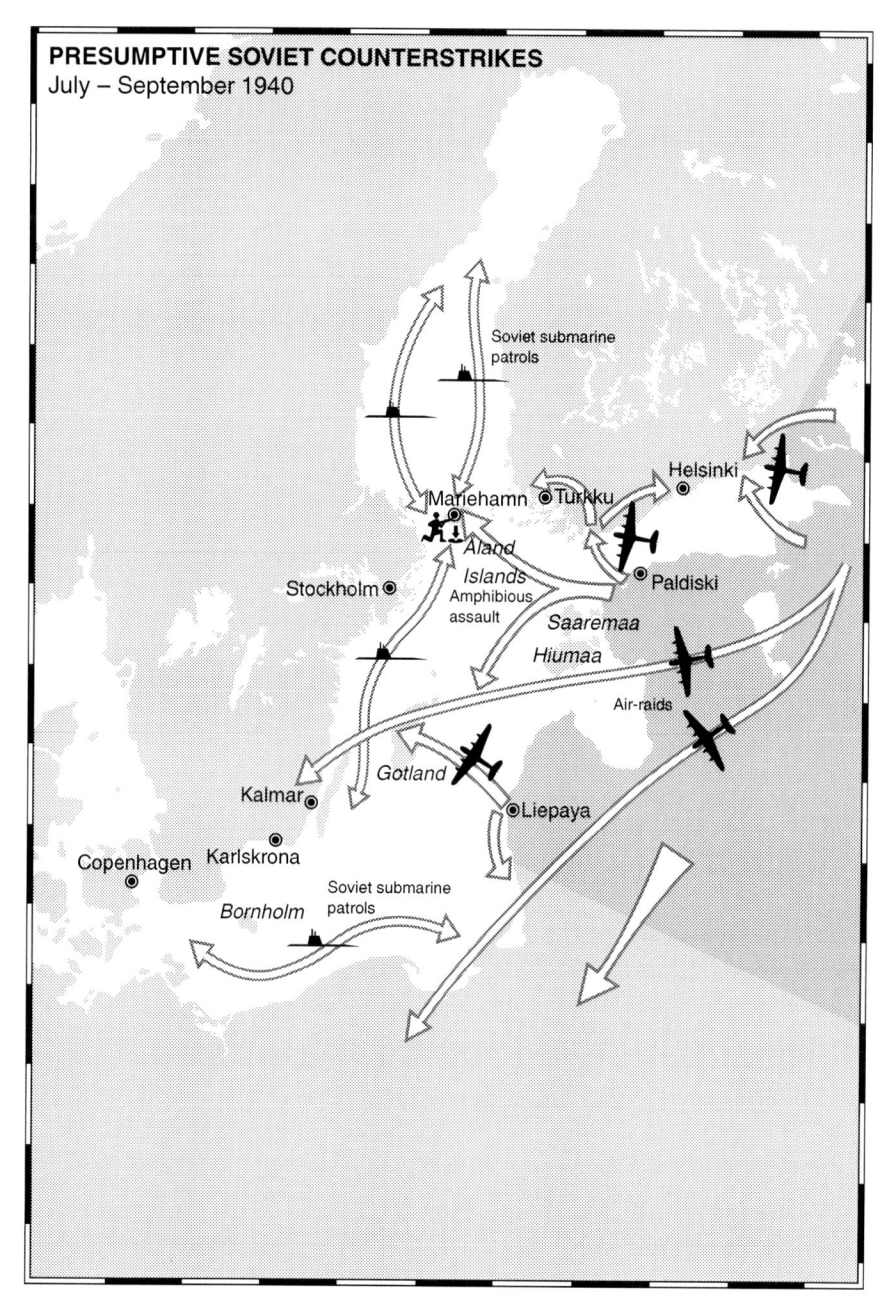

Map 5 Presumptive Soviet counterstrikes, 1940.

at the mouth. Thus, the Baltic Fleet could look more optimistically on the future. In a series of reports to Stalin, Molotov and Zhdanov on 5 April 1940, Kuznetsov stated that the Baltic Fleet in the future would conduct its operations as far west as possible. This, of course, must also affect the fleet's organization. The fleet soviet and the fleet staff must move from Kronstadt to Paldiski in Estonia.[51]

However, transferring command and control functions to Paldiski would take some time. Until the Paldiski base was fully operational in 1943, ships would have to return all the way to Kronstadt, some 250 miles eastwards, for maintenance, repair and replenishment of fuel and supplies. During winter this would not only be impractical, but impossible. Until the facilities at Paldiski had been completed, Tallinn would therefore serve as fleet headquarters.[52]

Finally, in the summer of 1940, Soviet naval planning in the Baltic seemed to have caught up with the offensive doctrine the RKKA had been cultivating for years. In July, Kuznetsov issued new planning directives to the Baltic Fleet Staff, ordering it both to defend the mouth of the Gulf of Finland and to keep control over the northern Baltic. The enemy's bases and ships were to be destroyed, his sea lines of communication severed and the advance of the RKKA supported through a series of surface, submarine and air operations.[53]

On 20–21 August, the first war games were held in the new geographical setting and with the new operational directives. As soon as the enemy's intention to attack had been established, the task of the defending 'Red' side was to carry out a lightning attack against Swedish, German and Finnish air and naval installations. Then, the fleet fell back on its defensive positions along the Baltic coast and at the mouth of the Gulf.[54]

Clearly, the preparations for preemptive strikes went beyond theoretical thinking. Thanks to a temporary deciphering breakthrough in the summer of 1940, Swedish radio intelligence could establish that the Baltic Fleet trained to lay mines outside Swedish ports.[55] In mid-August, the head of the Baltic Fleet's Intelligence Section delivered maps and aerial photographs over Stockholm, or 'target number 55621c' as the Swedish capital was labeled, to the fleet air arm.[56] The new operational plan also stated that mines were to be laid by submarines and aircraft outside Swedish ports and in the Baltic approaches, and submarines were to patrol Swedish coastal waters.[57]

In September 1940, the Baltic Fleet Staff presented a detailed plan for the capture of the Åland Islands, with one infantry division supported by two battalions of naval infantry and one battalion of paratroopers. To deceive the enemy, the embarkation of a minor landing force was to be staged in Liepaya. These ships would sail for the island of Gotland and only in a later stage turn north toward the Åland Islands. The main landing would be supported through air attacks against Stockholm and Turku.[58]

The problems of jointness

Just as before, however, offensive operations posed serious problems. The Baltic Fleet's strategic location may have improved, but its fighting capability still left much to be desired. When assessing the results of the 1940 war games, commentators stressed that participants had been ignorant of geographic conditions outside Soviet home waters, and had demonstrated poor knowledge of archipelago operations. There had also been a deplorable lack of depth in the deployment of forces. Without depth, joint operations between air, surface and submarine units would be difficult.[59]

The problems of jointness also overshadowed the discussions during the Naval War College conference in Leningrad in October 1940. How were the functions of command and control to be exercised in modern operations?

Captain Vladimir Rutkovsky, associate professor at the Naval War College's department of operations, claimed that the effect of Soviet submarine operations during the war against Finland had been considerably reduced due to the confused command structure. Orders had been delayed for hours or simply disappeared on the way. The tactical command was supposed to be in the hands of the squadron commanders at sea, but the latter had no wireless communication with their units. All instructions from the squadron commander to his ships had thus to be transmitted through the fleet staff in Kronstadt, which frequently changed orders without informing him.[60]

Although most participants agreed on concentrating powers with the squadron commanders at sea, there were still different opinions on whether there should be a special chief of submarine operations in the fleet. Another matter of discussion was the lack of supply ships in the Baltic Fleet. Most submarines in the Baltic Theater belonged to the middle and small-size categories. The reason for this was that Leningrad could be relied on for supply. Conditions were different in the Pacific Theater, where distances were vast and civilian infrastructure sparse. Here, submarines had to be big. However, the need for submarines in the Baltic to return frequently to base for replenishment also made it difficult to maintain an efficient blockade.[61] Admiral Isakov understood the need for more supply ships in the Baltic, he said, but due to the great oceanic naval program there was at present no space available in the Soviet shipyards. Supply ships had a construction time of two years and required a staple bed the same size as a cruiser.[62]

When it came to air–naval cooperation, the main presentation was done by Commander Petrovsky, deputy commandant of the college and head of scientific research. As the Germans had demonstrated, it was important to concentrate air resources. Organizationally, the Germans solved this by centralizing all aircraft to the *Luftwaffe*. Not even the pilots flying hydroplanes aboard German battleships belonged to the *Kriegsmarine*. The Soviets, on their part, had returned naval aviation to the navy in 1935 after having practiced the German system for many years. Was this good or bad?[63]

The Soviets knew that to solve its wartime missions the Navy would need air support from the regular VVS anyhow. At mobilization, the greater part of the VVS was to be subjugated to the different front commanders. In 1939–40, the VVS had been reorganized into regiments and divisions, partly with the aim of creating mixed formations like the Germans had with both fighter, reconnaissance and bomber squadrons. There were some worries among naval aviators that they would have to follow this example. Major-General Suvorov, head of the Naval Aviation Advanced Command Course in Peterhof, pointed out that such units could well be created within a military district with eight or nine air force divisions, each of them composed of five to six air force regiments. The navy had much fewer aircraft and, as a rule, no single fleet more than one or two complete regiments of fighters or bombers. If those units were to be dissolved, there would be no competent tactical commanders at any level.[64]

Colonel Kolesnikov, head of operations in the air arm directorate of the Naval Staff, made another worrying observation pertaining to the scale of modern operations. During one year of warfare, the German *Luftwaffe* had reportedly carried out some 3,500 strikes against various targets, which equaled an average of 9.7 operations per day. The Soviets on their part planned for one or two major bomb raids each day, and that would probably be the limit of their ability. In view of the distance between the western border zone and the military industrial centers of the country, and in view of the fact that during the initial weeks of war railways in the European part of the Soviet Union would be clogged with transports for the RKKA, the Baltic Fleet aviators could not expect any additional supplies or spare parts during the first two or three months of a campaign. To manage that long, they had to revise thoroughly their daily consumption norms for ammunition and fuel.[65]

Several speakers also emphasized that naval pilots must train on attacking targets at sea. Reconnoitering, protecting Soviet naval bases or bombing the bases of the enemy – those missions could always be entrusted to regular VVS pilots. Sinking a warship at sea, however, demanded specialist skills. In his concluding remarks to the discussion on air–naval cooperation, Admiral Isakov was blunt enough to formulate the matter from the perspective of service rivalry:

> The main task of our aviation is to know how to defeat the enemy at sea, in cooperation with our fleet. If anywhere in a real situation we should fail to cooperate operationally and tactically in a correct way, and subsequently [fail] to destroy in concentrated blows an enemy fleet crossing the sea...no one would forgive us. They would ask: 'For what reason were you to have an air arm?'[66]

However, as Isakov pointed out on this occasion and later in December when he talked to the naval command in Moscow, the growing role of air power in modern warfare should not lead to exaggerated formalism on the part of the Soviet Navy. The forces of dialectic materialism, according to which every successful weapon system would inspire equally successful countermeasures, ensured that the only correct approach to modern warfare was that of careful, unprejudiced study. No modern operation could be conceived without air power, but air power was not enough. The Baltic Fleet air arm had not succeeded in eliminating the Finnish coast defense battleships, nor had *Luftwaffe* defeated Britain. Not even the classical theories of sea power, which had gained some popularity among the younger generation of Soviet naval officers recently, could provide solutions in every situation. The Germans had succeeded in Norway before the eyes of the Royal Navy, in spite of British mastery at sea.[67]

The October conference also included special reports on the cooperation between ground and naval forces and between surface ships and other categories of naval forces. It should be noticed that the presenters – Vladimir Belli and Sergey Stavitsky – were both representatives of the old, pre-revolutionary officer corps. Belli emphasized that the Soviets must be able to land at several places simultaneously, in rough weather at a long distance from their bases – just as the Germans had succeeded in doing in Norway. The tame exercises that the Baltic Fleet held in the Gulf of Finland would not do as preparation. Support from paratroopers was necessary. Having seized a bridgehead – in the Åland Islands, for instance – troops must be prepared to hold it against enemy counterattacks.[68] During the following discussion, the Baltic Fleet naval infantry commander, Brigadier Nikolay Yulyanovich Denisevich, pointed out that his men were taught drill, shooting and guard duty by instructors from the Red Army, but there were no specialists to teach them how to disembark from a landing craft. During the war against Finland, fresh recruits from the naval training squadron had in fact performed better in combat than the naval infantry. In the future, the navy must recognize amphibious operations as a specialization in its own right.[69]

It should be noticed that during the entire conference at the Naval War College, discussions centered around the use of submarines and aircraft, and around joint operations with other services. Although more than half of the future tonnage of the Soviet Navy was to consist of heavy artillery ships, there was a strange silence regarding battleships and cruisers, as if they had no real role to play in the navy's future operations. In his lecture, Stavitsky explained that the heavy warships were 'capable of delivering heavy blows, supporting other forces at sea, aviation especially, serving as command posts, directing submarines. Consequently, their role is greater than only supporting the light forces'. Nonetheless, small warships could infiltrate the enemy's formation more easily than big warships and were better at keeping up pressure against the enemy for extended periods because of their greater numbers. 'Consequently', Stavitsky concluded, 'if you say that surface forces are more capable at exploiting success, then among them the most capable are the light forces'. At the December conference in Moscow, Isakov stated that flank support to the army by heavy artillery ships would be too risky in modern wars, if the enemy had any submarines or aircraft in the area.[70]

No one present seemed to be of a different opinion. The ocean-going fleet may have played a prominent role in political rhetoric, but it was clearly of secondary importance when the Soviet admirals made concrete plans for war.

Practical matters, such as cooperating with the RKKA, appeared more imminent. 'We do not know what the army men want, and we do not know how to help them', Brigadier Denisevich complained during his intervention. Two months later, when the naval command gathered for renewed discussions in Moscow, the commander of the Black Sea Fleet, Rear-Admiral Filipp Oktyabrsky, made similar remarks.[71] Immediately after this meeting, chief of the Naval Staff Isakov wrote to his RKKA counterpart General Meretskov. Isakov pointed out that in the Baltic Theater there were no plans for cooperation between the Baltic Fleet and the LVO. Could Isakov and Meretskov really leave it to the regional level to work out such important matters? Was the RKKA at all preparing to defend the newly acquired naval bases in Latvia? To plan for operations in the theater, Isakov wrote, the navy must have answers to these questions.[72]

Later, Nikolay Kuznetsov was to complain in his memoirs that central directives regarding the cooperation between fleets and military districts had been issued only in February 1941. Then, it had been too late to prepare properly for the German onslaught. When the war began in June, there was great confusion in the local chain of command.[73]

Conclusion

Although the Soviet oceanic naval program was revised repeatedly between 1936 and 1940, it still promised a tremendous expansion of the Soviet naval forces. The plan also signified the resurrection of the Soviet Navy as an independent fighting service after years of subjugation with its own people's commissariat, its own naval staff and its own people's commissariat for ordnance. Still, the Soviet School – the shift toward an offensive, big-ship fleet – seems more difficult to explain from the perspective of organizational conflict than the previous stages in doctrinal developments – the Old School and the Young School.

The gigantic construction program was shrouded in secrecy and initiated from above. Although the powerful new fleet would need new bases in better locations, Soviet naval leaders only played a subordinate role in the autumn of 1939 when it came to planning and carrying out the negotiations with the Balts and the Finns for base treaties. Moreover, the creation of an entirely new system of ports and airstrips further west assured that a substantial portion of their budget would be locked up in infrastructure development for years to come. Finally, as the new ships and the new bases would not be operational before the mid-1940s, it was still uncertain whether the Baltic Fleet could counter the threat posed from Germany and its allies. Especially the fleet's air arm seemed too weak for the many missions it was expected to solve.

In the winter of 1939–40, the war against Finland confirmed the fleet's insufficient preparedness. Soviet submarines proved incapable of operating outside the Gulf of Finland for extended periods, the fleet air arm could not attack moving targets at sea, the fleet's amphibious force hardly existed at all. In the aftermath of the war, naval doctrine and training were therefore thoroughly revised. Although the new base system in Estonia and Latvia would not be in function before 1943, it at least made it realistic to plan for operations outside the Gulf of Finland. At last, the navy's preparations for war were in line with the offensive thinking of the Red Army. According to the planning which evolved from the summer of

1940, preemptive air strikes, submarine and amphibious operations would be carried out in the enemy's own home waters.

But could the Baltic Fleet – in view of its recent experience against the Finns – really solve such complicated missions? Soviet admirals seemed far from convinced, discussing their problems with surprising frankness. Nor did they see the many battleships and heavy cruisers they would possess in a few years as a solution. During the naval command conferences in October–December 1940, discussions focused on air power, submarines, amphibious forces and their combined use in joint operations.

Notes

1. Monakov, 'Sudba doktrin i teory, 8', pp. 39–42; Rowher and Monakov, *Stalin's Ocean-going Fleet*, pp. 62–4.
2. Kuznetsov, *Nakanune*, p. 257; Gribovsky, 'Na puti k "bolshomu morskomu i okeanskomu flotu" ', pp. 12–13.
3. Berezovsky, *et al.*, *Boevaya letopis*, pp. 607–8, 611–12, 614, 619; Zonin, *Admiral L. M. Galler*, pp. 281–2.
4. Voroshilov to Stalin and Molotov, September 1937, f. r-1877, o. 1, d. 435, list 28–9.
5. Smirnov and Galler to Stalin and Molotov, 27 February 1938, f. r-1877, o. 1, d. 435, list 35, 40.
6. Kuznetsov to Stalin, Molotov, Zhdanov and Voroshilov, October 1939, f. r-1877, o. 1, d. 97, list 38–9.
7. Barsukov and Zolotarev (eds), *Russky arkhiv*, vol. I.2 pp. 309–10; for an overview of the ships included in the 1936–39 naval construction programs, see Rohwer and Monakov, *Stalin's Ocean-going Fleet*, pp. 74–7, 85–106, 119–21.
8. 'Orienterovichnye raschetnye materialy po rezheniyu otdelnykh zadach flotov na dalnevostochnom, balticheskom i severomorskom teatrakh', 25 May 1938, f. r-1877, d. 30, o. 1, list 22; directive from the People's Commissariat for Defense on the subordination in wartime of various fleets and flotillas under military districts and armies, 27 February 1939, f. r-1877, o. 1, d. 77, list 2–3.
9. Levchenko to Smirnov, 26 April 1938, f. r-1877, o. 1, d. 39, list 3–4.
10. 'Orienterovichnye raschetnye materialy po rezheniyu otdelnykh zadach flotov na dalnevostochnom, balticheskom i severomorskom teatrakh', 25 May 1938, f. r-1877, o. 1, d. 30, list 23–30, 39–41; for Tributs's report to Galler, 19 April 1938, on the winter defenses of Kronstadt, see f. r-1877, o.1, d. 38.
11. Smirnov to the Baltic Fleet Soviet, 9 April 1938, f. r-1877, o. 1, d. 31, list 1–3; order by Levchenko, Chief of Staff Tributs and Commissar Vulyshkin, 19 April 1938, ibid., list 4–6.
12. Zonin, *Admiral L. M. Galler*, pp. 303–4; Berezovsky *et al.*, *Boevaya letopis*, pp. 620–2.
13. Protocol notes, 5 May 1939, f. r-1877, o. 1, d. 40, list 145–7.
14. Yegorov to Galler and Shaposhnikov, 30 December 1936, f. r-2041, o.1, d. 19, list 15–17; also in f. r-92, o. 2, d. 297, list 1–3.
15. Shaposhnikov to Galler, 13 January 1937, f. r-92, o. 2, d. 297, list 4–7.
16. Sivkov to Yegorov, 11 May 1937, f. r-2041, o. 1, d. 76, list 83–4.
17. Sivkov and Isakov to Yegorov and Dybenko, 9 June 1937, f. r-2041, o. 1, d. 76, list 103–7; on the Kotka landing operation see Captain 3rd rank Zuykov's study, 29 April 1937, ibid., list 85–94.
18. Isakov to the Baltic Fleet Soviet, 8 July 1937, f. r-1285, o. 2, d. 1, list 268; Shaposhnikov to Isakov, 10 August 1937, f. r-92, o. 2, d. 297, list 48–9; Isakov to Shaposhnikov, 29 August 1937, f. r-2041, o. 1, d. 76, list 124–7.

19 'Orienterovichnye raschetnye materialy po rezheniyu otdelnykh zadach flotov na dalnevostochnom, balticheskom i severomorskom teatrakh', 25 May 1938, f. r-1877, o. 1, d. 30, list 31–8.
20 Tributs to Levchenko, 14 April 1938, 'Otchet po operativnoy igre KBF provedennoy 25–26 marta 1938 g.', f. r-92, o. 2, d. 432, list 276–96.
21 For Kuznetsov's definition of the 'main body' (*boevoe yadro* – 'pryzvannoe k rezheniyu samostayatelnykh operativnykh zadach v masshtabe teatra, v otryve ot baz'), see Kuznetsov to Stalin, Molotov and Zhdanov, 5 April 1940, f. r-1678, o. 1, d. 162, list 362.
22 Berezovsky *et al.*, *Boevaya letopis*, pp. 620–1.
23 Voroshilov and Shapsohnikov to the Naval Staff, 27 February 1939, f. 1877, o. 1, d. 77, list 2; Isakov to the Baltic Fleet Soviet, 22 March 1939, ibid., d. 80, list 2–3; Kuznetsov to the Baltic Fleet Soviet, 2 August 1939, ibid., list 8–10.
24 Yegorov to Molotov, 5 August 1937, f. r-2041, o. 1, d. 76, list 115–17.
25 Galler, 10 June 1939, f. r-1877, o. 1, d. 97, list 1–13.
26 Kuznetsov to Molotov, 7 September 1939, f. r-1877, o. 1, d. 97, list 92–6; memorandum by Galler, 31 August 1939, ibid., list 97–102.
27 Kuznetsov, *Krutye povoroty*, p. 47; Zonin, *Admiral L. M. Galler*, p. 309; Crowe, *Baltic States and the Great Powers*, p. 90.
28 Yury Gorkov, *Kreml, stavka, genshtab* (Tver: Rif [LTD], 1995), pp. 242–3.
29 Komplektov *et al.* (eds), *Polpredy soobshchayut...*, pp. 105–13, 220–7; Crowe, *Baltic States and the Great Powers*, pp. 90–8.
30 On the fleet's general dispositions in Estonia and Latvia, see Petrov, 'Osvoenie Pribaltiki'.
31 Kuznetsov to Stalin, Voroshilov and Zhdanov, 26 October 1939, f. r-1877, o. 1, d. 97, list 38–62; cf. Stavitsky *et al.*, 16 October 1939, 'Artilleriskaya sistema oborony poberezha baltiskogo morya i vynesennogo vpered bazirovaniya KBF', f. r-1877, o. 1, d. 40, list 251–61; order by Kuznetsov, 19 November 1939, ibid., list 317; Barsukov and Zolotarev (eds), *Russky arkhiv*, vol. 1.2, p. 375.
32 Galler, 21 November 1939, f. r-1877, o. 1, d. 97, list 107–18.
33 Pitersky and Barashuk, 21 November 1939, 'Obyazatelnaya zapiska k planu razvitiya VVS KBF 1940–1943 gg.', f. r-1877, o. 1, d. 97, list 119.
34 Berezovsky *et al.*, *Boyevaya letopis*, pp. 636–8, Ekman, 'Sjöstridskrafterna', vol. I, p. 172; C. E. Bruun, 'Luftstridskrafterna', in Henrik Ekberg (ed.), *Finland i krig 1939–1945*, vol. I (Helsinki: Holger Schildts förlag, 1986), p. 196.; Pavel Petrov, 'Voenno-morskie sily Finlandii (1918–1939 gg.)', *Tayfun*, no. 4 (2000).
35 Kuznetsov, *Nakanune*, p. 280.
36 Petrov, 'Krasnoznamenny baltisky flot', chapter 2.
37 Kuznetsov to Baltic Fleet Soviet, 23 November 1939, f. r-1877, o. 1, d. 91, list 115–21; extract from directives by the People's Commissar for Defense, 2 December 1939, ibid., d. 93, list 12; however, there were several civilian casualties due to Soviet bombing after this date as well; cf. Kai Brunila, 'Hemmatrupperna', in Henrik Ekberg (ed.), *Finland i krig, 1939–1945*, vol. I (Helsinki: Holger Schildts förlag, 1986), p. 167.
38 Petrov, 'Krasnoznamenny baltisky flot', chapter 2; cf. *idem*, 'Baltika, noyabr 1939-god: Materialy boevogo planirovaniya KBF', *Russkoe Proshloe*, no. 8 (1999).
39 Ekman, 'Vinterkriget till sjöss', pp. 188–90; Pavel V. Petrov, 'Bronenostsy beregovoy oborony *Väinömöinen* i *Ilmarinen*', *Tayfun*, no. 12 (2000), p. 10.
40 Stupnikov (ed.), *Dvazhdi*, pp. 166–7; Berezovsky *et al.*, *Boevaya letopis*, p. 650.
41 Isakov to Kuznetsov, no date, f. r-1678, o.1, d. 115, list 157–8; on the decoration of *S-1*, see Berezovsky *et al.*, *Boevaya letopis*, p. 648; Stalin's proposal – Kuznetsov, *Nakanune*, pp. 279–80; *idem*, *Krutye povoroty*, p. 54.
42 Isakov to Kuznetsov, no date, f. r-1678, o.1, d. 115, list 157–8.
43 Isakov to Kuznetsov, 13 February 1940, f. r-1678, o. 1, d. 115, list 64–5.
44 Ekman, 'Vinterkriget till sjöss', p. 189.

45 Pavel Petrov, 'Linkory protiv batarey: operatsii eskadry KBF v bierskom arkhipelage', *Tayfun*, no. 3 (1999); Berezovsky *et al.*, *Boevaya letopis*, pp. 639–42; Ekman, 'Vinterkriget till sjöss', pp. 174–84; Ohto Manninen, 'Pervy period boev', in Oleg A. Rzheshevsky and O. Vehviljainen (eds), *Zimnyaya voyna: Politicheskaya istoriya* (Moscow: Nauka, 1999), p. 158.
46 Kuznetsov's order to the Baltic Fleet, 23 November 1939, f. r-1877, o. 1, d. 91, list 115–21; Berezovsky *et al.*, *Boevaya letopis*, pp. 636–8; Ekman, 'Vinterkriget till sjöss', p. 174.
47 Barsukov and Zolotarev (eds), *Russky arkhiv*, vol. I.2, p. 186.
48 Stupnikov (ed.), *Dvazhdy*, pp. 167–8; Berezovsky *et al.*, *Boevaya letopis*, pp. 646–7.
49 Kuznetsov to Baltic Fleet Soviet, 14 February 1940, f. r-1877, o. 1, d. 97, list 142.
50 G. F. Krivosheyev (ed.), *Grif sekretnosti snyat: Poteri vooruzhennikh sil SSSR v voynakh, boevikh deystvyakh i voennykh konfliktakh* (Moscow: Voenizdat, 1993), pp. 120–1; Berezovsky *et al.*, *Boevaya letopis*, p. 661; Carl Van Dyke, 'The Timoshenko Reforms: March–July 1940', *Journal of Slavic Military Studies*, vol. 9 (1) (March 1996), pp. 73–4.
51 Kuznetsov to Stalin, Molotov and Zhdanov, 5 April 1940, f. r-1678, o. 1, d. 162, list 362.
52 Kuznetsov to Stalin, Molotov, Voroshilov and Zhdanov, 23 June 1940, f. r-1678, o. 1, d. 162, list 631–3; Berezovsky *et al.*, *Boevaya letopis*, p. 661.
53 Kuznetsov to the Baltic Fleet Soviet, 25 July 1940, f. r-1877, o. 1, d. 80, list 22–4.
54 Material on the 1940 war games in f. r-92, o. 2, d. 756.
55 Erik Norberg, 'Sjökrig i Östersjön: Sovjetiska planer och tysk aktivitet inför uppgörelsen 1941', in Bo Hugemark (ed.), *I orkanens öga: 1941 – osäker neutralitet* (Stockholm: Probus, 1992), p. 169; on Swedish radio intelligence, see Bengt Beckman, *Svenska kryptobedrifter* (Stockholm: Albert Bonniers förlag, 1996).
56 Filippovsky to Baltic Fleet chief of staff and Baltic Fleet air arm chief of staff, 14 August 1940, f. r-92, o. 2, d. 771, list 1.
57 The 1940 campaign plan can be found in f. r-92, o. 2, d. 660.
58 The plan for the Åland operation in f. r-92, o. 2, d. 669; cf. Ohto Manninen, *Molotovin cocktail – Hitlerin sateenvarjo*, pp. 114–22.
59 See f. r-92, o. 2, d. 756, list 125–30, 135–9.
60 Barsukov and Zolotarev (eds), *Russky arkhiv*, vol. I.2, pp. 40–8.
61 Ibid., pp. 48–80.
62 Ibid., pp. 83–4.
63 Ibid., pp. 88–105.
64 Ibid., pp. 126–30.
65 Ibid., pp. 117–20.
66 Ibid., p. 148.
67 Ibid., pp. 254–8.
68 Ibid., pp.152–62; 181–95.
69 Ibid., pp. 175–8.
70 Ibid., pp. 155, 223–5; cf. pp. 243–50.
71 Ibid., pp. 294–5; cf. Kuznetsov, *Krutye povoroty*, pp. 77, 94–5.
72 Isakov to Meretskov, 14 December 1940, f. r-92, o. 2, d. 97, list 327–8.
73 Kuznetsov, *Nakanune*, pp. 255–6; idem, *Krutye povoroty*, pp. 45–6, 48–50, 77, 96.

13

THE NAVY OF THE SOVIET ADMIRALS

In November 1936, the Supreme Soviet gathered for an extra session to approve the country's new constitution, which established that the Soviet Union was a developed socialist state where antagonism between classes no longer existed. The first part of the road to Communist Utopia had now been successfully completed. The constitution contained regulations on the government's accountability to parliament and established that parliament – the Supreme Soviet – was to be a federal assembly with two chambers, directly elected by the people. It also provided a supreme court, civil rights for 'alien social elements' (hitherto excluded from suffrage) and equality for women. In several ways, the constitution of 1936 signaled a return to normality after the long endurance of total mobilization during the five-year plans. The struggle for industrialization had been won, the remnants of the old society had been defeated and daily life promised to become easier.[1]

Although on the surface the Soviet Union in many respects adapted to international normality during the late 1930s, in reality life was far from normal. Food rationing had been abolished in early 1935, but a wide range of basic foodstuffs and consumer goods remained scarce or inaccessible, as did housing. The shortage of trained labor in industry remained, which led to the introduction of truly draconian disciplinary measures. As from December 1938, arrival 20 minutes late would be considered as absence without leave, and was to be punished with immediate discharge. Workers were also to carry special workbooks in which their performance was recorded. From June 1940, absence without leave (arrival 20 minutes late) could result in up to four months of hard labor.[2]

Moreover, in 1937–38 the country experienced one of the worst periods of state terror in the history of any nation, a purge known as the *Yezhoshchina* after Nikolay Yezhov, head of the NKVD (Narodny Kommissariat Vnutrennikh Del = People's Commissariat for Internal Affairs) in the period. The *Yezhovshchina* was intimately linked to the constitutional reform, which created fears that formerly deported persons could now return to society from deportation and 'instigate anti-Soviet crimes'. To prevent this, in July 1937 the Politbureau approved the NKVD's operational order No. 00447 'concerning the punishment of former kulaks, criminals and other anti-soviet elements'. J. Arch Getty and Oleg Naumov describe this directive 'as one of the most chilling documents of modern history'. It established special quotas for the number of people who were to be shot or sent to prison camps in each republic, territory and region of the country. The campaign was to be administered by local troikas, consisting of the local party secretary, the NKVD chief and the procurator. According to the original plan, some 72,950 were to be shot and another 177,500 exiled.[3] According to a secret Soviet investigation from 1953, however, the final toll was 681,692 people shot and some 2.5 million arrested. The total number of victims remains in dispute.[4]

In November 1938, when Lavrenty Beriya replaced Yezhov (who was subsequently arrested and executed) the terror started to subside. At that point, most people in authority had been replaced. In 1939, the average age among the members of the Council of People's Commissars was 39, which made the Soviet cabinet the youngest in the world. Among the 1,966 delegates at the XVIIth Party Congress in 1934, more than 56 percent had been arrested. So had 114 of the 139 members the XVIIth Party Congress had elected to the Central Committee, and eight of the 15 members it had elected to the Politburo. Of course, millions of ordinary people, outside the ruling elite, had also had their lives shattered.[5]

Historians working within the so-called 'totalitarian paradigm' have generally regarded the terror as a logical consequence of Marxist–Leninist ideology, as a conscious strategy by the regime to maintain power and even to rejuvenate bureaucracy. Stalin is attributed a central role as the architect behind the repression.[6]

Their colleagues among the pluralists–revisionists have presented another version, where the terror is at least partly initiated from below, a kind of grass-roots revolt against bureaucracy and officialdom. Stalin is often portrayed as an arbitrator, balancing rival party factions against each other, reacting to events rather than initiating them, seriously believing – like most other people in the Soviet Union at the time – that the alleged conspiracies were real.[7] The new sources that have become available in recent years point both ways. It is clear that the purge was initiated from above, that Stalin knew what was going on and that his signature can be found under tens of thousands of death sentences. On the other hand, the complexity of events is also apparent. Locally, the process of identifying and hunting down 'enemies of the people' soon acquired a momentum of its own and increased the number of victims many times.[8]

Large-scale repression in the armed forces began with the so-called Tukhachevsky affair in May–June 1937, when Deputy People's Commissar for Defense Marshal Tukhachevsky was arrested together with seven other superior commanders, suspected of a 'military-political conspiracy against Soviet Power… stimulated and financed by German Fascists', convicted and shot. For a long time, it was generally believed that during the following year and a half some 35,000 officers – between a third and half of the Soviet officer corps – suffered a similar fate. Also, this self-inflicted massacre was seen as a major reason behind the military disaster in 1941. Later, post-glasnost research has reduced the number of repressed officers. The total number of commanding personnel in 1937–38 was much greater than hitherto estimated, and many of those purged were later rehabilitated and allowed to return to service. According to Roger R. Reese, the victims were not 35,000 out of 70,000 but rather some 23,000 out of 206,000. Moreover, most of the purged were not executed but merely discharged from service. In most cases, the reason for their dismissal was not political but had do with incompetence, drinking or petty criminality. It should also be noticed that the military authorities played an active role in identifying 'wreckers' and 'enemies of the people' among their own. The armed forces were no passive victims of state terror but cooperated in full with the repressive organs. Finally, when explaining the military setbacks in 1939–41, current research is more interested in the Red Army's many structural weaknesses before the war: the low level of general education among personnel, the shortage of competent NCOs and the rapid organizational expansion in the late 1930s, which necessitated the promotion of inexperienced people to senior rank. Roger Reese offers the following characterization of the Red Army officer corps in 1941:

> They came from homes with no electricity or plumbing. Growing up, they had had little exposure to automative or other complex machinery. As officers they were thrust into a quasi-urban social setting, with responsibility for supervising others in doing things that they themselves had not been prepared for. It seems as though every officer wanted results from his subordinates while he fended off his superiors as he attended to his tasks. The result: low morale, high turnover, and many duties performed poorly or not at all.[9]

All this having been said, it is nonetheless true that in 1937–38 thousands of experienced, loyal and competent military leaders were falsely accused of treason and espionage, executed or sent off to prison camps, and that no other Great power army had to suffer similar devastation on the verge of World War II.

The navy and normalization

One of several signs of normalization during the Supreme Soviet's congress in November 1936 was Defense Commissar Voroshilov's announcement that the country was going to build an ocean-going fleet. As Molotov would declare later, just like any other Great power the 'powerful Soviet state must have a sea-going and ocean-going fleet, consistent with its interests, worthy of our great task.'[10]

During an evening in Stalin's dacha in 1939, the newly appointed People's Commissar for the Navy, Nikolay Kuznetsov, expressed doubts that huge battleships would be of much use in a narrow inland sea like the Baltic. Hearing this, the *Vozhd* just pressed some more tobacco into his pipe, stared at Kuznetsov and declared emphatically: 'We shall collect the money kopeck by kopeck and build them.' Later, Kuznetsov would describe the oceanic naval construction program as a gigantic waste of money, which in the end had contributed little to national security.[11]

However, although from a strategic viewpoint the 'Big Ship' navy may have been dubious, in the context of strategic culture, it made perfect sense. Battleship construction was the logical parallel to other developments in Soviet society at the time: the introduction of school uniforms, patriotic history teaching and school fees for secondary education, the return of neoclassical ideals in art and architecture, the shift toward a more conservative legislation on marriage and abortion, etc. In all these areas, the Soviet Union adapted to European 'normality' during the late 1930s. At the Spithead naval review during King George VI's coronation in May 1937, the *Marat* represented the Soviet government.[12]

A further step in normalization was a decree by the Council of People's Commissars and the Politburo on 22 June 1939, according to which the last Sunday in July would henceforth be celebrated as the 'Day of the Soviet Navy'. The official motive was to secure 'mobilization of the great working masses' around the nation's navy, but the time for celebration was not chosen randomly. On 26–7 July 1714, the Russian Navy under the command of Peter the Great and Admiral Apraksin had won its first great victory against the Swedes in the Battle of Gangut (*Hanko* in Finnish). The issue of *Morskoy Sbornik* which proclaimed the great news about the Navy Day also contained the first of two articles on the Gangut battle, appearing under the heading 'From the Combat Past of the Russian Navy'. Clearly, the Soviet Navy was not so much a weapon of the international proletariat any longer as as part of the Soviet Union's national arsenal. When the newly appointed commander in the Baltic, Vladimir Tributs, presented the Baltic Fleet in a special article in the same issue, he mentioned as its first heroic deed not the storming of the Winter Palace or the battles of the Civil War, but the victory at Gangut.[13]

New directives for the naming of warships, issued by the Soviet government in September 1940, further underlined the changed conceptualization of national identity. Battleships, regarded as the navy's most prestigious warships, were to be named after the union republics (*Sovetskaya Rossiya*, *Sovetskaya Ukraina*, *Sovetskaya Gruziya*), a practice identical to that of, for instance, the US Navy. The new class of heavy cruisers were to have names after the main naval bases (*Kronshtadt*, *Sevastopol*, *Vladivostok*, etc.) and destroyer leaders after major cities and the capitals of the republics (*Moskva*, *Leningrad*, *Tashkent*). Soviet destroyers were to be named after masculine adjectives (*Gnevny*, 'furious'; *Stremitelny*, 'energetic'; *Opytny*, 'experienced'), a practice identical to that of the Imperial Navy. Like the submarines in the Imperial Navy, patrol ships were to be named after predators (*Tigr*, *Leopard*, *Oryol*, 'eagle'). The only major warships which were to be named after revolutionary heroes in the future were light cruisers (the *Kirov* class and its successors) and minesweepers (a category of ships for whom were to be reserved the names of sailors fallen during the Civil War).[14] Soviet heroes were to be commemorated, but Marat or the Paris Commune were no longer suitable as sources of inspiration.

The Soviet admirals

Another sign of the Soviet armed forces' adherence to international norms was the introduction of regular generals' and admirals' titles, approved in early

May 1940. About a month later, on one and the same day (4 June) no less than 1,056 army and navy officers were promoted to these ranks. In the navy there were four lieutenant-generals (one in the naval air force and three in the coastal artillery) and some 30 major generals appointed, as were three full admirals (Lev Galler, Ivan Isakov and Nikolay Kuznetsov) seven vice-admirals (Gordey Levchenko, Sergey Stavitsky and Vladimir Tributs among them) and 63 rear-admirals and engineer rear-admirals (among them Vladimir Belli).[15]

The leaders of the so-called Soviet School could all be found among these 'admirals of 1940.'

Robert Herrick identifies Vladimir Belli (1887–1981) as the Soviet School's leading architect. A former tsarist officer serving aboard the battleship *Tsesarevich* during World War I, he was in reality a representative of the Old School. Belli had joined the Bolsheviks at an early stage, participated in the evacuation of the Baltic Fleet in 1918 and later commanded his own destroyer (named *Kapitan Belli*). After a period as naval attaché to China and as head of the foreign section of the Naval Staff, he went to the Naval War College as a professor of strategy in 1926. With the exception of the 15 months in 1930–31 when he was imprisoned, he remained there until his retirement in 1949.

It was through his position as college professor that Belli had the opportunity to influence the doctrinal development of the Soviet Navy. In the early 1930s, when he had had to denounce the theory of command of the sea after his return from imprisonment, his teachings were in accordance with Young School orthodoxy. In 1933, together with Alexander Alexandrov and Ivan Isakov, he published a book on German submarine operations during World War I which criticized the notion of 'the general engagement' and suggested that all operations in the future would be joint. Towards the end of the 1930s, however, Belli began introducing a modified version of the Old School, according to which the notion of command of the sea could still be usable in the context of a confined theater of operations during a limited period of time.[16] For a short period during the Great Terror in 1937, the course in strategy and operational art at the Naval War College was cut down to a mere 100 study hours, and expected to include an introduction to 'the Marxist–Leninist study of war'. Having to reduce the teaching of strategic theory to a minimum, Belli chose to lecture on Clausewitz rather than on any Soviet author. In 1939, he had replaced all Soviet naval strategists in the reading list with classical Anglo-Saxon thinkers like Mahan and Colomb, authors who had been strictly prohibited only a few years before.[17] In the summer of 1940, when Belli analyzed the initial phase of World War II in *Morskoy Sbornik*, his concept of 'limited command of the sea' became fully established.[18]

A man with a similar role to Belli's, that of a teacher conveying the intellectual heritage of the old Imperial Navy to the younger generation, was Sergey Petrovich Stavitsky (1886–1953). Stavitsky had graduated as an artillery officer in 1912 and served the Baltic during World War I. After joining the Bolsheviks in 1917 and participating in the Baltic Fleet's evacuation in the spring of 1918, he commanded the battleships *Sevastopol* (*Parizhkaya Kommuna*) and *Petropavlovsk* (*Marat*) during the Civil War. In the early 1920s, he served as head of operations in the Baltic Fleet and then in the Naval Staff. From 1924 until 1941, he was mainly active as a professor at the Naval War College. His only extramural assignment was in 1926–27, when he commanded the Baltic Fleet battleship squadron. Stavitsky was one of the main authors of the 1937 Naval Fighting Regulation and also wrote an influential 'Introduction to the Tactics of Naval Forces' which appeared in November 1940.[19]

Two other survivors of the Imperial Navy who played leading roles during the Soviet School era were Galler and Isakov. As we have seen, Lev Mikhailovich Galler (1883–1950) had played an important role already during the Old School period, in the 1920s. He was, however, more of an administrator than a writer. In 1937, he was promoted to deputy naval commander and in 1938 to chief of the resurrected Naval Staff. In 1940, he became Deputy People's Commissar for the Navy, responsible for ship construction.[20]

Ivan Stepanovich Isakov (1894–1967) had graduated from the Naval Guards School in the spring of 1917, just a few weeks after the fall of the monarchy. He saw action against the Germans in the battle of Moonsund in 1917, participated in the evacuation of the Baltic Fleet in 1918 and served in both the Baltic and in the Caspian Sea during the Civil War. After extensive service in the Black Sea during the 1920s, Isakov attended the Naval War College in 1927–28. Having served in the section of operations of the RKKA General Staff, he was chief of staff in the Baltic 1933–35. After a tenure as professor and dean at the Naval War College, he returned to this position in January 1937 and was appointed Baltic Fleet commander later the same year. He was appointed commandant of the Naval War College in 1938 and Deputy People's Commissar for the Navy in 1939. Isakov's literary production includes novels and naval history, but little military theory. Like Galler, he was more a naval practitioner than a theoretician. When the Soviet Navy evaluated the experience of modern war in Moscow in December 1940, Isakov emphasized that the theory of command of the sea was a rational theory, but it must not be taken for a recipe which could be applied in every situation in life. Rather than engaging in yet another round of fruitless theoretical discussions on doctrine, he said, the Soviet Navy should instead study the context of each operation and search for practical lessons.[21]

Isakov's successor as commander of the Baltic Fleet in 1938 was Gordey Ivanovich Levchenko (1897–1981) Levchenko had entered the Imperial Navy in 1913 as a sailor and participated in World War I aboard the cruisers *Grombovoy* and *Admiral Nakhimov*. He fought in the Civil War against Yudenich's troops, and then went to the Naval Academy, graduating as one of first Soviet naval officers in 1922. Having commanded the Baltic training squadron, the Caspian Flotilla, the Baltic battleship squadron and the Black Sea destroyer squadron, in 1937–39 Levchenko became chief of staff in the Baltic Fleet, then fleet commander and later Deputy People's Commissar.[22]

If Levchenko succeeded Isakov as commander in Kronstadt, he in turn was succeeded by Vladimir Fillopovich Tributs (1900–77). Tributs had also fought as a sailor in the Civil War in the Caspian and Volga Theaters. He graduated from the Frunze Naval Academy in 1926 and from the Naval War College in 1932. Tributs served in senior positions aboard the battleships *Parizhkaya Kommuna* and *Marat* in the late 1920s and early 1930s, and then commanded his own destroyer in the Baltic (*Jakov Sverdlov*). In 1938–39 he succeeded Levchenko first as chief of staff and then as commander of the Baltic Fleet, remaining in the later position throughout World War II.[23]

The youngest leader of the Soviet School was Nikolay Gerasimovich Kuznetsov (1902–74), who had entered the Northern Dvina flotilla as a volunteer during the Civil War and graduated from the Frunze Naval Academy in 1926. After service aboard the cruiser *Chervona Ukraina* (ex-*Profintern*) in the Black Sea, he was appointed commander of this ship in 1934. On Revolution Day 1935, he was portrayed in the armed forces' daily, *Krasnaya Zvezda* as the 'youngest captain of any navy in the world'. In 1936–37, he served as naval attaché and military advisor to the Republican government in Spain. After his return, he was appointed deputy commander of the Pacific Fleet and later took over full command. From this position, he was called to Moscow to become People's Commissar for the Navy in March 1939, at the age of 37.[24]

As can be gathered from these short biographies, Belli, Stavitsky, Galler and Isakov were all born in the 1880s and 1890s and had begun their career in the Imperial Navy. Levchenko, Tributs and Kuznetsov, on the other hand, were born around the turn of the century and were products of the Civil War. As would be appropriate in a country where class conflict had been officially abolished, the old imperial officer corps and the young red commanders seemed to cooperate together in perfect harmony under the Soviet School. With the exception of Isakov, the role of the members in the senior group before World War II was that of theoreticians, teachers and administrators. Like their predecessors in the Old School of the 1920s, they had mainly served aboard artillery ships during their active career. Again, Isakov, who had specialized as a torpedo officer and served aboard destroyers, was an exception. Moreover, they had all participated under Rear-Admiral Shchastny in the Baltic Fleet's great escape in 1918, when the navy aligned with the Bolsheviks. The less experienced red commanders in the junior group filled the active command positions, but were not yet expected to contribute to the theoretical development of doctrine. In most organizations, this would seem a rational distribution of work. The *spezedstvo*, 'specialist-bashing', ideology which had brought the Young School to power during the first five-year plan was no longer *à la mode*. Also, the Red Young Commanders of the Soviet School differed from their predecessors during the previous decade in that their careers had taken place outside the PUR. Their professional competence was primarily military. Although Lechenko had joined the Communist Party as early as 1919, Tributs and Kuznetsov were not recruited until the mid-1920s. None of them had experienced the Civil War in commanding positions, but in the ranks.

In short, this stage of the Soviet Navy's doctrinal development was characterized by a certain balance between theoretical insight and practical experience. However, it was a long way before the service would be even remotely close to the inflated, self-admiring image presented in official propaganda.

Political control through terror and dual command

Between 1922 and 1937, no less than 6,245 commanders and specialists had graduated from Soviet naval academies and schools. Nonetheless, the chronic shortage of trained personnel remained, so central authorities usually urged for restraint when it came to purges in the naval forces. After the repressive wave in 1930–31, naval commander Orlov did what he could to rehabilitate victims. In a speech before the party organisation of the People's Commissariat for Defense in March 1937, he told how he himself had recently examined a great number of proposed discharges in the Black Sea Fleet. Not in one single case had he found the requests to be well founded.[25]

Only a couple of months later, in May 1937, the Great Terror began. Before it ended in November 1938, the navy had been deprived of some 3,000 officers.[26] Most of those people were simply fired, but a considerable number were also shot or sent off to prisons and camps with long-term sentences. We do not know how many were executed and how many were imprisoned, nor how many were later allowed to return to service. Many of those who were afflicted by repression were obviously incompetent, had drinking problems or were over-aged and would have been forced to retire in any navy – albeit with less inhumane methods. However, several others were highly competent, conscientious and hard working and therefore hard to replace.

It is tempting to see the purges as a way to eliminate the Young School and pave the way for a new, battleship-oriented generation of naval commanders. In August 1938, an article in the navy daily *Krasny Flot* by A. Yevseyev branded the 'enemy agents' of the Young School, who under the disguise of revolutionary phraseology had propagated defeatism and 'strategic mental vacuum and fault-finding'.[27] After his return from Spain in the autumn of 1937, the leading Young School theoretician Alexander Alexandrov was discharged from the navy and later arrested. Belli, who suspected Alexandrov of having orchestrated his own arrest back in 1930, paid him back by denouncing him as an enemy of the people in the August 1939 issue of *Morskoy Sbornik*. In February 1940, however, Alexandrov was suddenly released and allowed to enter service again.[28] While Alexandrov survived the repression physically, Old School battleship enthusiasts like Zof, Pantserzhansky and Petrov, who had long since left active service in the navy, were arrested and shot. All in all, it is therefore difficult to discern any logical pattern behind these persecutions, nor to see what the victims had in common except their bad luck.

Among those executed were two People's Commissars and one Deputy People's Commissar, two naval commanders and one deputy naval commander, six fleet and flotilla commanders, five chiefs of fleet staffs or deputy chiefs of fleet staffs, six heads of sections in the central apparatus, 15 heads or chief specialists in fleet staffs, 32 commanders of units and chiefs of staffs of units, 22 commanders of 1st and 2nd class warships (artillery ships and torpedo craft), as well as the commandant of the Naval War College.[29]

The decimation of experienced staff created problems in many areas. The serious crisis in personnel, however, followed from the navy's rapid expansion under the oceanic naval construction program. From the summer of 1936 to the winter of 1938, the number of officers, NCOs and enlisted personnel grew from 9,640 to 28,450 people.[30] According to Oleg Suvenirov, about a third of the navy's commanding positions (4,195 out of 13,662) were vacant on 1 January 1938.[31] Sergey Ignatiev, Deputy People's Commissar for the Navy responsible for personnel, gave somewhat different figures on the personnel strength at the naval command's conference in Moscow in December 1940. On 1 January 1938, Ignatiev claimed, the number of personnel had been 19,500, on 1 October 1939 28,753 and on 1 December 1940 35,977. What matters here are not the exact numbers but that Ignatiev's report confirms the high number of vacancies. As there were only 24,750 in the rolls in the autumn of 1940, according to Ignatiev, the navy lacked about 10,000 men.[32]

In the Baltic Fleet, the situation had become urgent already in the autumn of 1938. Apart from the 478 men who had been discharged since the spring of 1937 because of the purges, some 84 officers had been promoted from middle to senior ranks during the summer and an additional 44 from junior to middle ranks. All these people left vacancies at lower levels in the hierarchy that had to be filled. There were 19 ship commanders missing, 41 deputy ship commanders, some 50 commanders of supply units, etc. In addition, about 300 men were scheduled for studies at various naval schools. The commander of the Baltic Fleet's Intelligence Section complained to the Naval Intelligence Directorate in Moscow that he would be short of commanding personnel, even if he limited his ambitions to manning only the previous, much smaller organization. For this reason, he asked for permission to keep some of his staff until this year's graduation at the naval academies. In sum, in the autumn of 1938 there were 896 vacant positions in the fleet and no more than 381 replacements coming in.[33]

The alleged existence of a military conspiracy in the Soviet armed forces justified a reintroduction of the dual command system. According to a decree on 15 August 1937, the need for the commissar's signature was hence to be required on every order by the military commander at the level of regimental units (squadrons in the Navy) and above. Together with the unit's military commander, the commissar was to protect the unit from 'enemies of the people, spies, saboteurs and wreckers', and educate the personnel in 'unswerving loyalty to the Fatherland and Soviet power and merciless struggle against the enemies of the people'.[34]

In April 1940, after the ill-fated war against Finland, Marshal Semyon Timoshenko (who had led the final breakthrough of the Finnish fortifications on the Karelian Isthmus), replaced Voroshilov as People's Commissar for Defense. Timoshenko was bent on resurrecting the autonomy and status of the officer corps. The dual-command system, which had demonstrated its harmful effects in the recent war, was abolished through a government decree on 12 August 1940. At the same time, the 'Political Directorate' (*Politicheskoe Upravlenie* = PU) in the Navy was renamed as the 'Main Directorate for Political Propaganda' (*Glavnoe Upravlenie Politicheskoy Propagandy* = GUPP).[35]

A few days before the decree was passed, on 7 August, Belsky of the Baltic Fleet Political Administration discussed the role of commissars at a conference in Moscow for navy political personnel. He pointed out that some of the Baltic Fleet's commissars had misunderstood their position and acted as if they were deputy commanders of their ship or their unit. They undermined the authority of the military commander by revoking his orders or buried themselves in administrative work, instead of attending to propaganda. He quoted the diary of one of his men, a wing commissar in the fleet air arm, who worked 14 hours a day but spent less than four hours on political work. This, of course, was not the way it should be. Since the band of military conspirators had been purged, Belsky asserted, the Red Army and Navy could count on a new generation of loyal and competent commanders in leading positions. These people could be trusted with running daily affairs, while the political leadership should concentrate its efforts on moral and ideological education.[36]

Apparently, the return to the old system of unified command did not go as smoothly as Belsky's description would suggest. When the naval leadership assembled in December 1940, there were complaints about commissars who refused to step down from their earlier functions as deputy commanders, continuing to neglect party work and propaganda. Also, some military commanders were accused of hostile demonstrations and jubilant malice when hearing of Timoshenko's decree. A staff officer in one of the Black Sea Fleet's submarine squadrons had told the unit's political instructor: 'Well, now there is nothing more for you to do than to take your bag and go begging.'[37]

Ideological leadership in war

At lower levels in the Baltic Fleet, the purges seem to have affected order and discipline. During September 1937, 110 sailors, 27 junior commanders, 24 middle commanders and even one senior commander were arrested for various criminal charges. No less than 128 of them (79 percent) were guilty of disorderly conduct in public, drunkenness or street fighting. According to the fleet's chief attorney Shturman, the passivity of commanders and PUR staff were to blame.[38]

It is reasonable to assume that in the autumn of 1937, when no accusation seemed too ridiculous to be taken seriously, a passive, nonprovocatory stance toward subordinates was a perfectly rational strategy for persons in authority.

A first test of how the discipline and combat qualities of the Baltic Fleet had been affected by the purges came after the signing of base treaties with Estonia and Latvia. On 14 October 1939, People's Commissar for the Navy Kuznetsov issued special instructions regarding the behavior of navy personnel stationed in the Baltic republics. Their mission would require 'the greatest revolutionary vigilance, attentiveness and a conduct worthy a warrior of the Great Soviet

Union'. Consequently, in all their contacts with local inhabitants, Soviet sailors must demonstrate military professionalism and a high level of culture. Under no circumstances should they appear as victors or conquerors, insult the national feelings of Estonians and Latvians, agitate or try to undermine the social and economic systems of these two countries. The commissars and the Komsomol were expected to prevent any form of disorderly conduct. Provocations from anti-Soviet elements should be avoided, as should all discussions with local inhabitants on military matters. As the Soviet Union's stock of foreign currency was limited, no private shopping could be allowed. All supplies were to be provided through the local Soviet trade representative. Similar instructions were later issued to army and air force personnel.[39]

A few weeks later, the Baltic Fleet went into action against the Finns. Again, discipline and combat qualities were tested. The Central Navy PUR had issued instructions to the Baltic Fleet PUR, listing its main preoccupations during the conflict:

- Keeping personnel oriented about the character of the war, the objectives of the Soviet Union and the tasks of the Baltic Fleet
- Ensuring that party members would behave as examples to others in combat
- Strengthening the vigilance of personnel and the protection of military secrets
- Safeguarding the supply and the communications of the fleet
- Supervising combat activities
- Conducting work among the families of commanding personnel
- Attending to the relationship to the (Finnish) population and to prisoners
- Issuing directives for agitation work among units.

Just like everybody else, the Baltic PUR (PU Balt) expected a quick Soviet victory. During the first days of the campaign, it issued directives to the commissars to watch out for especially brave and heroic men, who – provided the commissar had known the person for at least a year – could be recommended for party membership. After the recent purges, the ranks needed to be filled up with reliable people. About two weeks later, when the task of subduing the 'White Finns' had proven less simple than expected, the PU Balt issued another directive which urged for vigilance and discipline, and struggle against disorganization, cowardice and 'the incorrect putting of questions'.[40]

There were indeed examples of outstanding heroism in the Baltic Fleet during the campaign. Some 22 'Heroes of the Soviet Union' were awarded (17 to airmen – of whom two belonged to the PU Balt – three to submarine commanders and two to infantrymen).[41] There were, however, also people who did not live up to expectations. In a special message on 25 December 1939, fleet commander Tributs took the submariners to task for spreading demoralizing rumors about defects in the latest series of submarines of the 'Shch' class. This was an act of treason which would be severely punished.[42] On 10 January 1940, the commander of the OLS,

Captain 1st rank Ptokhov, was relieved of his command, accused of having appeared drunk and of making an unauthorized trip to Riga. He was later dishonorably discharged and expelled from the party.[43]

In the navy, the evaluation of the war experience started immediately afterwards. Within the Navy PUR, it focused on the performance of the commissars. As a result, new directives were issued for the Navy's political work in the summer of 1940. One of the problems identified was that in the Soviet armed forces, squad leaders and their equivalents had no special training or sense of identity in relation to the rank and file. They were merely senior conscripts, who often used their position to bully fresh recruits but could not be employed as instructors or enforcers of discipline. Rather than sending the most suitable conscripts on squad leader training, unit commanders saw these courses an an opportunity to get rid of indisciplined conscripts, Deputy People's Commissar Ignatiev complained when he assessed the navy's personnel situation in December 1940 (the Baltic Fleet lacked 719 NCOs and 1,217 squad leaders on 1 October 1940). In the revised instructions for the Navy's political work, raising the status of junior NCOs was therefore pointed out as one of the main tasks.[44]

In early August 1940, navy senior political commanders had convened in Moscow under the chairmanship of the Supreme Political Commissar of the Navy, Deputy People's Commissar Ivan V. Rogov. After Rogov had delivered a critical survey of political work in the navy in general and in the Baltic Fleet in particular, Belsky of the Baltic PU took the floor. Belsky – who was versed in Bolshevik etiquette – admitted that Rogov's critical remarks had been justified, and then went on to give his analysis of political work in the Baltic Fleet. Toward the end of his report, when he forgot himself and began depicting the efforts of his subordinates during the war against Finland in too bright colors, Rogov brusquely interrupted him from the audience, disrespectfully addressing him in the personal form (*ty*): 'You'd better tell us why there are so many extraordinary events taking place among you, why your people work so badly, why they don't listen to you, how propaganda is directed. These things you have to speak about.'[45] Rogov's dissatisfaction with the Baltic Fleet was apparent also at the conference in Moscow in December, when he accused fleet commander Tributs of concealing unpleasant facts. On this occasion, it was the Baltic Fleet's chief commissar Mark Yakobenko who had to demonstrate proper self-criticism.[46]

During the August conference, Belsky admitted that some people in the PU Balt had demonstrated lack of initiative and sense of duty during the war. Navy personnel had been listening to Finnish radio and read Finnish propaganda leaflets. In Estonia and Latvia, the Soviet Union had been dishonored through cases of drunkenness, association with 'questionable elements' and even desertion. Softness and 'democratism' had led to a rapid growth of disciplinary offenses, even among communists and Komsomol members. If the Baltic Fleet was to regain its fighting capacity, Belsky said, tough commanders with an iron will were urgently needed.[47]

Apart from stricter discipline, the fleet also needed commissars who knew how to handle people. Belsky mentioned the case of a recruit who had confessed to the unit's party secretary that he was afraid to go to the front. Instead of having a chance to overcome his fear by being sent to the front, the recruit was expelled from the Komsomol, accused of treason, cowardice and refusal to obey orders. This, Belsky said, was not the proper way to go about things.[48]

Another example of incompetent behavior, according to Belsky, was offered by political instructor Feshchenko of the battleship *Oktyabrskaya Revolutsiya*. In May 1940, Feshchenko, the ship's doctor Vinogradov and the party secretary Bubnov all knew that Red Navy man Panyushkin, a first-year conscript and a non-party member, was depressed and contemplated suicide. Feshchenko had even got his hands on a farewell note that Panyushkin had written to his mother. Instead of offering the unhappy man some friendly counseling, Feshchenko gathered the crew, read the letter aloud and tore it to pieces, probably to castigate suicide as cowardly and immoral. That same night, Panyushkin threw himself overboard. Before he drowned, he swam for approximately ten minutes in full view from the ship's bridge, without the officer on watch reacting.[49]

As a part of Timoshenko's efforts to strengthen discipline in the armed forces, a new military penal code system was introduced in July 1940. From now on, absence without leave would result in trial before a comrade tribunal which had the right to meet out disciplinary penalties. If the offence was repeated, or if the crime consisted of more than two hours' absence, the delinquent would be transferred to a disciplinary battalion for six months up to two years (in time of war the punishment would be 3–7 years' imprisonment). If someone was missing for more than 24 hours, this would be regarded as desertion, punishable with 5–10 years' imprisonment (in war execution by a firing squad and confiscation of property).[50]

Indeed, these draconian regulations had some effect. The number of navy personnel punished for absence without leave decreased from 482 in September 1940 to 359 in October and to 116 in November. However, no less than 41 percent of all disciplinary infringements during 1940 still fell within that category. Out of 1,249 cases in the navy, no less than 578 occurred in the Baltic Fleet. Also, the general level of criminality and indiscipline in the navy seemed to explode – from 833 sentences in 1939 to 3,336 sentences in 1940. Out of those convicted, 385 were NCOs and 124 officers. All categories of crimes grew: neglect of orders (567 cases against 92 cases in 1939), infringement of the watch regulation (71 cases against 40 cases in 1939), hooliganism (129 cases against 52 in 1939), theft and embezzlement (172 cases against 87 in 1939).

In addition, there were some 83 sentences for anti-Soviet agitation, with another 70 cases in this category under investigation by December 1940. According to the navy chief attorney, division juror Georgy Alexeyev, recent decrees which had stirred up anti-Soviet slander among the Red Navy men pertained to the introduction of admirals' ranks, the prolongation of service time for navy conscripts, the stricter disciplinary regulations and above all – the 1940 uniform regulation. For the first time, Soviet Navy personnel were issued with special winter clothing as well as a special dress uniform. On the other hand, conscripts would no longer be allowed to keep their uniforms after discharge.

According to Alexeyev, the exchange of uniforms had proceeded more slowly in the Baltic Fleet than in the other fleets and therefore caused more discontent there. By the end of 1940, convicts had to wait for months to serve their time in the navy guardhouses. Also, the number of suicides among navy personnel had grown to an alarming level (110 cases in 1940 compared to 97 cases in 1939). Alexeyev thought this had to do with the habit of commanders threatening conscripts with prison when they had done something wrong. 'You can imagine yourselves,' Kuznetsov, told the assembled naval command at the December conference in Moscow: 'If they came to you and said: "Tomorrow they will give you five years." How would you feel? And put yourself in the place of the Red Navy man, who believes in it.'[51]

Modernization: in quest of 'good, civilized documents'

The struggle for modernization in the Baltic Fleet could be illustrated by the example of the intelligence section, where in 1936–37 substantial efforts were made to overcome educational deficiencies among the staff. In January 1936, the section consisted of the staff section in Kronstadt and of 'naval frontier intelligence posts' numbers 1 and 2 on the mainland. While the staff section was responsible for analysis, the naval frontier intelligence posts handled the collection of raw intelligence. Just like the rest of the Baltic Fleet, the section was expanded and experienced growing demands on its performance as the Soviet Union prepared to acquire an ocean-going fleet. Out of ten commanders' and specialists' posts in the analysis section, four were vacant, as were eight out of 18 posts in the naval frontier intelligence posts.[52]

There was a lack of people, and the people employed were regarded as poorly educated. Therefore, during the first half of 1936 personnel were sent for supplementary training courses. The commanding personnel assembled in Kronstadt, while the others formed two study groups in Leningrad. The training program consisted of 210 study hours (two days per week during January and February and one half day per week during March and April). Among the subjects were operations and tactics, knowledge of the enemy, knowledge of the Soviet side and staff work. In addition to these subjects came foreign languages (two hours per week), Marxism–Leninism (two hours per week) and shooting and physical training (one hour per week).

One of the three groups consisted of people whose general education was especially weak. But the curricula of the two 'advanced' groups were hardly impressive either, but focused on the dissemination of rather basic military knowledge: elementary staff work, tactics, the Soviet Navy and foreign navies and military geography. The course concluded with an operational war game, simulating defense in the Gulf of Finland.[53] Even among the more literate personnel, the level of professional competence seems to have been quite modest.

In December 1936, three Baltic Fleet radio intelligence operators were awarded the Order of the Red Banner for accomplishments in connection with the Soviet intervention in Spain.[54] Nonetheless, those rewards could not hide fundamental flaws in Baltic Fleet intelligence. In a letter to the head of the section, Alexander Yevseyev, in April 1936, Bogovoy of the fleet staff severely criticized the intelligence section's monthly intelligence estimates: 'Although not so bad from a formal point of view, with regard to their content these documents cannot aspire even for the grade of "pass".' According to Bogovoy, the quality of analysis, style and language must be improved immediately so that the Baltic Fleet's intelligence surveys could be regarded as 'good, civilized [*kulturnye*] documents.'[55]

Similar criticism came from the GRU in Moscow. For instance, there was little proof of the Baltic Fleet's assertion that the Finns were constructing airstrips to receive assistance from abroad, and although quantitative data on enemy fleets were frequent, there was little comparison with the situation in previous years or any general discussion of their weak and strong points.[56]

To some extent, these deficiencies could probably be explained by the fact that Yevseyev had been suffering from bad health for some time. In the summer of 1936, Nikolay Timofeyev took over as head of the section. As we learnt in Chapter 9, there was reason to suspect serious leaks in security in the past, and Timofeyev soon appointed a special investigation into the handling of classified documents under his predecessor.[57]

In May 1937, these investigators presented their report, which contained severe criticism of sloppy adminstrative routines and lax security. Whole series of classified documents could no longer be found in the files, or only after extensive search. Secret documents and the keys to safes had been left unattended. From now on, the storage of classified documents in drawers would be forbidden, even temporarily. Those culpable would be let off with a warning this time, as the missing material was no longer of immediate interest and would soon have been weeded out anyway. One co-worker, Shatalov, would be excused because of his lack of experience. In the future however, there would be no leniency.[58]

Furthermore, Timofeyev tried to speed up the publication of dictionaries on foreign fleets. During 1937, special leaflets on the Royal Navy and on the Baltic, Finnish, Swedish and Polish navies were in preparation. However, the Baltic Fleet Staff had not reserved any funds for their printing. The book on the German Navy, which should have been published in May 1937, had not yet appeared by September.[59] Timofeyev also tried to ensure that cameras with telephoto lenses would be available aboard all Soviet ships when they went to sea. In a letter to the chief of staff, Isakov, in September 1937, he described a recent incident when a Soviet submarine had encountered the Swedish submarine *Nordkaparen* at sea: '...we could only photograph her because one of the commanding personnel had brought his own private "Leica". At the same time, we ourselves were immediately photographed from the Swedish submarine by no less than 4 men.'[60]

In conclusion, we can see that Timofeyev made substantial efforts to professionalize the fleet's intelligence work. In doing so, he probably made excessive demands of his people. In the appendix of this book, it is argued that dissatisfaction from below with Timofeyev's modernization attempts contributed to his perishing in the purges in December 1937. It is true that navy personnel – and among navy personnel those assigned for intelligence – formed an educational elite in the Soviet military. Still, far from all officers had a complete secondary education. Many of Timofeyev's subordinates in the intelligence section seem hardly to have known how to read a map and were ignorant of basic archival routines. They were unable to produce simple publications on time and had problems in writing intelligible reports. Through the repeated inquiries into the social composition of the Baltic Fleet personnel which were organized during the *Yezhovshchina*, we have an idea of the educational background of the intelligence section during 1938. In February, there were 17 privates and junior NCOs serving in the section (about a quarter of private and junior NCO positions were vacant). Fourteen of these men were workers, 12 members or candidate members of the party or the Komsomol, but only seven had spent more than four years at school, only two more than seven years.[61] Out of 22 officers and senior technicians serving in November 1938, only ten had two years' experience of intelligence work or more, and just as many less than one year.[62] The impression of professional competence is not overwhelming.

After Timofeyev's arrest, his deputy, Alexander Fillipovsky, succeeded him. In an austere message to his people on 17 December 1937, the new commander explained:

> As a result of the harmful direction during the past two years by the enemy of the people and spy Timofeyev, the Baltic Fleet intelligence section does not solve the missions it has been assigned…Timofeyev's wrecking espionage work has even liquidated the few miserable results which have indeed been accomplished.

The section must now quickly be reorganized and intelligence work in the Baltic Fleet brought up to a suitable level: 'This our party, the government and the entire country demand from us.' Quite a few co-workers had not yet realized the nature of this formidable task but preferred to spend their day in idleness. From now on, the frontier intelligence posts should work from 10.00 a.m. to 11.00 p.m., including a two-hour lunch break and half an hour for language studies. In Kronstadt, work was to go on from 9.00 a.m. to 10.00 p.m. with a one-hour lunch break. One day a week should be reserved for individual supplementary training, with time for preparations the evening before from 6.00 p.m. The day before one's weekday off was also to be free from 6.00 p.m.[63]

As we can see, Fillipovsky took care not to criticize his subordinates without first blaming Timofeyev and his harmful rule. He also used the same description of the irresponsible co-workers who had fallen under Timofeyev's influence – as idle and uninterested wreckers – as he had used when characterizing his predecessor at a meeting with the party cell two weeks before.[64]

In his first New Year's message to the section in 1938, however, Fillipovsky no longer tried to mitigate his criticism. While the Communist Party and the people were enthusiastically supporting the great oceanic naval program, he complained, the personnel of the intelligence section seemed disinterested.[65] A few days later, Fillipovsky learnt that even his deputy, Junior Lieutenant Frumkin, had left secret documents unattended. In view of Frumkin's good work in the past, Fillipovsky stated in a special message to his subordinates, this infringement of security would not lead to any reappraisals but neither Frumkin nor anyone else should expect leniency if this happened again.[66]

Fillipovsky's readiness to openly disavow his deputy did not improve discipline much. Two months later, when he made an unannounced inspection tour of the premises, Fillipovsky was shocked by what he saw:

> During this inspection, I discovered a complete chaos on the desks of most workers. On their desks one can find wrapping paper, various drafts, naval literature, notebooks, collars, ties, radio equipment and similar items. In such a disorder, one can not rule out that official documents or elaborated drafts are also left unattended. Furthermore, the heads of the section dedicate little attention to the foreign newspapers they receive on behalf of the section. Such newspapers can be seen lying around everywhere, without anyone studying them or taking care of them as would be appropriate. In the premises where the workers reside there is a sense of destititution. One gets no impression of an organized workplace.[67]

The intelligence section was certainly not the only part of the Baltic Fleet with similar problems.

In February 1937, the commissar of the Baltic Fleet battleship squadron reported that in his unit (two battleships with a total crew of about 2,300 men), there were 785 sailors and NCOs who had not yet completed the first year of middle school (5th grade), the level of education considered necessary to serve in the Soviet naval forces. A special training program had been organized with one group of 1st graders, nine groups of 2nd graders, 22 groups of 3rd graders, 25 groups of 4th graders and four groups of 5th graders. The ordinary service did not allow for more than two lessons a week, lessons that had to take place aboard the ships and with almost no teaching material. Aboard the *Marat*, 5–6 men had to share one book between them. Although many sailors would like to continue further than 5th grade, there were no teachers available. Only a few conscripts had a complete (10th grade) or incomplete (8th grade) secondary education. Therefore, Commissar Sokolov (later in the year a victim of the purges) pleaded that a special training program for teachers must be organized.[68]

On 1 September 1939, the same day that Nazi Germany initiated World War II by invading Poland, the Soviet Union introduced its new national service law. From now on, the defense of the Fatherland was to be the duty of every male Soviet citizen, regardless of his social background. As the navy's official handbook concluded, persons with a secondary or university education would no longer be exempted: 'This will mean a powerful reinforcement of the ranks of the Navy.'[69]

Already in May, the time of service in the navy had been differentiated. In the fleet it was expanded to five years, in the coastal artillery and the naval air arm reduced to three years. After the draftees had been examined, those in need of preparatory education were sent off for a year of ordinary elementary school. Conscripts with a university diploma could be sent directly to a reserve officer training program. After four years of service as ensigns, they would receive the rank of junior lieutenant and join the reserve. Conscripts with a complete secondary education could do the same after two years as privates in specialist positions.[70]

As has been mentioned, the navy's rapid expansion under the ocean naval construction program created a shortage of officers in all parts of the navy. Between 1936 and 1940, the number of naval academies tripled from four to 12, and the quality of training suffered. At some of the new institutions, more than half of the teaching positions were vacant. There was talk of cadets who in their third year did not know what a destroyer was, could not read a sea chart or even sail.[71]

It was in the midst of this process that the Baltic Fleet was thrown into the war against Finland, with predictable results. A number of Soviet warships had had arms and equipment which the crew did not know how to operate.[72] On Christmas Day 1939, Fleet Commander Tributs issued an order to his submarine commanders, telling them that 'every submarine commander has to know that it is a little thing to wish to defeat the enemy, to only have boldness, bravery and courage'. Seamanship and knowledge of equipment was also required, as was knowledge of the enemy and the theater of operations.[73] In a special report in August 1940, Kuznetsov proposed to the government that the Baltic Fleet's officers should be sent out on a secret reconnaissance cruise in the Gulf of Bothnia, as 'fighting with the White Finns in the Baltic demonstrated poor knowledge of the theater' among personnel.[74]

Out of the five ships sunk by Soviet submarines during the war, only one was sunk by torpedoes, the rest by artillery fire. At the Naval War College's conference in October 1940, Associate Professor Anatoly Tomashevich blamed the lack of proper exercises, asserting that Soviet submarine commanders could not recognize foreign ships, were ignorant of range finding and could only hit moving targets if they moved on a steady course. The submariners of the Imperial Navy, he said, had been superior by far. In those days, collisions with submarines were unheard of. In the Soviet era, training had become less demanding.[75]

During 1939–40, the Soviet Navy lost 667 men in accidents. Another 1,107 were injured. The number of aircraft crashed during training amounted to two entire regiments – 122 aircraft – (48 in the Baltic Fleet). It should be noticed, however, that some speakers at the October conference regarded a minor number of accidents as a necessary price to pay for realism in training. The alternative would be to abstain from training for operations in rough weather or at night. With regard to aviation, Captain 2nd rank Titov, head of the Baltic Fleet anti-air artillery, suggested that a unit which did not suffer a single crash during training had not been trained properly.[76]

Another complaint expressed by several speakers during the Leningrad conference was that the Soviet military academies did not produce independent commanders. Was it even possible to imagine Soviet naval officers behaving like the commander of the German pocket battleship *Admiral Graf Spee* or his British opponent on the *Exeter*?[77] When Isakov tried to explain the moral factors behind Germany's recent victory over France, he mentioned Germany's youth. While the French had rested on their laurels since 1918 and conserved their decadent bourgeois democracy – even keeping some of the leaders from those days in power – the Germans had built an entirely new society under fascism, a culture without holy old men. Although the present German leaders were veterans of World War I, they were not like Weygand, Pétain and Gamelin but represented a fresh outlook and new, powerful ideas. More important from a Marxist point of view – thanks to the Treaty of Versailles, the German military machine could be constructed on a modern material base. By forbidding Germany from keeping tanks, aircraft and submarines, the allies ensured that Germany would have equipment superior to their own in the next war. When German rearmament began in 1935, it was based entirely on the latest technology, and it also become possible for the German military leaders to develop a more modern doctrine.[78]

What is interesting in Isakov's analysis is that his description of Nazi Germany came close to the national self-image of the Soviet Union, that of a vital society with an entirely new way of thinking. He described the Soviets as rich in new ideas, 'as we are no law-abiding dogmatists of the past, but the creators of a new way of life'.[79] Moreover, in the years to come the Soviet Navy planned to renew its material base on a scale unknown to all other navies in the world. What prospects of doctrinal development lay ahead, the audience must well have asked itself.

However, even if Isakov's discreet parallel between the Soviet Union and Germany may look like an attempt to boost the Soviet Navy's self-confidence, the conference participants all agreed that they did not live up to the expectations of 'modern flagmen, modern commanders, modern staffs matching the conditions of war at sea under modern conditions'.[80] Instead, they perceived themselves as inferior to the Germans in this regard: 'As a rule, the state of organization is a sign of culture. We should study the situations, methods and forms of organization which can bring our state of organization to a higher level'.[81]

Naval Aviator Major-General Suvorov pointed out that although there was an abundant literature on recent wars available to Soviet officers, no one cared to read it: 'Literature attracts the educated, civilized person, while the uneducated does not take any interest even in the books on his own bookshelf.'[82]

Navy Commissar Rogov, always an eager spokesman for the necessity of honest self-criticism, went even further:

> I must say that the basic fault in our management is weak organization and very weak culture. The level of our military and political training, I would even say our general level, is still suffering. In this, we have little to be proud of.[83]

Conclusion

After the traumatic experience of collectivization and forced industrialization, Soviet policy during the late 1930s was characterized by an ambition to adapt to superficial 'normality' – domestically as well as internationally. It is in this cultural context that the sudden urge to have an ocean-going battleship fleet should be seen. The Soviet Union was adapting to Great power standards. Other signs of adaption were the return to principles from the tsarist period for naming new warships, the reintroduction of admirals' ranks and the amalgamation of 'military specialists' and 'red commanders' into a new group of naval leaders.

Parallel to 'normalization', waves of terror spread chaos and fear – through the navy as well as through other sectors of Soviet society. Together with the navy's rapid expansion, the removal of experienced and competent leaders at different levels in the service led to serious problems. In early 1938, a third of all positions in the navy were unmanned. In August 1937, the purges and the demands for increased vigilance that came with them led to the return of dual command. However, in 1939–40 the war against Finland suggested that this system was just as impractical as could be suspected, so it was soon abolished again. Moreover, the efforts of the commissar to strengthen morale and discipline seemed to have little effect if the personnel had no confidence in their training or in the competence of their leaders.

As is demonstrated by the Baltic Fleet intelligence section, although tremendous work was done to raise educational levels among the staff and to modernize administrative routines, little seemed to have been achieved. In the autumn of 1940, when the naval command assembled for its autumn conferences, the number of disciplinary infringements and fatal accidents during training had reached truly worrying levels. The Soviet admirals and their commissars simply had to accept that modernity could not be acquired through terror, through harsher disciplinary regulations or intensified agitation. That the Red Navy men lacked the fighting qualities their superiors wished to see in them had to do with alleged cultural weaknesses in Russian society, which almost a quarter of a century of Soviet power had done little to remedy. Ocean-going battleships or not, the perceived gap between Russia and the surrounding world remained, as did feelings of inferiority.

Notes

1. Hildermeier, *Geschichte der Sowjetunion*, pp. 436–38; Thurston, *Life and Terror*, pp. 1–15.
2. Kotkin, *Magnetic Mountain*, pp. 259–79; Hildermeier, *Geschichte der Sowjetunion*, p. 521.
3. Operational order 00447 and documents relevant to this decision can be found in J. Arch Getty and Oleg Naumov, *The Road to Terror: Stalin and the Self-Destruction of the Bolsheviks, 1932–1939* (New Haven, CT: Yale University Press, 1999), pp. 470–80, quote from p. 471.

4 Figures from Getty *et al.* 'Victims of the Soviet Penal System'; a higher total number of victims suggested by Alexander N. Yakovlev, *A Century of Violence in Soviet Russia* (New Haven, CT: Yale University Press, 2002).
5 Hildermeier, *Geschichte der Sowjetunion*, pp. 444–68.
6 Important contributions within the totalitarian tradition are Robert Conquest, *The Great Terror: Stalin's Purge in the 1930s* (London: Macmillan, 1968); *idem*, *The Great Terror: A reassessment* (New York: Oxford University Press, 1990); Tucker, *Stalin in Power*; cf. also Carl J. Friedrich and Zbigniew Brezinski, *Totalitarian Dictatorship and Autocracy* (Cambridge, MA: Harvard University Press, 1965).
7 J. Arch Getty, *Origins of the Great Purges: The Soviet Communist Party Reconsidered, 1933–1938* (Cambridge: Cambridge University Press, 1985); Gábor Rittersporn, *Stalinist Simplifications and Soviet Complications: Social Tensions and Political Conflicts in the U.S.S.R., 1933–1953* (Chur: Harwood Academic Publishers, 1991).
8 J. Arch Getty and Roberta Thompson Manning (eds), *Stalinist Terror: New Perspectives* (Cambridge: Cambridge University Press, 1993); Getty and Naumov, *Road to Terror*; Thurston, *Life and Terror*.
9 Reese, *Stalin's Reluctant Soldiers*, p. 203; Reese is a prominent spokesman for the revisionist interpretation – cf. his 'The Red Army and the Great Purges', in J. Arch Getty and Robert Thompson Manning (eds), *Stalinist Terror: New Perspectives* (Cambridge: Cambridge university press, 1993); the authoritative Russian study on the subject so far is Suvenirov, *Tragediya RKKA* (Moscow: Terra, 1998).
10 The translation to English from Erickson, *Soviet High Command*, p. 475.
11 Kuznetsov, *Nakanune*, pp. 258–60, cf. *idem*, *Krutye povoroty*, pp. 37, 41–2.
12 Hildermeier, *Geschichte der Sowjetunion*, pp. 545–54, 563–80; on the *Marat* in Spithead, see Berezovsky *et al.*, *Boevaya letopis*, p. 609.
13 Novikov, 'Gangutskaya pobeda'; Vladimir Tributs, 'Krasnoznamenny baltflot na strazhe rodiny', *Morskoy Sbornik*, vol. 92(12) (1939).
14 Order by the People's Commissar for the Navy, 25 September 1940, f. r-1549, o. 1, d. 71, list 139–41.
15 L. I. Mandelstam (ed.), *Sbornik zakonov SSSR i ukazov prezidiuma verkhnogo soveta SSSR 1938–1956* (Moscow: Gosudarstvennoe izdatelstvo yuridecheskoy literatury, 1956), pp. 197–8; Suvenirov, *RKKA nakanune*, pp. 228–9; Berezovsky *et al.*, *Boevaya letopis*, pp. 660–1.
16 Herrick, *Soviet Naval Theory and Strategy*, pp. 65–6, 76–7, 110–24.
17 Dotsenko, *Morskoy biograficheskiy slovar*, p. 55; Belli, Memoirs, r-2224, o. 1, d. 4, list 195–7; I. V. Kasatonov, *Flot vychodit v okean: povest ob admirale flota V. A. Kasatonove* (St Petersburg: Lyuks, 1995), p. 49.
18 Herrick, *Soviet Naval Theory*, pp. 126–37.
19 Dotsenko, *Morskoy biograficheskiy slovar*, p. 388.
20 Zonin, *Admiral L. M. Galler*, pp. 276–7, 281–2, 291–2; Dotsenko, *Morskoy biograficheskiy slovar*, pp. 111–12.
21 Dotsenko, *Morskoy biograficheskiy slovar*, p. 184; Barsukov and Zolotarev (eds), *Russky arkhiv*, vol. I.2, pp. 256–7; a selection of Isakov's articles, as well as a complete bibliography of his works, can be found I. S. Isakov, *Izbrannye trudy: Okeanologiya, geografiya i voennaya istoriya* (Moscow: Izdatelstvo Nauka, 1984).
22 Dotsenko, *Morskoy biograficheskiy slovar*, p 247.
23 Ibid., pp. 407–8.
24 Kuznetsov, *Nakanune*, passim; Dotsenko, *Morskoy biograficheskiy slovar*, pp. 234–5; on Kuznetsov in *Krasnaya Zvezda*, see Suvenirov, *RKKA nakanune*, pp. 181–2.
25 Suvenirov, *RKKA nakanune*, p. 176.
26 Monakov, 'Sudba doktrin i teory, 8', p. 42.
27 A. Yevseyev, 'Do kontsa razgromit vracheskie teorii v morskoy strategii', *Krasny Flot*, 28 August 1938, quoted from Herrick, *Soviet Naval Theory and Strategy*, p. 97.

28 Herrick, *Soviet Naval Theory and Strategy*, p. 138 n.15; during the first monhs of the war – in November 1941 – Alexandrov was again to experience arrest and expulsion from the Party, followed by sudden rehabilitation – Barsukov and Zolotarev (eds), *Russky arkhiv*, vol. I.2 p. 384.
29 Monakov, 'Sudba doktrin i teory, 8', p. 42.
30 Ibid., p. 42.
31 Suvenirov, *RKKA nakanune*, pp. 216–17.
32 Barsukov and Zolotarev (eds), *Russky arkhiv*, vol. I.2 pp. 375–7.
33 'Spisok kommandnogo i nachalstvuyeoshchego sostava 1. BRO', f. r-1883, o. 1, d. 58, list 63; 'Vedomost nalichiya mladshego nachalstvuyeoshchego i ryadavogo sostava 1 BRO', ibid., list 64; Fillipovisky to the head of naval intelligence Yakimychev, 2 April 1938, ibid., list 46; Kireyev, 22 August 1938, 'Svedeniya o kolichestve uvolennogo, arrestovannogo, vydvinutogo komnachsostava po KBF', f. r-2185, o. 2, d. 3, list 34–5.
34 Suvenirov, *RKKA nakanune*, p. 202; the text of this decree can be found in A. I. Barsukov and V. A. Zolotarev (eds), *Russky arkhiv: Velikaya Otechestvennaya voyna. Prikazy i direktivy narodnogo komissara oborony SSSR*, vol. II.1 (Moscow: Terra 1994), pp. 24–5.
35 Van Dyke, 'Timoshenko Reforms', Suvenirov, *RKKA nakanune*, pp. 231–2; Berezovsky et al., *Boevaya letopis*, pp. 662, 664.
36 Stenographic protocol from the meeting of the senior and superior political personnel of the navy, evening session, 7 August 1940, f. r-1549, o. 1, d. 173, list 13–17.
37 Barsukov and Zolotarev (eds), *Russky arkhiv*, vol. I.2, pp. 429–31, 437–8 quote from p. 429.
38 Fleet Procurator Shturman to Fleet Commander Isakov, 19 October 1937, f. r-2185 o. 2, d. 210, list 114.
39 Kuznetsov to the Baltic Fleet Soviet, 14 October 1939, f.-92 o. 2, d. 464, list, 2–4, 7–9; on Voroshilov's directives, see Komplektov et al. (eds), *Polpredy soobschayut...*, pp. 147–52.
40 Stenographic protocol from the meeting of the senior and superior political personnel of the navy, evening session, 7 August 1940, f. r-1549, o. 1, d. 173, list 26–7.
41 Cf. the list of awards in Stupnikov (ed.), *Dvazhdi*, pp. 315–20.
42 Tributs to submarine commanders and commissars, 25 December 1939, f. r-1877, o. 1, d. 91, list 111–12.
43 Stenographic protocol from the meeting of the senior and superior political personnel of the navy, evening session, 7 August 1940, f. r-1549, o. 1, d. 173, list 6.
44 Ibid., list 17–18; Barsukov and Zolotarev (eds), *Russky arkhiv*, vol. I.2, pp. 379–80.
45 Stenographic protocol from the meeting of the senior and superior political personnel of the navy, evening session, 7 August 1940, f. r-1549, o. 1, d. 173, list 32.
46 Barsukov and Zolotarev (eds), *Russky arkhiv*, vol. I.2, pp. 381–3, 442–4.
47 Stenographic protocol from the meeting of the senior and superior political personnel of the navy, evening session, 7 August 1940, f. r-1549, o. 1, d. 173, list 12–15, 19–20.
48 Ibid., list 21.
49 Ibid., list 22.
50 Barsukov and Zolotarev (eds), *Russky arkhiv*, vol. I.2, pp. 154–7.
51 Ibid., pp. 468–75 (Kuznetsov quote p. 475); on the 1940 uniform regulation M. M. Khrenov et al., *Voennaya odezhda Vooruzhennikh Sil SSSR i Rossii (1917–1990-e gody)* (Moscow: Voenizdat, 1999), pp. 126–32; Kuznetsov, *Krutye povoroty*, pp. 37–8.
52 A. Yevseyev, 14 January 1936, 'Prikaz nachalnika razvedivatelnogo otdela Krasnoznamnenogo balticheskogo flota', f. r-1883, o. 2, d. 3, list 1–2.
53 Order by Isakov, 22 November 1935, f. r-1883, o. 2, d. 4, list 1–2; order by Isakov, 25 November 1935, ibid., list 3–4; order by Yevseyev, 26 January 1936, ibid., list 12–13; study plan by the head of the Baltic Fleet operational section Rechister (no date), ibid., list 9–11.
54 Order by the head of GRU Uritsky, 20 December 1936, f. r-1883, o.1, d. 28, list 161–5.

55 Bogovoy to Yevseyev, 22 April 1936, f. r-1883, o. 1, d. 28, list 16–17.
56 Deputy heads GRU Nikonov and Martinson to Yevseyev, 7 July 1936, f. r-1883, o. 1, d. 28, list 32–3; the assertions made with regard to Finnish airstrips are probably those in the March survey that year, see ibid., list 12.
57 Order by Timofeyev, 14 February 1936; f. r-1883, o. 2, d. 4, list 14; order by Timofeyev, 25 December 1936, ibid., list 47.
58 Order by Timofeyev, 20 May 1937, f. r-1883, o. 2, d. 5, list 1; the investigation same date, ibid., list 3–4.
59 Timofeyev to the deputy head of GRU (RU RKKA) Gendits, 21 September 1937, f. r-1883, o. 1, d. 55, list 64; Timofeyev to Gendits, 26 September 1937, ibid., list 63.
60 Timofeyev to Isakov, 20 September 1937, f. r-1883, o. 1, d. 55, list 62.
61 Filippovsky, 10 February 1938, 'Socialno-demograficheskaya charakteristika mladsego nachalstvuyushchego i ryadogo sostava RKKA, Razved.otdel KBF', f. r-1883, o. 1, d. 58, list 17; cf. Filippovsky, 15 March 1938, ibid., list 29–31; Filippovsky to the head of Naval Intelligence Directorate Nefodov, 19 August 1938, ibid., list 132–8.
62 Filippovsky, 1 November 1938, f. r-1883, o. 2, d. 7, list 15–15b.
63 Order by Filippovsky, 17 December 1937, f. r-1883, o. 2, d. 5, list 6.
64 Cf. appendix.
65 Order by Filippovsky, 1 January 1938, f. r-1883, o. 2, d. 6, list 1–3.
66 Ibid., 11 January 1938, f. r-1883, o. 2, d. 7, list 2; for Frumkin's service record, see Filippovsky, 1 November 1938, ibid., list 15–15b.
67 Order by Filippovsky, 10 March 1938, f. r-1883, o. 2, d. 6, list 9.
68 Sokolov to PUR KBF, 10 February 1937, f. r-34, o. 2, d. 1568, list 46–7.
69 Mandelstam (ed.), *Sbornik zakonov SSR*, pp. 177–187; B. I. Smirnov, *Voenno-morskoy flot* (Leningrad: Voennomorizdat, 1941), p. 7.
70 Mandelstam (ed.), *Sbornik zakonov SSR*, p. 187; Smirnov, *Voenno-morskoy flot*, pp. 10–12.
71 Barsukov and Zolotarev (eds), *Russky arkhiv*, vol. I.2, pp. 420–3, 438.
72 Ibid., pp. 163–4.
73 Tributs to submarine commanders and commissars, 25 December, 1939, f. r-1877, o. 1, d. 91, list 111–12.
74 Kuznetsov to Molotov, 9 August 1940, f. r-1678, o. 1, d. 162, list 766.
75 Barsukov and Zolotarev (eds), *Russky arkhiv*, vol. I.2, pp. 55–61.
76 Ibid., p. 443, statistics on accidents, Titov's statement, p. 137; cf. naval airman Colonel Shuginin, pp. 113–16.
77 Ibid., vol. I.2, p. 174; cf. interventions by Sergeyev, Pavlovich and Laukhin, pp.131–6, 163–9.
78 Ibid., pp. 30–1,
79 Ibid., p. 37.
80 Ibid., p. 265.
81 Ibid., p. 38.
82 Ibid., p. 129.
83 Ibid., p. 443.

14

THE LESSONS OF WAR AND PEACE

In his classical work *On War*, the Prussian General Carl von Clausewitz made his famous dictum on war as a continuation of politics by other means. He also identified the three fundamental aspects of modern war: reason – expressed through its subordination to politics; 'chance and probability' – best mastered by the creative genius of the military commander; and 'primordial violence, hatred and enmity' – reflecting the people and its passions. The difficulty of balancing these incompatible forces against each other was what made war dangerous and risky, and the successful war leader worthy of admiration. Clearly, there is a correspondence between this Clausewitzean triad and the three themes that have been the focal points of the present book. The cold rationality of strategic thought represents the statesman's perspective. At the level of operational planning and organizational rivalry the creative genius of the military leader will be required. At the tactical level, in the midst of battle, the culturally conditioned emotions of fighting men seem to be the most influential force at play.[1]

In this light, it is easy to see how Clausewitz identified the core problem of war by defining it as a continuation of politics, as a 'true political instrument'. A war objective, whose logic and rationality may seem crystal clear at the strategic level, tends to get increasingly blurred when implemented at operational and tactical levels of decision, when theory is confronted with the frictions and conflicting rationality of practical life, with ordinary people of flesh and blood. As Deputy People's Commissar for the Navy Admiral Isakov admitted during the Naval War College's conference in October 1940:

> We have no lack of new ideas or fresh thinking, as we are no law-abiding dogmatists of the past, but the creators of a new way of life... However, there is a field of work where we are at a standstill. As soon as it comes to practical execution, we are quite bad.[2]

In the preceding pages, we have seen numerous examples of this gap between theory and practice which Isakov referred to. How could the evolution of Soviet naval doctrine between the world wars be analyzed in the context of strategy, organizational rivalry and culture?

Strategy

In Chapters 5, 8 and 11, we studied the strategic dimension – the relationship between the Baltic Fleet's preparations for war and Soviet foreign policy objectives.

During the early 1920s, the 'offensive' Old School thrived on the dreams of world revolution. When this thinking had become unfashionable, the need to seize the Baltic approaches to keep the Western powers out of the region instead came to the fore.

From 1928–30, however, the emphasis in Soviet foreign policy was on coexistence and collective security. Although threat assessments remained much the same, the new course suggested a more defensive emphasis in Soviet military planning. Now, the defensive Young School took over. A few years later, Hitler's rise to power in Germany made the turn toward a defensive naval doctrine somewhat problematic, especially since Britain in 1935 allowed Germany to rearm its navy.

This new threat perception formed an important motive for Stalin's oceanic naval program and the rise of the Soviet School. However, in the autumn of 1940, Nazi Germany's inability to win a decisive victory over Britain made the Soviet naval command reconsider the balance of power in Europe once again. The battleship program was temporarily halted.

Consequently, the shifts in naval doctrine did coincide with changes in Soviet foreign policy during the period. This, perhaps, is only what could be expected.

Organizational rivalry

Chapters 6, 9 and 12 investigated naval doctrine from the perspective of organizational rivalry. How could the evolution of doctrine be explained against the background of inter-service competition and the conflict between the regional and central levels in the Soviet navy hierarchy? It was argued that in a littoral sea region like the Baltic – sparsely populated, with a difficult terrain and only a few good roads – the projection of military power has always demanded a comparatively high degree of joint planning between land and sea forces. With the rise of air power in the first half of the twentieth century, this need was further accentuated, which tended to increase organizational friction. During the 1920s, the Old School made determined efforts to preserve the navy as an independent service with its own distinct missions and capital ships as the main weapon system.

Under the circumstances, however, the coastal-defense doctrine of the Young School proved better adapted to political reality, as it advocated a cheaper navy that would coordinate its operations with the ground forces. Although fairly consistent plans existed for the defense of Leningrad, the demands to support the Red Army's offensive operations into Finland and Estonia were harder to meet. The ships of the Baltic Fleet must maneuver along the shallow coasts of the Gulf of Finland, while supporting fast-moving mechanized forces ashore with powerful artillery fire.

The Soviet School era, which saw a huge rise in naval spending and the resurrection of an independent People's Commissariat for the Navy, signified the service's return to political grace. Just as before, however, the Baltic Fleet's primary mission would be to support the Red Army's offensive operations. Could the fleet's weak air arm meet the demands of modern warfare, and would the fleet's resources suffice for the construction of new base facilities in the Baltic Theater? Although the war against Finland in 1939–40 demonstrated serious deficiencies, the fleet's campaign planning became even more offensive in character in the following months, when new bases had been acquired in the west. Now, the Baltic Fleet calculated with preemptive air strikes and submarine attacks against the enemy in the initial phase of a war. These plans notwithstanding, Soviet naval leaders were uncertain of their success.

As we can see, there was thus also some link between the internal, bureaucratic struggle in the Soviet armed forces and the shifts between different naval doctrines. However, the great oceanic program and the resurrection of the navy in 1937–38 were initiated from above. Soviet naval leaders did not orchestrate the expansion of their own missions and responsibilities, but were worried and anxious about that development and not particularly interested in battleships.

Culture

Chapters 7, 10 and 13 focused on the cultural aspects of Soviet naval doctrine in the period. In these chapters, the relationship between the Communist Party and the navy constituted a central theme, as did the complicated image in Russian/Soviet tradition of the West and of Modernity. Although they saw the capitalist world as essentially inferior, caught in a historical stage from which Russia had already triumphantly emerged, the Soviets also acknowledged the fact that for the time being their country lagged behind. Before the Soviet Union had caught up and could aspire for a position as a major modern military power, the civilizing work that had to be accomplished seemed enormous.

During the NEP era, the former tsarist officers who dominated the service were allowed to continue cultivating the traditions of the Imperial Navy. The regime realized its dependence on bourgeois experts in this as in other fields, and trusted political commissars to control the old elite until a new generation of Soviet trained naval officers could take over. This was the cultural significance of the Old School era.

Later, when the first five-year plan called for general mobilization and rapid progress, red commanders replaced the former military specialists, who were criticized for their caution and conservatism. The civil war veterans who came instead may have had little qualified military training, but were still accredited with fresh ideas on naval warfare and became known as the Young School. While the Old School had symbolized continuity from the former regime, the Young School heralded the emergence of a genuine Soviet self-consciousness which rejected tradition and believed itself to be superior in its own right, combining futurist notions of joint operations with ideological zeal. Although its spokesmen were seemingly ignorant of naval tactics, their doctrine was in fact better adapted to the peculiar geography of the Baltic.

The return to traditional blue-water thinking under the Soviet School reflected general ideological trends in Soviet society in the late 1930s. As the Soviet state claimed equality with the West it should – like any modern great power – also have an ocean-going fleet. During this phase, the former military specialists and the new red commanders were finally successfully amalgamated into a homogenous officer corps. The 'Great Terror' in 1937–38, which offered the navy an opportunity to rid itself of unwanted personnel in commanding positions, may have contributed to that result, but the purges also afflicted highly competent and loyal people. An even more important cause of the lack of competent personnel in the navy on the eve of World War II was the service's rapid organizational expansion under the great oceanic naval construction program. As was demonstrated by the poor performance during the conflict with the Finns, the great project of educating the navy in the ways of modern warfare was largely unfinished by 1941.

1941: the 'Real War'

In comparison with earlier studies on the Soviet Navy between the world wars, this book has dedicated fairly limited interest to the 'hardware' – to the ships and aircraft, the artillery and armor, or to the technological changes behind the evolution of different weapon systems. Still, the dividing issue between the rival naval schools in the Soviet Union in the 1920s and 1930s could best be described as a conflict over the interpretation of technological developments. How had the coming of submarines and air power affected the future prospects of big artillery ships? Had the increased vulnerability of those ships made them obsolete, or would the introduction of effective countermeasures soon neutralize any disadvantages, size proving to be crucial to survival of warships in a modern combat environment? Without the experience of a major war at sea – which occurred only in 1939–45 – this remained a disputed matter.

Here is not the place for a detailed account of naval operations in the Baltic during the summer and autumn of 1941. What follows in the next few pages is only a brief outline of events from June to December, intended to illustrate how the 'real war' differed from the war which the Baltic Fleet had prepared for during the 1920s and 1930s.

The Baltic Fleet was not taken by surprise by the attack on 22 June. The number of air space violations over naval bases had grown during the spring, and already in late March, People's Commissar Kuznetsov had forbidden the navy to open fire against foreign aircraft. From the second week of May, the Soviets increased their own reconnaissance at the mouth of the Gulf of Finland and off the Swedish island of Gotland. In mid-June, reports spoke of German troops concentrating in Finnish ports and of Finnish civilians evacuating the surroundings of the Soviet base at Hanko. Also, it was noticed, German cargo ships were in a hurry to leave Soviet ports.[3]

On 14 June, when the Soviet news agency TASS issued a communiqué emphatically denying all rumors of an impending Soviet–German war, seven German minelayers hid in the Finnish archipelago. During the night between the 21st and the 22nd, they laid out mines at the mouth of the Gulf of Finland (minefields codenamed *Apolda*) and off the Soviet base in Paldiski (minefields codenamed *Corbetha*). During the previous three nights, four other minelayers from Pillau had laid out mines between Memel (Latvian Klaipeda) and the Swedish island of Öland (minefields codenamed *Wartburg*). In the early hours of the 22 June, Finnish submarines also mined the Estonian archipelago. After the beginning of hostilities, Germans and Finns laid additional minefields in Riga Bay and off Hanko, and the Swedes were made to lay mines on their side of the borderline in connection to the *Wartburg* fields. The southern Baltic, the Latvian coast and the Gulf of Finland were then completely sealed off.[4]

In June 1941, the Baltic Fleet consisted of two battleships, two cruisers, one old training cruiser, one old minelayer, two destroyer leaders, 19 destroyers (out of which 12 were modern – six more destroyers were commissioned during the autumn), nine patrol ships (out of which one had been taken over by the Estonian Navy), 33 minesweepers (out of which 17 were modern – one additional minesweeper was commissioned in August), 11 big, 36 medium (out of which all but four were modern – two more medium submarines were commissioned during the autumn) and 23 small submarines, 656 aircraft (172 bombers and torpedo bombers, 353 fighter and 131 reconnaissance aircraft). The personnel numbered some 58,000. The fleet was concentrated in three main areas: the OLS commanded by Rear-Admiral Valentin Drozd, deployed at Ust–Dvinsk outside Riga and in Liepaya close to the border (cruisers *Kirov* and *Maxim Gorky*, two squadrons of destroyers, 1st Submarine Squadron, some MTBs and minesweepers); the *eskadra* commanded by Rear-Admiral V. D. Vdovitchenko at Tallinn (battleship *Oktyabrskaya Revolutsiya*, destroyer leaders *Leningrad* and *Minsk*, two squadrons of destroyers, some MTBs and minesweepers); the remaining ships at Kronstadt (battleship *Marat*, two squadrons of destroyers and 2nd and 3rd Submarine Squadrons among them).[5]

Although combat readiness level 1 had been proclaimed shortly before midnight on the 21st, the Baltic Fleet was slow to go to war. During the early hours of the 22nd, at least one Soviet destroyer and three patrol ships passed within sight of German minelayers laying the *Apolda* barrage, but did not react. Only at 02.28, German minelayer *Brummer* (ex-Norwegian *Olav Tryggvason*) and an escorting MTB were fired upon by two Soviet reconnaissance aircraft. These shots from two MBR-2 flying boats of the 44rd Air Squadron were the first that the Baltic Fleet fired in the war against Germany. About an hour later, a Soviet cargo ship reported being attacked by German MTBs east off Gotland. Shortly afterwards, German aircraft appeared in the sky above Oranienbaum and Kronstadt, and at 04.47 above Liepaya. Soviet anti-air artillery opened fire. Not until 05.17 did the Fleet Soviet inform all units that the Germans were attacking. Not until 06.30 was the order to lay a protective mine barrier issued. It was executed between 22 and 24 June, with some 3,000 mines and 500 sweeping obstacles.[6]

This improvised GOR did not follow the established perimeter of the 1920s and 1930s between Stirsudden and Shepelev but was drawn further west, between the newly founded Soviet bases at Hanko in Finland and Hiiumaa Island in Estonia, not far from where the Germans had laid their *Apolda* barrage the night before. To stiffen the Hanko–Hiumaa line, cruiser *Maxim Gorky* and three destroyers were drawn north from Riga Bay. Although a Soviet patrol ship had reported that German minelayers had been active in the area, this force sailed right into the *Apolda* minefields in the early hours of 23 June: the destroyer *Gnevny* was sunk and the cruiser *Maxim Gorky* damaged for the duration of the war. Minesweeper *T-208/Shkiv*, which sailed out from Tallinn to assist *Maxim Gorky*, was also destroyed. *Maxim Gorky* and her escorts should have brought their own minesweepers with them, but the two ships available were old and slow – former Latvian and Lithuanian minesweepers making six knots per hour – and had been left behind.[7]

For at least a decade, the lack of modern minesweepers had been pointed out as a serious weakness in the Baltic Fleet.

The fall of Liepaya

Another old weakness in the Baltic Fleet, the failing coordination with the RKKA, was also demonstrated during the first days of the war. The plan for defending the forward base in Liepaya had been improvised in great haste, and the fleet staff in Tallinn and the Eighth Army of the Baltic Military District had never agreed on how to divide responsibility between the naval base commander, Captain 1st rank M. S. Klevensky, and the commander of the ground forces, Major-General N. A. Dedayev of the 67th Rifle Division. Moreover, in line with the Baltic Fleet's general scenario, the defense plan only calculated with an attack from the sea. That German tanks would be threatening Liepaya from the rear within 24 hours came as a complete surprise. When nine cargo ships evacuated supplies and civilians to Tallinn on the 23th, panic broke out. First, the ammunition and fuel dumps were blown up, then the destroyer *Lenin* and five submarines (*S-1*, *M-71*, *M-80* and the former Latvian submarines *Ronis* and *Spidola*). The crews were sent to fight as infantry outside the city. Three submarines managed to escape, but two of them (*M-78* and *S-3*) were later sunk off the coast by German submarines, and the third (*M-83*) scuttled by her crew at sea. On the evening of the 24th, Major-General Dedayev was dead and the German Eighteenth Army had encircled Liepaya. Now, the remaining ships were scuttled. On 29 June, the Germans entered the city. Two cargo ships, loaded with refugees and materiel, were captured on the shore.[8]

Now, the Baltic Fleet evacuated its remaining bases in Riga Bay. With the assistance of a dredger and a tugboat, cruiser *Kirov*, three destroyers and seven submarines escaped from Riga to Tallinn through the narrow Moon Sound, only hours before German troops marched into the city on 1 July.[9]

On the offensive

In control of the Latvian coast, the Germans could start supplying their rapidly advancing ground forces by sea. The Soviets tried to disturb this traffic by sending destroyers through the Moon Sound into Riga Bay. Supported by aircraft operating from Saaremaa Island and by fire from the coastal batteries on Hiiumaa Island, these destroyers attacked both German transport ships and supply columns ashore. Also, air raids were made on Berlin from Saaremaa Island. Together with units from the RKKA air arm, *DB-3* bombers of the Baltic Fleet 1st Mine-Torpedo Regiment made repeated attacks on the German capital from 8 August to 4 September, dropping hundreds of thousands of leaflets and 36 tons of bombs. This period, from mid-July to late August, was the only stage during the 1941 campaign when the Baltic Fleet was able to take to the offensive. In the best traditions of the Young School, naval, ground and air units fought jointly. However, the price was heavy. Three modern destroyers were sunk during the raids into Riga Bay: *Serdity* by air bombing, *Smely* by torpedoes from German MTB *S 54* and *Statny* by a mine. Out of 33 bombers participating in the raids on Berlin, as many as 17 were lost.[10]

The evacuation of Tallinn

The reason why the Baltic Fleet's offensive operations in Riga Bay were eventually halted was that the fleet's main base in Tallinn had come under attack. On 7 August, the German Eighteenth Army had reached the Gulf of Finland at Kunda, 50 miles east of Tallinn, splitting the Soviet forces in Estonia in two. To prevent the forces around Tallinn from evacuating, German and Finnish minelayers laid a barrage off Juminda with some 2,400 mines and explosive buoys. During the following weeks, while the Germans closed in on Tallinn from three directions, the Baltic Fleet began evacuating civilians and military materiel from the city. Transports had to be hidden not only from the enemy but also from the local NKVD representatives, who were suspicious of everything that looked like desertion. Altogether, 17,000 civilians, 9,000 wounded and some 15,000 tons of materiel (including arms, ammunition and equipment for ship repair) were shipped out. However, during the attempts to clear a route back to Kronstadt through the Juminda minefields 8–24 August, heavy losses were suffered. The destroyer *Karl Marx* and steamer *Sibir* were sunk by aerial bombing, the destroyer *Engels*, minesweepers *T-202/Buy*, *T-209/Knekht*, *T-213/Krambol* and *T-214/Bugel* by mines. Steamer *S/S Vyacheslav Molotov* – with 3,500 passengers aboard – also hit a mine but kept floating.[11]

The worst was yet to come – the *Tallinnsky perekhod* (the Tallinn Crossing), also known as 'Russia's Dunkirk'.

The decision to evacuate Tallinn was made on 26 August. On the afternoon the next day, a major counterattack was launched outside the city to push the German troops back. Covered by intensive fire from the warships and the coastal artillery batteries in the harbor, some 23,000 men of the Eighth Army's Xth Corps, the Baltic Naval Infantry Brigade and the Baltic Fleet headquarters then embarked aboard 128 warships and 67 cargo ships. Members of the government and party leadership of Soviet Estonia also went aboard. Divided into four separate echelons, this force set sail for Kronstadt. Due to rough weather, the first ships could not leave until the afternoon on the 28th. This delay meant that the Juminda minefields had to be passed during darkness. The result was disastrous, and enemy *Stuka* bombers, coastal batteries and MTBs inflicted additional losses. Out of 29 large cargo ships, one made it to Kronstadt, three ran aground in Hogland and 25 were sunk. Out of 38 minor cargo ships, 9 were sunk. The Baltic Fleet lost five old destroyers (*Skory, Jakov Sverdlov, Kalinin, Artem, Volodarsky*), two patrol ships (*Sneg, Tsiklon*), one patrol craft (*Saturn*), two submarines (*S-5* and *Sch-301*) and some minor vessels. Leader destroyer *Minsk* was severely damaged. Estimates of the number of people killed and drowned vary from 5,000 to 14,000.[12]

In Soviet historiography, the *tallinnsky perekhod* has usually been described as a victorious 'breakthrough', a daring action without parallel in naval history. The Baltic Fleet was saved from capture, and the ship artillery and the 18,000 soldiers who were transported out of Talllinn could reinforce the garrison of Leningrad. Only during the 1990s did this heroic image began to give way to a more critical appraisal, which portrayed events off Juminda as a senseless massacre that could have been avoided. The decision to evacuate Tallinn could have been made earlier. Fleet commander Vice-Admiral Tributs – who personally led the operation aboard the cruiser *Kirov* – could have chosen a less dangerous route closer to the coast. The air cover could have been stronger.[13]

Clearly, there were also other, structural causes for the disaster. The shortage of minesweepers in the Baltic Fleet has already been mentioned. By the end of August, Tributs had lost about a third of the minesweepers which had been under his command on 22 June (apart from losses already mentioned *T-298/Imanta, T-216, T-201/Zaryad, T-212/Shtag* and *T-51/Pirmunas*; the first four ships were destroyed by mines, while the *T-51* was sunk by German MTB *S 54*). Eight of the lost minesweepers belonged to the modern *Fugas* class, of which there were now only ten ships left.[14]

Moreover, as we have learnt in the preceding chapters, the Baltic Fleet staff had serious deficiencies in training. Out of 72 officers serving there in 1941, only six held a degree from the Naval War College.[15] To improvise an operation of this scale at such short notice would have been beyond the capacity of most naval staffs. In this light, the evacuation of Tallinn may perhaps still be considered a remarkable achievement.

Under siege

After their escape, the ships of the Baltic Fleet were deployed in the inner part of the Gulf of Finland, where they gave valuable fire support to the defenders of Leningrad. The main force was anchored in the waters between Oranienbaum and Kronstadt, and consisted of battleships *Marat* and *Oktyabrskaya Revolutsiya*, cruiser *Kirov*, destroyer leaders *Minsk* and *Leningrad*, five destroyers (*Surovy, Smetlivy, Silny, Steregushchy, Gordy*) and six gunboats (*Amgun, Volga, Kama, Moskva, Selemdzha, Krasnoe Znamya*). Minor vessels (destroyers *Grozhyashchy, Slavny*, the unfinished destroyers *Strogy, Stroyny* and *Opytny* and the gunboats *Sestroretsk*, *Oka* and *Zeya*) were anchored on the river Neva, firing in support of Leningrad's southwestern defenses. Cruisers *Maxim Gorky* and *Petropavlovsk* (unfinished, ex-German *Lützow*) and three destroyers (*Storozhevoy*, *Strastny*, *Stoyky*) were deployed in the city's port as a mobile reserve. Coastal batteries included, the fleet contributed some 345 artillery pieces to Leningrad's defense, firing more than 70,000 shells between 30 August and 31 December 1941.[16]

Supporting the ground forces was not a new mission to the Baltic Fleet, and backing up the static front around Leningrad was clearly a less complicated job than the mission envisaged before the war – assisting Soviet mechanized forces when they advanced in high speed deep into enemy territory. However, big ships at anchors were also very vulnerable. When German artillery deployed on the southern shore of the gulf and started firing back against Kronstadt, the *Oktyabrskaya Revolutsiya*, the *Kirov* and four of the destroyers had to be drawn back to Leningrad in the beginning of October. In Leningrad's port, the unfinished cruiser *Petropavlovsk* was sunk by German artillery on the 18 September (she was later salvaged, renamed *Tallinn* and used as accommodation hulk). In early November, submarine *L-1* suffered the same fate.[17]

According to Kuznetsov, in mid-September Stalin stated the fleet must be scuttled should the enemy conquer Leningrad.[18] Other solutions were also contemplated. On 15 September, German intelligence picked up a telegram from Tributs to his colleague in the Black Sea, Vice-Admiral Oktyabrsky, describing the Baltic Fleet's situation as desperate and internment in neutral Sweden as a better alternative than capture. Fearing that the Baltic Fleet would break out, Hitler on 20 September ordered the *Seekriegsleutung* to prevent an escape to Sweden with all possible means. On 23–5 September 1941, battleship *Tirpitz*, cruisers *Admiral Scheer*, *Köln* and *Nürnberg*, three destroyers and 10 MTBs were deployed around the Åland Islands, while cruisers *Emden* and *Leipzig* and a couple of MTBs were stationed around Liepaya. This was the only time during World War II when German surface forces were concentrated in the Baltic.[19]

Within 48 hours, the German warships could return their bases. *Luftwaffe* had taken care of the matter. In a series of devastating raids from 19 to 30 September, planes from the VIIIth *Fliegerkorps* attacked the Baltic Fleet's major surface units around Kronstadt and Leningrad and crippled them for a considerable time. The *Marat* was hit by a 1,000-kilo bomb in her front and sunk in shallow waters. Although the old battleship would continue to serve as a floating battery (from 1943 under her original name *Petropavlovsk*), she would never go to sea again (when hearing the news, the head of the Swedish Naval Staff's section of operations, Commander Rutger Croneborg, noticed with envy in his diary: 'The Swedish torpedo officer's dream for decades past of sinking one of these ships has now been accomplished by German airmen.'). The other battleship, *Oktyabrskaya Revolutsiya* and the cruisers *Kirov* and *Maxim Gorky* all suffered varying degrees of damage, as did destroyers *Gordy*, *Grozhchyashchy*, and *Silny*. The leader destroyer, *Minsk*, the destroyer *Steregushchy*, the submarine *M-74*, patrol ship *Vikhr* 22 and the gunboat *Pioner* were all sunk, but could later be salvaged.[20]

After the fall of Tallinn, the only remaining positions of the Baltic Fleet outside the Gulf of Finland were the coastal artillery positions in Moonsund archipelago (Saarema, Hiiumaa, Worms and Muhu Islands) and Hanko, at the mouth of the Gulf. From 9 September to 22 October, German army and navy units conquered the Moonsund archipelago in a bitter struggle (during a deception maneuver in support of this operation, the Finnish coastal battleship *Ilmarinen* was sunk by a mine). After the fall of the Moonsund archipelago, with winter approaching, the Soviets evacuated Hanko. Between 26 October and 2 December, 22,803 men, a considerable amount of heavy equipment (26 tanks, 72 artillery pieces, 56 mortars) and 1,756 tons of provisions were brought out. The operation cost them heavily: three modern destroyers (*Smetlivy*, *Surovy* and *Gordy*), three minesweepers (*T-203/Patron*, *T-206/Verp* and *T-56/Klyuz*) and one patrol ship (*T-297/Virsailis*) were sunk by mines. Altogether, some 5,000 lives were lost, most of them during the last convoy when passenger ship *Iosif Stalin* with 5,500 troops aboard hit a mine.[21]

Balance sheet

With the evacuation of Hanko, the Baltic Fleet's operations during 1941 were over. Operations like this one probably constituted the fleet's most important contribution to the Soviet defensive effort during this catastrophic year. Apart from Tallinn and Hanko, naval units had evacuated the garrisons at Björkö (1–2 September: 27,000 soldiers, 188 artillery-pieces, 950 cars, 2,000 horses), Björkö Islands (1 November: 6,547 soldiers, 74 artillery-pieces, 110 horses) and Hogland with adjacent islands (29 October–6 November: 3,247 soldiers, 4 tanks, 49 artillery-pieces, 98 horses, 2,000 tons of provisions). In addition, the Ladoga Flotilla had evacuated troops and civilians from the western parts of the Lake Ladoga area (15–27 August and 17–20 September: 25,000 troops, 18,000 civilians, 9 tanks, 260 artillery-pieces and mortars, 536 cars, 4,647 horses, etc.).[22]

The fleet's losses had been horrendous: one out of two battleships, one out two destroyer leaders (later salvaged), 16 out of (originally) 19 destroyers (one later salvaged), four out of nine patrol ships (one later salvaged), 13 out of (originally) 33 minesweepers, one unfinished cruiser and a number of smaller vessels. In addition, 28 out of 70 submarines had been scuttled or sunk (apart from those already mentioned above, big submarines *P-1* and *L-2*, medium submarines *S-6*, *S-8*, *S-10*, *S-11*, *Sch-319*, *Shch-322*, *Shch-324* and ex-Estonian *Kalev*, small submarines *M-81*, *M-94*, *M-98*, *M-99* and *M-103*; submarines *M-94* and *M-99* had been torpedoed by German submarines and *S-10* disappeared from unknown causes; all the others had been sunk by mines).[23]

When it comes to human devastation, the Baltic Fleet had lost some 25,455 men during the period 22 June–30 September alone. Out of these, 10,662 were 'irretrievable' losses (dead or missing). In addition came the losses suffered during October–December in the battle for the Moonsund Islands and the evacuation of Hanko. All in all, the Soviet Navy suffered 81,589 casualties during 1941,

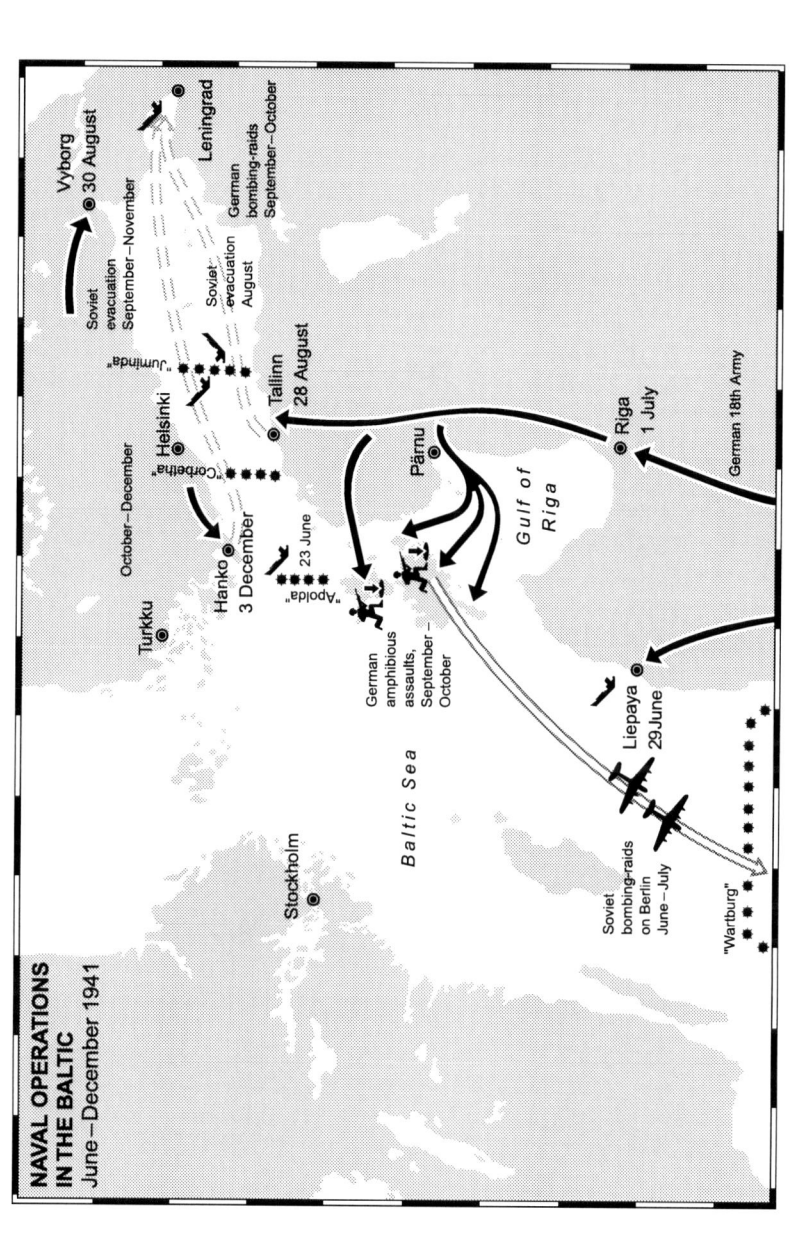

Map 6 Naval operations in the Baltic, 1941.

of which 59,803 were 'irretrievable'. Most of them were suffered during October–December, when four newly organized naval infantry brigades fought in the battle of Moscow, and other naval units participated in the liberation of Rostov and in the defense of Sevastopol.[24]

The 1941 campaign ended in a strategic fiasco, with the Baltic Fleet being bottled up in the Gulf of Finland for most of the remaining war. The Soviets had expanded into the Baltic States and fought their costly war against Finland to prevent exactly this from happening. However, they had not predicted German behavior correctly. For years, the Baltic Fleet had practiced defending Leningrad against a superior fleet of capital ships or prepared to fight off landing attempts on the shores of Kaporsky Bay and Luzhky Bay. But the German naval command was not interested in that kind of war. The *Seekriegsleutung* saw the British as their main enemy, the Atlantic and the Mediterranean as the main theaters of war. Their mission in the Baltic were limited to defending the German coast, protecting supply transports for Army Group North and preventing Soviet ships from escaping to Sweden. There were no resources for a large-scale assault against the coasts of Estonia and Latvia.[25] Consequently, there was no concentration of ships in German and Scandinavian ports before the attack. The expected warning did not come. Nor were there any fat targets for Soviet preemptive strikes.

During the campaign, the Germans committed naval forces that were inferior to the Baltic Fleet, but they coordinated them with their forces on land and in the air in a far superior way. They sunk Soviet warships with mines, torpedoes, aerial bombs and artillery fire from ashore. It was almost as if the *Kriegsmarine* had studied the doctrine of the Soviet Young School. Only during a few days in September, when the *Tirpitz* and her escorting cruisers gathered outside the Gulf of Finland, the old Soviet threat scenario seemed to become realistic, Leningrad being threaten by a mighty fleet of capital ships. Then, the Germans called in the *Luftwaffe* instead, and the war in the Baltic returned to twentieth-century reality. Only the Soviets used naval artillery to any extent during the campaign – to defend Leningrad – and were then taught how vulnerable big ships were from the air.

The inter-war period in perspective

After 1945, the naval schools from the inter-war period repeated themselves to some extent. There was a 'second Old School' from 1945 to the mid-1950s, a 'second Young School' from the mid-1950s to the mid-1960s and a 'second Soviet School' which reigned from the late 1960s until the demise of the Soviet Union. In the nuclear age, however, the implications of these doctrines were different than they had been during the 1920s and 1930s, not least for the Baltic Fleet.

The war left the Soviets determined not to be bottled up again in the Baltic, nor to allow hostile powers to dominate the region in the future. In the annexed city of Königsberg in East Prussia, later renamed Kaliningrad, they founded the new main base of the Baltic Fleet, outside the Gulf of Finland. In addition, Soviet influence in Poland, the GDR and Finland ensured that the immediate neighbors could no longer serve as bridgeheads for an invasion. In spite of an overwhelming military dominance in the region, however, Soviet feelings of weakness and inferiority remained. In the post-1945 era, strategic calculations had to be made in a global context. Superiority in one part of the world could easily be leveled in another.

Nor did the navy benefit particularly from Stalin's interest in 'big ships' after the war. In February 1946, the People's Commissariat for the Navy was again incorporated into the People's Commissariat for Armed Forces (which in March 1946 was renamed the Ministry for the Armed Forces, when all the Soviet governmental ministries dropped the name 'People's Commissariat'). The naval command also suffered new purges. Together with three other top-ranking admirals (Galler, Alafusov and Stepanov), Kuznetsov was charged with leaking secrets to the British and demoted to fleet commander in the Pacific. His alleged co-conspirators were all sentenced to ten years (Galler died in prison).[26] In 1951, Kuznetsov was brought back from the cold and reinstated as naval commander in the reestablished naval ministry. A rather ambitious construction program was launched with cruisers, destroyers, frigates, submarines and shore-based aviation.[27] Still, the 'Second Old School' did not claim an independent strategic role for the navy, like its predecessor had done in the 1920s. The impact of air power, nuclear weapons and rocket technology made such claims difficult to maintain. Kuznetsov failed to get aircraft carriers included in the shipbuilding programs, came into conflict with Defense Minister Marshal Zhukov and was finally discharged in December 1955, blamed for the loss of a battleship in the Black Sea.[28]

Kuznetsov's successor was Sergey S. Gorshkov (1910–88), who represented the 'Brezhnev generation' in the Soviet Navy. Like their 'fellow-Brezhnevites' in other sectors of society, these people were born a few years into the twentieth century, had no experience of the Civil War and but vague memories of the world before 1917. The purges and the rapid organizational expansion of the 1930s had moved them up in the world. They had little reason to feel anything but loyalty to a political system that had rewarded them so generously. They would continue to rule the Soviet empire until its incipient demise in the 1980s. Like his comrade from the class of 1931 at the Frunze Naval Academy – Igor Kasatonov (1910–89, deputy naval commander in the 1970s) – Gorshkov witnessed the Soviet Navy's evolution from a steam-driven, coastal defense force in the early 1930s to a nuclear-propelled, ocean-going fleet in the 1980s.[29]

First, however, the Soviet Navy had to go through its 'Second Young School' phase under Nikita Khrushchev. Only ten days after Stalin's death, the Ministry for the Navy was again incorporated into the newly created Ministry for Defense. In the following year, the construction of cruisers was halted. As Krushchev told the XXIst Party Congress in 1960, nuclear weapons would be the decisive weapon system in the future. Khrushchev also designated the newly established service of the Strategic Rocket Troops as the main branch of the armed forces, adding that the Soviet conventional forces, especially the navy, must be reduced in the future. In 1956, as the armed forces were restructured to meet the threat of a nuclear attack, the naval air force had to surrender its fighter squadrons to the newly created Air Defense Service.[30] In the late 1950s, the prospects of the Soviet Navy seemed gloomier than at any time since the time after the Civil War, when Lenin and Trotsky had questioned its continued existence.

However, the introduction of intercontinental ballistic missiles in the 1960s also contained the seeds of a Second Coming of the Soviet School. If the Soviet Navy was to assist in the protection against nuclear attack, not only must it have the capacity to hunt and destroy NATO strategic submarines on the high seas, but also the capacity to deliver a second-strike. This required a strategic submarine fleet. Furthermore, the humiliating outcome of the Cuban missile crisis in 1962 demonstrated that sea power had a political role to play. Admiral Gorshkov argued the need for a 'balanced navy' able to protect socialism and Soviet economic interests around the globe.[31]

In the 1970s, for the first time in history Russia became the world's second sea power. Now, it could be argued, a 'mature version' of the Soviet School ruled the waves, albeit with large nuclear submarines instead of battleships. However, this development did not particularly benefit the Baltic Fleet, but the Northern and Pacific Fleets.[32] At the end of the Cold War, the Baltic's strategic value was entirely dependent on its function as a flanking area to the North Atlantic and central Europe. When the doctrinal developments of the inter-war period repeated themselves in the nuclear age, this confined inland water was of little significance.

The 1920s and 1930s was the real age of greatness for the Soviet Baltic Fleet. Still, as we have seen, those years had their share of trouble and anxiety.

Notes

1 Carl von Clausewitz, *On War* (Princeton, NJ: Princeton University Press, 1984 [1976]), p. 89.
2 Barsukov and Zolotarev (eds), *Russky arkhiv*, vol. I.2, p. 37.
3 Berezovsky *et al.*, *Boevaya letopis*, pp. 671–4; Kuznetsov, *Nakanune*, pp. 320–2.
4 P. O. Ekman, *Sjöfront: Sjökrigshändelser i Norra Östersjöområdet 1941–1944* (Helsinki: Schildts, 1981), pp. 27–48; *idem*, 'Sjöstridskrafterna', vol. II, pp. 100–7; by the end of 1941, the Germans had lost at least ten cargo ships and two minesweepers in the *Wartburg* minefields. In addition, three minelayers had been sunk in the Swedish minefield off Öland – see Meister, *Der Seekrieg*, p. 11.
5 Rohwer and Monakov, *Stalin's Ocean-going Fleet*, pp. 136–7; Ekman, *Sjöfront*, p. 15; Stupnikov (ed.) *Dvazhdy*, p.172; Krivosheyev (ed.), *Grif sekretnosti snyat*, p. 162. The Soviet-made ships in the Baltic Fleet had the following specification: **Battleships** (*Gangut* class battleships *Marat* and *Oktyabrskaya Revolutsiya*, commissioned in 1914 but modernized in 1931–33): *normal displacement*: 25,000 tons; *length*: 185 m; *speed*: 23 knots; *crew*: 1,300–400; *armament* (mm): $4 \times \text{III-305}$, 16×120, 6×76, 4×450 (torpedoes), 1 aircraft. **Cruisers** (*Kirov* commissioned 1938, *Maxim Gorky* 1940): *normal displacement*: 7,880–8,177 tons; *length*: 191 m; *speed*: 36 knots; *crew*: 734; *armament* (mm): 3×180; $6 \times 1\text{-}100$; 9×45, $2 \times \text{III-533}$ torpedoes, 2 aircraft. **Minelayer** (*Marti*, converted 1933–36 from the former imperial yacht *Shtandart*, commissioned in 1899): *normal displacement*: 5,565 tons; *length*: 122 m; *speed* 14–19 knots; *crew*: 390; *armament* (mm); 4×130, 7×76, 3×45, 3×12.7, 780 mines.

Destroyer leaders (*Leningrad* commissioned 1936, *Minsk* 1938): *normal displacement*: 2,050–280 tons; *length*: 128 m; *speed*: 40–3 knots; *crew*: 250; *armament* (mm): 5 × I-130, 2–3 × I-76, 2 × I-45 (*Leningrad*) and 6 × II-37 (*Minsk*), 2 × III torpedoes, 76 mines. **Destroyers project 7** (*Gnevny, Grozyashchy, Gordy, Steregushchy* and *Smetlivy* commissioned 1938–39): *normal displacement*: 1,855 tons; *length*: 113 m; *speed*: 37 knots; *crew*: 246: *armament* (mm): 4 × I-130, 2 × I-76, 2 × I-45, 2 × III-533 torpedoes, 56 mines. **Destroyers project 7-U** (*Storozhevoy, Serdity, Stoyky, Silny, Surovy, Slavny* and *Smely* commissioned 1940–41; *Strashny, Skory, Statny, Svirepy, Stroyny* and *Strogy* commissioned 22 June–22 September 1941): *normal displacement*: 1,834 tons; *length*: 113 m; *speed*: 38 knots; *crew*: 200; *armament* (mm): 4 × I-130, 2 × I-76, 3 × I-45, 2 × III-533 torpedoes. **Patrol ships projects 2 and 39** (*Tayfun, Tsiklon, Vikhr, Purga, Vyuga, Burya* commissioned 1931–38, *Sneg* and *Tucha* of project 39 1938): *normal displacement*: 580–90 tons; *length*: 71 m; *speed*: 24 knots; *crew*: 72; *armament* (mm): 2 × 120, 2 × 45, 1 × 450 torpedoes, 24 mines. **Minesweepers project 3** (*T-201/Zaryad, T-202/Buy , T-203/ Patron* and *T-204/Fugas* commissioned 1936–38): *normal displacement*: 428 tons; *length* 62 m; *speed*: 18 knots; *crew*: 52; *armament* (mm) 1 × 100, 1 × 45, 30 mines. **Minesweepers project 53U** (*T-205/Gafel, T-206/Verp, T-207/ Shpil, T-208/Shkiv, T-209/Knekht, T-210/Gak, T-211/Rym, T-212/Shtag, T-213/Krambol, T-214/Bugel, T-215, T-216* and *T-218* commissioned 1939–40, *T-217/Kontradmiral Yurkovsky* commissioned in August 1941): *normal displacement*: 417 tons; *length*: 62 m; *speed*: 14 knots; *crew*: 69; *armament*: 1 × 100, 1 × 45, 10–20 mines. **Big submarines series I** (*D-2/Narodvolets* commissioned in 1931): *displacement*: 934 tons; *length*: 78 m; *range*: 8,950 nautical miles; *speed*: 14 knots; *crew*: 53–5; *armament* (mm): 8 + 533 torpedoes (14 torpedoes), 8 mines, 1 × 100, 1 × 45, 1 × 7.62. **Big submarines series II** (*L-1/Leninets, L-2/Stalinets* and *L-3/Frunsovets* commissioned in 1933): *total displacement*: 1,025 tons; *length*: 81 m; *range*: 7,400 nautical miles; *speed*: 14 knots; *crew*: 52; *armament* (mm): 6 + 533 torpedoes (12 torpedoes), 14–20 mines, 1 × 100, 1 × 7.62, 1 × 45. **Big submarine series IV** (*P-1/Pravda, P-2/Zvezda* and *P-3/Iskra* commissioned in 1936): *normal displacement*: 931 tons; *length*: 90 m; *range*: 5,753 nautical miles; *speed*: 20 knots; *crew*: 56; *armament*: 4 + 2-533 torpedoes (10 torpedoes), 2 × 100, 1 × 45. **Big submarines series XIV** (*K-3, K-21, K-22, K-23* commissioned in 1940): *normal displacement*: 1,500 tons; *length*: 98 m; *range*: 16,500 nautical miles; *speed*: 23 knots; *crew*: 65; *armament* (mm): 4+2-533 torpedoes (10 torpedoes), 2 × 100, 1 × 45. **Medium submarines series III** (*Shch-301/Shchuka, Shch-302/Okun, Shch-303/Ershch* and *Shch-304/Komsomolets* commissioned in 1933–34): *normal displacement*: 572 tons; *length*: 57 m; *range*: 3,130 nautical miles; *speed*: 12 knots; *crew*: 40; *armament* (mm): 4+2-533 torpedoes (10 torpedoes), 1 × 45. **Medium submarines series Vb and Vb2** (*Shch-305/Voistvyushchy, Bezbozhnik* and *Shch-308/Semga* commissioned in 1934–35, *Shch-306/Piksha, Shch-307/Treshka, Shch-309/Delfin, Shch-310/Belukha* and *Shch-311/Kumzha* of project Vb2 in 1935–36): *normal displacement*: 592–3 tons; *length*: 59 m; *range*: 3,130 nautical miles; *speed*: 14 knots; *crew*: 40; *armament* (mm): 4+2–533 torpedoes (10 torpedoes), 2 × 45. **Medium submarines series IX and IXb** (*S-1* and *S-3* commissioned in 1936, *S-4, S-5, S-6, S-7, S-8, S-9, S-10, S-11, S-101* and *S-102* of series IXb in 1939–41): *normal displacement*: 828–37 tons; *length*: 78 m; *range*: 9,860 nautical miles; *speed*: 20 knots; *crew*: 45; *armament* (mm): 4 × 2–533 torpedoes (12 torpedoes), 1 × 100, 1 × 45. **Medium submarines series X and Xb** (*Shch-317, Shch-318, Shch-319, Shch-320, Shch-322, Shch-323* and *Shch-324* commissioned in 1936, *Shch-405* and *Shch-406* commissioned in 1941, *Shch-407* and *Shch-408* in October 1941): *normal displacement*: 828–37 tons; *length*: 78 m; *range*: ?; *speed*: 20 knots; *crew*: 45; *armament* (mm): 4+2-533 torpedoes (12 torpedoes), 1 × 100, 1 × 45. **Small submarines series VI-b** (*M-71, M-72, M-73, M-74, M-75, M-76, M-77, M-78, M-79, M-80, M-81, M-82* and *M-83* commissioned in 1935–36): *normal* *displacement*: 161 tons; *length*: 38 m; *range*: 1,065 nautical miles; *speed*: 13 knots; *crew*: 19; *armament* (mm): 2+0-533 torpedoes (2 torpedoes), 1×45. **Small submarines series XII** (*M-90, M-94, M-95, M-96, M-97, M-98, M-99, M-102* and *M-103* commissioned in 1939–40): *normal displacement*: 206 tons; *length*: 45 m; *range*: 3,330 nautical miles; *speed*: 14 knots; *crew*: 20; *armament* (mm): 2+0-533 torpedoes (2 torpedoes), 1×45. Rowher and Monakov, *Stalin's Ocean-going Fleet*, pp. 91–4, 99–101, 136, 232–53.

6 Ekman, *Sjöfront*, p. 36; idem, 'Sjöstridskrafterna', vol. II, p. 108; Vasilyev, 'Pervy boevoy pokhod', p. 50; Kuznetsov, *Nakanune*, pp. 337–8.

7 Ekman, *Sjöfront*, p. 40; Vasilyev: 'Pervy boevoy pokhod', pp. 52–9.

8 Kuznetsov, *Krutye povoroty*, p. 96; Dotsenko, *Flot*, pp. 64–5; Stupnikov (ed.), *Dvazhdy*, pp. 173–4; Rohwer and Monakov, *Stalin's Ocean-going* Fleet, p. 262; Achkasov et al., *Boevoy put*, pp. 413–15.

9 Ekman, *Sjöfront*, pp. 63–4; idem, 'Sjöstridskrafterna', vol. II, p. 115; Rohwer and Monakov, *Stalin's Ocean-going Fleet*, pp. 263–4.

10 Ekman, *Sjöfront*, p. 64; Achkasov et al., *Boevoy put*, p. 242; Michael Salewski, *Die Deutsche Seekriegsleitung 1935–1945*, vol. I, *1935–1941* (Frankfurt: Bernhard & Graefe Verlag für Wehrwesen, 1970), p. 420; Horst Boog et al., *Das Deutsche Reich und der Zweite Weltkrieg*, vol. IV, *Der Angriff auf die Sowjetunion* (Stuttgart: Deutsche Verlags-Anstalt, 1983), pp. 549, 561; Rohwer and Monakov, *Stalin's Ocean-going Fleet*, p. 262.

11 Dotsenko, *Flot*, p. 70; Ekman, *Sjöfront*, pp. 67–8; Rohwer & Monakov, *Stalin's Ocean-going Fleet*, pp. 262, 264.

12 Ekman, *Sjöfront*, pp. 70–9; Achkasov et al., *Boevoy put*, pp. 244–9; Dotsenko, *Flot*, pp. 66–8; Stupnikov (ed.), *Dvazhdy*, pp.176–80.

13 The traditional Soviet view: Achkasov et al., *Boevoy put*, p. 249; Stupnikov (ed.), *Dvazhdy*, pp. 179–80; critical views in Dotsenko, *Flot*, pp. 68–71.

14 Rohwer and Monakov, *Stalin's Ocean-going Navy*, pp. 136, 264.

15 Dotsenko, *Flot*, p. 70.

16 Ekman, *Sjöfront*, p. 97; Dotsenko, *Flot*, pp. 77–9; Achkasov et al., *Boevoy put*, pp. 257–62.

17 Dotsenko, *Flot*, pp. 78–9; Ekman, *Sjöfront*, p. 98; Rohwer and Monakov, *Stalin's Ocean-going Navy*, pp. 262–3.

18 Kuznetsov, *Nakanune*, p. 342.

19 Boog et al., *Das Deutsche Reich*, p. 564; Salewski, *Die Deutsche Seekriegsleutung*, p. 423.

20 Boog et al., *Das Deutsche Reich*, p. 686; Ekman, *Sjöfront*, pp.102–3; Dotsenko, *Flot*, p. 78; Rohwer and Monakov, *Stalin's Ocean-going Fleet*, pp. 262–4; Croneborg quoted in Alf W. Johansson, 'Transiteringar, eskorteringar och det svenska territorialvattnet: Marina frågor I de svensk–tyska relationerna 1941–1942', in Stig Ekman (ed.), *Småstatspolitik och stormaktstryck: Aspekter på svensk politik under andra världskriget* (Stockholm: Liber 1986), p. 138.

21 Ekman, *Sjöfront*, pp. 106–23.

22 Dotsenko, *Flot*, pp. 75, 242.

23 Rohwer and Monakov, *Stalin's Ocean-going Fleet*, pp. 262–4.

24 Krivosheyev, *Grif sekretnosti snyat*, pp. 162, 168; Achkasov et al., *Boevoy put*, pp. 323–36, 418–26.

25 Salewski, *Die Deutsche Seekriegsleitung*, pp. 366–8, 373; Boog et al., *Das Deutsche Reich*, pp. 319–26.

26 Vladimir Shlomin and Vadim Messoylidi, 'Ataka na flot', *Leningradskaya Panorama*, no. 6 (1990).

27 Ranft and Till, *Sea in Soviet Strategy*, pp. 90–1; Herrick, *Soviet Naval Strategy*, chapter 6; Rohwer and Monakov, *Stalin's Ocean-going Fleet*, pp. 178–217.

28 Rohwer and Monakov, *Stalin's Ocean-going Fleet*, pp. 216–17.
29 Gorshkov's memoirs appeared posthumously in 1996: *Vo flotskom stroyu* (St Petersburg: Logos, 1996).
30 Ranft and Till, *Sea in Soviet Strategy*, p. 114.
31 Gorshkov, *Sea Power of the State*; some of Gorshkov's articles in *Morskoy Sbornik* were published in Preston (ed.), *Red Star Rising at Sea*.
32 Skogan, 'Evolution of the Four Soviet Fleets'; Andolf and Johansson, 'The Baltic' pp. 232–44; Agrell, 'Strategisk förändring', p. 223.

APPENDIX
The Great Terror in the Baltic Fleet

The sources for studying the Great Terror in the Baltic Fleet are limited, as the records of the Baltic Fleet Revolutionary Tribunal—the special court organized in 1919 to fight counterrevolution—are missing for the years 1935–38. The archives of the Baltic Fleet PU and personnel sections contain information on those individuals who were discharged, but only occasionally let us know if they were also arrested and punished. Another way to study the effects of the repression is to look at the changes in the membership cadres of the Communist Party in the Baltic Fleet. Purges were a regular feature of party life, aimed at liberating the cadres from allegedly passive or morally degenerate members. As late as in 1935–36, party members and candidate members admitted after 1926 had had their membership cards attested in a massive campaign all over the country. Out of 8,652 people checked in the Baltic Fleet, some 453 had been expelled. Some 194 successfully appealed the decision, bringing the final number of expelled party members down to 259.[1]

Although the number of victims of this bloodless cleansing could be compared to that claimed by the *Yezhovshchina*, the consequences of expulsion in 1937–38 were far worse.

The scale of the purges

The first arrests in the Baltic Fleet had occurred in the early spring of 1937. In the beginning of April, the chief of the RKKA General Staff, Yegorov, rebuked fleet commander Sivkov for having allowed individuals to see the operational plan who had later been arrested by the NKVD. Among them were the fleet chief engineer Nikolay Alexandrovich Maximov. In the future, Yegorov wrote, every precaution must be taken so that only reliable people were trusted with sensitive documents. In difficult cases, Sivkov should consult the PUR.[2] A few days later, the NKVD made two more arrests in the Baltic Fleet. Before the end of May, there had been four more. In a country where the security police normally made several thousand arrests every month, there was probably little to say about this. In June, however, after Deputy People's Commissar for Defense Marshal Mikhail Tukhachevsky and seven other leading army officers had been arrested as members of a fascist-military plot against the Soviet government, numbers began to rise dramatically. Between 16 June and 23 July, no less than 61 men were relieved from duty in the Baltic Fleet. About half of those were arrested, bringing the total number of arrested people since 1 April up to 38.[3]

It is hard to discern a systematic plan behind this sudden wave of repression. Just as with the general purge in Soviet society, it wandered back and forth in an irregular pattern. By the end of July, the NKVD had arrested the head of section for ordinance and planning and the deputy chief mechanic from the fleet staff; the deputy commander of the battleship *Oktyabrskaya Revolutsiya* and the commander of the minesweeper *T-56/Klyuz* from the sailing fleet; from the air arm the commander himself, division commander Mikhail Alekseyevich Gorbunov, one wing and one squadron commander as well as the commandant of the 105th Junior Specialist Flying School; from the fleet's construction service apart from the chief engineer, Maximov, the commander, 1st Intendent Nikolay Nikolayevich Alexandrov and the head of the 109th Construction Battalion; from installations and units ashore the chief technician of the Oranienbaum naval base, the head of the medical service at the Fleet Machinist School, one of the teachers at the Electrical School, the chief engineer of the Izhorsk Fortress Area, the artillery commander in Kronstadt and his deputy, the commander of the special signals company etc. In addition to those arrested among regular navy personnel, 11 men had been arrested in the PUR: the chief political officer of the 1st Submarine Squadron, the chief political officer in the battleships squadron, the political officers aboard the two battleships, the chief political officer of the minesweeping squadron, the chief political officer of the construction troops in the Kronstadt area as well as three battalion political officers and two company political officers. Furthermore, 28 officers and men in the sailing fleet and the PUR, from the rank of captain 3rd rank/major downwards, had been proposed for discharge.[4]

By this time, the head of the construction service, Alexandrov, had confessed that he and the fleet chief engineer Maximov were members of a 'Trotskist military sabotage unit' that had received instructions from the recently disclosed enemy of the people, Gamarnik (head of the PUR RKKA), systematically to sabotage airstrips, hangars and barracks.[5]

After the head of the Baltic Fleet PUR, Alexander Sergeyevich Grishin, had taken his life,[6] attention soon turned toward the fleet commander, Alexander Kusmich Sivkov, a former nobleman and imperial officer who had survived remarkably well under the Soviet regime. In July, however, his wife was suddenly arrested for having concealed that her father had been a colonel in the tsarist army. On 1 August, Sivkov himself was arrested as a member of an alleged 'anti-big-ship conspiracy' among the students of the class of 1927 at the Naval War College. He was convicted and executed on 22 February 1938. His brother, who was a doctor at a naval school, was also arrested and shot.[7]

According to a report by the fleet commissar, Bulyshkin, between 26 August and 1 November 1937 an additional 31 men were discharged from the regular fleet. Of these, no less than 15 were arrested. During November and early December, the NVKD also arrested the commander of the battleship squadron, the commander of the destroyer flotilla, one of the submarine squadron commanders, the deputy head of anti-air defenses and the commander of the Main Base Defense Force.[8] Altogether during 1937, 187 officers were discharged from the Baltic Fleet. Out of these, no less than 120 were arrested. In August 1938, when Bulyshkin had been relieved from his post too, an additional 291 had been discharged, of whom 112 had been arrested. Another 35 were proposed for discharge.[9]

How did the purges affect the membership structure of the fleet party organization? During 1938, a total of 160 party, candidate and Komsomol members were expelled. Out of these, five were women. Most of those expelled were officers (42), civilian construction personnel (27), engineers-technicians (24) and PUR instructors (20). Junior commanders (ten) and NCOs (ten) were rather few. The most common reason for expulsion was 'espionage' (39), being an 'enemy of the people' (32), 'maintaining relations with enemies of the people' (32), or displaying 'general moral decadence' (21). Political deviations such as 'infringements of party and state discipline' (10) 'Trotskyism' (8) or 'rightist deviation' (3) came far down on the list.

Who were the surviving party members? Only five of the 5,635 full members in 1938 had joined before 1917, 2,157 between 1917 and 1929, 2,687 in 1930–32 – and only 12 (!) in the years 1933–36. The reason for this steep fall was most likely the reduced recruitment after 1933 together with the lowered age for conscription in 1934, which meant that most recruits were under 21 when they entered the ranks of the RKKA. In 1937, recruitment started to increase again with 185 new members and as many as 589 in 1938. Although about half the cadre still consisted of people who had joined during of the first five-year plan, so had about half of those who were expelled in 1938. Moreover, the balance would tip further in the next few years. No less than 78 percent of the 3,887 candidate members had been recruited during the course of 1938![10] The ranks of the Baltic Fleet party organization had been refilled with loyal 'Stalinist disciples'.

Getting rid of unwanted people

When individual cases are examined more closely, it does seem as if the Baltic Fleet used the purges to get rid of unwanted people, and that many who were deprived of their party card lost it so that they could be fired more easily.

In June 1937, the battleship squadron requested the discharge of several officers aboard the *Oktyabrskaya Revolutsiya* who had been recently expelled from the party. The head of the electromechanical section had concealed that his father had been a major landowner (with dozens of horses and cattle and four employees) who had committed suicide during 'the dekulakization campaign' in 1930. Furthermore, he also entertained contacts with Trotskyist elements in the crew. The head of supplies had sent money to his ex-wife, who in turn maintained relations with her brother, a suspect spy whom the NKVD had deported from Leningrad. One of the battery commanders had concealed that his father had owned a bakery with many workers. In passing, it was stated about all three men that they were indifferent to their work,[11] but this accusation may well have been just as discriminatory.

In July 1937, Ship Engineer Tambyar was denounced as a wrecker and reactionary by one of technicians aboard the ship where he served. The technician had found Tambyar's diary, which revealed that he was responsible for some recent machine wreckage and harbored a decadent moral attitude. Tambyar thought about suicide and held 'the mass of Red Navy men' in secret contempt, thinking they deserved to be 'flogged with leather strips the way you flog Chinese'. Also in Tambyar's case, it was noticed that for some time he had shown indifference to his duties.[12]

The conductor of the Kronstadt fortress band, Peter Matveich Bucharsky, drank and gambled and had beaten up a tram conductor in Leningrad. According to the NKVD – one of Bucharsky's former employers – he had concealed a heavy criminal record when he entered the ranks of the Baltic Fleet in 1934. Since he was kicked out of the party in 1923 for having criticized NEP, Bucharsky had shown a marked lack of interest in politics. Nonetheless, he at times had demonstrated 'compassion with enemies of the people' and lamented some of the recent executions. According to the commandant of Kronstadt, the fortress band had to get rid of Bucharsky to 'recover morally'. Similar problems plagued the 1st Submarine Squadron's band, whose musical leader spent most of his time either drunk or in the guardhouse for disorderly behavior. He was also discharged during the summer of 1937.[13]

By cleansing its ranks of unwanted co-workers, the navy was able to raise the level of professionalization. 'Purged from abominable spies and traitors, the Soviet Navy steadily improves the level of combat training', *Morskoy Sbornik* announced in November 1938.[14] After all, it could be argued that only those in the Baltic Fleet who lived up to a certain level of military competence, who mastered the art of modern war, the technology and the bureaucratic routine that came with it, could be defined as really good communists.

The relationship between notions of moral soundness and professional competence is especially apparent from the case of 59-year-old Isidor Arkhipovich Abramenkov, head of one of the intelligence section's radio-reconnaissance units. When the commander of the Baltic Fleet Levchenko wrote to the People's Commissariat for the Navy in July 1938 and asked that Abramenkov should be discharged, the primary arguments dealt with his alleged political unreliability, his relatives in Estonia and the fact that he had recently been expelled from the party. However, when a few days before Abramenkov's superior, Filippovsky, had requested his discharge, it was the man's shortcomings as intelligence operative that had come to the fore. Abramenkov's political offenses were only mentioned in passing. Modern radio intelligence required 'energetic, operationally well prepared and well educated leadership', according to Filippovsky. Abramenkov had served on his post since 1927 and received decorations in the past but was no longer up to the mark. He lacked the ability to concentrate and tended to bury himself in details. In addition, he was rude and tactless to subordinates, which indicated a 'low level of political education'.[15]

Clearly, all those who were eliminated from the ranks of the Baltic Fleet in 1937–38 were not as expendable as Abramenkov may have been. Already in early July 1937, the Baltic Fleet chief of staff, Isakov, complained that since his head of ordinance and planning Manturov had been arrested, all work in the fleet staff connected to the third five-year plan was virtually paralyzed.[16] Later, the head of the staff training section, Evgeny Konstantinovich Prestin (a former imperial officer), was also arrested, convicted and shot.[17]

After the *Yezhovshchina*, less-educated and able personnel continued to dominate among those who were purged from the navy. Out of the 487 people discharged during 1940 (a figure which did not include 147 people sacked from the naval air force), less than 10 percent (45) had a complete naval academy degree. As many as 63 percent (305) were promoted NCOs or had no formal military education. The most common motivation for discharge was drinking (180 cases or 37 percent). As many as 99 (20 percent) were simply considered incompetent for the position they held. Only 53 (11 percent) were discharged because a military tribunal had sentenced them.[18]

The Great Terror: the case of the intelligence section

On 29 November 1937, the NKVD arrested Nikolay Timofeyev, head of the Baltic Fleet intelligence section. Thanks to the preserved minutes from a closed meeting with the intelligence section's primary party organization (or party cell, as these organizational bodies were called until 1934), held about a week later on 4 December, we can gain a glimpse of the circumstances surrounding Timofeyev's fall.[19]

The document is fragile, the text faded and some words more or less illegible. Many of the allusions that are made to people, places and events can only vaguely be understood or not at all. Still, the testimonies from Timofeyev's former subordinates are worth quoting at some length as they bring to life the eery atmosphere of the Great Terror and help us understand the mechanisms at the local level behind these tragic events.

Timofeyev was not the first to be arrested in the section. On 28 October 1937, Junior Lieutenant Georgy Georgevich Chuchkag had been taken.[20] It may have been this arrest that triggered a massive purge of the intelligence section's party cell in the autumn of 1937. Among those expelled was the organization's secretary. Apparently, Timofeyev had been unwilling to condemn those expelled or remove them from their posts. He may have tried to help some of them materially, or gone to Moscow to plead their case. During the meeting on 4 December, several speakers referred to Timofeyev's generosity toward certain shady individuals and to a suspect trip he had made to Moscow shortly before his arrest.

When the meeting of the party cell opened, the chairman, Lieutenant N. S. Frumkin, proposed that negotiations should be postponed to the next day so that the matter could be treated in a broader context, taking into account the full consequences of Timofeyev's crimes and how one could best assist the security organs and the party in liquidating them. That motion, however, was not seconded.

Then followed a short report on Timofeyev's arrest by the deputy head of the section, Filippovsky, now acting commander. Afterwards, each member was expected to give an account of his relations with Timofeyev. Obviously, the purpose of this exercise was to demonstrate continued loyalty to the party and vigilance against its enemies, but also a readiness for self-criticism. Although it was important to distance oneself from the fallen comrade, this must not be taken for an attempt to reduce one's own share of the collective responsibility. To appear too anxious to clear oneself would seem like an effort to escape closer examination. At an earlier meeting after Timofeyev's arrest, one of the co-workers, Berendt, had stated that from now on one must look for enemies of the people in each and every individual. Some speakers now criticized that statement as irresponsible and dangerous.

G. I. Lebedev, who had become deputy head of the section after Timofeyev's arrest, started by pointing out that Timofeyev had been a double-dealer. After Junior Lieutenant Chuckhag's arrest by the NKVD, Timofeyev had still characterized him as a good comrade. Timofeyev had known Chuchkag since childhood, had served together with him and had probably embezzled the intelligence section's funds to help him financially. Lebedev reminded his comrades how at a recent party meeting he had urged them to look for hidden wreckers, although he had never dreamt that corruption in the section had reached this scale. He concluded by pointing out that he himself was not responsible for recruiting Timofeyev, nor was he an enemy of the people.

Pavlov, who worked in radio intelligence, stated that the low quality of the section's work at present was next to criminal. Timofeyev had sent one of the Baltic Fleet's expensive American radio receivers off to the Far East and taken another foreign receiver with him to his home. In his dacha, he had suspect friends living at the state's expense, and his renovation of the section's garage had been allowed to drag on the entire summer.

Another radio-intelligence analyst, D. L. Shteynbakh, complained that Timofeyev had been unwilling to assist him in his work. He had only corrected the grammar in his reports and snubbed him for writing 'like a Jew'. They should speak less of Timofeyev, Shteynbakh thought, and more of the many shortcomings in the section's work and clear out everything that was unsound. Shteynbakh, who had installed a radio receiver in Timofeyev's apartment on his orders, was one of those who disagreed with comrade Berendt's statement that enemies must be looked for in each and every individual. In fact, there had been many signs of Timofeyev's individual guilt, but the collective had not reacted in time.

The chairman, Junior Lieutenant Frumkin, disagreed with Shteynbakh. It was important to speak of Timofeyev and his wrecking activities, as they still plagued the section. Timofeyev had told his personnel not to trust the NKVD and had probably planted hostile elements among them. Wherever work did not go well, the enemy must be identified and rooted out. Regrettably, there were numerous comrades who were unable to see facts or individuals as they were, or to lift the discussion to the level of principle where the necessary conclusions could be drawn. Everything and everyone connected to Timofeyev must now be checked, and any new officers who were appointed must be free of foreign acquaintances. Frumkin found it necessary to point out that there had been no slanderous talk against the party at a certain meeting at which he had been present.

Charkevich, who served aboard the reconnaissance boats in the Gulf of Finland, reported that only three such patrols had taken place during the autumn and the plans for winter had had to be changed because of Timofeyev. He had in reality never concerned himself much with this part of the section's work.

Then, Timofeyev's deputy and successor Filippovsky took the floor. Their commander, he told the meeting, had spent most of his working day in Kronstadt with idle talk, putting his signature on papers while totally neglecting organized work or his real duties. He had sabotaged the training courses for military interpreters by calling them off for no reason. He had allowed the reconnaissance boats to be employed in an incorrect way. He had been ambiguous toward the expulsion of certain party members and prevented their removal from sensitive posts. Rumor had it that he had been protected by the head of the Baltic Fleet PUR, Alexander Grishin, an exposed enemy of the people, who had used Timofeyev's apartment to hide secret documents. Like many speakers before him, Filippovsky concluded by pointing out that he had not recruited Timofeyev, nor had Timofeyev recruited him.

Yeremeyev, who was the section's political officer, emphasized that Timofeyev had had an improper attitude to party work. The head of personnel, Andreyev, had similar tendencies, and the relations between him and Timofeyev must now be thoroughly investigated. Timofeyev had created an unsound environment in the workplace and forced Yeremeyev out of his office. Furthermore, he had refrained from reporting to the NKVD when Yeremeyev told him of an anti-Soviet person who lived in Yeremeyev's mother's apartment. Yeremeyev also pointed out that he himself had no personal relations with Timofeyev and reminded the meeting of the anti-party conduct of comrade Shatalov, who had known of Timofeyev's undermining work but done nothing.

Prokazov began by admitting his guilt. As an old worker and former commissar he had relied too much on Timofeyev and been blind to his many faults and felonies. Timofeyev had allowed enemies of the people to serve on important posts. Now, the intelligence section was probably ridden with spies: 'Timofeyev has planted his deputy here in the section, of this we can be certain.' Prokazov had an idea who the secret wrecker could be: Yakovlev, the head of operational intelligence work, had had good relations with Timofeyev and had even been prepared to vouch for his honesty.

V. P. Sychev, newly appointed as party secretary in the cell, had attended an evening conference in Timofeyev's home in 1936. He went home immediately afterwards, disappointed with the collective. Timofeyev had been able to impress them with empty talk. When Sychev really needed instructions, however, Timofeyev was unable to give any and had only talked about the need to act independently. According to Sychev, this could hardly be regarded as leadership. The way in which Timofeyev protected expelled party members, the fact that he brought

Andreyev to the section against the will of Moscow, all this made it important to examine everything related to Timofeyev and to find out who his covert successor was. For a long time, Sychev had suspected Yakovlev but had no evidence. Sychev concluded by saying that he himself was nothing but an honest communist. He had not recruited Timofeyev, nor had Timofeyev recruited him.

Berendt, who at an earlier meeting had talked of the need to search for enemies everywhere, now apologized for this statement. An apologetic intervention by a previous speaker had led him astray. All he had meant to say was that the enemy should be sought out wherever there were signs of inefficient work. Timofeyev was not responsible for everything. Andreyev had been in charge of personnel in the section and had severely neglected recruitment, supplementary training courses and the relations between co-workers. Only after his trip to Moscow had Timofeyev stopped protecting Andreyev. Like many others before him, Berendt found it necessary to point out that he had not recruited Timofeyev.

B. S. Antoshchenko pointed out that it was a waste of governmental funds – equal to wrecking – to keep a person working on the section when he was completely useless. Timofeyev had known this all along but done nothing about certain co-workers. He had not been interested in the 'little people', nor had he tried to 'lead' them. His relationship to Andreyev must be investigated further. Timofeyev had also staged lavish parties, according to Antoshchenko. If he had not embezzled state funds, where did the money come from? Antoshchenko also wanted to stress that he had had no personal relationship to Timofeyev.

The next speaker was Shatalov, who earlier in the year had been spared from punishment by Timofeyev because of his alleged 'inexperience'. In the present discussion he had been accused of anti-party behavior by the political officer, Yeremeyev. Shatalov began by pointing out that he had been selected to work in the intelligence section not by Timofeyev but by Filippovsky. He had hardly had any contact with Timofeyev, whose weak style of leadership had undermined discipline. Following orders, Shatalov had many times together with other comrades done what were in reality private errands for Timofeyev and the former fleet commander, the exposed enemy of the people Sivkov. When Shatalov took over the administration of the section's funds, he found that money was missing. Only during November, some 500–600 rubles had disappeared. Apparently, Timofeyev had continued his secret game until the end, and possibly used government means to support 'enemies of the people' as well. The only one who had understood what was going on was comrade Sychev, who apparently preferred fighting alone as he was 'smarter than others.'

Nechaev confirmed that Timofeyev had managed things in Kronstadt in a bad way, turning more often to the traitor fleet commander Sivkov than to the chief of staff, Isakov (since the 1935 reorganization the intelligence section was no longer a part of the fleet staff but subordinate to the fleet commander, so this routine really made sense). Timofeyev had also protected the enemies of the party and those who were lazy. He had kept those with good records away from supplementary training courses and sent incompetent people in their place. He had spread hostile propaganda against the NKVD. To Nechaev, it was clear that comrades Sychev, Prokazov and Berendt were not giving all the facts, as they had known about the wrecking but had not alerted the NKVD. Therefore, everyone in the section must be investigated. Nechaev concluded by saying that he had not been recruited by anyone.

After Nechaev's intervention, the time had come to pass a resolution. Unanimously, the meeting voted to expel Timofeyev ('an enemy of the people and a spy') and to demand increased vigilance of every party member in order to expose and eliminate the consequences of Timofeyev's treason. Comrades Filippovsky and Lebedev were to examine the autobiographies and personal circumstances of certain members, whereas comrades Prokazov, Berendt and Antoshchenko were to look especially into Andreyev's and Yakovlev's past and investigate their relationship to Timofeyev. Furthermore, each party member must show more discipline and less indifference in his daily work and write an individual report on personal observations in connection with Timofeyev and his sabotage. Through comrade Lebedev, these reports were to be the handed over to the security organs. Finally, comrade Shteynbakh was to inform the Komsomol members at their upcoming meeting.[21]

At subsequent meetings with the party bureau, the party organization in the Baltic Fleet Staff and the Baltic Fleet Party Commission, the expulsion of Timofeyev was confirmed. The motives given were based on the critique which his co-workers had formulated at the cell meeting on 4 December: party activities, Marxist–Leninist education, supplementary training courses for commanding personnel and all operational intelligence work in the intelligence section had come to a standstill during his time in office. Timofeyev had entertained a secret network of spies and wreckers, fomented hostility against the NKVD and allowed irresponsible attitudes to spread. His leadership had created tensions among his staff and threatened discipline.[22]

Timofeyev was formally dismissed from service in the Baltic Fleet on 7 February 1938. A junior lieutenant in radio intelligence was dismissed on the same occasion, but so far Timofeyev and Chuchkag were the only people in the intelligence section who had been arrested by the NKVD.[23] Of Timofeyev's subsequent fate we have no information, but in view of the sensitive position he held it is reasonable to assume that he was shot.

As we are familiar from Chapter 13 with Timofeyev's work during 1936–37 and the administrative changes he initiated, we can imagine that many of his subordinates felt their work was not appreciated, and that they were blamed for inadequacies that really had structural causes. To many, it must have been a relief to see their zealous and overbearing boss disappear. First, however, he had to be unmasked as a traitor and double-dealer, as someone who had in reality favored lazy and inefficient subordinates, a leader who had been insensitive to the 'little people' and their problems, who had spent most of his day idly behind his desk, expecting initiative from below instead of commanding from the front in true Stalinist manner. At the same time, the men in the intelligence section knew that

Timofeyev was right – their work did not live up to modern standards. When their commander was revealed as an enemy of the people, it was convenient to blame him for all that had gone awry. This way, morale and social cohesion in the workplace could be preserved. When young Shteynbakh suggested to the meeting that they should talk less of Timofeyev's crimes and more of the many structural deficiencies in the section's work, he was immediately rebuked. It is worth noticing that those who had positions of authority (section commander Filippovsky, deputy section commander Lebedev, party cell chairman Frumkin, political officer Yeremeyev, party secretary Sychev), were especially eager to keep the discussion focused on Timofeyev as an individual. Nechaev made a dangerous remark in his concluding intervention: some comrades had been in such positions that they should have known what was going on during Timofeyev's reign. This was probably also the reason why so many speakers found it urgent to point out that they themselves had had nothing to do with Timofeyev's recruitment. Andreyev and Yakovlev, two subsection leaders who apparently were not present at the meeting, were frequently pointed out a suitable targets for continued cleansing. A year later, when the *Yezhovshchina* started to subside, at least Andreyev was still on the personnel list and had thus managed to survive so far.

The Baltic Fleet intelligence section offers a telling example of how 'small people' during the Great Terror stepped forward to settle personal accounts with unpopular bosses and colleagues, transforming their small grievances and petty conflicts into something greater and more heroic. The countless ordinary people who eagerly assisted were not necessarily misled victims of the totalitarian system, nor engaged in rational defense of their 'objective interests' against white-collar bureaucrats and administrators.

Regardless of whether Stalin consciously planned the purges or only responded to pressure from below, the Great Terror would not have been possible without the psychological prerequisites at hand in Soviet society. In most Soviet workplaces in the late 1930s, a sense of emergency had been reigning for years, caused by material shortage, human inadequacy and a continuous turnover of employees. Frustrated people could contrast their miserable everyday situation with how official propaganda depicted the reality in which they lived.

When the purges opened an opportunity to vindicate years of hardship, suffering and humiliation, they gratefully took it, in the Baltic Fleet intelligence section as well as in other places.

Notes

1 Suvenirov, *RKKA nakanune*, p. 75.
2 Yegorov to Sivkov, 4 April, 9 April 1937, f. r-92, o. 2, d. 297, list 40–1.
3 Colonel Plotsin, 23 July 1937, report on discharged commanding personnel since 1 April 1937, f. r-2185 o. 2, d. 1, list 231–41; on the connections between the Tukhachevsky plot and arrests in the navy, see Shoshkov, *Repressirovannoe OSTEKHBYURO*.
4 Colonel Plotsin, 23 July 1937, report on discharged commanding personnel since 1 April 1937, f. r-2185, o. 2, d. 1, list 231–41.

5 Baltic Fleet procurator Sturman to the Baltic Fleet Soviet, 14 July 1937, f. r-2185, o. 2, d. 1, list 305.
6 The time of Grishin's suicide is not known, but the end of his term as head of the Baltic Fleet PU is given as 11 May 1937. Cf. Suvenirov, *RKKA nakanune*, p. 322; Berezovsky et al., *Boevaya letopis*, p. 680.
7 Shoshkov, *Repressirovannoe OSTEKHBYURO*, p. 168; after Sivkov's arrest, his name was erased from many documents in the Baltic Fleet archive; see, for instance, Shaposhnikov to Sivkov, 9 April 1937, f. r-92, o. 2, d. 297, list 50.
8 Bulyshkin to the Supreme Soviet of the RKKA Naval Forces, 20 November 1937, f. r-2185, o. 2 d. 2, list 296–9; Kireyev to UMS RKKA, 7 December 1937, ibid., list 344.
9 Kireyev, 22 August 1938, 'Svedeniya o kolichestve uvolennogo, arrestovannogo, vydvinutogo komnachsostava po KBF', f. r-2185, o. 2, d. 3, list 34–5.
10 Baltic Fleet Commissar Muravyev, 14 January 1939, statistical surveys of Baltic Fleet personnel, f. r-1549, o. 1, d. 29, list 1–6, 77–80.
11 Battleship squadron commander Samoilov and battleship squadron commissar Sokolov to fleet commander Sivkov (whose name has been deleted after his purge), 14 June 1937, f. r-2185, o. 2, d. 1, list 299–301; cf. also acting fleet commander Isakov and fleet commissar Bulyshkin, 7 July 1937, ibid., list 296–7; Izhorsk commandant Palunin to Baltic Fleet Soviet, 22 August 1937, ibid., list 377–89.
12 Head of training Kuznetsov and Regimental Commissar Gavrilov to acting Baltic Fleet commander Isakov, 28 July 1937, f. r-2185, o. 2, d. 1, list 427–8.
13 The commander of Kronstadt fortress, Mushnov, 22 June 1937, f. r-2185, o. 2, d. 1, list 251–2; commander 1st Submarine Squadron Samborsky, 9 June 1937, ibid., list 306.
14 'Pod znamenem partii Lenina–Stalina', *Morskoy Sbornik*, vol. 91(10) (1938), p. 6.
15 Intelligence section commissar Yeremeyev to fleet staff commissar Kuznetsov, 20 July 1938, f. r-2185, o. 2, d. 4, list 386; Filippovsky to Baltic Fleet commander Levchenko, 26 July 1938, ibid., list 387; Filippovsky's characterization of Abramenkov, 5 July 1938, ibid., list 388; Baltic Fleet commissar Muravyev and Baltic Fleet commander Levchenko to the Deputy People's Commissar for the Navy Smirnov, ibid., list 389.
16 Isakov to the Baltic Fleet Soviet, 8 July 1937, f. r-2185, o. 2, d. 1, list 268.
17 Shoshkov, *Repressirovannoe OSTEKHBYURO*, pp. 235–6.
18 Barsukov and Zolotarev (eds), *Russky arkhiv*, vol. I. 2, pp. 377–8.
19 Minutes from the closed meeting with primary party organization of the RO KBF (*Razvedyvatelny otdel Krasnoznamennogo Baltiyskogo Flota* = intelligence section Baltic Fleet), 4 December 1938, r-34, o. 12, d. 'Timofeyev, Nikolay Petrovich, r. 1897', list 4–9.
20 Filippovsky to Bulyshkin, 15 February 1938, f. r-1883, o. 1, d. 58, list 20.
21 Minutes from the closed meeting with the primary party organization of the RO KBF, 4 December 1938, r-34, o. 12, d. 'Timofeyev, Nikolay Petrovich, r. 1897', list 4–9.
22 Extract from protocol 57 of the Baltic Fleet Party Commission point 4, 11 February 1938, list 1; extract from protocol 5 closed meeting with Baltic Fleet Staff party organization, 15 November (*sic*! Should be December) 1937; extract from protocol 7 from meeting with Baltic Fleet Staff party organization, PUR and Baltic Fleet, no date, list 2.
23 Extract from order by the People's Commissar for the Navy, 7 February 1938, f. r-1883, o. 1, d. 58, list 22; Filippovsky to Bulyshkin, 15 February 1938, ibid., list 20.

BIBLIOGRAPHY

Archival material
Russian State Archive of the Army (RGVA), Moscow
fond 33988 (*Revolutsionny Voenny Soviet*)

Russian State Archives of the Navy (RGAVMF), St Petersburg
fond 479 (*shtab komanduyushchego flotom baltiskogo morya*)
r-1 (*shtab RKKF*)
r-34 (*Politicheskoe upravlenie KBF*)
r-92 (*shtab KBF*)
r-1483 (*Upravlenie morskikh sil RKKA*)
r-1529 (*istorichesky otdel glavnogo morskoga shtaba*)
r-1543 (*OsoAviaKhim*)
r-1678 (*narodny kommissariat VMF*)
r-2041 (*morskoy otdel generalnogo shtaba RKKA*)
r-1877 (*glavny morskoy shtab VMF*)
r-1549 (*Glavnoe upravlenie politpropagandy VMF*)
r-1883 (*razvedyvatelny otdel KBF*)
r-2224 (*Vladimir Belli*)
r-2185 (*otdel lichnogo sostava shtaba KBF*)

Published documents

A. I. Barsukov and V. A. Zolotarev (eds), *Russky arkhiv: Velikaya Otechestvennaya Voyna. Prikazy i direktivy narodnogo komissara oborony SSSR*, vol. II.1 (Moscow: Terra, 1994).

A. I. Barsukov and V. A. Zolotarev (eds), *Russky arkhiv: Velikaya Otechestvennaya Voyna. Prikazy i direktivy narodnogo komissara VMF v gody Velikoy Otechestvennoy voyny*, vol. X. 10 (Moscow: Terra, 1996).

A. I. Barsukov and V. A. Zolotarev (eds), *Russky arkhiv: Velikaya Otechestvennaya Voyna, nakanune voyny: Materialy soveshchany vyshego rukovodyashchyego sostava VMF SSSR v kontse, 1940 goda,* vol. I.2 (Moscow: Terra, 1997).

Berezovsky N. Yu. (ed.), 'Postanovlenie revvoensoveta SSSR ot 8 maya, 1928 g. O znachenii i zadachakh morskikh sil v sisteme vooruzhennykh sil strany', *Voenno-Istorichesky Zhurnal*, vol. 49(5) (1988).

Berezovsky, N. Yu. (ed.), 'Na borbu s limotrofami', *Voenno-istorichesky zhurnal*, vol. 54(4) (1993).

Berezovsky, N. Yu. (ed.), ' "Dlya kakikh tseley stroit flot?" Proekt pyatletnego plana RKKF, 1925 g.', *Istorichesky Arkhiv*, (4) (1996).

Dyakov, Yury and Bushuyeva, Tatyana (eds), *The Red Army and the Wehrmacht: How the Soviets Militarized Germany 1922–1933 and Paved the Way for Fascism. From the Secret Archives of the Soviet Union* (New York: Prometheus Books, 1995).

Grava-Kreituse, I. et al. (eds), *The Occupation and Annexation of Latvia, 1939–1940: Documents and Materials* (Riga: Latvijas Vestures fonds, 1995).

Holtsmark, Sven G. (ed.), *Norge og Sovjetunionen, 1917–1955: En utenrikespolitisk dokumentation* (Oslo: Cappelen, 1995).

Komplektov, V. G. et al. (eds), *Polpredy soobshchayut...Sbornik dokumentov ob otnosheniyakh SSSR s Latviey, Litvoy i Estoniey: avgust, 1939 g.–avgust, 1940 g.* (Moscow: Ministerstvo Innostranikh del, 1990).

Kvasonkin, A. V. (ed.), *Sovetskoe rukovodstvo: Perepiska, 1928–1941* (Moscow: Rosspen, 1999).

Mandelstam, L. I. (ed.), *Sbornik zakonov SSSR i ukazov preziduma verkhnogo soveta SSSR 1938–1956* (Moscow: Gosudarstvennoe izdatelstvo yuridecheskoy literatury, 1956).

Meijer, J. M. (ed.), *The Trotsky Papers*, vol. II, *1917–1922* (The Hague: Mouton, 1971).

Rossiyisky Gosudarstvenny Arkhiv Voenno-Morskogo Flota v fondakh (1917–1940 gg.) (St Petersburg: [Russian State Archives of the Navy], 1995).

Savinkin, A. E. et al. (eds), *Voenno-morskaya ideya Rossii: Dukhovnoe nasledie Imperatorskogo flota* (Moscow: Russky put, 1999).

Woodward, E. L. and Butler, R. (eds), *Documents on British Foreign Policy, 1919–1939*, series 3, vol. VII (London: Her Majesty's Stationery Office, 1954).

Woodward, E. L. and Butler, R. (eds), *Documents on British Foreign Policy 1919–1939*, series 1, vol. VIII (London: Her Majesty's Stationery Office, 1958).

Contemporary published sources

Aleksandrov, A. P., 'Oborona sovetskoy strany', *Morskoy Sbornik*, vol. 79(5) (1926).

Alyakrinsky, N., 'O bolshikh oshibkakh v korotkom doklade', *Morskoy Sbornik*, vol. 79(5) (1926).

Anonymous, 'Alandskie ostrova (geograficheskaya spravka)', *Morskoy Sbornik*, vol. 92 (12) (1939).

Bykov, P., 'K voprosy o prepodavanii v.-m. istoricheskikh predmetov', *Morskoy Sbornik*, vol. 79(5) (1926).

Från Röda Armén: Översättning av 1929 års fälttjänstreglemente jämte kort översikt av krigsorganisationen (Stockholm: Militärlitteraturföreningens förlag no. 156, 1930).

Frunze, Mikhail, 'Nam nuzhen silny baltisky flot', *Krasnaya Zvezda*, 3 July 1925.

Gorsky, N., 'Flot i aviatsiya', *Morskoy Sbornik*, vol. 75(11) (1922).

Isakov, I. S., 'Belomorsko-baltiskaya vodnaya magistral: Naznachenie i mashtaby stroitelstva' (1932), in *Izbrannye trudy: Okeanologiya, geografiya i voennaya istoriya* (Moscow: Izdatelstvo Nauka, 1984).

Ivanov, L., 'Problema Alandskikh ostrovov', *Morskoy Sbornik*, vol. 92(12) (1939).
Jane's Fighting Ships, 1928 (London: Jane's Yearbooks, 1928).
Kozhanov, I., 'Sootvestvovali organisatsiya i metody maloy voyny strategicheskim zadacham nemtsev i obstanovke v protsesse razvitiya ot nachala do kontsa, 1914 goda?', *Morskoy Sbornik*, vol. 79(5) (1926).
Melenkovsky, A., 'Poltirabota v flote', *Morskoy Sbornik*, vol. 79(5) (1926).
Novikov, N. V., 'Problema oborony za rubezhom v, 1925 godu', *Morskoy Sbornik*, vol. 79(5) (1926).
Novikov, N., 'Gangutskaya pobeda: Kampanii, 1713 i 1714 gg. na Finlandskom teatre i gangutskaya operatsiya', *Morskoy Sbornik*, vol. 92(12) (1939).
Petrov, Mikhail, 'Po povodu manevrov balticheskogo flota', *Morskoy Sbornik*, vol. 75(11) (1922).
Peyron, E. W. 'Årsberättelse av föredragande i sjökrigsvetenskap', *Krigsvetenskapsakademiens handlingar*, vol. 125 (1923).
'Pod znamenem partii Lenina-Stalina', *Morskoy Sbornik*, vol. 91(10) (1938).
's', Några ord om Sveriges lant- och sjöförsvar', *Krigsvetenskapsakademiens Tidskrift*, vol. 127(1) (1925).
Shvede, Evgeny, 'Yeszhyo neskolko slov po povodu spora mezhdu lineynym korablem i vozdushnym apparatom', *Morskoy Sbornik*, vol. 75(11) (1922).
Smirnov, B. I., *Voenno-morskoy flot* (Leningrad: Voenmorizdat, 1941).
Smirnov, P. I. 'K itogam spora o morskom i vozdushnom flotakh', *Morskoy Sbornik*, vol. 79(5) (1926).
Svechin, Alexander, *Strategiya* (Moscow: Gosvoenizdat, 1927).
Tributs, V., 'Krasnoznamenny baltflot na strazhe rodiny', *Morskoy Sbornik*, vol. 92(12) (1939).
Veygelin, K., 'Sili vozdushnie i morskie', *Morskoy Sbornik*, vol. 75(11) (1922).
Zakharov, M. V. (ed.), *Voprosy strategii i operativnogo isskustva v sovetskikh voennikh trudakh (1917–1940 gg.)* (Moscow: Voenizdat, 1965).

Unpublished literature

Blinov, A. M., introduction to the archive catalogue of f. r-92, o. 1, shtab KBF (operativny otdel), in RGAVMF, St Petersburg.
Petrov, Pavel V., 'Krasnoznamenny baltisky flot v sovetsko-finlandskoy voyne, 1939–1940 gg.' (unpublished dissertation, St Petersburg State University, Department of Russian History, spring term 2000).

Literature

Achkasov, V. I. et al., *Boevoy put sovetskogo voenno-morskogo flota* (Moscow: Voenizdat, 1988).
Agrell, Wilhelm, *Alianspolitik och atombomber: Kontinuitet och förändring i den svenska försvarsdoktrinen, 1945–1982* (Lund: Liber, 1985).
Agrell, Wilhelm, 'Strategisk förändring och svensk-sovjetiska konflikter i Östersjöområdet efter 1945', *Scandia*, vol. 51 (1985).
Allison, Graham T., *Essence of Decision: Explaining the Cuban Missile Crises* (New York: HarperCollins, 1971).

Almond, Gabriel A. and Roselle, Laura, 'Model Fitting in Communism Studies', in Fleron, Frederic J., Jr. and Hoffman, Erik P. (eds), *Post-Communist Studies and Political Science: Methodology and Empirical Theory in Sovietology* (Boulder, CO: Oxford: Westview Press, 1993).

Andolf, Göran and Johansson, Bertil, 'The Baltic – a Sea of Peace? Swedish Views of Soviet Naval Policy in the Baltic', in Rystad, Göran, Böhme, Klaus R. and Carlgren, Wilhelm M. (eds), *In Quest of Trade and Security: The Baltic in Power Politics, 1500–1990, Vol. II, 1890–1990* (Stockholm: Probus, 1995).

Åselius, Gunnar, '"The Unskilled Fencer": Swedish Assessments of the Soviet Navy, 1921–1928', *Militärhistorisk Tidskrift*, vol. 13 (1991).

Åselius, Gunnar, 'Östersjöområdet i sovjetisk marindoktrin, 1920–1940', *Tidskrift i Sjöväsendet*, vol. 160(1) (1997).

Åselius, Gunnar, 'Preventivkrig mot Sverige? Sverige i rysk och sovjetisk marin planering, 1914–1940', *Tidskrift i Sjöväsendet*, vol. 162(4) (1999).

Åselius, Gunnar, 'Naval Theaters in Soviet Grand Strategic Assessments, 1920–1940', *Journal of Slavic Military Studies*, vol. 13(1) (2000).

Askgaard, Finn, *Kampen om Östersjön på Carl X Gustafs tid*, Carl X Gustaf-studier 6 (Stockholm: Militärhistoriska förlaget, 1974).

Baryshnikov, V. N., 'K voprosu o planirovanii Sovetskim baltiyskim flotom voennikh deystvy protiv Finlandii v 1930-e gg. (raschety i realnost)', in Koreneva, S. B. and Prokhorenko, A. V. (eds), *Rossiya i Finlandiya v xx veke: K 80-letiyu nezavisimosti Finlandskoy respubliki* (St Petersburg: Evropeysky dom; Vaduz: Topos Verlag, 1997).

Baryshnikov, Vladimir N., *Ot prokhladnogo mira k zimney voyne: Vostochnaya politika Finlandii v 1930-e gody* (St Petersburg: Izdatelstvo Sankt Peterburgskogo Universiteta 1997).

Bathurst, Robert B., *Intelligence and the Mirror* (London: Sage Publications, 1993).

Beaumont, R. A., *Joint Military Operations: A Short History* (Westport, CT: Greenwood Press, 1993).

Beckman, Bengt, *Svenska kryptobedrifter* (Stockholm: Albert Bonniers förlag, 1996).

Berezovsky, N. Yu., Berezhnoy, S. S. and Nikolayeva, Z. V., *Boevaya letopis sovetskogo voenno-morskogo flota, 1917–1941* (Moscow: Voenizdat, 1993).

Berge, Anders, *Sakkunskap och politisk rationalitet: Den svenska flottan och pansarfartygsfrågan, 1918–1939* (Stockholm: Almquist & Wiksell International, 1987).

Beznosov, A. B., 'Sekret Basis Nord', *Voenno-istoricheskij Zhurnal*, vol. 51(7) (1990).

Bikkenin, R. R., Glushchenko, A. A. and Partala, M. A., *Ocherki o svyazistakh rossiskogo flota: Kratkaya istoriya sozdaniya i razvitiya Sluzhby svyazi VMF v period, 1900–1930-ch g.* (St Petersburg: Dmitry Bulanin, 1998).

Björklund, Elis, 'Det ryska anfallsföretaget mot Sverige, 1914', *Svensk Tidskrift*, vol. 23 (1936).

Bond, Brian, 'British War Planning for Operations in the Baltic before the First and Second World Wars', in Rystad, Göran, Böhme, Klaus R. and Carlgren, Wilhelm M. (eds), *In Quest of Trade and Security: The Baltic in Power Politics, 1500–1990*, Vol. II, *1890–1990* (Stockholm: Probus, 1995).

Boog, Horst et al., *Das Deutsche Reich und der Zweite Weltkrieg*, Vol. IV, *Der Angriff auf die Sowjetunion* (Stuttgart: Deutsche Verlags-Anstalt, 1983).

Breyer, Siegfried, *Soviet Warship Development*, vol. I: *1917–1937* (London: Conway Maritime Press, 1992).

Brose, Eric Dorn, *The Kaiser's Army: The Politics of Military Technology in Germany during the Machine Age, 1870–1918* (Oxford: Oxford University Press, 2001).
Brunila, Kai, 'Hemmatrupperna', in Ekberg, Henrik (ed.), *Finland i krig, 1939–1945*, vol. I (Helsinki: Holger Schildts förlag, 1986).
Bruun, C. E., 'Luftstridskrafterna', in Ekberg, Henrik (ed.), *Finland i krig, 1939–1945*, vol. I (Helsinki: Holger Schildts förlag, 1986).
Bueb, Volkmar, *Die 'Junge Schule' der fransözösischen Marine: Strategie und Politik, 1875–1900* (Boppard am Rhein: Boldt, 1971).
Burev, V. N., *Otetchestvennoe voennoe korablostroenie v tretyem stolety svoey istorii* (St Petersburg: Sudostroenie, 1995).
Carlgren, Wilhelm M., *Svensk utrikespolitik, 1939–1945* (Stockholm: Allmänna förlaget, 1973).
Carlgren, Wilhelm M., *Varken–eller: Reflektioner kring Sveriges Ålandspolitik, 1938–1939* (Stockholm: Militärhistoriska förlaget, 1977).
Carlgren, Wilhelm M., 'Svek Sverige Finland?', *Historisk Tidskrift*, vol. 105(2) (1985).
Carlgren, Wilhelm, M., 'Den stora överraskningen: Regeringen och Moskvapakten', in Hugemark, Bo (ed.), *Stormvarning: Sverige inför andra världskriget* (Stockholm: Probus, 1989).
Castex, Raoul, *Strategic Theories*, ed. Eugenia C. Kiesling (Annapolis, MD: US Naval Institute, 1994).
Champonnois, Suzanne, 'The Baltic States as an Aspect of Franco-Soviet Relations, 1919–1934. A Policy or Several Policies?', in Hiden, John and Loit, Alexander (eds), *Contact or isolation? Soviet–Western Relations in the Interwar Period* (Stockholm: Studia Baltica Stockholmiensa, 1991).
Champs, Henri de, *Från gången tid* (Stockholm: Fritzes, 1948).
Chernavin, V. N. (ed.), *Voenno–morskoy slovar* (Moscow: Voenizdat, 1989).
Clausewitz, Carl von, *On War* (Princeton, NJ: Princeton University Press, 1984 [1976]).
Colton, Timothy J., *Commissars, Commanders and Civilian Authority* (Princeton, NJ: Princeton University Press, 1979).
Colton, Timothy J., 'Perspectives on Civil–Military Relations in the Soviet Union', in Colton, Timothy J. and Gustafson, Thane (eds), *Soldiers and the Soviet State: Civil–Military Relations from Breshnev and Gorbachev* (Princeton, NJ: Princeton University Press, 1990).
Conquest, Robert, *The Great Terror: Stalin's Purge in the 1930s* (London: Macmillan, 1968).
Conquest, Robert, *The Harvest of Sorrow: Soviet Collectivization and the Terror-Famine* (London: Hutchinson, 1986).
Conquest, Robert, *The Great Terror: A Reassessment* (New York: Oxford University Press, 1990).
Corbett, Julian S., *Some Principles of Maritime Strategy*, ed. Eric J. Grove (Annapolis, MD: US Naval Institute Press, 1988 [1911]).
Cronenberg, Arvid, *Militär intressegrupp-politik: Kretsen kring Ny Militär Tidskrift och dess väg till inflytande i 1930 års försvarskommission* (Kristianstad: Militärhistoriska förlaget, 1977).
Cronenberg, Arvid, 'Säkerhetspolitik och krigsplanering: Huvudlinjer i arméns operativa planering, 1906–1945', in Hugemark, Bo (ed.), *Neutralitet och försvar: Perspektiv på svensk säkerhetspolitik, 1809–1985* (Stockholm: Probus, 1986).
Crowe, David M., *The Baltic States and the Great Powers: Foreign Relations, 1938–1940* (Boulder, CO: Westview Press, 1993).

Dotsenko V. D., *Flot–Voyna–Pobeda, 1941–1945* (St Petersburg: Sudostroenie, 1995).
Dotsenko, V. D., *Morskoy biograficheskry slovar* (St Petersburg: Logos, 1995).
Earle, Edward. M., 'Lenin, Trotsky, Stalin: Soviet Concepts of War', in Earle, Edward M. (ed.), *Makers of Modern Strategy: Military Thought from Machiavelli to Hitler* (Princeton, NJ: Princeton University Press, 1944).
Ekman, P. O., *Sjöfront: Sjökrigshändelser i Norra Östersjöområdet 1941–1944* (Helsinki: Holger Schildts förlag, 1981).
Ekman, P. O., 'Sjöstridskrafterna', in Ekberg, Henrik (ed.), *Finland i krig, 1939–1945*, vol. I (Helsinki: Holger Schildts förlag, 1986).
Ekman, P. O., 'Vinterkriget till sjöss', in Ekberg, Henrik (ed.), *Finland i krig, 1939–1945*, vol. I (Helsinki: Holger Schildts förlag, 1986).
Ekman, P. O., Sjöstridskrafterna', in Ekberg, Henrik (ed.), *Finland i krig, 1939–1945*, vol. II (Esbo: Schildts, 2000).
Engström, Johan and Frantzén, Ole (eds), *Øresunds strategiske rolle i et historisk perspective: Föredrag hållna vid symposium på Revingehed i Skåne och på kastellet i København 3–7 juni 1996* (Stockholm: Armémuseum, 1998).
Erickson, John, *The Soviet High Command: A Military-Political History, 1918–1941* (London: Macmillan, 1962).
Eyre, Dana P. and Suchman, Mark C., 'Status, Norms and Proliferation of Conventional Weapons: An institutional Theory Approach', in Katzenstein Peter J. (ed.), *The Culture of National Security: Norms and Identity in World Politics* (New York: Columbia University Press, 1996).
Fitzpatrick, Sheila, *Cultural Revolution in Russia, 1928–1932* (Bloomington, IN: Indiana University Press, 1978).
Fitzpatrick, Sheila, *Education and Social Mobility in the Soviet Union, 1921–1934* (Cambridge: Cambridge University Press, 1979).
Fitzpatrick, Sheila, 'New Perspectives on Stalinism', *Russian Review*, vol. 45 (1986).
Fitzpatrick, Sheila, *The Cultural Front: Power and Culture in Revolutionary Russia* (Ithaca, NY: Cornell University Press, 1992).
Fleron, Fredric J. Jr. and Hoffman, Erik P. (eds), *Post-Communist Studies and Political Science: Methodology and Empirical Theory in Sovietology* (Boulder, CO: Westview Press, 1993).
Försvarets forskningsanstalt, *Rysk militär förmåga i ett tioårsperspektiv* (FOA-R–99–01151–170–SE, May 1999).
Friedrich, Carl J. and Brezinski, Zbigniew, *Totalitarian Dictatorship and Autocracy* (Cambridge, MA: Harvard University Press, 1965).
Gemzell, Carl-Axel, *Conflict, Organization and Innovation: A Study of German Naval Strategic Planning, 1880–1940* (Lund: Scandinavian University Books, 1973).
Gemzell, Carl-Axel, 'Warszawapakten, DDR och Danmark: Kampen för en maritim operationsplan', *Historisk Tidskrift*, vol. 96(1) (1996).
Gerner, Kristian, Hedlund, Stefan and Sundström, Niclas, *Hjärnridån: Det europeiska projektet och det gåtfulla Ryssland* (Stockholm: Fischer, 1995).
Getty, J. Arch, *Origins of the Great Purges: The Soviet Communist Party Reconsidered, 1933–1938* (Cambridge: Cambridge University Press, 1985).
Getty, J. Arch and Manning, Roberta Thompson (eds), *Stalinist Terror: New Perspectives* (Cambridge: Cambridge University Press, 1993).
Getty, J. Arch and Naumov, Oleg, *The Road to Terror: Stalin and the Self-Destruction of the Bolsheviks, 1932–1939* (New Haven, CT: Yale University Press, 1999).

Getty, J. Arch, Rittersporn, Gábor and Zemskov, N. N., 'Victims of the Soviet Penal System in the Prewar Years: A First Approach on the Basis of Archival Evidence', *American Historical Review*, vol. 98(4) (1993).

Glantz, David M., *The Military Strategy of the Soviet Union: A History* (London: Frank Cass, 1992).

Glantz, David M., *Barbarossa: Hitler's Invasion of Russia 1941* (Stroud: Tempus, 2001).

Glete, Jan, 'Kriget till sjöss, 1788–1790', in Artéus, Gunnar (ed.), *Gustav III:s ryska krig* (Stockholm: Probus, 1992).

Glete, Jan, 'Bridge and Bulwark: The Swedish Navy and the Baltic, 1500–1809', in Rystad, Göran, Böhme, Klaus R. and Carlgren Wilhelm M. (eds), *In Quest of Trade and Security: The Baltic in Power Politics, 1500–1990* vol. I, *1500–1890* (Stockholm: Probus, 1994).

Glete, Jan, 'Östersjön som maritimt operationsområde – ett historiskt perspektiv', *Tidskrift i Sjöväsendet*, vol. 162(3) (1999).

Goldrick, James and Hattendorf, John B. (eds), *Mahan Is Not Enough: The Proceedings of a Conference on the Works of Sir Julian Corbett and Admiral Sir Herbert Richmond* (Newport, RI: Naval War College Press, 1993).

Gooch, John, 'Maritime Command: Mahan and Corbett', in Gray, Colin S. and Barnett, Roger W. (eds), *Seapower and Strategy* (Annapolis, MD: US Naval Institute Press, 1989).

Gorkov, Yuriy, *Kreml, stavka, genshtab* (Tver: Rif LTD, 1995).

Gorodetsky, Gabriel, *The Precarious Truce: Anglo-Soviet Relations, 1924–27* (Cambridge: Cambridge University Press, 1977).

Gorshkov, Sergey G., *Sea Power of the State* (Oxford: Pergamon Press, 1979).

Gorshkov, Sergey G., *Vo flotskom stroyu* (St Petersburg: Logos, 1996).

Gribovsky, V. Yu, 'Na puti k "bolshomu morskomu i okeanskomu flotu"', *Gangut*, no. 9 (1995).

Hagen, Mark von, *Soldiers in the Proletarian Dictatorship: The Red Army and the Soviet Socialist State, 1917–1930* (Ithaca, NY: Cornell University Press, 1990).

Haslam, Jonathan, *Soviet Foreign Policy, 1930–33: The Impact of the Depression* (Cambridge: Macmillan, 1983).

Haslam, Jonathan, *The Soviet Union and the Struggle for Collective Security in Europe, 1933–39* (London: Macmillan, 1984).

Herrick, Robert W., *Soviet Naval Strategy: Fifty Years of Theory and Practice* (Annapolis, MD: US Naval Institute Press, 1968).

Herrick, Robert W., *Soviet Naval Theory and Strategy: Gorshkov's Inheritance* (Annapolis, MD: US Naval Institute Press, 1988).

Herspring, Dale R., *Russian Civil–Military Relations* (Bloomington, IN: Indiana University Press, 1996).

Highham, Robin, *Airpower: A Concise History* (Yuma, AZ: Sunflower University Press, 1988 [1972]).

Hildermeier, Manfred, *Geschichte der Sowjetunion, 1917–1991: Entstehung und Entwicklung der ersten sozialistischen Staates* (Göttingen: Verlag C. H. Beck, 1998).

Hofsten, Gustaf von and Waernberg, Jan, *Örlogsfartyg: Svenska maskindrivna fartyg under tretungad flagg* (Stockholm: Svenskt militärhistoriskt bibliotek, 2003).

Holmquist, Åke, *Flottans beredskap, 1938–1940* (Stockholm: Allmänna förlaget, 1972).

Hovi, K., 'The French Alliance Policy, 1917–1927: A Change of Mentality', in Hiden, John and Loit, Alexander (eds), *Contact or Isolation? Soviet–Western Relations in the Interwar Period* (Stockholm: Studia Baltica Stockholmiensa, 1991).

Hovi, Olavi, *The Baltic Area in British Policy, 1918–1921*, vol. I, *From the Compiégne Armistice to the Implementation of the Versailles Treaty, 11.11 1918–20.1. 1920* (Helsinki: Studia Historica Helsinki, 1980).

Hugemark, Bo, 'The Swedish Navy – Auxiliary Force or Strategic Factor?', in Rystad, Göran, Böhme, Klaus R. and Carlgren, Wilhelm M. (eds), *In Quest of Trade and Security: The Baltic in Power Politics, 1500–1990*, vol. II, *1890–1990* (Stockholm: Probus, 1995).

Hughes, Wayne P., *Fleet Tactics: Theory and Practice* (Annapolis, MD: US Naval Institute Press, 1986).

Hughes, Wayne P., 'The Strategy–Tactics Relationship', in Gray, Colin S. and Barnett, Roger W. (eds), *Seapower and Strategy* (Annapolis, MD: US Naval Institute Press, 1989).

Ireland, Bernhard, *Jane's Battleships of the 20th Century* (London: Harper Collins Publishers, 1996).

Jacobson, J., 'Essay and Reflection: On the Historiography of Soviet Foreign Relations in the 1920's', *International History Review*, vol. 18(2) (1996).

Jakobson, Max, *The Diplomacy of the Winter War: An Account of the Russo-Finnish War 1939–1940* (Cambridge, MA: Harvard University Press, 1965).

Johansson, Alf W., *Finlands sak: Svensk politik och opinion under vinterkriget 1939–1940* (Stockholm: Allmänna förlaget, 1973).

Johansson, Alf W., 'Östersjöproblematiken i ett historiskt perspektiv, sedd ur svensk synvinkel', *Gotlands roll i Östersjön i historiskt perspektiv och nutid*. Appendix to *Kungl. krigsvetenskapsakademiens handlingar och tidskrift*, vol. 190 (1986).

Johansson, Alf W., 'Transiteringar, eskorteringar och det svenska territorialvattnet: Marina frågor i de svensk–tyska relationerna 1941–1942', in Ekman, Stig (ed.), *Småstatspolitik och stormaktstryck: Aspekter på svensk politik under andra världskriget* (Stockholm: Liber, 1986).

Johnson, Bo, 'Kolliderande suveränitet: översikt över folkrättsliga problem i det nordiska närområdet', *Tidskrift i Sjöväsendet*, vol. 136(4) (1973).

Kalela, Jorma, *Grannar på skilda vägar: Svensk–finska relationer, 1921–1923* (Helsinki: Historiallisia tutkimuksia, 1971).

Kasatonov, I. V., *Flot vykhodit v okean: Povest ob admirale flota V. A. Kasatonove* (St Petersburg: Lyuks, 1995).

Kasatonov, I. V., *Flot vyshyol v okean* (Moscow: Andreyevsky flag, 1996).

Kasatonov I. V. et al. (eds), *Krasnoznamenny baltisky flot v Velikoy Otechestvennoy Voyny sovetskogo naroda, 1941–1945 gg.*, 5 vols (Moscow: Voenizdat, 1990–92).

Katzenstein, Peter J., 'Introduction: Alternative Perspectives on National Security', in Katzenstein, Peter J. (ed.), *The Culture of National Security: Norms and Identity in World Politics* (New York: Columbia University Press, 1996).

Katzenstein, Peter J. (ed.), *The Culture of National Security: Norms and Identity in World Politics* (New York: Columbia University Press, 1996).

Khrenov, M. M. et al., *Voennaya odezhda Vooruzhennikh Sil SSSR i Rossii (1917–1990–e gody)* (Moscow: Voenizdat, 1999).

Kier, Elisabeth, *Imagining War* (Princeton, NJ: Princeton University Press, 1997).

Kilin, Yu. M., 'Voenno-politicheskie aspekty sovetsko-finlandskikh otnosheny v 1920–1930-e gody', in Koreneva, S. B. and Prochorenko, A. V. (eds), *Rossiya i Finlandiya v XX veke* (St Petersburg: Evropeysky dom; Vaduz: Topos Verlag, 1997).

Kipp, Jacob W., 'The Development of Naval Aviation, 1908–1975', in Higham, Robin and Kipp, J. W. (eds), *Soviet Aviation and Air Power: A Historical View* (London: Brassey's, 1977).

Kolkowicz, Roman, *The Soviet Military and the Communist Party* (Princeton, NJ: Princeton University Press, 1967).

Kotkin, Stephen, *Magnetic Mountain: Stalinism as Civilization* (Berkeley, CA: University of California Press, 1995).

Krivosheyev, G. F. (ed.), *Grif sekretnosti snyat: Poteri vooruzhennikh sil SSSR v voynakh, boevikh deystvyakh i voennykh konfliktakh* (Moscow: Voenizdat, 1993).

Kuznetsov, Nikolay G., *Nakanune* (Moscow: Voenizdat, 1966).

Kuznetsov, Nikolay G., *Krutye povoroty: Is zapisok admirala* (Moscow: Molodaya gvardiya, 1995).

Leskinen, Jari, *Vaiettu Suomen Silta: Suomen ja Viron salainen sotilaainen yhtestoiminta Neuvostoliiton varalta vuosina, 1930–1939* (Helsinki: Suomen Historiallinen Seura, 1997).

Lewin, Moshe, *The Making of the Soviet System: Essays in the Social History of Inter-War Russia* (New York: Pantheon, 1985).

Lovett, Christopher C., 'Russian and Soviet Naval Aviation, 1908–1996', in Higham, Robin, Greenwood, J. T. and Hardesty, V. (eds), *Russian Aviation and Air Power in the Twentieth Century* (London: Frank Cass, 1998).

Mackintosh, J. M., 'The Red Army, 1920–1936', in Liddell-Hart, Basil H. (ed.), *The Soviet Army* (London: Weidenfeld & Nicolson, 1954).

Mahan, Alfred T., *Mahan on Naval Strategy*, ed. John B. Hattendorf (Annapolis, MD: US Naval Institute Press, 1991).

Malia, Martin, *The Soviet Tragedy: A History of Socialism in Russia, 1917–1991* (New York: Free Press, 1994).

Manninen, Ohto, *Molotovin cocktail – Hitlerin sateenvarjo: Toisen mailmansodan historian uudelleenkirjoitusta* (Helsinki: Painatuskeskus, 1994).

Manninen, Ohto, 'Pervy period boev', in Rzheshevsky, Oleg A. and Vehviljainen, O. (eds), *Zimnyaya voyna: Politicheskaya istoriya* (Moscow: Nauka, 1999).

Mawdsley, Evan B., *The Russian Revolution and the Baltic Fleet: War and Politics, February, 1917–April, 1918* (London: Macmillan, 1978).

Mawdsley, Evan, 'The Fate of Stalin's Naval Program', *Warship International*, vol. 27 (1990).

MccGwire, Michael, *Military Objectives in Soviet Foreign Policy* (Washington, DC.: Brookings Institution, 1987).

Meister, Jürg, *Der Seekrieg in den osteuropepäischen gewässern, 1941–1945* (Munich: Lehmanns, 1958).

Millet, Alan R., 'Assault from the Sea: The Development of Amphibious Warfare between the Wars', in Murray, W. and Millet, Alan R. (eds), *Military Innovation in the Interwar Period* (Cambridge: Cambridge University Press, 1995).

Mitchell, Donald W., *A History of Russian and Soviet Sea Power* (London: André Deutsch, 1974).

Mitchell, M., *The Maritime History of Russia, 848–1948* (London: Sidgwick & Jackson, 1949).

Monakov, Mikhail, 'Sudba doktrin i teory, 1: "Kakoy RSFR nuzhen flot?" 1922 g.', *Morskoy Sbornik*, vol. 143(11) (1990).

Monakov, Mikhail, 'Sudba doktrin i teory, 2: "Kakoy RSFR nuzhen flot?" 1923–1925 gg.', *Morskoy Sbornik*, vol. 143(12) (1990).

Monakov, Mikhail, 'Sudba doktrin i teory, 6: Tanki ili korabli? 1928–1930 gg.', *Morskoy Sbornik*, vol. 145(3) (1992).
Monakov, Mikhail, 'Sudba doktrin i teory, 7: Razgrom staroy shkoli, 1930–1931 gg.', *Morskoy Sbornik*, vol. 145(7) (1992).
Monakov, Mikhail, 'Sudba doktrin i teory, 8 [9]: Flot dlya "maloy voyny"', *Morskoy Sbornik*, vol. 147(3) (1994).
Monakov, Mikhail, 'Sudba doktrin i teory, 8: K bolshomu morskomu i okeanskomu flotu (1936–1939 gg.)', *Morskoy Sbornik*, vol. 147(5) (1994).
Monakov, Mikhail and Berezovsky, N. Yu., 'Sudba doktrin i teory, 4: "Flot dolzhen byt aktivnym." 1925–1928 gg.', *Morskoy Sbornik*, vol. 144(3) (1991).
Monakov, Mikhail and Berezovsky, N. Yu., 'Sudba doktrin i teory, 5: K istorii voprosa o "maloy voyne". 1927–1928 gg.', *Morskoy Sbornik*, vol. 144(4) (1991).
Monakov, Mikhail and Gribovsky, V., 'Sudba doktrin i teory, 9 [10]: Na poroge bolshoy voyny', *Morskoy Sbornik*, vol. 147(12) (1994).
Iver, B. Neumann, Iver B., Leira, Halvard and Heikka, Henrika 'The Concept of Strategic Culture: The Social Roots of Nordic State Strategies', *Cooperation and Conflict*, vol. 40(1) (2005).
Norberg, Erik, 'Sjökrig i Östersjön: Sovjetiska planer och tysk aktivitet inför uppgörelsen, 1941', in Hugemark, Bo (ed.), *I orkanens öga: 1941 – osäker neutralitet* (Stockholm: Probus, 1992).
Norman, Hans (ed.), *Skärgårdsflottan: Uppbyggnad, militär användning och förankring i det svenska samhället, 1700–1824* (Lund: Historiska Media, 2000).
Odom, William E., 'The Party Military Connection. A Critique', in Herspring, Dale R. and Volgyes, Ivan (eds), *Civil Military Relations in Communist Systems* (Boulder: Westview Press, 1978).
Overy, Richard J., *Russia's War* (London: Penguin, 1997).
Perechnev, Yu. G., 'Pered voyny', in Kasatonov, I. V. et al. (ed.), *Krasnoznamenny baltisky flot v Velikoy Otechestvennoy Voyny sovetskogo naroda, 1941–1945 gg.* vol. I, *Oborona Pribaltiki i Leningrada, 1941–1944 gg.* (Moscow: Nauka, 1990).
Petrov, Pavel V., 'Baltika, noyabr 1939-god: Materialy boevogo planirovaniya KBF', *Russkoe Proshloe*, no. 8 (1999).
Petrov, Pavel V., 'Linkory protiv batarey: Operatsii eskadry KBF v bierskom arkhipelage', *Tayfun*, no. 3 (1999).
Petrov, Pavel V., 'Osvoenie Pribaltiki: KBF v Estonii i Latvii (oktybabr, 1939–febral, 1940 gg.)', *Tayfun*, nos 3 and 4 (2000).
Petrov, Pavel V., 'Voenno-morskie sily Finlandii (1918–1939 gg.)', *Tayfun*, no. 4 (2000).
Petrov, Pavel V., 'Bronenostsy beregovoy oborony *Väinömöinen i Ilmarinen*', *Tayfun*, no. 12 (2000).
Philbin, Tobias R., III, *The Lure of Neptune: German–Soviet Naval Collaboration and Ambitions, 1919–1941* (Columbia, SC: University of South Carolina Press, 1994).
Podsoblyayev, Ye. F., 'Nuzhen li flot Sovetskoy Rossii? (po materialam diskussii, proshedshey posle pervoy mirovoy voyny)', *Novy Chasovoy*, no. 5 (1997).
Podsoblyayev, Ye. F., 'Kakoy flot nuzhen RSFR? (po materialam diskussii proshedshey posle Pervoy mirovoy voyny', *Novy Chasovoy*, no. 6 (1997).
Ponikarovsky, V. N. et al. (eds), *Voenno–morskaya akademiya (kratkaya istoriya)*, (Leningrad: TsKF VMF, 1991).
Posen, Barry R., *Explaining Military Doctrine: France, Britain and Germany between the Wars* (Ithaca, NY: Cornell University Press, 1984).

Preston, Herbert R. (ed.), *Red Star Rising at Sea* (Annapolis, MD: US Naval Institute Press, 1974).

Ranft, Bryan and Till, Geoffrey, *The Sea in Soviet Strategy* (London: Pinter, 1983).

Rebas, Hain, 'Probleme des kommunistischen Putschversuches in Tallinn am, 1. Dezember, 1924', *Annales Societatis Litterarum Estonicae in Svecia*, vol. 9 (1980–85).

Reese, Roger R., 'The Red Army and the Great Purges', in Getty, J. Arch and Manning, Roberta Thompson (eds), *Stalinist Terror: New Perspectives* (Cambridge: Cambridge University Press, 1993).

Reese, Roger R., *Stalin's Reluctant Soldiers: A Social History of the Red Army, 1925–1941* (Lawrence, MA: Sunflower Press, 1996).

Reese, Roger R., *The Soviet Military Experience: A History of the Soviet Army, 1917–1991* (London: Routledge 2000).

Rice, Condoleezza, 'The Making of Soviet Strategy', in Paret, Peter (ed.), *Makers of Modern Strategy: Military Thought from Machiavelli to the Nuclear Age* (Princeton, NJ: Princeton University Press, 1986).

Rittersporn, Gábor, *Stalinist Simplifications and Soviet Complications: Social Tensions and Political Conflicts in the U.S.S.R., 1933–1953* (Chur: Harwood Academic Publishers, 1991).

Roberts, Geoffrey, *The Soviet Union and the Origins of the Second World War: Russo-German Relations and the Road to War, 1933–1941* (London: Macmillan, 1993).

Rohwer, Jürgen, 'Russian and Soviet Naval Strategy', in Skogan, John and Brundtland, Arne (eds), *Soviet Sea Power in Northern Waters* (London: Pinter, 1990).

Rohwer, Jürgen and Monakov, Mikhail, *Stalin's Ocean-going Fleet:Soviet Naval Strategy and Shipbuilding Programmes, 1935–1953* (London: Frank Cass, 2001).

Ruge, Friedrich, *The Soviets as Naval Opponents, 1941–1945* (Annapolis, MD: US Naval Institute Press, 1979).

Rystad, Göran, 'The Åland Question and the Balance of Power in the Baltic during the First World War', in Rystad, Göran, Böhme, Klaus R. and Carlgren, Wilhelm M. (eds), *In Quest of Trade and Security: The Baltic in Power Politics, 1500–1990*, vol. II, *1890–1990* (Stockholm: Probus, 1995).

Salewski, Michael, *Die Deutsche Seekriegsleitung 1935–1945*, vol. I, *1935–1941* (Frankfurt: Bernhard & Graefe Verlag für Wehrwesen, 1970).

Salmon, Patrick, 'British Security Interests in Scandinavia and the Baltic, 1918–39', in Loit, Alexander (ed.), *The Baltic in International Relations between the Two World Wars* (Stockholm: Studia Baltica Stockholmiensa, 1988).

Salmon, Patrick J., 'Perceptions and Misperceptions: Great Britain and the Soviet Union in Scandinavia and the Baltic Region, 1918–1939', in Hiden, John and Loit, Alexander (eds), *Contact or Isolation? Soviet–Western Relations in the Interwar Period* (Stockholm: Studia Baltica Stockholmiensa, 1991).

Samuelson, Lennart, 'The Naval Dimension of Soviet Five Year Plans, 1925–1941', in McBride, W. M. and Reed, E. P. (eds), *New Interpretations in Naval History: Selected Papers from the Thirteenth Naval History Symposium* (Annapolis, MD: US Naval Institute Press, 1998).

Samuelson, Lennart, *Plans for Stalin's War Machine: Tukhachevskii and Soviet Defence Industry Planning, 1925–1941* (London: Macmillan, 1999).

Saul, Norman E., *Sailors in Revolt: The Russian Baltic Fleet in 1917* (Lawrence, KS: University Press of Kansas, 1978).

Scammel, Claire, 'The Royal Navy and the Strategic Origins of the Anglo-German Naval Agreement, 1935', *Journal of Strategic Studies*, vol. 20(2) (1997).

Shalagin, B., 'Sobiratel baltflota. K 130-letiyu so dnya rozhdeniya admirala N. O. Essena', *Morskoy Sbornik*, vol. 143(12) (1990).
Shimsoni, Jonathan, 'Technology, Military Advantage and World War I: A Case of Military Entrepreneurship', *International Security*, vol. 15(3) (1990–91).
Shlomin, Vladimir and Messoylidi, Vadim, 'Ataka na flot', *Leningradskaya Panorama*, no. 6 (1990).
Shoshkov, E. N., *Repressirovannoe OSTEKHBYURO* (St Petersburg: Nauchnoinformatsionnoe tsentr Memorial 3, 1995).
Skogan, John, 'The Evolution of the Four Soviet Fleets, 1968–1987', in Skogan John, and Brundtland, Arne (eds), *Soviet Sea Power in Northern Waters* (London: Pinter, 1990).
Snyder, Jack, *The Ideology of the Offensive: Military Decision Making and the Disasters of 1914* (Ithaca, NY: Cornell University Press, 1984).
Stalbo, K. A. (ed.), *Istoriya voenno-morskogo isskustva: Sovetskoe voenno-morskoe iskusstvo v grazhdanskoy voyne i v period postroeniya sotsialisma v SSSR (1917–1941 gg.)*, vol. II (Moscow: Voenizdat, 1963).
Stites, Richard, *Revolutionary Dreams: Utopian Visions and Experimental Life in the Russian Revolution* (Oxford: Oxford University Press, 1988).
Stupnikov, N. A. (ed.), *Dvazhdi Krasnoznamenny baltisky flot* (Voenizdat: Moscow, 1990).
Suvenirov, Oleg, *RKKA nakanune: Ocherki istorii politicheskogo vospitaniya lichnogo sostava krasnoy armii, 1929 g.–yuon, 1941 g.* (Moscow: Institut voennoy istorii ministerstvo oborony R.F., 1993).
Suvenirov, Oleg, *Tragediya RKKA, 1937–1938 gg.* (Moscow: Terra, 1998).
Sweet, David, 'The Baltic in British Diplomacy before the First World War', *Historical Journal*, vol. 13 (1970).
Thurston, Robert W., *Life and Terror in Stalin's Russia, 1934–1941* (New Haven, CT: Yale University Press, 1996).
Till, Geoffrey, 'The Great Powers and the Baltic', Rystad, Göran, Böhme, Klaus R. and Carlgren Wilhelm M. (eds), *In Quest of Trade and Security: The Baltic in Power Politics, 1500–1990 II: 1890–1990* (Stockholm: Probus, 1995).
Till, Geoffrey, 'Luxury Fleet? The Sea Power of (Soviet) Russia', Rodger, N. A. M. (ed.), *Naval Power in the Twentieth Century* (Annapolis, MD: Naval Institute Press, 1996).
Tomson, Edgar, *Kriegsbegriff und Kriegsrecht der Sowjetunion* (Berlin: Berlin Verlag, 1979).
Tucker, Robert C., *Stalin in Power: The Revolution from Above, 1928–1941* (New York: Norton, 1990).
Turtola, Martti, *Från Torne älv till Systerbäck: Hemligt försvarssamarbete mellan Finland och Sverige, 1923–1940* (Stockholm: Militärhistoriska förlaget, 1987).
Turtola, Martti, 'Aspects on Finnish–Estonian Military Relations in the 1920s and 1930s', in Hiden, John and Loit, Aleksander (ed.), *The Baltic in International Relations between the Two World Wars* (Stockholm: Studia Baltica Stockholmiensa, 1988).
Ueberschär, Gerd R. and Bezymensky, Lev A. (eds), *Der Deutsche Angriff auf die Sowjetunion, 1941: Die Kontroverse um die Präventivskriegsthese* (Darmstadt: Primus Verlag, 1998).
Ulam, Adam B., *Expansion and Coexistence: Soviet Foreign Policy, 1917–73* (New York: Holt, Rinehart & Winston, 1974 [1968]).
Ulfving, Lars, 'Sjökriget Sverige–Sovjetunionen: Det inofficiella kriget i Östersjön mellan Sovjetunionens ubåtsvapen och Sveriges flotta sommaren och hösten 1942', in Hugemark, Bo (ed.), *Vindkantring: 1942 – politisk kursändring* (Stockholm: Probus, 1992).

Ullman, Richard H., *Anglo-Soviet Relations, 1917–1921*, vol. II, *Britain and the Russian Civil War* (Princeton, NJ: Princeton University Press, 1968).

Van Dyke, Carl, 'The Timoshenko Reforms: March–July, 1940', *Journal of Slavic Military Studies*, vol. 9(1) (1996).

Van Dyke, Carl, *The Soviet Invasion of Finland, 1939–40* (London: Frank Cass, 1997).

Vasiliev, D. M., 'Pervy boevoy pokhod Otryada legkikh sil', *Gangut*, vol. 9 (1995).

Vego, Milan N., *Naval Strategy and Operations in Narrow Seas* (London: Frank Cass, 1999).

Wahlbäck, Krister, *Finlandsfrågan i svensk politik, 1937–1940* (Stockholm: Norstedts, 1964).

Westwood, J. N., *Russian Naval Construction, 1905–1945* (London: Macmillan Press, 1993).

Yakovlev, Alexander N., *A Century of Violence in Soviet Russia* (New Haven, CT: Yale University Press, 2002).

Yemelin, A., 'Sudba doktrin i teory, 3: Voennaya reforma, 1924–1928 gg.', *Morskoy sbornik*, vol. 144(2) (1991).

Zonin, Sergey A., *Admiral L. M. Galler: Zhizn i flotovodcheskaya deyatelnost* (Moscow: Voenizdat, 1991).

INDEX

Abramenkov, Isidor Arkhipovich 241–2
Airforce, Soviet *see* VVS
air power 179–80, 192, 195, 224, 229; influence 37–8; support 191
Åland Islands 120, 121, 161, 162, 164, 171, 181, 188, 190, 193; convention 1921 121, 161; demilitarized status 120, 121, 161, 162; treaty 121, 122
Alexandrov, Alexander Petrovich 141, 145, 202, 205
Alexandrov, Nikolay Nikolayevich 239
Alexeyev, Georgy 210–11
Alyakrinsky, Nikolay 107–8
Andreyev 244, 245, 246, 247
Anglo-German naval agreement, 1935 122
Antoshchenko, B. S. 245, 246
arrests: navy personnel 99, 109, 144, 205, 207, 238–40, 242, 243, 246; political 92, 199
Aube, Théophile 10

Baltic Fleet BOS (*Beregovoy Otryad Soprovozhdeniya*) 188
Baltic Fleet PUR 103, 106, 109, 144, 190, 208, 209
Baltic Fleet (Russia) 43–4
Baltic Fleet (Soviet) 3–4, 5, 6, 22, 34, 38, 50, 63, 66, 75, 76, 80, 82–3, 85–6, 104, 105, 133, 234; in action 184–5, 186, 188, 215, 225; battleships 7, 57, 61, 63, 72, 84, 132, 175, 176, 182, 186, 225, 228, 234; communists 105; deployment 183–4, 191; dual command system 46–7, 112, 206–7; educational efforts 106, 214–15, 217; evacuation 202, 227–8; exchange of uniforms 210–11; fall of Germany 232; fall of Tallinn 230; fighter planes (air arm) 77, 84, 185, 192; foreign policy 222; independent role 123; Intelligence Section 49, 121, 143, 146–7, 190, 206, 211–12, 213, 214, 217; losses 188, 215, 227, 230; maneuvers 60, 79, 80, 84, 131; minesweepers 76, 83, 101, 130, 133, 179, 180, 181, 184, 201, 225, 226, 227, 228, 230, 239; missions 86–7, 88, 158, 188, 194, 195, 228; modernization 212, 213; naval doctrine 29, 41, 88; new base 194, 223; one man command system 98–102, 145, 146, 152; operations 5, 34, 58, 79, 128, 130, 134, 162, 167, 168, 171, 177–8, 180, 181 208, 227; Order of Red Banner 95, 211; purges 207, 110–13, 213; ranks 148; with Red Army 120, 223, 227; relationship with LVO 31, 82, 83, 118, 121, 127, 148, 179; renaming 73, 95; staff 5, 35, 36, 46, 73, 77, 82, 83, 96, 99, 104, 105, 127, 131, 132, 141, 145–6, 151, 168, 175, 181, 186, 190, 203, 204, 207, 213, 216; support to communists 46, 49; war games 118, 120, 122, 161, 168; war scenarios 128–30
Baltic Theater 4, 7, 21, 23–7, 57, 58, 118, 121, 132, 133, 158, 194; mission 68; situation in 1940 167–71; war scenarios 177
battleship 10, 11, 14, 32, 130, 223, 234; campaign 78; construction 11; death 12; defense operations 75–9; defense squadron 79; names and types 23, 26, 33, 43, 44, 57, 84, 121, 176, 186, 202–3, 228, 229; naming of warships 94, 201; new ones 101, 175, 200; tonnage 57, 176

262

INDEX

Belli, Vladimir 16, 60, 61, 63, 64, 65, 67, 73, 86, 87, 94, 96, 99, 144, 145, 166–7, 188, 193, 201, 202
Berendt 57, 243, 245, 246
Berzin, Yan Karlovich 159, 160, 161
Björkö batteries 80–2, 87, 185, 186, 230
Black Sea Fleet 21–2, 25, 32, 38, 66, 73, 97, 98, 141, 142, 143, discharges 205; reorganization 181
Black Sea theater 21, 38, 85, 133
Blitzkrieg operation 49, 169–71
Boevaya letopis voennogo-morskogo flota 5–6
Bolshevik/s 47, 48, 102, 104, 107, 130, 146; ideology 49, 107, 146; regime 4, 92, 96, 111; stronghold 44; takeover 95, 97
Britain 137, 160, 164, 165, 192; military doctrine 20; naval power 57, 60–2, 67, 95, 118–20, 222
Bucharsky, Peter Matveich 241
Bukharin, Nikolay 138
Bulyshkin 239, 240

Castex, Raoul 11, 13
Center of Military History of the Soviet General Staff 5–6
Charkevich 244
Cheka (*Chrezvychaynaya kommissiya*) 73, 92, 98
Chuchkag, Georgy Georgevich 242, 243, 246
civil–military relations: Soviet 44–5
Civil War (Russia) 4, 15, 21, 28, 46, 48, 51, 76, 92, 98, 146, 151, 152, 203, 204, 223, 233, 234; veterans 142, 223
Cold War 4, 7, 13, 34, 44, 45, 52; post 6, 7, 45, 234
collective security 117, 222
collectivization 139, 149
command system: dual 46–7, 112, 206–7; one man 98–102, 145, 146, 152
Corbett, Julian 10–11, 12, 13, 14, 94
Crimean War 21, 25
'cultural revolution' 138, 139–40

Denmark 30, 57, 59, 122; German occupation 169; relations with Russia 63–4
Dobrolevsky 64–5, 66
Dotsenko, V. I. 5
Dushenov, Konstantin Ivanovich 141, 143

Engels 227
Engels, Friedrich 47, 67, 94, 138
Essen, Nikolay 33–4
Estonia 4, 6, 60, 61, 62, 63, 79, 86, 96, 117, 120, 121, 122, 130, 132, 159, 160, 161, 166, 167, 168, 178, 183, 194, 207, 209, 222, 225, 227, 232; 1920 peace treaty 163
European Union (EU) 6

Fakel 184–6, 188
Fillipovsky, Alexander 213–14, 243, 244, 245, 246, 247
Finland 4, 5, 25, 60, 61, 62, 64, 65, 79, 96, 117, 119, 121, 122, 132, 149, 159, 160, 161, 162, 165, 166, 167, 168, 171, 177, 182, 183, 186, 188, 191, 194, 206, 209, 215, 217, 222, 223, 228, 232
five year plans: first 139, 143, 157, 204, 223; second 126, 139, 157; third 133
France 10, 14, 20, 27, 29, 46, 60, 62, 67, 84, 107, 118, 119, 120, 122, 128, 131, 157, 160, 163, 164, 216
Frinovsky, Mikhail 162–3
Frumkin, N. S. 242, 243, 247
Frunze 33, 84, 85, 126
Frunze, Mikhail 25, 84, 93, 100, 111, 112, 152
Frunze Naval Academy 204, 233

Galler, Lev 26, 97–8, 130, 132, 133, 145, 161, 163, 175, 176, 179, 180, 181, 182, 183, 186, 203, 204, 233
Gamarnik, Yan 239
Germany 5, 6, 12, 63, 118, 122–3, 126, 132, 157, 159, 160, 161, 162, 166, 167, 168, 169, 171, 177, 188, 193, 194, 222, 224; Nazi 20, 214, 216, 222; Weimar 58, 66–7, 68, 121
Gorbunov, Mikhail Alekseyevich 239
Gorshkov, Sergey S. 5, 233, 234
Gosplan 'Industrial Party' 139, 144
GPU (Gosudarstvennoe Politicheskoe Upravlenie) 73, 83, 92, 99
Great Terror *see* purges
Grishin, Alexander Sergeyevich 239, 244
GRU (*Glavnoe Razvedyvatelnoe Upravlenie*) 63, 73, 122, 123, 159, 212
Gusev, V. I. 72–3, 93

Herrick, Robert W. 4, 5, 13, 140, 202
Hitler, Adolf 18, 121, 123, 160, 169
hostile neutrals 63–6

263

INDEX

Ignatiev, Sergey 206, 209
Isakov, Ivan 131, 163, 169, 182, 185, 186, 188, 191, 192, 193, 194, 202, 203, 204, 216, 242, 245

Japan 33, 36, 38, 43, 77, 127, 134, 157, 169, 181, 222, 223, 227
Jeune École see Young School

Karelian Isthmus 3, 130, 165, 186, 188
Keller, Captain 35–6
Kellogg–Briand Pact 117
Kholodovsky, S. 62–3, 66–7
Klado, Nikolay Lavrentivich 95, 97
Koivisto batteries *see* Björkö batteries
Komsomol (*Kommunisticheskiy Soyuz Molodezhi*) 100, 104, 111–12, 150, 208, 210, 213
Kronstadt 98, 105, 131, 188, 191, 194, 203; 1921 mutiny 4, 47, 59, 60, 72, 87, 98, 105; navy base 3, 4, 21, 22, 25, 58, 73, 77–9, 80, 83, 86, 103, 108, 162, 177–81, 182, 184, 211, 213
Kuznetsov, Nikolay 3, 5, 7, 22, 142, 164, 166, 167, 168, 175, 176, 179, 181, 182, 184, 185, 186, 188, 190, 194, 200, 204, 207, 211, 215, 224, 229, 233

Latvia 4, 6, 60, 62, 63, 117, 121, 159, 160, 161, 165, 166, 167, 168, 177, 183, 194, 207, 209, 225, 232
Lausanne Treaty 21–2, 57
League of Nations 57, 65, 117, 119
Lebedev, G. I. 243, 246, 247
Lenin, Vladimir 47, 72, 92, 100, 104, 126, 149, 234
Leningrad 3, 12, 25, 104, 117, 123, 126, 134, 158, 160, 169, 178, 185, 191, 211, 222, 228
Levchenko, Gordey Ivanovich 178, 203, 204, 241
Lithuania 6, 60, 62, 63, 120, 161
Litvinov, Maxim 117, 164
Locarno Treaty 117
Ludri, Ivan Martynovich 140–1, 144, 175

Mahan, Alfred T. 10, 12, 30, 43, 79, 94, 95, 96, 202
Manturov 242
'mare clausum' 23
'mare liberum' 23, 25
Marx, Karl 47, 138

Marxist – Leninist ideology 44, 49, 51, 96, 107, 143, 199, 202, 211
Maxim Gorky 3, 225, 226, 229
Maximov, Nikolay Alexandrovich 238, 239
Meretskov, Kirill Afanasevich 182, 194
military doctrine 8, 13, 30, 31, 41, 48, 49; defensive 14, 21, 29; deterrent 14, 21; operational level 8, 14, 20, 29, 37, 38, 42, 221; strategic level 8, 14, 20, 21, 42, 221; tactical level 8, 15, 20, 42, 50, 51, 221
minesweepers 61, 76, 83, 101, 130, 133, 179, 180, 181, 184, 201, 225, 226, 227, 228, 230, 239
Molotov–Ribbentrop Pact 158–9, 164, 182
Monakov, Mikhail 5, 7, 157, 158
Moonsund archipelago 4, 230
Morskoy biograficheskyy slovar 5
Morskoy Sbornik 5, 16, 74, 75, 77, 78, 101, 102, 104, 107, 108, 131, 140, 141, 142, 144, 148, 162, 201, 202, 205, 241
Moscow Peace Treaty, 1940 188

Napoleonic Wars 24, 26, 34, 74–5
naval construction program, 1921 32–3, 59, 85, 175, 176, 200, 215, 225
naval doctrine (Soviet) 41, 42, 177, 178, 223; defensive 13, 27, 32, 43, 57, 74–6, 77, 79, 88, 93, 119, 121, 123, 128–30, 134, 158, 169; offensive 13, 27, 34, 57–8, 68–9, 74, 76, 79, 80, 85, 93, 119, 130, 134, 164, 169, 177; organizational level 8, 15, 38, 177, 221, 222; strategic level 8, 15, 27, 58, 158, 194, 202, 221, 222; tactical level 8, 9, 15, 41, 42, 217, 221, 223
Naval Fighting Regulation, 1930 (BU-30) 13
Naval Fighting Regulation, 1937 (BU-37) 13
naval history (Soviet): literature 4–6, 15–16
Naval War College: faculty 74, 94, 95, 97, 101, 118, 139, 143, 144, 166, 175, 191; graduates 96, 129, 140, 142, 145; war games 86, 103, 149
naval/y (Soviet): ranks 133–4, 147–8, 152, 201–2; reorganization 84–5; tactics 9, 13
Navy Day 201

INDEX

Nechaev 245–6, 247
Nemits, Alexander 57–8, 72, 97, 99, 169
New Economic Policy (NEP) 48, 92, 93–4, 107, 111, 149, 223
Nikonov 122–3, 158, 159, 160
Nikonov–Steynbryuk report 122–3
NKVD (Narodny Kommissariat Vnutrennikh Del) 196, 198–9, 227, 238, 239, 240, 241, 242, 243, 244, 245–6
NMO-40 (*Nastavlenie Morskikh Operatsii*) 13
North Atlantic Treaty Organization (NATO) 6
Northern theater 23, 97, 127
Norway 64, 159, 193

ocean-going fleet 5, 41, 133, 157, 159, 200, 214, 217, 223, 224, 233
OGPU (*Obyedinyonnoe Gosudarstvennoe Politicheskoe Upravlenie*) 92, 144, 149
'Old School' 12, 14, 57, 67, 68–9, 72, 74, 75, 77–8, 87, 94, 95, 98, 111, 119, 129, 139, 140, 142, 152, 194, 202, 203, 222, 223; second 232, 233, 234
Operation Barbarossa 3
Order of Red Banner 95, 211
Orlov, Vladimir Mitrofanovich 122, 142, 143, 175, 205
OsoAviaKhim 150–1, 152

Pacific Fleet 7, 204, 233, 234
Pacific theater 2, 127, 131, 133, 191
Panteleyev, Y. A. 168
Pantserzhansky, Eduard Samuilovich 97, 143, 205
Pavlov 243
Petrov, Mikhail 22, 61, 67, 74, 77, 85, 95, 96, 97, 140, 144, 205
Petrov, Pavel V. 5, 188
Plotkin 163
Poland 23, 59, 60, 62, 63, 79, 117, 118, 120, 121, 122, 126, 159, 166, 167, 182, 214, 232
political commissars 46, 47, 51, 111
Poltava see Frunze
Posen, Barry R. 20, 21
Pravda 64–5
Prestin, Evgeny Konstantinovich 242
Prokazov 244, 246

PUR (*Politicheskoe Upravlenie RKKA*) 16, 45–6, 51, 72, 101, 103, 142, 145, 146, 148, 149, 150, 204, 207
purges 126, 139, 144–6, 198, 200, 205–9, 213, 219, 224, 233

Rechister, Dimitry 132–3, 161
Red Army 4, 25, 38, 59, 73, 79, 84, 85, 86, 104, 112, 120, 126, 134, 177, 178, 193, 194, 207, 222, 223
Red Navy 44, 101, 109–10, 147–8
Reese, Roger R. 199–200
RKKA (*Raboche-Krestyanskaya Krasnaya Armiya*) 16, 45, 46, 50, 59, 83, 98, 100, 102, 111, 118, 127, 149, 150–1, 168, 175, 176, 182, 184, 190, 193, 194, 226, 227
Rodionov, Konstantin 128–9
Rogov, Ivan V. 209, 216
Royal Navy (Britain) 25–6, 10, 61, 193, 213
RVS (*Revolutsionny Voenny Soviet*) 15, 22, 67, 68, 69, 72, 79, 84, 85, 87, 97, 118, 126, 148, 150

Sandler, Rickard 161, 165
Shaposhnikov, Boris Michailovich 126, 162, 163–4, 179, 180, 182
Shatalov 244, 245
'shock workers' 139
Shteynbakh, D. L. 243, 246, 247
Shteynbryuk 122, 123, 158, 159
Sivkov, Alexander Kusmich 180, 238, 239, 245
'small wars' 74–5, 86, 87, 88, 141–2
Smirnov, Peter 109–11, 178, 179
Sokolnikov, B. A. 82, 83
Soviet School 14, 175, 194, 202, 203, 222, 224
Spanish Civil War 157, 167, 171
Stalin, Joseph 13, 93, 137, 149, 158, 165–6, 167, 175, 182, 186, 190, 199, 233, 247
Stalin's Ocean-going Fleet 5
Stavitsky, Sergey Petrovich 202, 203, 204
Stirsudden–Shepelev line 118, 129, 130, 178, 225
Stockholm Plan 161–2
St Petersburg 26, 80

submarines 3, 6, 12, 13, 14, 34, 159, 176, 185–6, 207, 224, 234; Baltic Fleet 61, 63, 66, 71, 73, 86, 87, 94, 96, 101, 119, 120, 122; collision 215; defects 208; naming 140
Supreme Soviet 198, 200
Svechin, Alexander 25, 93, 94, 141, 144
Sweden 63–4, 65, 66, 120, 122, 160, 162, 165–6, 167, 171, 177, 185, 186
Sychev, V. P. 244–5, 246, 247

Tallinn 3, 4, 87, 164, 181, 227
Tambyar 241
TASS 224
Timofeyev, Nikolay 212–13, 242–7
Timoshenko, Semyon 206, 207, 210
Toshakov, Arkady 58–9, 61, 75–6, 77, 79, 84, 97, 127, 169
Treaty of Versailles 216
Tributs, Vladimir 3, 168, 169, 181, 184, 203–4, 215, 228, 229
Trotsky, Lev 46, 72, 84, 93, 96, 100, 104, 138, 234
Tukhachevsky, Mikhail 22, 61, 67–8, 84, 85, 93, 94, 97, 130, 131, 178, 238

UVMS (*Upravlenie Morskikh Sil RKKA*) 16, 127, 133, 144, 175, 176

Veygelin, K. 77–8
Viktorov, Mikhail Vladimirovich 98, 99, 145
von Clausewitz, Carl 11, 47, 202, 221
Voroshilov, Kliment 121, 127, 132, 147, 160, 161, 162, 206

VVS (*Voenno–Vozdushnye Sili*) 38, 133, 191; antisubmarine warfare (ASW) resources 76; pilots 192

war games 19, 120, 121, 129, 149, 168, 181, 190; joint 60, 63, 118, 119
Warsaw Pact 3
Westwood, J. N. 4, 5
'White Guard Organizations' 119
World War I 11, 75, 93, 166, 202, 204, 216
World War II 4, 5, 9, 11, 13, 15, 20, 33, 140, 141, 163, 171, 179, 200, 202, 204, 214, 224, 229

Yakimychev, Alexander 142
Yakovlev 244, 245, 246, 247
Yegorov, Alexander 175, 238
Yeremeyev 244, 245, 247
Yevseyev, Alexander 146, 179, 205, 212
Yezhovshchina 213
Young School 12, 14, 117, 118, 119, 121, 123, 126, 127, 134, 139, 140, 142, 143, 152, 158, 194, 202, 204, 205, 222, 223; second 232, 233

Zherve, Boris 74, 95–6, 140, 141, 143, 144, 145
Zinovyev 94, 127
Zof, Vladimir 85
Zof, Vyatcheslav Ivanovich 98, 105, 109, 142, 143, 205
Zonin, Sergey 5, 179, 182